P9-CQE-741

Historians on History

Readings edited and introduced by

JOHN TOSH

Second Edition

PEARSON
Longman

Harlow, England • London • New York • Boston • San Francisco • Toronto
Sydney • Tokyo • Singapore • Hong Kong • Seoul • Taipei • New Delhi
Cape Town • Madrid • Mexico City • Amsterdam • Munich • Paris • Milan

PEARSON EDUCATION LIMITED

Edinburgh Gate
Harlow CM20 2JE
United Kingdom
Tel: +44 (0)1279 623623
Fax: +44 (0)1279 431059
Website: www.pearsoned.co.uk

First edition published in 2000
Second edition published in Great Britain in 2009

© Pearson Education Limited 2000, 2009

The right of John Tosh to be identified as author of this work has been asserted
by him in accordance with the Copyright, Designs and Patents Act 1988.

ISBN: 978-1-4058-0168-3

British Library Cataloguing in Publication Data
A CIP catalogue record for this book can be obtained from the British Library

Library of Congress Cataloging-in-Publication Data
Historians on history : readings / edited and introduced by John Tosh. – 2nd ed.
    p. cm.
  Includes index.
  ISBN 978-1-4058-0168-3 (pbk.)
  1. History–Philosophy.   2. Historiography.   I. Tosh, John.
  D16.8.H6241742 2009
  901–dc22

                                                                    2008023720

All rights reserved; no part of this publication may be reproduced, stored
in a retrieval system, or transmitted in any form or by any means, electronic,
mechanical, photocopying, recording, or otherwise without either the prior
written permission of the Publishers or a licence permitting restricted copying
in the United Kingdom issued by the Copyright Licensing Agency Ltd, Saffron
House, 6–10 Kirby Street, London EC1N 8TS. This book may not be lent,
resold, hired out or otherwise disposed of by way of trade in any form of
binding or cover other than that in which it is published, without the prior
consent of the Publishers.

10 9 8 7 6 5 4 3 2 1
12 11 10 09 08

Set by 35 in 11/13pt Bulmer MT
Printed and bound in Malaysia (CTP-VVP)

The Publisher's policy is to use paper manufactured from sustainable forests.

Contents

Historians on History

Preface to the Second Edition

This edition has been revised and expanded in the light of comments made by students, colleagues and three very perceptive publisher's readers. I have remodelled the section on 'Race' to reflect the broader agenda of Postcolonialism. The content of the section on People's History has been adjusted to correspond with its new title, History from Below. The biggest change comes towards the end of the book. In Part Six I try to do justice to the Cultural Turn in historical studies, including the considerable current interest in memory. This is at the expense of the extended treatment given in the first edition to the polemics surrounding Postmodernism, now represented by just three extracts. I have made some revisions to the editorial matter, and I have added a guide to further reading.

John Tosh
London, November 2007

Author's Acknowledgements

This anthology is in many ways a by-product of my book, *The Pursuit of History: Aims, Methods and New Directions in the Study of Modern History* (4th edn, Longman, 2006). Many of the debts which I should acknowledge are recorded there. I am particularly grateful to Kathy Castle, Chris Clark, Michael Pinnock, Michael Roper and Bob Shoemaker for their advice on the selection of readings.

I owe a special debt to Andrew MacLennan, formerly of Longman, who enthusiastically welcomed this proposal, and to Heather McCallum for seeing it through to publication.

John Tosh
London, October 1999

Publisher's Acknowledgements

The publishers are grateful to the following for permission to reproduce copyright material:

MARXISM AND HISTORY by Christopher Hill (Copyright © Christopher Hill, 1948) Reprinted by permission of A.M. Heath & Co. Ltd; Allan Lane for the article 'The Great Cat Massacre and Other Episodes' in *FRENCH CULTURAL HISTORY* by Robert Darnton (Penguin Books 1986, 2001). Copyright © Robert Darnton, 1984; 'The Great Cat Massacre and Other Episodes' in *FRENCH CULTURAL HISTORY* by Robert Darnton, Basic Books, 1984. Reprinted by permission of Basic Books, a member of Perseus Books Group; Howard Zinn for extracts from *THE POLITICS OF HISTORY*, Beacon Press, 1970. Used by kind permission of Howard Zinn; Gisela Bok, 'Women's History and Gender History' in *GENDER & HISTORY* 1, 1989. Reprinted with permission from Wiley Blackwell; 'Postcoloniality and the Artifice of History: Who Speaks for "Indian" Pasts?' by Dipesh Chakrabarty in *REPRESENTATIONS*. Copyright 1992 by University of California Press – Journals. Reproduced with permission of University of California Press – Journals in the format Tradebook via Copyright Clearance Center; Extract from pages 1–11 in Herbert Butterfield, *THE ENGLISHMAN AND HIS HISTORY*, 1944 © Cambridge University Press, reproduced with permission; Carnegie Mellon University for 'Personal history and the history of the emotions' by Theodore Zeldin in *JOURNAL OF SOCIAL HISTORY* 15 (1981/2) © Peter N. Stearns; University of Chicago Press for extracts from *THE GENIUS OF AMERICAN POLITICS* by Daniel Boorstin © 1953, 1962 by The University of Chicago. All rights reserved. University of Chicago Press for extracts from 'History and the Social Sciences' by Fernard Braudel in *ON HISTORY*, 1980, translated by Sarah Matthews © 1980 by The University of Chicago. All rights reserved; Columbia University Press for 'Gender: a useful category of historical analysis' from *GENDER AND THE POLITICS OF HISTORY* by Joan Scott. Copyright © 1988 Columbia University Press. Reprinted with permission of the publisher and extracts from *CULTURAL HISTORY AND POSTMODERNITY: DISCIPLINARY READINGS AND CHALLENGES* by Mark Poster. Copyright © 1997 Columbia University Press. Reprinted with permission of the publisher; Reprinted from Philip Abrams, *HISTORICAL SOCIOLOGY*. Copyright © 1982 by Mrs. Sheila Abrams. Used by permission of Cornell University Press and Sheila Abrams; *WHAT IS HISTORY?* Reproduced by permission of Curtis Brown Group Ltd, London on behalf of E.H. Carr. Copyright © E.H. Carr 1961; Editions Gallimard for extracts from *THE TERRITORY OF THE HISTORIAN*, Emmanuel Le Roy Ladurie © Editions Gallimard, Paris, and extracts from *'BETWEEN MEMORY AND HISTORY: LES LIEUX DE MÉMOIRE'*, Pierre Nora © Editions Gallimard, Paris; G.R. Elton, *THE PRACTICE OF HISTORY*, 1st Edition, 1969, Fontana. Copyright © G.R. Elton 1969, reproduced with permission of Wiley-Blackwell; C.V. Wedgwood, from 'The Sense of the Past', the Leslie Stephen Lecture for 1957, reprinted in *HISTORY AND HOPE*, Fontana, 1987. The Principal and Fellows of Lady Margaret Hall., Oxford, on behalf of the Estate of C.V. Wedgwood; From A. Adu Boahen: *CLIO AND NATION-BUILDING IN AFRICA*, Ghana Universities Press, Accra; 'Has History ceased to be relevant?' by Allan Bullock in *THE HISTORIAN* 43, 1994. Used by kind permission of the Honourable Adrian Bullock for the Estate of Lord Alan Bullock; J.H. Plumb, *THE DEATH OF THE PAST*, 1969, Palgrave Macmillan, reproduced with permission of Palgrave Macmillan; Richard Hofstadter, 'History and the social sciences' in *VARIETIES OF HISTORY* by Fritz Stern, 1970, Palgrave Macmillan. Used by kind permission of Beatrice K. Hofstadter; Manchester University Press for an extract from *THE HISTORIAN'S CRAFT* by Marc Bloch © Manchester University Press 1954; Methuen Publishing Ltd for 'New Ages don't begin all at once' by Bertolt Brecht (Methuen Publishing, London) and 'Questions From A Worker Who Reads' by Bertolt Brecht (translated by Michael Hamburger) from *POEMS 1913–56* (Methuen Publishing Ltd, London); Oxford University Press for extracts from Richard Cobb, 'Experiences of an Anglo-French Historian' from *A SECOND IDENTITY: ESSAYS ON FRANCE AND FRENCH HISTORY* (OUP, 1969) by permission of Oxford University Press, extracts from H.R. Trevor-Roper, 'The Past and the Present: History and Sociology' in *PAST AND PRESENT* 42, 1969. Reproduced with permission of the

Past and Present Society, extracts from Lawrence Stone, 'The revival of narrative: reflections on a new old history' in *PAST AND PRESENT* 85, 1969. Reproduced with permission of the Past and Present Society, and extracts from Gerda Lerner, 'The Necessity of History' from *WHY HISTORY MATTERS* (OUP, 1982) by permission of Oxford University Press, Inc; Reproduced by permission of Oxford University Press India, New Delhi. 'On Some Aspects of the Historiography of Colonial India' by Ranajit Guha in *SUBALTERN STUDIES I*, 1981, Oxford University Press India; Excerpt from 'History: Professional and lay' by H.R. Trevor-Roper (© H.R. Trevor Roper) from *HISTORY AND IMAGINATION* is reproduced by permission of PFD (www.pfd.co.uk) on behalf of H.R. Trevor-Roper; 'Women's history', by Joan Scott in Peter Burke (ed.), *NEW PERSPECTIVES ON HISTORICAL WRITING*. Reproduced by permission of Polity Press; LUDTKE, ALF; *THE HISTORY OF EVERYDAY LIFE*. © 1989 CAMPUS VERLAG GMBH, FRANKFURT/MAIN ENGLISH TRANS. © 1995 Princeton University Press. Reprinted by permission of Princeton University Press; From *IN RED AND BLACK: MARXIAN EXPLORATIONS IN SOUTHERN AND AFRO-AMERICAN HISTORY* by Eugene Genovese, copyright © 1968, 1969, 1970, 1971 by Eugene Genovese. Used by permission of Pantheon Books, a division of Random House, Inc; From 'Beyond chaos: black history and the search for the New Land' by Vincent Harding in *AMISTAD* 1 (1970), Vintage books, a division of Random House, Inc. Used by permission of Vincent Harding, a Professor Emeritus of Religion and Human Transformation, and The Chairperson of The Veterans of Hope Project in Denver, Co at the Iliff School of Theology; From *DISORDERLY CONDUCT* by Carroll Smith-Rosenberg, copyright 1985 by Carroll Smith-Rosenberg. Used by permission of Alfred A. Knopf, a division of Random House, Inc; Taylor & Francis Ltd for the poem that begins 'New Ages don't begin all at once', and 'Questions of a studious working man' by Bertolt Brecht, Copyright (1997) From (*BERTOLT BRECHT: POEMS 1913–1956*) by (Bertolt Brecht). Reproduced by permission of Routledge, Inc, a division of Informa plc, extracts from *CONTESTED PASTS*, Katherine Hodgkin and Susannah Radstone, Copyright © 2003 Routledge. Reproduced by permission of Taylor & Francis Books UK, extracts from 'Histories, empires and the post-colonial moment' by Catherine Hall in *THE POST-COLONIAL QUESTION: COMMON SKIES, DIVIDED HORIZONS* by Iain Chambers and Lidia Curti, extracts from 'The end of social history?', Patrick Joyce, *SOCIAL HISTORY* 20, 1995, reprinted by permission of the publisher (Taylor & Francis Ltd, http://www.informaworld.com), extracts from *THE WORLD WE HAVE LOST*, Peter Laslett, Copyright © 1965 Methuen.

Reproduced by permission of Taylor & Francis Books UK and Janet Laslett for the Estate of Peter Laslett, and *PEOPLE'S HISTORY AND SOCIALIST THEORY*, Raphael Samuel, Copyright © 1965 Routledge Journals. Reproduced by permission of Taylor & Francis Books UK and Alison Light for the Estate of Raphael Samuel; From *TELLING THE TRUTH ABOUT HISTORY* by Joyce Appleby, Lynn Hunt, and Margaret Jacob. Copyright © 1994 by Joyce Appleby, Lynn Hunt, and Margaret Jacob. Used by permission of W.W. Norton & Company, Inc; E.J. Hobsbawm for extracts from the article 'Marx and History' in *NEW LEFT REVIEW* Journal Issue 143, February 1984 © E.J. Hobsbawn 1983/2008; Yale University Press London for Michael Howard, *THE LESSONS OF HISTORY*, © 1989 by Yale University Press. All rights reserved, and Robert William Fogel, "Scientific" history and traditional history', in *WHICH ROAD TO THE PAST?*, © 1983 by Yale University Press. All rights reserved.

We have been unable to trace the copyright holders of *INTRODUCTION TO THE STUDY OF HISTORY* by V.H. Galbraith and would appreciate any information which would enable us to do so.

A Note on the Texts

In this book I offer a large number of short extracts instead of a small number of long ones. This is partly in order to represent as wide a cross-section of the debates as possible, and partly on account of the brevity of many important statements: working historians tend not to write treatises on the nature of their craft.

My selection is for the most part confined to the English-speaking world: Britain, the United States, India and Ghana. A small number of French and German historians are included, whose work in translation has become a familiar and influential part of historical debate in the English-speaking world.

The extracts can be taken as they stand. For the most part no specialist historical knowledge should be needed to follow the arguments. For the sake of accessibility I have not included those statements which are enmeshed in ongoing debates.

Footnotes have in most cases been simplified and reduced in number. A few additional footnotes have been included by the editor (marked ED). The list of permissions provided gives full details of the original place of publication, to which readers can refer for the full version.

Introduction

Historians in general are not much disposed to reflect in public on the nature of their craft. They are often happiest in the archives, and most ill at ease when called upon to evaluate the claims of their discipline in general terms. When they do so, they are most likely to pronounce on matters of method and technique. Yet no enterprise as laborious and long drawn-out as historical research can be pursued without deeply held convictions as to its purpose and significance. History is studied and read because it feeds certain human aspirations, and our response to a particular work of history will inevitably be influenced by its writer's stance in this regard. This anthology does not address the issue of how history is studied, but the governing rationale of the discipline as a whole. Thirty-eight historians have been drawn from the English-speaking world over the past fifty years to reflect the views which students today are most likely to encounter in the history they read. None of these writers regarded reflection on the nature of history as their principal interest; all were – or are – working historians, and the reflections gathered together in this volume were incidental to their main work. Academics expend a good deal of energy demolishing the views of those with whom they disagree; in this selection I have given priority to statements which affirm rather than attack.

Historians do not, of course, inhabit a self-contained professional niche. Some of the concerns documented here are traditional to the discipline of history – for instance the aspiration to re-create the past, or the search for trajectories of change and growth. Others reflect the place of historians in a wider political and cultural milieu. Socialism, feminism and multi-culturalism have each owed their initial impact on historians to the efforts of activists committed to a radical political agenda. In recent years the articulation of a Postmodernist historiography has been most zealously pursued by scholars from philosophy and from literary and cultural studies. In this volume, however, the views of writers like Michel Foucault, Edward Said and Hayden White appear only in the form in which they have been incorporated by historians themselves. The selection is intended to offer insight into the mentality of historians, rather than to reveal the full range of critical perspectives on history which critics from outside the profession have explored.

Seen though the eyes of historians, the current ferment of debate about the proper cultural role of their discipline is not quite so innovative as it may appear. Historians have long taken up varied – even contradictory – attitudes to the status of their subject, and these have a habit of recurring again and again in forms which may be strongly coloured by wider debates, but which owe quite as much to the structure of historical discourse itself. In this Introduction I discuss four longstanding and influential aspirations of historians, and then consider to what extent they continue to be reflected in current debate.

I

The first aspiration is one to which nearly all historians would own: to discover what happened in the past and what it was like to live in the past. Some such objective is the prerequisite for any attempt to make use of the past, but for many historians it is an end in itself; the process of research then becomes like a detective enquiry, or a venture in resurrection. This attitude to the past became commonplace during the Renaissance, when knowledge about the ancient world of Greece and Rome was highly valued for its own sake. It was elevated into a rigorous scholarly method during the nineteenth century, its intellectual respectability indicated by the coining of a new term, *historicism*. Led by the German historian, Leopold von Ranke, the historicists emphasised before all else the otherness of the past. It was dead and gone, and it was also fundamentally different from the present. Hence exceptional powers of the mind were required to bring it to life

– to achieve what Pieter Geyl called 'a disinterested understanding of what is alien to you'.[1]

The historicists emphasised two aspects of the historian's craft. First, they laid down rigorous procedures for the interpretation of the primary sources, by which they meant in practice the documents surviving from the period studied (visual and oral sources and the landscape were not seriously exploited until the twentieth century). To be steeped in the texts of a period was the mark of the true scholar; textual study was the principal training of the apprentice historian, and scholarly reputations were built on the preparation of scholarly editions of chronicles and state documents. If this had been the only prescription of the historicists, the outcome would have been a great deal of dry-as-dust technical history. But the documentary emphasis was combined with an appeal to the powers of the imagination. The gulf which separates our time from the past could only be crossed, it was claimed, by the historian who strove to place him/herself on the other side of the gulf, by, as it were, stepping into the shoes of people in the past and seeing the world through their eyes. Without this effort of empathy the aspiration to re-create the past would be in vain.

Historicism is alive and well in our own time. Since the existence of a profession of historians was largely an invention of the historicists, it is not surprising that the occupational identity of modern historians is still grounded in their research programme. Command of the sources not only continues to be the principal test of historical scholarship; for some it is a source of inspiration to posterity quite independent of the attempt to construct a coherent account of the past [extract 2]. Imagination is less often discussed, partly because of the danger that it may be confused with lack of rigour or with creative invention. Those who stress their imaginative skills tend to be the more individualistic – even eccentric – scholars [extracts 3, 4]. All of the writers represented in Part One are historicists in the further sense that they have little or no interest in the uses to which their historical knowledge might be put. For them knowledge of the past is an end in itself, and they have a lofty indifference to the claims of social utility. The most that writers in this tradition are likely to concede is that history is a cultural resource, a storehouse of accumulated human experience for our contemplation and delight. Anything more applied is suspect, as implying that historians should tailor their enquiries to an ignorant call for 'relevance'. It follows that the standard-bearers of historicism tend to be hostile to some of the more topical areas of historical work which reflect that call, particularly in the social and cultural fields.[2]

II

If historicism has come to seem the 'common sense' of historical work, it has not always been so. A much older reason for studying the past is the completely antithetical one of uncovering the shape of human destiny: what pattern does history fall into, and to what goal is it proceeding? For many centuries in Europe these questions were understood in sacred terms. To the Christian writers of the Middle Ages it was axiomatic that human life was a passage from the Creation to the Last Judgement, and historical knowledge must inevitably bear witness to this grand theme. From the seventeenth century onwards the authority of the Christian world view crumbled, as a result of the divisions in Christendom and the rise of free thought and science. In its place arose a secularised interpretation of history in which human rather than divine activity took centre-stage. The historians of the Enlightenment in the eighteenth century were confident that the human record was one of material and moral improvement, and that their society stood at a pinnacle of achievement. As the evidence of economic progress became more dramatic during the succeeding century, belief in progress became, if anything, more pronounced: Lord Macaulay, writing in the 1850s, advanced an exclusive British claim to be the progressive force in the world; Lord Acton at the end of the century invoked the authority of science to underwrite the concept of progress in human affairs. That kind of confidence may depend on a blinkered view of the world, but it cannot be sustained in the teeth of decline or collapse. Belief in progress has been one of the principal casualties of the catastrophes of the twentieth century – two world wars, the Slump of the 1930s, the threat of nuclear destruction, and the squandering of the natural environment. By the 1960s, when the last major professions of progress were made, the defensive tone is unmistakable. J.H. Plumb [extract 5] proclaimed his faith in the power of reason, and of historical study as a means of enhancing humanity's reasoning power. E.H. Carr [extract 6] drew back from any definition of the goal of history, settling instead for the proposition that the goal must be expected to change as history moved forward, and with it the angle of the historian's vision.

The last – and for a long time the strongest – version of progress was Marxism. Marx's division of all history into the successive phases of ancient, feudal, capitalist and socialist, each more 'progressive' than the last, marks him out clearly as a son of the Enlightenment. What endowed Marx with so much appeal for a hundred years after his death was his prioritisation of economic or 'material' life as the benchmark of progress, and his belief that progressive change came out of revolutionary conflict. These ideas held out the promise of an effective politics to radical political movements in the Western bourgeois world. But they also had major implications for the writing of history. Some historians, particularly those belonging to the Communist Party, fully subscribed to Marx's distinctive take on 'progress', and hoped that their own work would offer further illumination of the revolutionary path which the advanced world was destined to tread in the future. The majority, while no doubt sympathising with Marx's political radicalism, valued his theory for other reasons. Marx's theory of society was above all an integrated one, linking the 'superstructure' of politics, law and art with the economic 'base' of 'forces' and 'relations' of production. He understood major political change in the same way – as the expression of deeply seated tensions in the socio-economic order. Thus both the English Revolution of the 1640s and the French Revolution in 1789 were not primarily about competitive politics among the elite; both, in Marx's view, were manifestations of the transition from feudalism to capitalism – the central progressive change in modern times. For historians who wished to overcome the confines of specialised work and move towards what would later be called 'total history', Marxism offered a theoretical framework of great power. During the 1960s and 1970s political engagement with the Left was common among historians in the Western world, and this, combined with the fissiparous tendency of so much technical history, gave Marxism an immense appeal [extracts 11, 12]. More recently the discrediting of Marxism as a force in world politics since 1989 and the rise of Postmodernism have not only reduced this appeal but have caused some historians to renounce Marxism altogether [extracts 35, 36]. But these acts of renunciation are unlikely to signal the disappearance of Marxist history-writing. The problems to which Marx offered such persuasive and comprehensive answers still remain, and no other theory has stepped into the breach.

III

....

Uncovering the shape of human destiny has certainly been the most ambitious way in which historians have sought to claim a broad significance for their work, but much more widespread has been the subordination of historical writing to immediate political objectives. Since classical times the legitimacy of political institutions and political leaders has been thought to depend on their demonstrable connection with a glorious past. During the Middle Ages every state in Europe encouraged the writing of official histories dominated by the law-givers, saints and warrior-kings of the past. Sometimes the moral of the tale was good government and internal order; sometimes it was superiority over other countries (especially traditional rivals). Some of this history amounted to little more than cynical improvisation on the part of writers seeking political patronage. But much of it reflected and embellished the common knowledge of the time. No society can sustain an identity or a common sense of purpose without 'social memory' – that is, an agreed picture of a shared past, which in most cases will be positive, if not inspiring. This was a pronounced feature of the popular cultural nationalism which spread across Europe during and after the Napoleonic era. As self-proclaimed experts in the past, nineteenth-century historians were under strong pressure to give academic weight to popular traditions of the heroic and the tragic, or to highlight unique national achievements. In wartime particularly, historians may heed the call for history of this kind, however remote it may seem from the kind they normally practise [extract 7].

History-writing has been most in thrall to nationalism when the nation-state is new or in the making – as in America in the early decades of the Republic, or in Germany around the time of unification in the mid-nineteenth century. The same pattern can be discerned in the former colonies which have regained their political independence since the Second World War, as the experience of sub-Saharan Africa shows [extract 9]. No less a nationalist than Julius Nyerere of Tanzania felt compelled to reprove the historians at Dar es Salaam University for exaggerating facts about the African past simply because colonial historians had ignored them.[3] On the other hand in Britain and America, where the stability and endurance of the nation are much more taken for granted, the nationalist tone tends to be less strident.[4] But histories which emphasise American 'exceptionalism' or British commercial and colonial growth are still cast in a nationalist framework, and they invite the charge of politically motivated distortion from the very groups which they exclude or stereotype [extracts 7, 8].

IV

There remains one other stance towards the past to consider. Historians may, like most historicists, disclaim all relevance; they may, like the Marxists, place their labours in the service of a grand model of human history; or they may actively promote a specific political loyalty. But what of the claim that history offers insights and lessons which arise from the historical record itself, and which historians alone are qualified to teach? This claim also has a long history, but in a form which modern historians find unacceptable. From the Renaissance until the eighteenth century history was thought to teach chiefly by example. Ancient Greece and Rome were regarded as an essential source of moral precedents – both good ones to be emulated and bad ones to be shunned. Apprentices to political power, like the sons of the gentry in England, were urged to draw lessons in practical statecraft from the ancients, amplified by modern commentators like Machiavelli. To historians since Ranke this approach seems completely misconceived. For examples drawn from an earlier age to have any authority assumes that the relevant conditions of life and thought are the same. But this is just what cannot be assumed: the lapse of time means that the context now is different, and what was estimable or practicable then cannot be taken as a guide for present practice. The same problem arises with the attempt to act on the belief that history repeats itself. It may do so in a superficial sense. But economic slumps or revolutions – to name two areas which attract crystal-ball gazing – do not occur in isolation, but within a constellation of contingent factors unique to the time in question. Historians are correct to argue that their enquiries into slumps or revolutions in the past cannot yield firm predictions about the future [extracts 26, 27].

When lay people look to history to provide 'answers' it is usually analogies or predictions that they have in mind. Since these approaches are so
antithetical to the historical outlook, it is not surprising that historians are
wary about admitting to any practical wisdom. When they do so, it is on
carefully defined terms. To be convincing, advocates of the relevance of
history must start from the truth that all social experience is historically
constructed and therefore subject to change. This does not mean that
everything is continually changing: Marc Bloch was right to point out
the inertia which characterises some of our social creations [extract 22].
But even the history which 'almost stands still'[5] is set more against the
rapid changes happening concurrently; and those changes create the gulf
between our own age and every previous one. It is the very strangeness of
the past which makes it so valuable as a perspective on the present. History
can tell us a great deal about what is unprecedented in our condition, as
well as make us aware of forgotten alternatives, and these insights can be
applied to international relations or to the institution of the family [extract
23]. History can also be read as a cautionary tale. Given the ample record
of erroneous predictions and unforeseen outcomes, one lesson of history is
surely the danger of making any firm assumptions about the world around
us: the future is always open and we need to cultivate a readiness for all
contingencies [extract 27]. Michael Howard draws attention to a reason
for studying history which is often neglected today, and that is the insight
it gives us into other countries: both the experience which has made them
what they are, and the attitudes prevalent today which were usually formed
by earlier history: the British paid for their ignorance of central Europe in
the 1930s, just as they continue today to pay for their ignorance about the
Irish past [extract 24]. Howard Zinn applies the same kind of thinking
to those aspects of the past of our own society which can jolt us out of
our complacency and passivity [extract 25]. Perspective, rather than
prophecy, is the contribution historians can make to the rational understanding of the contemporary world.

V

The last thirty years have seen more innovation and more debate about
first principles among historians than at any time since the emergence of

the discipline in the mid-nineteenth century. The range of political perspectives from which history is written has greatly expanded; serious
attempts have been made to practise history as a social science, employing
both theoretical models and quantitative method; and Postmodernism has
brought into question the traditional concern of historians with extended
narrative, social identity and textual authenticity. Amid this confusion of
influences, it is easy to see history as lacking any definition – an empty
space open to colonisation by other, more powerful interests. But the
reason why the current debates matter so much to historians is that they
impinge directly on the basic fourfold rationale for the study of history
which I have just outlined. From this perspective the contemporary intellectual ferment, while certainly hectic and turbulent, belongs squarely to a
long-established tradition of self-questioning and reappraisal.

One of the most marked features of Western society since the 1960s
has been the success of excluded social groups in securing access to the
instruments of cultural power. Creating and disseminating the appropriate
social memory is one of the most important of these. Nationalist history
has often been valued by the politically dominant classes precisely because
it excludes other, more subversive memories. Conversely, subordinate
or 'invisible' groups, like women and blacks and sexual minorities, have
recognised that their own political prospects depend on contesting the
national consensus and acquiring a dignified – or 'usable' – past of their
own. One reason why Marxist history was so popular at this time was its
position as the intellectual arm of organised socialism. Equally Black
Power in America and the women's movement on both sides of the Atlantic
have given rise to some highly effective work, designed to raise political
consciousness and give their supporters a sense of empowerment [extracts
14, 16, 17]. Identity-based history is a necessity not only for the nation,
but for any groups or interests within it which feel disfranchised or
excluded from the mainstream.

Historians who stand outside these political constituencies view politically engaged history of a radical kind with mixed feelings. Conservatives,
of whom there are many in the profession, reject it with outrage. Those
who are more open to new influences, and who recognise the claims of
the excluded, are excited by the expanding scope of history. But – like
President Nyerere – they are worried that too much political commitment
will lead to self-serving accounts of the past based on exaggeration and

over-selectivity. The historic role of the group may be exaggerated and its enemies traduced. Also, an identity across time may be claimed with distant predecessors which on closer inspection proves spurious. Indeed, the historian's response to history of this kind is to point out that no identity persists as an unchanging essence; it evolves over time, often changing character radically, and the role of the scholar is to uncover this process rather than salute those who have gone before as 'forebears'. Most academic historians value their intellectual autonomy above political relevance.

In fact the growth of women's history, black history and the rest has followed a much more interesting trajectory than the political bias highlighted by the critics. It would be quite wrong to suggest that all history written in the 1960s and 1970s in association with liberationist political movements was unscholarly. Many writers were able historians who applied their professional skills to new objectives and were genuinely excited by what they found [extract 16]. Political activists viewed with mixed feelings the entry of academic historians into these politically sensitive fields, fearing a loss of cutting edge. But the outcome for the practice of history was highly positive. Not only were social and political history reinvigorated by the arrival of new actors on the historical scene. The explanatory concepts available to historians were also significantly enlarged. Marxism is of course the classic instance of a politically marginal perspective transforming the questions which historians of the mainstream ask. What 'class' was to the labour movement, 'gender' was to the women's movement. The practice of women's history generated a new perspective in which all people and all structures in the past invite analysis from the perspective of gender [extract 18].

Postcolonial scholarship achieved a comparable feat with regard to the historical relationship between the colonising powers and the peoples of the colonial periphery. The outcome has been not only to restore agency to the peoples of the Third World, but to identify the ways in which Western historical scholarship itself has been complicit in the colonial project. Historians from South Asia in particular demand that the voice of the subaltern be heard in the historical record, as a means of empowerment in the present [extracts 19, 20]. As in the case of women's history, what began as a movement of ideologically motivated protest has paid rich dividends in historical understanding.

VI

....

The second area of debate concerns history's relationship to the social sciences. Ever since the Enlightenment the affiliation of the discipline has been in contention between the humanities and the social sciences. Is history of value primarily as a source of cultural and personal enrichment, or does it hold the key to understanding society and planning social change? The first proposition places history among the humanities, and this is the attitude of scholars in the historicist tradition. The second positions history alongside sociology and economics, as a 'scientific' endeavour to furnish social data for the understanding of current problems – the sluggishness of manufacturing industry, or the rise in divorce, or racial tension in our cities. Until the 1960s the loyalty of most historians was to the humanities. But with the upsurge of student radicalism and the call for 'relevance' – both of which enhanced the appeal of sociology at the expense of history – the subject was increasingly seen to fall under the aegis of the social sciences.

Some intellectual dependence on the social sciences was inevitable. The student of the great price inflation of sixteenth-century Europe would have been foolish to resist the expertise of the economist, just as anyone tackling the subject of witchcraft in early modern England was bound, sooner or later, to turn to anthropology for guidance.[6] To that extent, the vogue for social science merely reflected the broadening scope of historical enquiry. But the implications went very much further. The social sciences are characterised by their generalising ambitions. Economists are concerned with the broad principles of economic behaviour, not merely with the record of particular sectors or countries; sociologists conduct a great deal of face-to-face research in narrowly defined localities, but their discipline retains the imprint of its nineteenth-century founders who aimed to grasp the transition to modernity as a process common to the advanced societies of the world. The more historians step back from primary research to identify long-term trends and to make comparisons *between* societies, the more need they have of the concepts of the social scientist. Indeed the scholar studying the process of industrialisation in three European countries might with equal justice be claimed by history, economics and sociology.

To traditionalists history as social science is objectionable because it does not value the particular or the individual [extract 4]. The positive way of identifying the same issue is to say that the sociologically inclined historian is interested in *structure*. Structure is a means of drawing attention to the regularities of behaviour which we share with many others, whether as consumers or voters or followers of fashion. To speak of people in this way does not diminish their individuality, which comprises every facet of their life; it does, however, make their social actions intelligible. Historians who study whole societies or large social collectivities necessarily employ generalising language too, and the social sciences provide a rich conceptual stock [extract 28]. The same is true of change over time. Once structures of behaviour are perceived to shift or to endure through time, the models of social change developed by the social sciences become relevant too. Marxism offers the most striking instance of this; other models include Max Weber on bureaucratisation, and Alexis de Tocqueville on democracy.[7] Much of the suspicion towards this kind of work comes from the fear that the social sciences are imposing their explanatory frameworks, that history will lose its autonomy. It would be closer to the mark to describe the process as dialogue rather than surrender. Historians regard the concepts of sociology and economics as hypotheses to be tested against research, not tablets from heaven. The point is, as E.P. Thompson put it, to conduct 'a quarrel between the model and the actuality'.[8]

VII

The kinds of debates which were raging twenty years ago about history's position relative to the social sciences today seem very dated. They have been almost entirely eclipsed by the current furore over Postmodernism. Here the intellectual reference point lies within the humanities once more, but in a climate which is very hostile to traditional historicism. Much has been written – not least by historians themselves – about the destructive implications of the new ways of thinking. The central issue is what has come to be called 'the linguistic turn'. Postmodernism elevates language as the key to all experience, while at the same time denying that its meaning can be known with any certainty or authenticity: texts are opaque, authors beyond our reach, and 'readings' are determined by the cultural context and ideological inclination of the reader. The most the scholar can hope for is to situate a given text discursively – that is, within a number of intersecting discourses. At one level this set of propositions completely undermines the practice of source criticism as usually understood by historians. But almost every other aspect of historical work unravels as well. If historians cannot read 'their' as opposed to 'our' meanings in the documents, it follows that the 'otherness' of the past cannot be recovered. If language structures experience rather than the other way round, it no longer makes sense to speak of large collectivities (like class and nation) as historical actors with a group identity enduring through time. In fact Postmodernism regards the whole idea of a 'grand narrative' (i.e. a historical process like the spread of the Reformation or the rise of the bourgeoisie) as a discursive construct rather than a historical reality. Ultimately history as practised until now is dismissed as a spurious project to endow our lives in the present with meaning.[9]

Surprisingly, a few historians have enthusiastically signed up to the death of their discipline.[10] But of the positive responses to Postmodernism, the most interesting are those which see the potential for new kinds of history in the midst of the destructive rhetoric. The linguistic turn certainly opens up more subtle and suggestive ways of interpreting texts, and especially the relationship between them ('intertextuality'). Historians have been much influenced by Michel Foucault's theory of 'power/knowledge' with its insistence that discourse is a controlling, repressive force; both the history of the body and the history of revolutions bear witness to this insight.[11]

These new developments are generally grouped together as instances of 'the cultural turn'. This terminology arises from the much broader meanings which are now given to 'culture' within the humanities. Any study primarily concerned with meaning and representation in the past can now be termed 'cultural history'. Such studies account today for a significant proportion of historical work, especially by younger scholars. By opening up the texts of the past to the play of deconstruction, Postmodernism has broadened the scope of cultural interpretation to encompass sometimes wholly novel readings [extract 38]. At the same time, Postmodernism has undermined the confidence with which historians reconstruct events and human agency in the past, leading to the assumption that provisional interpretations of representation are all that can legitimately be attempted.

Historians have expended a great deal of effort on considering the relationship between the cultural turn and the social history which was previously in the ascendant [extract 38]. One consequence has been to turn the spotlight on social identity. Shared identities which issue in collective action are the stuff of social history, but how those identities are constructed and how they inform each other belong to the sphere of culture. The basic categories of social history – notably class and gender – which used to be regarded as fixed and enduring are now seen as fluid and contingent, founded more on the perception of a changing 'other' than on any essential quality of their own [extracts 35, 36].

Cultural history has had a major impact on one other dimension of history previously taken for granted, and that is memory. What people remember – and especially what they remember in common with their neighbours or their fellow citizens – is not just a matter of psychology, but is mediated by their changing circumstances and by the cultural influences to which they are exposed over time. The status of oral history has shifted in line with this view. Previously hailed as the authentic 'voice of the past', first-hand individual testimony is now seen to reflect the way in which memories are subtly modified by the experience which the informant has lived through, and the ways in which that experience has been represented in popular culture. When the content is public and contentious, memory is contested [extract 41].

History-writing is itself one mechanism of public memory. But it is a very self-conscious one, and as subject to manipulation as any other memory device [extract 40]. But whereas the fallibility of individual and collective memory is widely recognised, there is a common presumption that history should be 'true'. Historians themselves may hope that their work will be treated as an objective perspective on the present, but its reception is partly determined by the shape of popular culture and the contests to which that gives rise. These perspectives on collective memory ensure that, if for no other reason, the cultural turn continues to be an immensely important genre of historical writing.

VIII

At the close of the twentieth century debate about the nature and proper scope of historical enquiry is more lively than ever. On one level this is a conflict between rival disciplines for possession of history, as the social science tradition fights it out with Postmodernism. At a deeper level, it elaborates fundamental issues which have exercised historians for more than 200 years. Is the driving force of historical enquiry to bring the past to life or to illuminate the modern world? Should the historian cultivate a passionless detachment or a sympathetic engagement with the people of the past? Is history about what men and women have done, or only about how they represented and constructed their lives? And is history about the doings of individuals who are so richly documented, or about the evolution of society whose traces are so ambiguous and patchy? The vigour of historical scholarship can be partly judged by how openly these issues are debated. On that score historians may have some grounds for optimism about the future of their subject.

Yet, as the last two extracts show, historians have to do more than argue these questions among themselves. Nor is it enough to conduct a debate with intellectuals in adjacent disciplines. In the last resort, the readership of history and the extent of public support for its study will depend on the impact which historians make on the wider public [extracts 42, 43]. The number of academics who bring major historical issues before a general audience, in a way that is accessible without being condescending, is small.[12] Historians cannot affirm the importance of their work without taking steps to secure its dissemination. Only then will they begin to make a reality of the varied aspirations recorded in this volume.

Notes

1 Pieter Geyl, *Debates With Historians*, Fontana, 1962, p. 29.
2 Notably, for example, G.R. Elton, *The Practice of History*, Fontana, 1969.
3 J.K. Nyerere, quoted in C.C. Wrigley, 'Historicism in Africa', *African Affairs* 70 (1971).
4 There are of course exceptions. See Elton's two inaugural lectures, reprinted in his *Return to Essentials*, Cambridge University Press, 1991.
5 Fernand Braudel, 'History and the social sciences: the longue durée', in his *On History*, Weidenfeld & Nicolson, 1980, pp. 25–52.
6 Keith Thomas, *Religion and the Decline of Magic*, Weidenfeld & Nicolson, 1971.
7 See Peter Burke, *History and Social Theory*, Polity, 1992.

8 E.P. Thompson, *The Poverty of Theory*, Merlin Press, 1978, p. 78.
9 For a brief introduction, see John Tosh, *The Pursuit of History: Aims, Methods and New Directions in the Study of Modern History*, 4th edn, Longman, 2006, pp. 193–208. For a fuller and more sympathetic account, see Alun Munslow, *Deconstructing History*, Routledge, 1997.
10 See especially Keith Jenkins, *On 'What Is History?': From Carr and Elton to Rorty and White*, Routledge, 1995.
11 For a useful introductory selection, see Paul Rabinow (ed.), *The Foucault Reader*, Penguin, 1986.
12 For an evaluation of historians' performance in this respect, see John Tosh, *Why History Matters*, Palgrave Macmillan, 2008.

Part One

History for its own Sake

Fidelity to the sources

When historians feel the need to demonstrate their claim to exclusive expertise, they usually base it on their command of the primary sources (rather than, say, their powers of explanation or synthesis). V.H. Galbraith was a distinguished Medievalist whose reputation rested almost entirely on his critical studies of important documents, like Domesday Book and the chronicles of St Albans Abbey. He maintained that the principal value of studying history lay in a direct encounter with the primary sources; by comparison the interpretations of historians were fundamentally transient. G.R. Elton, Tudor scholar and noted controversialist from the 1960s to the 1980s, placed much more faith in the value of historical exposition than Galbraith did, but only if it was disciplined by the requirements of a rigorous historical method: the historian's agenda must be driven by the surviving sources of the past, not the intrusive questions of a present-minded enquirer. Elton returned to this theme many times, latterly in his *Return to Essentials* (1991).

Vivian Hunter

1. V.H. Galbraith

[from An Introduction to the Study of History, *C.A. Watts, 1964, pp. 61–74, 79–82]*

The study of history is a personal activity – it is an individual reading the sources of history for himself. History is, or ought to be, the least authoritarian of the sciences (if that is the right word). Its essential value lies in the shock and excitement aroused by the impact of the very ways and thought of the past upon the mind, and it is for this reason that actual original documents – themselves a physical survival of that past – exercise such fascination upon those who have caught something of its secret. The late canon Foster, writing of the marvellous riches of the archives of Lincoln Cathedral, has perfectly expressed the nature of this emotion. Acknowledging the debt of inspiration he owed to a brother historian, to whom he had written about them, he says: 'Soon afterwards he paid me a visit in Lincolnshire, and it will be long before I shall forget his wonder and delight as I opened before his eyes box after box of the original charters. Each moment I expected to hear from his lips the famous "Pro-di-gi-ous" of the enthusiastic and simple-minded Dominie.' The lectures and the textbooks are a necessary preliminary, a grammar of the subject; but the purpose of all this grammar is to lead the student himself to the sources, from the study of which whatever power our writing and talking has is derived. Where this object is not achieved, we have failed. In my youth it was still common for reviewers to state that *A* or *B* had said 'the last word' on the difficult question of *X, Y* or *Z.* The same fantastic conception still led historians to regard the sources as some dirty coal-mine, from which a precious deposit was recovered, leaving behind a vast, useless slag-heap. I would not be misunderstood: bibliography and historiography are, in their place, of the utmost importance; but the most brilliant reconstructions of the past can never lessen the immediate value of the sources of individual study.

The conception of research as synonymous with the very study of history is not really pedantic: but in fact that much-abused word has long since been identified in our common thinking with a system of higher degrees granted for theses embodying an 'original contribution to knowledge'. With one or two honourable exceptions, a deep line is drawn in British universities between under-graduate and post-graduate students. The writing of these theses is normally confined to the post-graduate students, who usually attempt one of the higher degrees, either the B.Litt. or the Ph.D. The system is largely borrowed from America (where, however, it is far more highly organised), which in turn took it from Germany. The practice of granting higher degrees has much to be said for it, and it has in any case come to stay. Nevertheless I cannot think it altogether congenial to our native outlook, and perhaps we should do well to take stock of it before it becomes quite as much an *incubus* upon English learning as it has already become in America. These 'original' theses are compiled in a very short time – one, two or at most three years: they are done by young people who have scarcely attained the equipment of a scholar by the time the thesis is completed: the choice of a subject is a perennial and notorious difficulty; and the result, at its best, is apt to be the publication of an immature monograph, much less readable than it would have been if more slowly evolved; while a very serious situation may arise for the student if, by an unlucky choice of subject, he fails to attain the degree. More generally, the student works in an atmosphere of anxiety and haste, at the very time in his career when leisure and time to think are most essential. He passes from the superficial study of wide periods (in which undergraduate work largely consists) to a specialisation that is too narrow, too intense and too hurried.

Higher degrees are bound up with the rapid development of historical teaching into a considerable profession. The demand for teachers has introduced competition which in turn threatens to commercialise historical study. It is rightly felt that the best teachers will be drawn from scholars familiar with the original sources, and the easiest proof of such familiarity is a thesis, and preferably a published thesis. Our young scholars are hard put to it to maintain the necessary quantity of 'original' research, while legitimate ambition or economic pressure urges them to hasty publication. The problem is a practical one, and to make even small changes in existing procedure would be a most complicated and difficult task. But having ventured to express my doubts about its adequacy, I will offer three general but still practical suggestions.

1. Something more should be done to efface the hard line generally drawn between under-graduate work and 'research'. Some insight into the raw material of history and the process by which the slick narrative of the textbooks is evolved should be given to all honours students before they get their degrees.

Experience has proved that this can be done, possibly, though not necessarily, by a thesis or exercise, which should not expect, though it might in exceptional cases obtain, publication.

2. The transcribing and editing of texts and documents should be encouraged as subjects for these degrees. At present the subjects are commonly too ambitious, and in the craze for originality the really vital and responsible work of preserving the past by publishing transcripts and calendars is commonly regarded as too humble for the grant of a higher degree. The supplicants for higher degrees would be most usefully employed in doing work for local societies, and such work, just because it is well within their compass, would lay the foundations of a surer and ultimately a wider scholarship than is achieved by the present practice. I am tempted to strengthen my case by a long list of great historians who served their apprenticeship by copying and editing texts, a list that might begin with the names of Stubbs and Maitland. But 'perhaps', wrote Maitland, 'our imaginary student is not he that should come, not the great man for the great book. To be frank with him this is at least probable. . . . But short of the very greatest work, there is good work to be done of many sorts and kinds. . . . At least he can copy, at least he can arrange, digest, make serviceable.'

3. Post-graduate scholarships for research should be freely tenable without any obligation or pressure upon the student to enter for higher degrees. Indeed, I see no reason why theses should not be offered for these degrees, if and when they are completed, without any of the present preliminaries – in exactly the same way as those of riper years now supplicate for the D.Litt. degree. Such an arrangement would make it far easier for the examiners to insist on the proper standard, which is one of the crucial difficulties of the existing system. It would also discourage the too-hasty publication of research in book form, in favour of articles or notes in the reviews. The thesis is commonly far too long and too elaborate, the writer's single talent being hardly discoverable in the napkin of already well-ascertained truth by which it is enveloped. The contribution made by nine out of ten of these theses would go easily into a very few pages, and the verbosity which we all deplore – it must be added – is encouraged by the existing regulations.

I have sometimes wondered whether a great deal of historical research is not vitiated by our insistence upon its originality. Although we pay lip service in our bibliographies to the just division of all historical writings into primary and secondary authorities, we are too apt to forget in practice that the true purpose of writing books about the past is not to supersede the original authorities, but to make their study more significant for our successors. What matters is that history should be studied, as soon and as far as possible, in the original sources; the originality of the result can safely be left to take care of itself, and is in any case beyond our control. The very conception of research is borrowed from the natural sciences, and it is arguable that in learning the method of science we have too slavishly copied its methods. It is obvious that the historical material available for research is strictly limited in amount, and there is a limit to the methods of inquiry which can be employed. On those aspects of history which are most central and worthy of study, original work in the sense of discovery must surely be the exception rather than the rule. On most lines of inquiry a prolonged study of the original sources is needed merely to reach, or to try to reach, the level of our predecessors. The greater part of such work is not 'original', but it is not therefore useless. Viewed across a lifetime, it is rather the main part of one's research, the condition of those occasional publications, which are in reality its by-products. If this be true, it follows that the subjects treated by aspirants to higher degrees become, and must become increasingly, trivial and abstruse, owing to the current demand for originality. I confess myself to be in imperfect sympathy with the popular conception of an army of young and eager experts, organised and equipped for the conquest of History, methodically dividing up among themselves the country to be occupied, and never resting until the last foot of ground is con-quered. One may even doubt whether significant research can be done to order at all. There is something of the accidental about all discovery, which has often only an oblique connexion with the study which led to it. The attempt to organise and direct the human mind on its highest level of activity removes the spontaneity which is its essence, and finds the motive for research in the result to be obtained instead of in the process and the activity themselves. To look back at the vast researches of our predecessors is to realise that their results, important as they were, are in some degree ephemeral, and though much stands fast for future generations, perhaps more is superseded. The activity of research, on the other hand, invaluable to those who pursue it, and to their generation, is perennial, unchanging and significant. Behind the obvious criticisms to which the system of higher degrees is, like any system, open, there is, in my mind at any rate, this deeper uneasiness.

The thoughts of men are never at a stand, they change from generation to generation; and if institutions or doctrines appear to survive for centuries, it is only with an ever-changing meaning. The past is dead – dead as the men who made it. To sink oneself in even the recent past, then, is a hard discipline, but a necessary one if written history is not to be a vast anachronism.

[To approach history as it were from the other end, is to learn humility at the cost of conviction and conceit. To live in any period of the past is to be so over-whelmed with the sense of difference as to confess oneself unable to conceive how the present has become what it is: it is, above all, to regard the study of the original sources not as a preliminary drudgery to the making of 'history', but as its most significant function] Such an attitude, it must be allowed, is not likely to produce a Gibbon or even a Macaulay. But if it makes the writing of history far more difficult, it informs the teaching of history with a new life and reality. The learning of history from the very beginning may become a sort of research whose primary object is an imaginative reconstruction of a different world: a personal effort to make the past, as it was, as much alive as the present. This can only be done by the study of the original sources. It is significant that Keats, who caught the nature of history in a famous sonnet, found his highest inspiration not in the Mr Mitford of his day, but in Homer.

In a conception of this kind what really matters in the long run is not so much what we write about history now, or what others have written, as the original sources themselves. They are an inexhaustible and an invaluable inheritance, to every part of which the historians of each succeeding genera-tion will perpetually refer, if knowledge is to avoid that touch of perversion and monstrosity familiar to us from the periods when it was studied at second hand. The power of unlimited inspiration to successive generations lies in the original sources, and the work of reconstructing the past will end only with the destruction of the evidence for it. A great awakening to the value of the sources for history was indeed a mark of the nineteenth century, and a series of Royal Commissions, the latest of which reported early in the present century, effected most salutary reforms in the custody of the 'public records and of local records of a public nature'. Beyond these lies a vast category of private records, far richer than any other country can boast, which have never been subjected to any form of regulation. These private records are no less valuable for his-torical study than the public records themselves, and it would be the greatest mistake to imagine that even the history of the State itself and of public admin-istration can be studied without them. Yet their very extent is unknown; they are often inaccessible; they are not always properly preserved from decay or the danger of fire, and, above all, the finest collections are continually being dispersed by sale. The Master of the Rolls, it is true, has already given a lead in the preservation of manorial Court Rolls, and a great deal is being done by the British Records Association, the Council for the Preservation of Business Archives and the numerous local record societies. But however much is done by individuals, some form of State regulation and financial assistance is also necessary. At present our governors, though well meaning, are still museum-bound and millionaire-minded. At their best they are collectors who can be induced to buy, but only to buy exhibition pieces, whose value is a scarcity value. The purchase of old pictures, medieval psalters, original signatures, first editions, and the maintenance of derelict castles and abbeys are a sign of goodwill. But this sub-literate interest in the past, excellent in itself, should be the beginning rather than the end of governmental generosity. The safety and integrity of private collections are a much more pressing need.

Not less important than the immediate physical preservation of the original sources of history is the task of putting them into print. The history of classical Greece and Rome reminds us that only that material survives which exists in many copies. More recently, we may recall the irreparable loss to Irish history by the destruction of the records in the Four Courts, or the wastage that must be going on today in Spain and in China. These are very real dangers and very near. Here again we have a right to expect that the enthusiasm and labour of historians should be helped out by more systematic and better-planned financial assistance from the government. The printing of the national archives is the task of H.M. Public Record Office. At the present rate of expenditure, so far from catching up on the past, which was the original intention in printing them, we are actually losing ground. If this continues, the progress of historical knowledge will gradually slow down. Each generation of scholars must look forward to being in a worse position than that which preceded it. The printed material, easily available for study, will become ever less and less in relation to the task to be performed by historians, and the work of synthesising the vast accumulation of material in monographs will in time become impossible. Meanwhile, as knowledge suffers, the danger of a breach in our historical tradition increases. At a modest estimate we have thirteen hundred years of continuous written records behind us. By far the greater portion of that record is still unprinted, and therefore in jeopardy. In the precarious international situation of today what is required is an effort to secure its only final preservation in print, not relatively equal to that of the Victorian age of splendid isolation, but an effort and expenditure relatively ten times greater. With each generation the tradition lengthens, and with the labours of our historical writers it also deepens. But we can only postulate for our descendants a fuller understanding of national history than we possess if we do everything in our power to preserve its past intact.

2. G.R. Elton

[from The Practice of History, *Fontana, 1969, pp. 15–19, 65–9]*

The amount of history that is written today (quite apart from the amount that, though studied, never gets written), and the number of people engaged in various ways in the investigation of the past, should frighten or exhilarate, according to temperament and the phase of the moon. Moreover, like every good service industry, history has something for everybody. Individual craftsmen, working for the few, exist side by side with mass-production factories supplying the needs of the many. All the signs are of health. The university departments are full of students; and teachers of history, laid end to end, might even reach from premise to conclusion. Publishers fall over each other in the rush for historians: even academic historians have at last realized that they own a marketable commodity and need not be quite so awed by the publisher's chequebook. The series multiply. The whole business is beginning to show the marks of a runaway boom: hectic production leading to dilution of quality, price inflation, and ever more insistent warnings from the apprehensive that all good things must come to an end. Indeed, there are signs that we may be reaching that crisis of confidence which can precipitate a slump. At every turn one encounters visceral investigation; the working historian's life is increasingly beset by the specialists in moral exhortation and the prophets of doom.

In some sense, this unsystematic debate is itself a sign of life, though it cannot be denied that life, as usual, involves occasional touches of disease or malformation. Nor is there a great deal that is new in all these doubts and warnings. A good many critics demand that historians should leave the shelter of their muniment rooms and libraries in order to play their part in creating a general intellectual climate; but do they know that they are only repeating the arguments of Voltaire and the eighteenth-century philosophical historians against the antiquarians whose researches they despised?[1] Those who preach the virtues of statistical, sociological or other 'scientific' methods are only reviving, after an interval so short as not quite to excuse their ignorance of the fact, the weary argument whether history is an art or science. Because its materials are necessarily partial, and the products emerging from individual minds more partial still, history always has posed and always will pose the sort of problems which give rise to dispute, acrimony, and the writing of hostile reviews. Why, at the very beginning of our science stands the prototype of all these arguments: history had barely begun when Thucydides attacked the methods and purposes of Herodotus. Debates among historians are coeval with the writing of history, and like the heresies of Christianity all the possible positions were worked out quite early, to be repeated in resounding counterpoint through ages of controversy.

Above all, historians have always wondered just why they do this thing – why they study history. It may be true that a concern with the past is a widely found human characteristic, but that does not dispose of the question. It only puts it one stage back: why should people be interested in the past, and especially why should they be sufficiently interested either to devote an intellectual existence to it or to support the lives of those who do? The question why society should wish to nourish historians leads to its corollary: what should historians do to justify their existence to their society? The simple answer that to study and write history is a pleasant occupation, that it satisfies the practitioners and does no harm to anyone else, is not only too obviously narrow and selfish but may not even be true. Historical writings can do harm; they have done so; and any thoughtful historian must at times ask himself whether he has a purpose beyond his own satisfaction.

The questions may be eternal; the answers tend to go in waves of fashion, cannoning off each other in often predictable reactions to the predominant theory of the moment. Since historians are naturally given to sharpness of tongue, the debate is likely to look savage to the outsider: it is not only in intellectual ascendancy that historical studies prove themselves to have supplanted medieval theology. Nevertheless, a little bit of perspective can fairly be demanded of men who claim to be concerned with the development of things and ideas through time. Thus when we are told, by an historian now in his early thirties, that in the first half of the present century English historians had 'temporarily lost their bearings' because the political and constitutional preoccupations proper when Britain ruled the world had ceased to be valid while nothing else had taken their place,[2] we should point out to him, gently, that he has merely failed to consider the question in a proper historical light. The many good historians whom he thus relegates to confusion and intellectual poverty did not, it is true, happen to hold certain beliefs that are fashionable now. They did not necessarily suppose that only social analysis has value in the study of history, and they did not, on the whole, suppose that they must justify their labours by reference to some non-intellectual effect upon society. But this does not mean that they were not possessed of principles and creeds as definite, and as potentially limiting, as those proclaimed by their critics. The first half of this century was dominated among English historians by a conviction that the principles of respectable historiography could be reduced to one main precept: to study history for its own sake. Though this austere rule could and did produce a fair amount of narrow tedium, it also resulted in some most remarkable monuments of the historian's craft. It is, so far, by no means clear that those who react against it are likely to write history anything like so well founded, so careful in its pursuit of the truth, or so uninfluenced by pre-conceived ideas and ready-made answers. Their chances of doing so are at present hard to judge because after quite a few years of manifestoes and occasional learned articles they have notched up a still surprisingly small amount of identifiable achievement.

....

            Mr Carr and Dr Plumb[3] are, at heart, 'whigs', looking into the past for reassurance; they begin with the assumption of a social purpose stated (that the historian must offer to society a demonstration of its power to advance itself) and they then eliminate any use of history which does not contribute to this purpose. For this reason they do fall into the deterministic error of choosing from the variety of history the line of events and detail which leads to their own present position, their preconceived end; everything else, if they do not ignore it, they explain away. The right approach would surely start from the other end. We must first explain in what manner the past can truly be studied – that is, we must accept the despised tenet that the past must be studied for its own sake – and then enquire whether this study has any contribution to make to the present.

    In short, we are once again faced with the autonomy of history: the study of history is legitimate in itself, and any use of it for another purpose is secondary. That secondary use will be laudable or deplorable in proportion as the autonomous purpose has been served well or ill. If I have rather more respect for the progress doctrines of Dr Plumb or Mr Carr than I have for the historical racialism of Rosenberg or the historical inevitabilities of Marxism, it is because I think their history better; if I have my reservations about their preferred interpretations, and especially about their prescriptions to other historians, it is because in my view they still ignore far too much about the past. The task of history is to understand the past, and if the past is to be understood it must be given full respect in its own right. And unless it is properly understood, any use of it in the present must be suspect and can be dangerous. One cannot use a corrupt means to a worthy end. And the creation of the sound instrument involves not only obvious things like doing the serious work of study, avoiding anachronism both in interpretation and judgment, devoting attention to the defeated as well as to the victors; it involves, above all, the deliberate abandonment of the present. The historian studying the past is concerned with the later event only in so far as it throws light on the part of the past that he is studying. It is the cardinal error to reverse this process and study the past for the light it throws on the present.

However, it does not in the least follow from this that the study of history, treated as autonomous and justified within itself, has no contribution to make beyond its frontiers. In the first place, let it be remembered that this pursuit of history in its own right is not only morally just but also agreeable. A good many people simply want to know about the past, for emotional or intellectual satisfaction, and the professional historian fulfils a useful 'social' function when he helps them to know better. He is also, of course, satisfying his own desire for knowledge, and he also is, after all, a part of society. This might be supposed to reduce the historian to a mere entertainer, but in fact it gives him a cultural role: he contributes to the complex of non-practical activities which make up the culture of a society. When he stimulates and satisfies the imagination he does not differ essentially from the poet or artist, which is not to say that he should be picturesque. There is an emotional satisfaction of a high order to be gained from extending the comprehending intelligence to include the past.

Next, it would certainly be untrue to suppose that history can teach no practical lessons. It enlarges the area of individual experience by teaching about human behaviour, about man in relationship to other men, about the interaction of circumstances and conditions in their effect upon individual and social fortunes. Its lessons are not straightforward didactic precepts, either instructions for action (the search for parallels to a given situation) or universal norms (history teaches that every thing progresses, history teaches the triumph – or futility – of moral principles); there is far too much variety about the past, far too much confused singularity about the event, to produce such simple results. Nevertheless, a sound acquaintance with the prehistory of a situation or problem does illumine them and does assist in making present decisions; and though history cannot prophesy, it can often make reasonable predictions. Historical knowledge gives solidity to the understanding of the present and may suggest guiding lines for the future.

Yet these emotional and practical uses of history are not its main contribution to the purpose of man. The study of history is an intellectual pursuit, an activity of the reasoning mind, and, as one should expect, its main service lies in its essence. Like all sciences, history, to be worthy of itself and beyond itself, must concentrate on one thing: the search for truth. Its real value as a social activity lies in the training it provides, the standards it sets, in this singularly human concern. Reason distinguishes man from the rest of creation, and the study of history justifies itself in so far as it assists reason to work and improve itself. Like all rational activities, the study of history, regarded as an autonomous enterprise, contributes to the improvement of man, and it does so by seeking the truth within the confines of its particular province, which happens to be the rational reconstruction of the past. In this larger purpose it has no sort of monopoly, for this it shares with every form of intellectual investigation, but it happens to have certain advantages in that it attracts a wide variety of intelligences, can do its work without too much demand on technical specialization in the learner, and can rest its capacity to train on its capacity to entertain.

In these advantages, which it possesses over both the natural and the social sciences, lie its temptations and perils: absence of technical specialization can lead to lack of rigour, entertainment to meretricious superficiality, variety of appeal to bias and propaganda. But the dangers do not deny the advantages; the possibility of corruption does not cast out the possibility of excellence. Integrity, resting on professional training and professional attitudes, is the safeguard. All historical work which satisfies the conditions of professional competence and integrity fulfils the historian's very important social duty; none that falls short of that standard can be trusted to fulfil any social duty safely, however conscious it may be of its obligations or however earnestly it may preach progress, the goodness of man, or the inevitability of revolutions. The quality of an historian's work must, as I have said, be judged purely by intellectual standards; the same is true of his contribution to society, though moral consequences may well flow from adherence to these principles of the reasoning capacity. It is not the problems they study or the lessons they teach that distinguish the historical sheep from the goats, but only the manner of their study, the precision of their minds, and the degree to which they approximate to the ultimate standards of intellectual honesty and intellectual penetration. *Omnia veritas.*

Notes

1 A.D. Momigliano, *Studies in Historiography*, Weidenfeld & Nicolson, 1966.
2 Keith Thomas in *Times Literary Supplement*, 7 April 1966, p. 275.
3 E.H. Carr, *What Is History?*, Penguin, 1964; J.H. Plumb, *The Death of the Past*, Macmillan, 1969. Both argued for a 'progressive' role for historians. See below, extracts 5 and 6 (ED).

Empathy and imagination

To some historians the documentary ideal has seemed inadequate. If the past is to come alive and speak to us directly, it must be approached with imagination as well as technical expertise. The historian's subjectivity is central to the idea of re-creation or resurrection, but it is a subjectivity in the service of the past, not the present. As the passage from C.V. Wedgwood makes clear, this way of thinking was most fully developed by the Romantics, particularly Sir Walter Scott. In her fine accounts of seventeenth-century England – particularly *The King's Peace* (1955) and *The King's War* (1958) – Wedgwood herself acknowledged the importance of place and ambience in kindling the historian's imaginative identification with the people of the past. For Richard Cobb the explanatory side of history is completely subordinated to the vivid evocation of obscure lives in the past. In order to be as receptive as possible to the voices encountered in the documents, he immersed himself in French life, acquiring what he called 'a second identity'. In books like *Death in Paris* (1978) Cobb brought the human aspects of revolutionary France uniquely to life.

3.   C.V. Wedgwood

[from 'The Sense of the Past', the Leslie Stephen Lecture for 1957, reprinted in her History and Hope, *Fontana, 1987, pp. 416–18, 420–3]*

Ralph Penderel, the hero of that tantalizingly unfinished fragment by Henry James, *The Sense of the Past*, had written – it was his only literary achievement – an unpretending work called *An Essay in Aid of the Reading of History*. From all we ever hear of this work it sounds a not very original consideration of the magic of old places and old things, redeemed by the extraordinary intensity with which its author experienced a relatively commonplace romantic emotion. 'There are particular places', Ralph Penderel is supposed to have written, 'where things have happened, places enclosed and ordered and subject to the continuity of life mostly, that seem to put us into communication, and the spell is sometimes made to work by the imposition of hands, if it be patient enough, on an old object or an old surface.' There is nothing very remarkable in the sentiment, but we are asked to believe that Ralph Penderel's attachment to the past, or rather to surviving objects of the past, was a faith strong enough to work a miracle, and transfer him back a century in time.

Even in fiction such miracles are to be distrusted, although the surviving pages of *The Sense of the Past* suggest that Henry James would have explored the impossible situation with a rare subtlety. But I have pirated his title because it indicates the nature of a problem, part historical, part literary, which has increasingly concerned students of the past. Is there anything to be said for the cultivation of the sense of the past, for the attempt to make the imaginative leap from our own epoch to an earlier one? Is it helpful to serious historical inquiry to encourage some play of the imagination; is it a dangerous folly or an essential exercise? The frontier between scholarship and creative literature is a disputed one, over which there has been much verbal combat. In this particular problem, that of historical imagination, literature has made significant contributions to scholarship and scholarship to literature.

We learn from the preface of the first edition to Henry James's posthumous fragment *The Sense of the Past* that he turned to this historical ghost story partly to take his mind off the troubles of the contemporary world during the First World War. His hero, too, found in the contemplation of the past a relief from the difficulties of the present. The desire for withdrawal, admitted or not, is often a powerful motive in driving the student, whether he be an amateur or a professional, towards the study of history. This element of escape implies also a certain lack of realism, which easily becomes a desire to idealize or at least to romanticize the past. The serious student of history, if he has, or is aware of, this weakness, has to be constantly on guard against it. On the other hand, without this romantic impetus, without this desire to remove from one age into another, to imagine and to share in the thoughts and feelings of a time remote from the present, historical inquiry would lack an essential element. Historical knowledge is in debt to the romantic writers, not so much for what they themselves did (though some of them made considerable advances in the study of the past), as for the deeper and wider scope that they gave to historical inquiry.

The summoning up of emotion like that of Henry James's hero, over some particular object or some particular place, hallowed by some great or supposedly great event, was not of course peculiar to the romantic or post-romantic epoch. Cicero spoke of 'the power of admonition that is in places'. Montaigne pondered on this way of feeling, in the sixteenth century: 'Is it nature, or by some error of fantasy, that the seeing of places that we know to have been frequented or inhabited by men whose memory is esteemed or mentioned in stories doth in some sort move and stir us up as much or more than hearing their noble deeds?'

Even the unsentimental Gibbon who was not, as he himself said, 'very susceptible of enthusiasm', was moved in this way by his first visit to Rome. 'After a sleepless night, I trod with a lofty step the ruins of the Forum. Each memorable spot where Romulus stood, or Tully spoke, or Caesar fell, was at once present to my eye, and several days of intoxication were lost or enjoyed before I could descend to a cool or minute investigation.' But that 'cool or minute investigation' was the proper occupation of an inhabitant of the Age of Reason, and Gibbon took care to let the intoxication evaporate before he began on the serious business of inquiry. To judge by this passage, he was also doubtful if these days of intoxication, which he admits he enjoyed, were not, by a more severe judgment, to be accounted 'lost'.

Dr Johnson, on the other hand, did not hesitate to ascribe some value to these intoxicating emotions. 'Far from me and from my friends be such frigid philosophy as may conduct us indifferent and unmoved over any ground which has been dignified by wisdom, bravery or virtue. That man is little to be envied whose patriotism would not gain force upon the plain of Marathon or whose piety would not grow warmer among the ruins of Iona.' This is already very close indeed to the frankly romantic fervour of John Keats:

> There is a charm in footing slow across the silent plain
> Where patriot battle has been fought, where glory had the gain;
> This is a pleasure in the heath where Druids old have been
> Where mantles grey have rustled by and swept the nettled green . . .

Clearly the feelings experienced, or manufactured, by Johnson, by Keats, and by many others, owed much less to knowledge of the past than they did to modern emotions; they were using historic sites not to strengthen their vision of the past for its own intrinsic interest, but simply to heighten their contemporary sensations of patriotism or piety.

But place has a real as well as a spurious charm and the more serious student of history does often find fascination in visiting the site of an event, quite apart from the value as evidence which it may also possess. The charm exercised by objects can be equally powerful. There is a fascination in the continued physical existence of chairs, tables, spoons, goblets, trenchers – things that were used and handled, not necessarily by the rare and famous whose names have survived, but simply by some of the millions whose names are as dead and forgotten as they are themselves.

The massive editing of documents over the last century, and the increasing use of such modern aids to research as photostat and microfilm, have relieved the historian of the continual necessity of manuscript research, though there will always remain certain things about which the manuscript and the manuscript only can enlighten us. But it is not necessity alone which draws the student of history constantly back to manuscript documents. There is a peculiar pleasure in the mere contact of the hand with the paper. I can speak with assurance only for that epoch to which most of my manuscript researches have been confined, the seventeenth century. Nothing seems to bridge the gap of the years so much as the unfolding and reading of ancient letters; sometimes minute particles of sand which had long adhered in some thick down stroke where the ink had been wet, detach themselves after three hundred years to blow away and join with yesterday's dust. This feeling for objects not merely as evidence but *for themselves* is not logically defensible; the moment we think about it we see that they do not really bring the past any nearer simply because they have existed, in one form or another, over a period of ten, twenty or a hundred generations. Landscape alters continuously. Gibbon when he trod with lofty step the ruins of the Forum was treading for the most part twenty or thirty feet higher than the footsteps of antiquity, though he did not use 'lofty' in that sense. Allowing for erosion, preservation and repair, very few surfaces of ancient things are in fact wholly ancient, and neither the ink nor the paper of that distracted complaint of the indiscipline of the Royalist cavalry, which I was reading last week, look the same to me as they did to Colonel John Boys, the governor of Donnington Castle, who wrote it, or to Prince Rupert who received it, in the spring of 1644.

It is not always the place itself but some element in it which, fused with our living knowledge, may suddenly vitalize the past. Some years ago in Switzerland I came almost by accident on the birthplace of Zwingli in the Toggenburg. The wooden peasant's house had been a good deal smartened up and restored. It had also been carefully furnished – in the praiseworthy and instructive modern manner – with such objects as would give the visitor an idea of a typical farmhouse interior at the latter end of the fifteenth century. But the house and all in it were vivid for me because I had lived for some months in childhood in a relatively modern farmhouse on the farther side of Switzerland, which was built on exactly the same plan. This is interesting evidence no doubt of the continuity of tradition in the building of Swiss farmhouses. But its immediate importance for me was that it brought a whole section of the past into my line of vision, almost into my personal experience: because I knew what it was like to live in such a house; knew the snug comfort of the wooden walls with the shutters closed at night, and the genial warmth from the oven, and – making considerable allowances for the differences between life in the last quarter of the fifteenth century and life in the first quarter of the twentieth – there remained at least a certain overlapping experience between Ulrich Zwingli and me.

Marc Bloch has said in those valuable and fragmentary reflections on *The Historian's Craft*, which he wrote during his years in the Resistance, and which were published posthumously after his capture and death, that the historian can only, in the last analysis, reconstruct the past by borrowing from, and applying, his own daily experience of life. Jacob Burckhardt was expressing the same idea in a rather different form when he described the purpose of his lectures to his students in Basle: he wished, he said, 'to make every member of my audience feel and know that everyone may and must take independent possession of what appeals to him personally'. 'Take independent possession' is the key phrase; for ultimately the understanding of the past, in so far as it is achieved at all, has to be independently achieved, by a sustained effort of the imagination working on a personal accumulation of knowledge and experience.

It was just this imaginative effort which the Romantics forced upon – or bequeathed to – historical scholarship. The foremost figure in this development was Sir Walter Scott. Leslie Stephen put the matter briefly and effectively when he spoke of the great step made by Scott when he observed that our ancestors were once 'as really alive as we are now'. The fashion for Sir Walter Scott's novels, not in the British Isles alone but over all western Europe, probably did more than any other single influence to awaken the minds of educated people to the vitality of the past. This is attested by the strongest possible witness, all the more telling because he is not altogether a favourable one. Leopold von Ranke has recorded, in an autobiographical fragment, the effect which the works of Scott had on him as a young man.

> The romantic historical works of Sir Walter Scott, which were well known in all languages and to all nations [he writes], played a principal part in awakening my sympathy for the actions and passions of past ages. On me too they exercised their spell and I read his works more than once with the most lively interest. But I was also offended by them. Among other things it distressed me that in *Quentin Durward* he treated Charles the Bold and Louis XI in a manner quite contrary to historical evidence . . . Comparison convinced me that historical statements are more beautiful and in any case more interesting than romantic fiction. I turned away altogether from the latter and resolved that in my own works I would neither invent nor poeticize anything but would confine myself strictly to the facts.

There are two parts of this confession of Ranke, and the last half – the criticism of *Quentin Durward* – is very often quoted without reference to what precedes it. First Ranke admits and indeed emphasizes that Scott had made history a living interest to thousands of readers, and had therefore brought into being for the historian a larger and a more sympathetic audience than ever before. Only then does he go on to express his distress at the shortcomings of *Quentin Durward* as a work of history, and so to dedicate himself to the establishment of fact pure and unadorned. In the introduction to his first major work he reiterated this dedication in the form in which it is best known, and declared that it is the historian's task only to show what actually happened ('*Er will bloss zeigen wie es eigentlich gewesen*'). The ideal was not one that could be realized, but if Sir Walter Scott can claim the credit not only for awakening a new public but also for starting Ranke on his career of fruitful and massive achievement, our debt to him becomes greater than ever.

4. Richard Cobb

[from 'Experiences of an Anglo-French Historian', in his
A Second Identity: Essays on France and French History,
Oxford University Press, 1969, pp. 17–20, 43–7]

I have never understood history other than in terms of human relationships; and I have attempted to judge individuals in their own terms and from what they say about themselves, in their own language.

Most interesting of all, to me, is the individual unrelated to any group, the man, the girl, or the old woman alone in the city, the person who eats alone, though in company, who lives in a furnished room, who receives no mail, who has no visible occupation, and who spends much time wandering the streets. For, apart from the everlasting problem of violence, the principal one that faces a historian like myself is that of loneliness, especially loneliness in the urban context. Hence my inveterate taste for the *chronique judiciaire* of *Le Monde* and, in its day, of *Libération* (the realm of the marvellous, the generous Madeleine Jacob, the warmest of popular historians, the most at home of any in *la correctionelle*). Gaby, from Pézenas has committed suicide in a *chambre de bonne* in the XV*me*; the body of Micheline, scantily clad in black underwear, her throat slit, has been discovered in the bedroom of an *hôtel de passe*, rue des Acacias. Madeleine, a Lyonnaise, in Paris only for the previous three months, has been shot dead, coming out of a Cours Pigier. Marcelle has been found stabbed to death, in the Bois de Boulogne; she was from la Ferté-Bernard. And so on. The *concierge*, plied by reporters, can only say: 'Ce fut une jeune fille tranquille, une vraie jeune fille, je ne lui connaissais aucune liaison, elle ne recevait point de visites'. The parents, back home, are bewildered. Sooner or later, the *dossier* is closed. But not for the historian. What road, thus terminating in violence, has been followed by the daughter of a *cheminot* from Saint-Germain-des-Fossés? Into what fearful trap has the lonely provincial girl stumbled? For many years, my favourite historians have been the late Pierre

Bénard and Madeleine Jacob (to whom I am further indebted for much information concerning Marie Besnard [. . .] all of whose trials she attended).

For myself, history has never been an intellectual debate. This may be due in part to my own insufficiencies, for I am no debater; but also I have never felt the need of it. For historians should not 'intellectualize' about people often less sophisticated than themselves, and about societies less complicated than those in which we live. In history, intellectual debate can so often be a cover for over-simplification, lack of experience, insufficient culture, lack of involvement and of sympathy, and the impetus to compare and to generalize in cases where comparisons and generalizations are either irrelevant or positively misleading. Why, one wonders, when reading certain sections of *Past and Present*, why do historians spend so much time arguing, imposing definitions, proposing 'models', when they could be getting on with their research?

I have, then, worked on French history because I like being in France and have now reached the second generation of my French friends. To live in France is to live double, every moment counts, the light of the sky of the Île-de-France is unique and a source of joy, there is joy too in a small rectangle of sunshine at the top of a tall, greying, leprous building, the colour of Utrillo, and in the smell of chestnuts that brings the promise of autumn, *la Rentrée*, and the beloved repetition of the Paris year. There is joy in speaking French, and in listening to women, children, Louis Jouvet, and Michel Simon speaking it. Paris is the abode of love, as well as of violence; if, as Louis Chevalier reminds us, the Paris street *sent le poudre*, it is only sometimes, whereas love is there all the time, in a cat arching its back in the sun, and in the eyes of *la belle boulangère* in her white apron. To speak and to write in French is to acquire a second personality and to express oneself not only in another gear, but in a manner other than in one's first. I do not say the same things in French as I do in English, because I am not the same person. For nine years I dispensed with my initial nationality almost entirely, and without any great feeling of deprivation.

My sense of involvement has been further enlarged by the experience of events over a long period, by personal contacts, and by random reading, over the years, of such populist and regionalist novelists as Eugène Dabit (the Paris suburbs), Louis Guilloux (Saint-Brieuc), Maxence van der Meersch (Roubaix), Marc Bernard (Nîmes), Henri Béraud (Lyon), René Fallet (Villeneuve-Saint-Georges), Raymond Queneau (Le Havre, the northern suburbs of Paris, Paris itself), Hervé Bazin (the Craonnais), René Lefèvre (Paris), Julien Blanc (mostly *maisons de redressement* and prisons), Panaït Istrati, and Blaise Cendrars (especially on the subject of Marseille). History is a cultural subject that cannot be disassociated from literature and language.

And both resist the attempts of syllabus-merchants to impose upon each the iron frame of periodicity. A great deal of Paris eighteenth-century history, of Lyon nineteenth-century history can be walked, seen, and above all heard, in small restaurants, on the platform at the back of a bus, in cafés, or on the park bench. I have at times been so much aware of this that, in order to improve my chances as an investigator of the past and to cast deeper roots in France, I have been tempted to apply for naturalization. Fortunately, I have been deterred on each occasion by the slowly grinding mills of French bureaucracy, as well as by the thought that I would no more belong in a French institutional framework than in an English one. I have tried to have it both ways: to increase my sense of involvement, and to preserve my status of Lone Wolf. It has not always worked very well. But after the *13 mai*,[1] French naturalization lost all its attraction.

....

In *Rue du Havre*,[2] Paul Guimard describes the scene outside Saint-Lazare, between 7.30 and 9.30 a.m., as witnessed by an elderly man, something of a sentimentalist, who lives in a *chambre de bonne* in the XIIme and who, as a war veteran, takes up his daily stand as a lottery ticket salesman, at the street corner. The man, who is utterly lonely, embarks on a series of fantasies in which various regular passers-by in the morning rush are not only identified, but, through the intervention of the stationary witness, introduced to each other, so that their lives are permanently changed. At 7.55 each morning a tall blonde girl – she could be a *bretonne* – her fair hair bobbing in the fast-moving sea of commuters, is carried past the vendor on his raft. At 7.59 there follows a young man, bare-headed, who smokes a pipe. The lottery man becomes attached to the two, looks out for them each day, establishing for them an imaginary itinerary: the girl, he decrees, lives in le Pecq with her widowed mother – or perhaps her grandmother – she takes the train at le Pecq at 7.20, and works for an *agent de change* somewhere near the rue Vivienne. (He has at least been able to ascertain that, on leaving the rue du Havre, she crosses over, left-turns, and disappears behind Le Printemps.) The young man lives in Rueil, taking a direct train from there at 7.30 a.m. He too heads left after Le Printemps; he must be some sort of engineer, working for a big industrial firm. He is unmarried – the old man is sure of this – but does not wish to remain permanently so. The blonde too is thinking eventually in terms of a family, but she has not met the right man. The two can never meet on the same train, and they are never likely to find themselves jostled together in the early-morning crush. Four minutes separate, apparently for ever, the two lives. The witness is powerless, he would like to stop the girl, tell her not to hurry, to wait till she is left in the trough of the wave, to be carried forward in the next swell from the station. He longs for some minor accident: a power failure which would keep her train stuck in le Vésinet or in Chatou for $3\frac{1}{2}$ minutes. There are days when one or other is missing; there is an occasion when the girl is carried along in the 8.12 wave; the old man notices that she is looking pale. And then, after weeks, after months, the miracle happens: both emerge, almost level, at 8.1. The vendor plunges into the crowd, pulls the girl's sleeve, calls to the young man, it is all a matter of seconds, they disappear, talking together, round the left bend. Contact has been established, not only between the girl and the young man, but between what is now the beginnings of a couple and their introducer. All three lives are radically changed, and for a period at least the vendor is pulled out of his lone-liness; the young man, who is a *chef de rayon* in Le Printemps – for that is as far as he ever went – secures him a temporary job as Father Christmas in the toy department.

The situation of the old man is similar to that of the historian – or of a certain sort of historian – also a stationary witness, an observer of a swirling collectivity of which he is not a part. He too is lonely, given to fantasy, having to make do with a few scraps of evidence, in an effort to give life to the passing faces. In his passionate desire to know, to establish contacts, there is an ele-ment of self-identification; he is both the blonde girl *and* the young man, *and* the red-faced, leather-coated gas man in the peaked cap, *and* the hard-faced woman in her late 40s who looks as if she runs her own small business. He too is attempting to break out of loneliness, even if it is a matter of living with the dead. For, to live with the dead, he must live with the living. Loneliness gives him that extra perception, those qualities of curiosity, imagination, and compassion, that are the necessary tools of his trade. I can only speak from experience; and history is experience. One becomes a certain sort of historian because one is a certain sort of person. I have always been a very lonely person, and like others similarly placed, I have sat in restaurants, picking up fragments of conversation, have headed for the café open late at night. In this perpetual attempt to escape from loneliness, the people that one is most likely to meet are themselves lonely. So many of them, after the third or fourth glass of calvados, will push their hats back and begin to give forth, to reminisce and to complain.

The historian then, as I imagine him, is Guimard's hero. He is also the Commissaire Maigret, his old-fashioned Gladstone bag, hastily but neatly packed by Madame Maigret, in his right hand, as he walks through the *salle des pas perdus* [entrance hall] of a provincial station, heading for the place de la Gare: a pause to look at the *planisphère* and map out the town, a few indecisive steps to look through the doors of three or four cafés, before deciding on one for breakfast, over the local paper and with ears attuned. An hour or more walking through the town from end to end – the station at one end, the cathedral at the other, the *sous-préfecture* half-way down – for how many French provincial towns resemble thus the simple plan of Fontenay-le-Comte of *Au bout du rouleau*! Having thus completed the exploration of the backbone of the herring, there is time to look at the side streets, before finally heading, in Maigret's case, for a certain house, for an hotel, in the historian's, for the *mairie*. It is the period at which the Commissaire is content to put his nose to the wind, to establish an ambience and the hour-by-hour clockwork of a small provincial town. Later he will talk to people; but first he must get his bearings, then he can explore assumptions and relationships and find out who is important. It is the most exciting stage of his *enquête*, before anything begins to fall into place, and it is often the most exhilarating stage of research.

There is more too that can be learnt from Maigret, for the Commissaire knows how, with patience, to reconstruct a life, a pattern of work and leisure, even a *vie intime*, from a few scraps of evidence and the inflexion of a voice. He is already loaded with a considerable weight of experience, and he is easily at home with small people. He feels uneasy, on the other hand, with the wealthy, the fashionable, the snob; the only foreigners for whom he feels an affinity are the sort of people Simenon's mother used to lodge in Liège: students from Russia and Eastern Europe, Jewish tailors. Though he shouts loud, has a terrible temper, he is not without compassion. For his older customers, *vieux chevaux de retour*, semi-criminals who have made good, set themselves up in the restaurant business, he has a genuine affection, the sort that is derived from shared experiences in the past and from the recollection of old times. He is rather out of sympathy with the young, does not like change, makes no allowance for revolution, believes that things were better when he was a young man in the career; there were less clever chaps about then. The *commissaire* is an artist in his way who likes seeing things for himself, even if it means staying up most of the night in a café by the canal or opposite the quai des Orfèvres; he does not like paper-work, nor employing assistants. He is an amateur, for he has never been trained in techniques. He does not even use *fiches*. But he knows where to find them, at the top of the PJ [the building of the Police Judiciaire].

At 4 o'clock one morning in a *tabac* in the rue du Four, I met a very drunken couple. One was a civilian pilot, who was to fly the next morning, and who had already been threatened with the removal of his licence after a drunken landing. The other was a very well-dressed, rubicund man, with neatly brushed black hair, a hat with a dark band, well-kept hands, and a diamond pin in his tie. He looked professional, and was at first reticent. But by 5 o'clock he was anxious to speak of himself, and gave me a number of hints. 'I am a Belgian; I come to Paris for the summer; I only work here in July, August, and early September; I only work in the XVI*me* and the XVII*me*. My work involves me with Post Offices, female servants, and chauffeurs.' It did not seem very difficult; I told him he was a professional house-breaker. He was delighted, opened a handsome pigskin bag, displaying some hundred instruments on runners. He was a man who enjoyed his work, but he also liked talking about it, and needed an audience.

This is both a personal and an aesthetic view of history. There are, of course, many sorts of history, and the historian makes his choice, which will always be dictated to some extent by his own sense of involvement and by a certain feeling of identification with the period and with the country to which he devotes his research. Indeed, I believe that such a sense of involvement is not only inevitable but even necessary, for the historian is not a cold clinician, he is not dealing with steely concepts *à la Saint-Just*[3] nor with geological 'social structures', he is concerned primarily with human beings. Olwen Hufton can write with such sympathy of Bayeux because she was partly educated there, of women, because she is a woman, of the nuns, because she was taught by them, and she can understand what poverty means to the mother of a large family, because she is aware, from her own experience, of the preponderant place occupied by the Catholic Church in the lives of the female poor. Edward Thompson became the leading historian of a section of the English working class after living for more than fifteen years in Halifax. He also possesses literary gifts which are, unfortunately, rare in an historian.

It is possible to write history that is in no way human. Many economic historians and some diplomatic ones have demonstrated how this can be done. It is no doubt a necessary kind of history, as important as any other. But in the end, history being a cultural subject, one can only judge it by applying to it cultural values. I distrust, when applied to history, such words as 'laboratory', 'workshop', 'group project', just as I distrust those who speak of universities in terms of 'the plant'. Something very alarming occurred in France when, in each university, the old and meaningful title of 'Faculté des Lettres' was given the meaningless and baroque addition of 'et des Sciences Humaines'. For history is not a science, nor should it be written by teams. We can leave that to surgery. The writing of history is one of the fullest and most rewarding expressions of an individual personality.

The historian should, above all, be endlessly inquisitive and prying, constantly attempting to force the privacy of others, and to cross the frontiers of class, nationality, generation, period, and sex. His principal aim is to make the dead live. And, like the American 'mortician', he may allow himself a few artifices of the trade: a touch of rouge here, a pencil-stroke there, a little cotton wool in the cheeks, to make the operation more convincing. Of course, complete understanding is impossible and the historian of the common people, of popular movements, and of individualistic eccentrics can only scratch at the surface of things. He may recapture a mentality; but he cannot probe deeply. He can only make one man witness for many by the selective use of the individual 'case history' as a unit in historical impressionism.

I do not know what history is about, nor what social function it serves. I have never given the matter a thought. There is nothing more boring than books and articles on such themes as 'What is History?', 'The Use of History', 'History and Something Else'. I do, however, find enormous enjoyment in research and in the writing of history. I am happy in it, and that is the main thing.

Notes

1 13 May 1940 was the date of the German invasion of France (ED).
2 *Rue du Havre*, novel published in 1957 by Paul Guimard (ED).
3 Saint-Just was a principal architect of the Terror in the French Revolution (ED).

Political Histories

History as progress

Progress is often thought of as being self-evident, partly because most people like to believe that they live in an age of progress. Advocates of progress are not necessarily partisan, but their interpretation is always political in the sense that it depends on prioritising some social values at the expense of others. Beliefs in progress often underpin more explicitly political histories, as in the case of Marxism (see below).

Historians today are less prone than their eighteenth- and nineteenth-century forebears to invoke progress as the governing principle of their work, partly because they are less confident that the civilisation of their own day represents a peak of human achievement, and partly because they hesitate to condemn 'unprogressive' epochs in the past. J.H. Plumb was a historian of eighteenth-century England who in his more personal statements echoed some of the optimism of Enlightenment intellectuals. Having rejected the idea that historians should crudely minister to the powers-that-be, he declared that sound critical history was valuable primarily because it documented the triumphs of human rationality and thus gave grounds for confidence in the future. E.H. Carr, though coming from a very different political position, reached similar conclusions. In his celebrated polemic, *What Is History?* (1961), he instanced Marxism and Freudianism as evidence of the advance of human reason into previously obscure areas, and saluted the emancipation of the former colonies of the European powers as the most important progressive tendency in the political realm. Carr even restated the eighteenth-century belief that historians were in a uniquely privileged position to determine the likely direction of the future, but few historians have followed him.

5. J.H. Plumb

[from The Death of the Past, *Macmillan, 1969, pp. 105–6, 136–45]*

The aim of history I believe, is to understand men both as individuals and in their social relationships in time. Social embraces all of man's activities – economic, religious, political, artistic, legal, military, scientific – everything, indeed, that affects the life of mankind. And this, of course, is not a static study but a study of movement and change. It is not only necessary to discover, as accurately as the most sophisticated use of evidence will allow, things as they actually were, but also why they were so, and why they changed; for no human societies, not one, have ever stood still. Although we carry within ourselves and within our societies innumerable relics of the past, we have discarded, outgrown, neglected and lost far more. But we have been moulded by Time, all of us, from the naked Negrito in the Malayan forest to the Nobel prize-winners of the Rockefeller Institute. This is a truism, but how this happened poses a problem of exceptional intellectual complexity. The materials for its solution are the debris of Time itself – the records, the artefacts, the monuments, even the landscapes we live in and the languages we speak – materials that are infinite in their number and combination, yet capable of order and interpretation. The historical methods and techniques for the investigation of this process are comparatively young; most of them, such as archaeology, palaeography, topography, sociology, linguistics, demography and the like, have been used by historians for little more than a hundred years. The purpose of historical investigation is to produce answers, in the form of concepts and generalizations, to the fundamental problems of historical change in the social activities of men. These generalizations about societies will, of course, not be immutable but always tentative. They must, however, be as accurate, as scientific, as detailed research and a profound sense of human reality can make them. The historian's purpose, therefore, is to deepen understanding about men and society, not merely for its own sake, but in the hope that a profounder knowledge, a profounder awareness will help to mould human attitudes and human actions. Knowledge and understanding should not end in negation, but in action.

....

History began because scholars perceived a problem which faced no other civilization – the problem of the duality of Europe's past, its conflicting ideologies and of their different interpretations of human destiny. Once historical criticism developed, the Christian explanation of the past could not maintain its supremacy. It slowly collapsed under criticism, but just as slowly and just as surely did the interpretations which replaced it – the concept of progress, the manifest destinies of competitive nationalism, social Darwinism, or dialectical materialism. History, which is so deeply concerned with the past, has, in a sense, helped to destroy it as a social force, as a synthesizing and comprehensive statement of human destiny.

Because of this, most historians in this century have avoided any attempt to explain the history of man. This has been left to the journalists, the prophets or the philosophers, but some of those who have attempted it acquired great popular success. H.G. Wells, Oswald Spengler and Arnold Toynbee, who sought to mould history into a meaningful past, secured millions of readers but the almost universal condemnation of historians. Yet the reception of their books points to the need of ordinary people, as well as to the difficulty of fulfilling it.[1] Although the past manufactured by his ancestors will no longer do, it would seem that man in the West still seeks a meaningful past, one which will confer as much significance on his life as the Marxist past does for those who can believe in it. Can historians fulfil this need? And is it their rightful task?

The historian, I believe, has a twofold purpose. He must pursue and test the concepts with which he deals. And because of the amount of material and its complexity, these concepts are likely to be limited in time. Much of his life must be spent, therefore, working with, and writing for, fellow professionals. These, as yet, are very early days for exact, professional history. But this cannot be the historian's sole *raison d'être*. Some would argue that the training which experience, even a short experience, gives in the techniques of historical study is a sufficient argument for its existence. This is the old argument for classical studies in a new guise. It is, of course, true that historical study does exercise memory, capacity for argument and clarity of expression. And it is excellent that it should do so, but there are plenty of academic disciplines which can do this, perhaps better than history.[2] The study of history can, of course, and does extend human experience in a peculiarly vivid way, but so do literary studies, so should sociology or anthropology or the study of politics. Again, this is in no way peculiar to history. The combination of all these virtues would justify a minor academic discipline and fulfil a minor social role in satisfying curiosity and gratifying nostalgia. History as entertainment, whether of the intellectual or of the romantic housewife, would persist. If this, however, were all that a study of history could do, no one would insist that it fulfils a vital and major social role. Yet if the past is allowed to die, or, having died, a new one fails to be conceived, that will be the fate of history. Its place as the interpreter of man's destiny will be taken by the social sciences.

In many ways the historian of today is in the position of the historian of the Enlightenment. He cannot accept the interpretation of the past of his immediate ancestors or even of the mass of society in which he lives. Crude ideological interpretations, Marxist or nationalist, conservative or liberal, religious or agnostic, providential or progressive, cyclical or linear, are a violation of his discipline and an offence to his knowledge. Many historians, therefore, have taken refuge in the meaninglessness of history, in the belief that history can only make a personal or neutral statement; it is a game for professional players who make the rules. Others, more conservative, have taken refuge in its providential nature. The Christian myth dies hard. We need again a compulsive sense of the value of man's past, not only for ourselves as historians, but also for the world at large.

The historians of the Enlightenment could discover with delirious joy the antique past that beckoned them in Greece and Rome; the multiplicity of historical worlds that rose above their intellectual horizon – Egypt, Persia, India, China – gave them new stimulus, fresh ideas, and a deep sense of recovery, of escape into a fresher, more viable historical understanding. Alas, such an experience cannot revitalize the historian of this century. There are no new pasts to discover. They are all exposed and all peopled by professional experts, digging in their minute concessions in the hope of finding a new sherd. The very limitations of professional historical study make it difficult for historians to deal with any messages that might be derived from the vista of man's past, even if he believed in them. He does not look for them. He does not wish to lift his eyes from what he can see with clarity to what may be baffling, obscure and misleading. Philosophical history is at a discount, and antiquarianism, transmuted into scholarship, triumphs. After two world wars, after Hitler and Hiroshima, after the brutalities of Stalin and the sad failures in Africa, in India, in Indonesia, historians cannot help but look at the immediate, as well as the distant, past with foreboding and with pessimism.

But blind optimism has rarely been the fault of the perceptive historian; Voltaire and Gibbon, the greatest historians of the Enlightenment, were conscious enough of the follies, the iniquities, the stupidities of mankind. But they were sufficiently detached to qualify their pessimism and to use a balanced judgment. To them the gains made by mankind were obvious and remarkable. They still are. Any historian who is not blindly prejudiced cannot but admit that the ordinary man and woman, unless they should be caught up in a murderous field of war, are capable of securing a richer life than their ancestors. There is more food in the world, more opportunity of advancement, greater areas of liberty in ideas and in living than the world has ever known: art, music, literature can be enjoyed by tens of millions, not tens of thousands. This has been achieved not by clinging to conservative tradition or by relying on instinct or emotion, but by the application of human ingenuity, no matter what the underlying motive might be. The great extension of rationalism has been a cause and a consequence of this development. In field after field, rationalism has proved its worth. It still has vast areas left to conquer in politics and social organization which may prove beyond its capacity, owing to the aggressive instincts built so deeply into man's nature. Nevertheless, the historian must stress the success, as well as point out the failure. Here is a message of the past which is as clear, but far more true, than the message wrung from it by our ancestors. The past can be used to sanctify not authority nor morality but those qualities of the human mind which have raised us from the forest and swamp to the city, to build a qualified confidence in man's capacity to order his life and to stress the virtues of intellect, of rational behaviour. And this past is neither pagan nor Christian, it belongs to no nation and no class, it is universal; it is human in the widest sense of that term. But this past must not be too simple. Just as the Christian past stressed the complexity of the battle between good and evil, so should the historian's past dwell on the difficulties which have faced those who have fought for intellectual and moral enlightenment. Nor need we gloss their motives. The historian's duty is to reveal the complexities of human behaviour and the strangeness of events. The past which mankind needs is no longer a simple one. Experience as well as science has made the majority of literate men aware of the vast complexity of human existence, its subtle interrelations. What, however, is becoming less and less stressed is the nature of the past, not only its successes, but also the shadows it casts across our lives. History, the dimension of Time, is ignored too frequently by sociologists, economists, politicians and philosophers; even theologians wish to escape from its clutches.

Any past serviceable to society, therefore, must be complex even though its base may be simple. That simple base I have described above. It is to me the one truth of history – that the condition of mankind has improved, materially alas more than morally, but nevertheless both have improved. Progress has come by fits and starts; retrogressions are common. Man's success has derived from his application of reason, whether this has been to technical or to social questions. And it is the duty of the historian to teach this, to proclaim it, to demonstrate it in order to give humanity some confidence in a task that will still be cruel and long – the resolution of the tensions and antipathies that exist within the human species. These are limited objectives. Historians can use history to fulfil many of the social purposes which the old mythical pasts did so well. It can no longer provide sanctions for authority, nor for aristocratic or oligarchical élites, nor for inherent destinies clothed in national guise, but it can still teach wisdom, and it can teach it in a far deeper sense than was possible when wisdom had to be taught through the example of heroes.

Because of the complexities of its dual past – pagan and Christian – because of the collapse of the Roman Empire, because the Christian past after the Reformation became multiple, because of the impact of great civilizations with a past of their own, because of the discovery in Europe of the huge time-span of man's existence in the world, Western society has been forced not only to study but to accept the fact of social change, of not only the complexity and variety of human existence, but also of its restless social movement in time. As soon as history began to free itself from the past, it was this aspect which drew the best minds to history. It is as true of Gibbon as of Marx, of Michelet as of Bloch. And here lies the greatest contribution that the historian can make. History can teach all who are literate about the nature of social change; even to tell the mere story of social change would be a valuable educational process in itself and help to fulfil a need in present society of which we are all aware. Of course, there will not be agreement; historians will speak with different voices. This no more matters than the lack of unity in wisdom literature did in the past. The importance lies in the nature, the cogency, the presentation of argument. We need to teach people to think historically about social change, to make them alert to the cunning of history which, as Lenin emphasized, always contains a quality of surprise. We must add the depth of time to studies which so singularly lack it. And it should be remembered that history is constantly growing in insight and probing ever deeper into questions which affect our daily lives. The knowledge of the mechanics of historical change is far more profound than it was two generations ago. But much of the professionalism of history remains professional; in spite of the huge output of paperback histories, the results of professional history are not conveyed with the emphasis and cogency that society needs. The historians have, very rightly, been active agents in the destruction of the past to which society has so frequently turned to acquire either confidence or justification or both. This critical, destructive role is still necessary; illusions about the past, even in professional circles, are abundant enough, but the historian, as with other members of society, is being freed from the trammels of the past by the changes in society itself. Paradoxically, what allows the sociologist to ignore the past, enables the historian to see it more clearly. Hence the historian's opportunity is similar, although far from identical, to that of the philosophers of the Enlightenment. They too were slipping off the shackles of the past, destroying its pretensions and its follies, but they also attempted to create out of the debris a more extended, a more rational, a more detached sense of human destiny. And so by his writings, by his thinking, even by his example, the historian today should be similarly engaged.

The old past is dying, its force weakening, and so it should. Indeed, the historian should speed it on its way, for it was compounded of bigotry, of national vanity, of class domination. It was as absurd as that narrow Christian interpretation which Gibbon rightly scorned. May history step into its shoes, help to sustain man's confidence in his destiny, and create for us a new past as true, as exact, as we can make it, that will help us achieve our identity, not as Americans or Russians, Chinese or Britons, black or white, rich or poor, but as men.

Notes

1 Apart from the excellent and stimulating world history of William H. McNeill, *The Rise of the West* (Chicago University Press, 1963) the most successful attempts have been made by archaeologists – Carleton S. Coon and Gordon Childe.
2 On the argument for classical studies as a training for the intellect, see M.I. Finlay, 'Crisis in the Classics', in J.H. Plumb (ed.), *Crisis in the Humanities*, Penguin, 1964, pp. 18–19.

6.   E.H. Carr

[from What Is History?, *Penguin, 1964, pp. 113–19, 132]*

L et us for the moment suspend judgement on the question whether we are living in a period of progress or of decline, and examine a little more closely what is implied in the concept of progress, what assumptions lie behind it, and how far these have become untenable. I should like, first of all, to clear up the muddle about progress and evolution. The thinkers of the Enlightenment adopted two apparently incompatible views. They sought to vindicate man's place in the world of nature: the laws of history were equated with the laws of nature. On the other hand, they believed in progress. But what ground was there for treating nature as progressive, as constantly advancing towards a goal? Hegel met the difficulty by sharply distinguishing history, which was progressive, from nature, which was not. The Darwinian revolution appeared to remove all embarrassments by equating evolution and progress: nature, like history, turned out after all to be progressive. But this opened the way to a much graver misunderstanding, by confusing biological inheritance, which is the source of evolution, with social acquisition, which is the source of progress in history. The distinction is familiar and obvious. Put a European infant in a Chinese family, and the child will grow up with a white skin, but speaking Chinese. Pigmentation is a biological inheritance, language a social acquisition transmitted by the agency of the human brain. Evolution by inheritance has to be measured in millennia or in millions of years; no measurable biological change is known to have occurred in man since the beginning of written history. Progress by acquisition can be measured in generations. The essence of man as a rational being is that he develops his potential capacities by accumulating the experience of past generations. Modern man is said to have no larger a brain, and no greater innate capacity of thought, than his ancestor 5000 years ago. But the effectiveness of his thinking has been multiplied many times by learning and incorporating in his experience the experience of the intervening generations. The transmission of acquired characteristics, which is rejected by biologists, is the very foundation of social progress. History is progress through the transmission of acquired skills from one generation to another.

Secondly, we need not and should not conceive progress as having a finite beginning or end. The belief, popular less than fifty years ago, that civilization was invented in the Nile Valley in the fourth millennium B.C. is no more credible today than the chronology which placed the creation of the world in 4004 B.C. Civilization, the birth of which we may perhaps take as a starting-point for our hypothesis of progress, was surely not an invention, but an infinitely slow process of development, in which spectacular leaps probably occurred from time to time. We need not trouble ourselves with the question when progress – or civilization – began. The hypothesis of a finite end of progress has led to more serious misapprehension. Hegel has been rightly condemned for seeing the end of progress in the Prussian monarchy – apparently the result of an overstrained interpretation of his view of the impossibility of prediction. But Hegel's aberration was capped by that eminent Victorian, Arnold of Rugby, who in his inaugural lecture as Regius Professor of Modern History in Oxford in 1841 thought that modern history would be the last stage in the history of mankind: 'It appears to bear marks of the fullness of time, as if there would be no future history beyond it.'[1] Marx's prediction that the proletarian revolution would realize the ultimate aim of a classless society was logically and morally less vulnerable; but the presumption of an end of history has an eschatological ring more appropriate to the theologian than to the historian, and reverts to the fallacy of a goal outside history. No doubt a finite end has attractions for the human mind; and Acton's vision of the march of history as an unending progress towards liberty seems chilly and vague. But if the historian is to save his hypothesis of progress, I think he must be prepared to treat it as a process into which the demands and conditions of successive periods will put their own specific content. And this is what is meant by Acton's thesis that history is not only a record of progress but a 'progressive science', or, if you like, that history in both senses of the word – as the course of events and as the record of those events – is progressive. Let us recall Acton's description of the advance of liberty in history:

> It is by the combined efforts of the weak, made under compulsion, to resist the reign of force and constant wrong, that, in the rapid change but slow progress of four hundred years, liberty has been preserved, and secured, and extended, and finally understood.[2]

History as the course of events was conceived by Acton as progress towards liberty, history as the record of those events as progress towards the under-standing of liberty: the two processes advanced side by side. The philosopher

Bradley, writing in an age when analogies from evolution were fashionable, remarked that 'for religious faith the end of evolution is presented as that which . . . is already evolved'. For the historian the end of progress is not already evolved. It is something still infinitely remote; and pointers towards it come in sight only as we advance. This does not diminish its importance. A compass is a valuable and indeed indispensable guide. But it is not a chart of the route. The content of history can be realized only as we experience it.

My third point is that no sane person ever believed in a kind of progress which advanced in an unbroken straight line without reverses and deviations and breaks in continuity, so that even the sharpest reverse is not necessarily fatal to the belief. Clearly there are periods of regression as well as periods of progress. Moreover, it would be rash to assume that, after a retreat, the advance will be resumed from the same point or along the same line. Hegel's or Marx's four or three civilizations, Toynbee's twenty-one civilizations, the theory of a life-cycle of civilizations passing through rise, decline, and fall – such schemes make no sense in themselves. But they are symptomatic of the observed fact that the effort which is needed to drive civilization forward dies away in one place and is later resumed at another, so that whatever progress we can observe in history is certainly not continuous either in time or in place. Indeed, if I were addicted to formulating laws of history, one such law would be to the effect that the group – call it a class, a nation, a continent, a civilization, what you will – which plays the leading role in the advance of civilization in one period is unlikely to play a similar role in the next period, and this for the good reason that it will be too deeply imbued with the traditions, interests, and ideologies of the earlier period to be able to adapt itself to the demands and conditions of the next period.[3] Thus it may very well happen that what seems for one group a period of decline may seem to another the birth of a new advance. Progress does not and cannot mean equal and simultaneous progress for all. It is significant that almost all our latter-day prophets of decline, our sceptics who see no meaning in history and assume that progress is dead, belong to that sector of the world and to that class of society which have triumphantly played a leading and predominant part in the advance of civilization for several generations. It is no consolation to them to be told that the role which their group has played in the past will now pass to others. Clearly a history which has played so scurvy a trick on them cannot be a meaningful or rational process. But, if we are to retain the hypothesis of progress, we must, I think, accept the condition of the broken line.

Lastly, I come to the question what is the essential content of progress in terms of historical action. The people who struggle, say, to extend civil rights to all, or to reform penal practice, or to remove inequalities of race or wealth,

are consciously seeking to do just those things: they are not consciously seeking to 'progress', to realize some historical 'law' or 'hypothesis' of progress. It
is the historian who applies to their actions his hypothesis of progress, and
interprets their actions as progress. But this does not invalidate the concept of
progress. I am glad on this point to find myself in agreement with Sir Isaiah
Berlin that 'progress and reaction, however much the words may have been
abused, are not empty concepts'.[4] It is a presupposition of history that man is
capable of profiting (not that he necessarily profits) by the experience of his
predecessors, and that progress in history, unlike evolution in nature, rests
on the transmission of acquired assets. These assets include both material
possessions and the capacity to master, transform, and utilize one's environment. Indeed, the two factors are closely inter-connected, and react on one
another. Marx treats human labour as the foundation of the whole edifice; and
this formula seems acceptable if a sufficiently broad sense is attached to
'labour'. But the mere accumulation of resources will not avail unless it brings
with it not only increased technical and social knowledge and experience, but
increased mastery of man's environment in the broader sense. At the present
time, few people would, I think, question the fact of progress in the accumulation both of material resources and of scientific knowledge, of mastery over the
environment in the technological sense. What is questioned is whether there
has been in the twentieth century any progress in our ordering of society, in
our mastery of the social environment, national or international, whether
indeed there has not been a marked regression. Has not the evolution of man
as a social being lagged fatally behind the progress of technology?

The symptoms which inspire this question are obvious. But I suspect none
the less that it is wrongly put. History has known many turning-points, where
the leadership and initiative has passed from one group, from one sector of the
world, to another: the period of the rise of the modern state and the shift in the
centre of power from the Mediterranean to western Europe, and the period
of the French revolution, have been conspicuous modern examples. Such
periods are always times of violent upheavals and struggles for power. The
old authorities weaken, the old landmarks disappear; out of a bitter clash of
ambitions and resentments the new order emerges. What I would suggest is
that we are now passing through such a period. It appears to me simply untrue
to say that our understanding of the problems of social organization or our
good will to organize society in the light of that understanding have regressed:
indeed, I should venture to say that they have greatly increased. It is not
that our capacities have diminished, or our moral qualities declined. But the
period of conflict and upheaval, due to the shifting balance of power between
continents, nations, and classes, through which we are living has enormously

increased the strain on these capacities and qualities, and limited and frustrated their effectiveness for positive achievement. While I do not wish to underestimate the force of the challenge of the past fifty years to the belief in progress in the western world, I am still not convinced that progress in history has come to an end. But, if you press me further on the content of progress, I think I can only reply something like this. The notion of a finite and clearly definable goal of progress in history, so often postulated by nineteenth-century thinkers, has proved inapplicable and barren. Belief in progress means belief not in any automatic or inevitable process, but in the progressive development of human potentialities. Progress is an abstract term; and the concrete ends pursued by mankind arise from time to time out of the course of history, not from some source outside it. I profess no belief in the perfectibility of man or in a future paradise on earth. To this extent I would agree with the theologians and the mystics who assert that perfection is not realizable in history. But I shall be content with the possibility of unlimited progress – or progress subject to no limits that we can or need envisage – towards goals which can be defined only as we advance towards them, and the validity of which can be verified only in a process of attaining them. Nor do I know how, without some such conception of progress, society can survive. Every civilized society imposes sacrifices on the living generation for the sake of generations yet unborn. To justify these sacrifices in the name of a better world in the future is the secular counterpart of justifying them in the name of some divine purpose. In Bury's words, 'the principle of duty to posterity is a direct corollary of the idea of progress'.[5] Perhaps this duty does not require justification. If it does, I know of no other way to justify it.

....

I return therefore in conclusion to Acton's description of progress as 'the scientific hypothesis on which history is to be written'. You can, if you please, turn history into theology by making the meaning of the past depend on some extra-historical and super-rational power. You can, if you please, turn it into literature – a collection of stories and legends about the past without meaning or significance. History properly so-called can be written only by those who find and accept a sense of direction in history itself. The belief that we have come from somewhere is closely linked with the belief that we are going somewhere. A society which has lost belief in its capacity to progress in the future will quickly cease to concern itself with its progress in the past. As I said at the beginning of my first lecture, our view of history reflects our view of society. I now come back to my starting-point by declaring my faith in the future of society and in the future of history.

Notes

1 Thomas Arnold, *An Inaugural Lecture on the Study of Modern History*, J.H. Parker, 1841, p. 38.
2 Lord Acton, *Lectures on Modern History*, Macmillan, 1906, p. 51.
3 For a diagnosis of such a situation, see R.S. Lynd, *Knowledge for What?*, Princeton University Press, 1967, p. 88.
4 *Foreign Affairs* XXVIII, no. 3 (June 1950), p. 382.
5 J.B. Bury, *The Idea of Progress*, Macmillan, 1920, p. ix.

The nation

The idea of the nation has always been founded on a common past, expressed as a national history. Once the political concept of the nation became identified during the nineteenth century with a common cultural tradition and an act of self-determination, the link between nationalism and history became quite explicit. The extracts reproduced here reflect very different political contexts. Herbert Butterfield's reflections on 'the Englishman's alliance with his history' were his contribution to national morale during the Second World War, all the more remarkable because only ten years previously, in *The Whig Interpretation of History* (1933), he had denounced the study of the past 'with one eye on the present'.

Daniel Boorstin's argument is more subtle and his tone more relaxed. Writing during the Cold War, when the confidence of Americans in the superiority of their way of life was at its height, Boorstin shows how consensus and stability in the United States have been sustained by the popular assumption that the American political genius is a given, created for all time by the Founding Fathers of the Republic. In his own prolific writings for the general reader, Boorstin sought to disseminate this view of American history. Finally, in his inaugural lecture the Ghanaian historian A. Adu Boahen considers the contribution of historical scholarship to nation building in the countries of sub-Saharan Africa recently freed from colonial rule. The history taught and read by Africans, no less than the political or economic system, needs to be decolonised, drawing on the full range of sources to answer questions which are relevant to Africa rather than Europe. The fact that African history exists today as a recognised field of study is due in no small part to the efforts of scholars motivated by Boahen's concerns.

7. Herbert Butterfield

[from The Englishman and His History, *Cambridge University Press, 1944, pp. 1–11]*

Although history may often seem to be – like the natural sciences – an international study, transcending racial and political frontiers, its interpretation remains more profoundly national, more stubbornly local, than many of us realize or perhaps trouble to keep in mind. We may imagine that here in England we are free from the prejudices and enthusiasms of other nations. Sometimes we think that our history is the impartial narrative, and we hardly believe that we are performing an act of interpretation at all. But however much we refine and elaborate, it is not clear that we reach – or that without great intellectual endeavour we could hope to reach – more than the English view of Louis XIV. And our best biography of Napoleon is only the supreme expression of what is really the English version of the man's career. We teach and write the kind of history which is appropriate to our organization, congenial to the intellectual climate of our part of the world. We can scarcely help it if this kind of history is at the same time the one most adapted to the preservation of the existing regime.

Our initial object is to study the so-called whig interpretation of history, as an aspect of the English mind and as a product of the English tradition. We shall treat it not as a thing invented by some particularly wilful historian, but as part of the landscape of English life, like our country lanes or our November mists or our historic inns. Along with the English language and the British constitution and our national genius for compromise, it is itself a product of history, part of the inescapable inheritance of Englishmen. We can say that it moulded Englishmen before anybody moulded it or began to be conscious of it at all.

One man in the 18th century wrote essays on English history so full of the song of liberty that he has been called the founder of the whig interpretation;

yet he was none other than the politician Bolingbroke, notorious in his day and ever since as the wildest and wickedest of tories. The tories in fact do not escape the whig interpretation, though they may try to undermine it and they play tricks with it at times – they attempt for example to show that on occasion they themselves, rather than the whigs, were the real promotors of our present-day liberty. And there is not anything in England worth considering on the other side – there is not anything worth the name of 'the tory interpretation of English history'. It is really the 'English' interpretation that we are discussing therefore, and from the way in which it developed we may see that it is like the British constitution – itself the product of history and vicissitude. It provided the most obvious method by which Englishmen could make capital out of their own past and put the history of earlier centuries to practical use. It represented indeed the way in which Englishmen would naturally view their past in days when the historical sense had not been tuned and trained. Great originality of mind would have been required in Englishmen to enable them to escape the whig interpretation. And it has needed generations of historical research to make us understand how closely our forefathers were the prisoners of it.

Those who, amid the breeze and agitation of contemporary debate, affect to court a controversy with such diluted remnants of the whig interpretation as still keep their currency amongst us, must take heed when they sally forth in their carpet slippers against this entrenched tradition. They will find a more comfortable piece of coast for their commandos if they will carry their offensive, not against the whig tradition itself, but against surviving defects in historical method. It is not necessary or useful to deny that the theme of English political history is the story of our liberty; and while men think that freedom is worth singing songs about, from New York to Cape Town, from London to Canberra, it will always be true that in one important respect – in yesterday's meaning of the term at least – we are all of us exultant and unrepentant whigs. Those who, perhaps in the misguided austerity of youth, wish to drive out that whig interpretation (that particular thesis which controls our abridgment of English history) are sweeping a room which humanly speaking cannot long remain empty. They are opening the door for seven devils which, precisely because they are newcomers, are bound to be worse than the first.

 We, on the other hand, will not dream of wishing it away, but will rejoice in an interpretation of the past which has grown up with us, has grown up with the history itself, and has helped to make the history. New interpretations always come with crudeness and violence at first, as we shall see. They erupt upon the world as propaganda; they must make their way as fighting creeds.

They can become wise and urbane, perhaps even harmless, all of them, but only after they have submitted to the chastening effect of controversy, discipline and tradition. Therefore, though we seek to tear it asunder, and to make clear what we may call the mere mechanics of its rise and its operation, we will celebrate this whig inheritance of ours with a robust but regulated pride; observing the part which an interpretation of history has played in building up the centuries and creating the England that we know.

The Englishman's Alliance with his History

Although it might seem strange to us today that Macaulay should ever have imagined his *History of England* as transcending party prejudice, he gives almost at the opening of that work an explanation of whig and tory partisanship in the treatment of historical problems. His account seems to beg the essential question, but it must be mentioned since it raises a matter of genuine interest. It is a useful introduction to an enquiry into the origin of the whig interpretation.

Macaulay refers to the fact that England has always taken particular pride in the maintenance of her institutional continuity. Our statesmen and lawyers have been under the influence of the past to a greater degree than those of other countries. From the 17th century our greatest innovators have tried to show that they were not innovators at all but restorers of ancient ways. And so it is that even when we have a revolution we look to the past and try to carry it out in accordance with ancient precedents. It is different in France as Macaulay explains – different especially since the Revolution of 1789. A Frenchman has no need to exaggerate the power of Louis XIV or underrate the ancient rights of the Parlement of Paris. He can take the view that the year 1789 rules a line across the story, he can say that modern France has a new start at the Revolution; while in modern England, if an unusual problem arises, the procedure may have to be determined upon precedents that go back to the middle ages. So in all English controversies both parties have referred to history in order to discover what they wished to discover – both parties have had a colossal vested interest in the historical enquiries that were taking place.

That marriage between the present and the past which Macaulay describes has been an interesting feature of English life, English law and English politics – a side of our story rich with latent values, and a restful thing for the mind to reflect upon. We have maintained a curious respect for law sometimes, even in periods of severe internal stress. In periods of change we have learned not to rush heedlessly onwards but to walk with a due regard for precedent. Yet this respect for the past has been combined with (perhaps even it has been dependent on) what one might call a sublime and purposeful unhistoricity. We have not in fact – however sincere our illusions on the subject – been the slaves and the prisoners of the 'genuine antique', the dead hand of archaic custom. And if we have clung to the past it has been to a nicely chosen past – one which was conveniently and tidily disposed for our purposes.

In particular we must congratulate ourselves that our 17th-century fore-fathers, for all their antiquarian fervour, did not resurrect and fasten upon us the authentic middle ages. Those 'historic rights' to which Englishmen (espe-cially in the Stuart period) so loved to appeal – it was essential that they should not have been rigid, but should have moved with the centuries, that 'ancient custom' should have been a living thing, to save us from the pressure of a fossilized antiquity. The good terms that Englishmen have managed to keep with their own bygone centuries have been the counterpart of their ability to make the past move with them, so to speak. They have depended on the ability of our 17th-century ancestors to see the middle ages not – if one may use the phrase – 'as they really were', but in terms that were appropriate to the Stuart age.

The French were different. When in the *Fronde*, in the middle of the 17th century, they asserted 'historic rights' and 'ancient custom' against the king, it was a genuine piece of history, a genuine survival from the past, that reared itself up against the monarchy. In France there still existed over-mighty sub-jects, semi-feudal potentates, privileged corporations – all clinging to private rights that were rooted in a continuous tradition. And the French, having been too much the slaves of their own preceding centuries, set out to free themselves in 1789 – they ended in fact by cursing their middle ages and repudiating their past. French liberty springs from a revolt against history and tradition – a revolt that suffered a serious handicap because it was based on the abstract 'rights of man'. But in England we made peace with our middle ages by mis-construing them; and, therefore, we may say that 'wrong' history was one of our assets. The whig interpretation came at exactly the crucial moment and, whatever it may have done to our history, it had a wonderful effect on English politics. For this reason England did not need a revolution of 1789 to save her from the despotism of the past. We did not need to resort to abstract philosophy – our liberty is based on 'the historic rights of Englishmen'. We did not have to demolish a tradition which stood rigid like a wall, hindering the transmutation of custom. And though we did have a revolution in the 17th century it did not make us 'happy ever afterwards' – it only taught us to treasure more dearly the continuity of our history. We hastened to tie up the threads and reconstitute the customs which linked the past with the present. And consciously we seem to have determined never to let such an aberration take place again.

But, for this marriage between 'progress' and 'tradition' in the English story, the rôle of the Tudors was an absolute necessity. It is important that there was a period in English history when all the loyalty of the country was centred upon the monarch. We seemed to forget in the 16th century those 'ancient rights' which had once been asserted against the crown. If indeed those historic rights and traditional privileges were remembered at all, they were recognized to have been reactionary, aristocratic and dangerous, as we shall see. The Tudors, we may say, performed for England much of the work which the French Revolution achieved for France. It was they who represented the breach with the past and who liquidated those things in the middle ages which men were delighted to be parted from. Under the Tudors we see the end of the feudal epoch, the rise of the middle class to political significance, and the realization of 'the idea of the state'. And it was the Tudors who imposed upon the people a notion of public policy that transcended the older concepts of private rights. It was we in England who, in the 16th century, did not care even to remember the regime of private rights and feudal assertiveness out of which we had too recently emerged. We worshipped our Tudor monarchs precisely because they had repressed this kind of abuse.

And so, the notion of historic rights, forgotten for a time under the Tudors, had to be recaptured – as something lost awhile – by historical enquiry; and it came to its full blossoming in the historiography of the early 17th century. Historic rights had to be summoned to new life again, not, as in France, by semi-feudal potentates whose claims had a continuous tradition behind them, but by middle-class citizens interested in antiquarian research. And when they emerged they had not the flavour of the *ancien régime* – they did not appear as a reassertion of reactionary feudal privilege at all. Indeed it is quite a question whether the rights that were put forward in the 17th century were genuinely 'historical' in the sense we should give to the word. A conception of customary rights which had been the privilege and the glory of an aristocracy was taken over by the middle classes. Ancient 'liberties' became generalized in the process and were transmuted into modern 'liberty'. Rights that had once been inimical to the central government were harnessed and subdued to the idea of the state. Feudal limitations on the royal power were called to mind again in a world that knew not the historic feudalism, and they were curiously reconstrued. All the changes that had taken place in the order of society gave even the old terminology new implications and new power. And, precisely because they did not know the middle ages, the historians of the time gave the

17th century just the type of anachronism that it required. Roughly speaking, we may say that only after 1600 do the worship of *Magna Carta* (as the charter of middle-class freedom), the superstition for historic rights, and the whig interpretation of history, come into effective existence after the curious interval afforded by the Tudor period. All three were born out of the same complex of events and conditions. They are joint products of one live piece of history.

The necessary background to the history of the rise of the whig interpretation, then, is that Tudor period in which the common Englishman knew no better than to be thankful for his kings. It was a period in which the recent victory of the national monarchy would appear as the culmination, indeed the end, of whatever historical process men were conscious of. We start therefore with an extreme tory interpretation – one not darkly hinted at, but distinctly formulated by the writers of histories. We need not shudder at the thought that this, too, was proper in its time and place – was so to speak organic to the age itself. It represented something like the meaning of the history, as this had been unfolded up to date.

It is typical of the English that, retaining what was a good in the past, but reconstruing it – reconstruing the past itself if necessary – they have clung to the monarchy, and have maintained it down to the present, while changing its import and robbing it of the power to do harm. It is typical of them that from their 17th-century revolution itself and from the very experiment of an interregnum, they learned that there was still a subtle utility in kingship and they determined to reconstitute their traditions again, lest they should throw away the good with the bad. In all this there is something more profound than a mere sentimental unwillingness to part with a piece of ancient pageantry – a mere disinclination to sacrifice the ornament of a royal court. Here we have a token of that alliance of Englishmen with their history which has prevented the uprooting of things that have been organic to the development of the country; which has enriched our institutions with echoes and overtones; and which has proved – against the presumption and recklessness of blind revolutionary overthrows – the happier form of co-operation with Providence.

8. Daniel Boorstin

[from The Genius of American Politics, *University of Chicago Press, 1953, pp. 8–9, 10–16]*

The American must go outside his country and hear the voice of America to realize that his is one of the most spectacularly lopsided cultures in all history. The marvelous success and vitality of our institutions is equaled by the amazing poverty and inarticulateness of our theorizing about politics. No nation has ever believed more firmly that its political life was based on a perfect theory. And yet no nation has ever been less interested in political philosophy or produced less in the way of theory. If we can explain this paradox, we shall have a key to much that is characteristic – and much that is good – in our institutions.

In this chapter I shall attempt an explanation. I start from the notion that the two sides of the paradox explain each other. The very same facts which account for our belief that we actually possess a theory also explain why we have had little interest in political theories and have never bothered seriously to develop them.

For the belief that an explicit political theory is superfluous precisely because we already somehow possess a satisfactory equivalent, I propose the name 'givenness'. 'Givenness' is the belief that values in America are in some way or other automatically defined: *given* by certain facts of geography or history peculiar to us.

....

Now I shall begin by trying to explain what I have called the first axiom of 'givenness': the idea that values are a gift from our past. Here we face our conscious attitude toward our past and toward our way of inheriting from it. This particular aspect of the 'givenness' idea may be likened to the obsolete biological notion of 'pre-formation'. That is the idea that all parts of an organism pre-exist in perfect miniature in the seed. Biologists used to believe that if you could look at the seed of an apple under a strong enough microscope you would see in it a minute apple tree. Similarly, we seem still to believe that if we could understand the ideas of the earliest settlers – the Pilgrim Fathers or Founding Fathers – we would find in them no mere seventeenth- or eighteenth-century philosophy of government but the perfect embryo of the theory by which we now live. We believe, then, that the mature political ideals of the nation existed clearly conceived in the minds of our patriarchs. The notion is essentially static. It assumes that the values and theory of the nation were given once and for all in the very beginning.

What circumstances of American history have made such a view possible? The first is the obvious fact that, unlike western European countries, where the coming of the first white man is shrouded in prehistoric mist, civilization in the United States stems from people who came to the American continent at a definite period in recent history. For American political thought this fact has had the greatest significance. We have not found it necessary to invent an Aeneas, for we have had our William Bradford and John Winthrop, or, looking to a later period, our Benjamin Franklin and James Madison. We have needed no Virgil to make a myth of the first settlement of our land or the first founding of the Republic; the crude facts of history have been good enough.

The facts of our history have thus made it easy for us to assume that our national life, as distinguished from that of the European peoples who trace their identity to a remote era, has had a clear purpose. Life in America – appropriately called 'The American Experiment' – has again and again been described as the test or the proof of values supposed to have been clearly in the minds of the Founders. While, as we shall see, the temper of much of our thought has been antihistorical, it is nevertheless true that we have leaned heavily on history to clarify our image of ourselves. Perhaps never before, except conceivably in the modern state of Israel, has a nation so firmly believed that it was founded on a full-blown theory and hence that it might understand itself by recapturing a particular period in its past.

This idea is actually so familiar, so deeply imbedded in our thinking, that we have never quite recognized it as a characteristic, much less a peculiarity, of our political thought. Nor have we become aware of its implications. 'Four score and seven years ago,' Lincoln said at Gettysburg in 1863, 'our fathers brought forth on this continent, *a new nation, conceived in Liberty, and dedicated to the proposition that all men are created equal*'. We have forgotten that these words are less the statement of a political theory than an affirmation that an adequate theory already existed at the first epoch of national life. As we shall see in a later chapter, this belief itself helps account for the way in which the traditional, conservative, and inarticulate elements of our Revolution have been forgotten. A few slogans have been eagerly grasped as if they gave the essence of our history. While the conservative and legal aspect of our Revolution has remained hidden from popular view, schoolboys and popular orators (who seldom read beyond the preambles of legal documents) have conceived the Declaration of Independence as written primarily, if not exclusively, to vindicate man's equality and his 'inalienable rights to life, liberty, and the pursuit of happiness'.

Our determination to believe in a single logically complete theory as our heritage from the earliest settlers has thus actually kept us from grasping the *facts* of the early life of our nation. Strenuous efforts have been made to homogenize all the fathers of our country. A great deal of the popular misunderstanding of the New England Puritans, for example, can be traced to this desire. Tradition teaches us to treat the history of our nation from 1620 to 1789 as a series of labor pains, varying only in intensity. The Puritans, we are taught, came here for religious and political liberty; and the American Revolutionaries are supposed to have shown a pilgrim-like fervor and clarity of purpose.

If we compare our point of view with that of the historically conscious peoples of Europe, we shall begin to see some of its implications. The Europeans have, of course, had their interludes of nostalgia for some mythical heroic age, some Wagnerian Götterdämmerung. Mussolini sought to reincarnate the Roman Empire, Hitler to revive some prehistoric 'Aryan' community. But such efforts in Europe have been spasmodic. Europeans have not with any continuity attributed to their nameless 'earliest settlers' the mature ideals of their national life. In contrast, we have been consistently primitivistic. The brevity of our history has made this way of thinking easy. Yet that is not the whole story. We find it peculiarly congenial to claim possession of a perfect set of political ideas, especially when they have magical elusiveness and flexibility. Their mere existence seems to relieve us of an unwelcome task.

Our firm belief in a perfectly preformed theory helps us understand many things about ourselves. In particular, it helps us see how it has been that, while we in the United States have been unfertile in political theories, we have at the same time possessed an overweening sense of orthodoxy. The poverty of later theorizing has encouraged appeal to what we like to believe went before. In building an orthodoxy from sparse materials, of necessity we have left the penumbra of heresy vague. The inarticulate character of American political theory has thus actually facilitated heresy-hunts and tended to make them indiscriminate. The heresy-hunts which come at periods of national fear – the Alien and Sedition Acts of the age of the French Revolution, the Palmer raids of the age of the Russian Revolution, and similar activities of more recent times – are directed not so much against acts of espionage as against acts of irreverence toward that orthodox American creed, believed to have been born with the nation itself.

Among the factors which have induced us to presuppose an orthodoxy, to construct what I have called a 'preformation' theory, none has been more important than the heterogeneous character of our population. Our immigrants, who have often been the outcasts, the déclassés, and the persecuted of their native countries, are understandably anxious to become part of a new national life. Hence they are eager to believe that they can find here a simplicity of theory lacking in the countries from which they came. Immigrants, often stupidly blamed for breeding 'subversive' or 'un-American' ideas, have as much as any other group frenetically sought a 'pure' American doctrine. Where else has there been such a naïve sense of political orthodoxy? Who would think of using the word 'un-Italian' or 'un-French' as we use the word 'un-American'?

The fact that we have had a written constitution, and even our special way of interpreting it, has contributed to the 'preformation' notion. Changes in our policy or our institutions are read back into the ideas, and sometimes into the very words, of the Founding Fathers. Everybody knows that this had made of our federal Constitution an 'unwritten' document. What is more significant is the way in which we have justified the adaptation of the document to current needs: by attributing clarity, comprehensiveness, and a kind of mystical foresight to the social theory of the founders. In Great Britain, where there is an 'unwritten' constitution in a very different sense, constitutional theory has taken for granted the *gradual* formulation of a theory of society. No sensible Briton would say that his history is the unfolding of the truths implicit in Magna Charta and the Bill of Rights. Such documents are seen as only single steps in a continuing process of definition.

The difference is expressed in the attitudes of the highest courts in the two countries. In Great Britain the highest court of appeal, the House of Lords, has gradually come to the conclusion that it must be governed by its own earlier decisions. When the House of Lords decides a point of the constitution, it is thus frankly developing the constitution, and it must follow the line which it has previously taken, until the legislature marks out another. Not so in the United States. Our Supreme Court considers itself free to overrule its earlier decisions, to discover, that is, that the constitution which it is interpreting really has all along had a different meaning from what had been supposed.

The American view is actually closer to the British view during the Middle Ages, when the very idea of legislation was in its infancy and when each generation believed that it could do little more than increase its knowledge of the customs which already existed. In the United States, therefore, we see the strange fact that the more flexible we have made our constitution, the more rigid and unexperimental we have made our political theory. We are haunted by a fear that capricious changes in theory might imperil our institutions. This is our kind of conservatism.

Our theory of society is thus conceived as a kind of exoskeleton, like the shell of the lobster. We think of ourselves as growing *into* our skeleton, filling it out with the experience and resources of recent ages. But we always suppose that the outlines were rigidly drawn in the beginning. Our mission, then, is simply to demonstrate the truth – or rather the workability – of the original theory. This belief in a perfect original doctrine, one of the main qualities of which is practicality, may help us understand that unique combination of empiricism and idealism which has characterized American political life.

9.   A. Adu Boahen

[from Clio and Nation-Building in Africa, *Ghana Universities Press, 1975, pp. 9–12, 16–20, 22]*

It should be obvious from what we have learnt from Clio that almost all the nations in Europe, the Middle East, the Americas and in Africa before the era of partition were, initially, forged primarily as a result of wars aimed either at the imposition of the culture and language of a dynasty or a principality over the other groups or of the union of groups of peoples of the same cultural and linguistic traditions living in a geographical area or of a successful bid for independence. Secondly most of these wars took place in the eighteenth and nineteenth centuries, and especially the nineteenth, a century in which, according to Hugh Seton-Watson, 'the whole tradition of progressive political thought . . . was in favour of centralism and against local diversity'. But the spirit of our times is certainly against wars, even of a localized nature. Moreover, there is now great respect for peoples with distinctive cultures and institutions of their own, however insignificant numerically they may be. Thirdly, and the most important of all, if nations are to be forged by war, which of these groups comprising each of the African countries is to spearhead the attack or play the role of the Capetians, the Normans, the Muscovites, the Oyoko and the Sefuwa, of France, England, Russia, Asante and Bornu respectively? Nation-building through war in modern Africa could only have been resorted to by the Colonial powers who had the material resources to do so. With their expulsion, the possibility of achieving linguistic and cultural homogeneity in any of the new African states through war should be ruled out. Moreover, in view of the doggedness with which African states have been guarding their territorial integrity since independence, and above all of the adoption of the principle of 'respect for the sovereignty and territorial integrity of each member state and for its inalienable right to independent existence' by the O.A.U., it is obvious that nation-building can take place in Africa only within the existing political framework of states.

If war cannot and should not be resorted to and if state boundaries cannot be redrawn, then the lesson that Clio teaches us as far as nation-building is concerned is that we have to operate within the existing framework of states and allow our cultural, religious, social, ethnic and linguistic differences to take their natural course while simultaneously forging a sense of identity and loyalty to the state. We should develop common bonds and shared interests through a dynamic programme of social reform, through economic, industrial and rural development aimed at integrating the separate economies of the various areas into complementary and unified structures, through modernization, and above all, as in the case of America, through universal education.

It should be noted that I am *not* advocating a single culture and a single language for each modern state in Africa. Though both would be advantageous, indeed ideal, Clio's instruction is that they are really not necessary for the inculcation of a sense of identity, national cohesion and consciousness among peoples living in a state. The Swiss are as nationally conscious as any nation and yet they do not speak the same language. The Germans and the Austrians speak the same language but they are not a single nation. If a single language or culture does develop naturally in the course of time, well and good; but no single culture or language should be imposed by legislative fiat on the peoples of any African country.

In the meantime, what should be emphasized is not simply the learning of each other's language but rather the overall economic and social development and modernization of the various regions constituting the state. The importance of economic development in this exercise cannot be overemphasized. As a recent authority, Rivkin, has pointed out, 'Almost in direct proportion to the retardation of growth or stagnation of African economies, the cause of nation-building has been adversely affected, for both economic development and nation-building share the problems of modernization and the need at the heart of the modernization process for change in methods, attitudes of mind, and ways of thinking, in order to achieve their respective and inextricably related ends, national growth and cohesion'.

The constitutional and legal institutions to be set up should also be of such a nature as to ensure political stability and participation of the population in this task of nation-building. This would call for a careful examination of the nature and role of the Military, the type of constitution (whether unitary or federal), the type of local government system to be instituted and the role to be accorded the Press, the Civil Service and the Judiciary. Full participation of all sections of society in the affairs of the state and political stability are necessary prerequisites for nation-building – prerequisites to which our 'Men on horseback', to borrow Professor Finer's fine phrase, would do well to betake themselves.

In the effort at the development of national cohesion, Clio and this time in her African mammy cloth can come to our aid in yet more ways. It is my firm conviction that a good knowledge of the past of the different groups composing the states, of their cultures and institutions, and of their roots will promote mutual respect and understanding which will break down the barriers of fear, suspicion and distrust that keep the various groups apart. As Professor Ajayi has put it, 'Increased knowledge of the actual state and development of the cultures of different African peoples in the past will not foretell the future, but it will provide understanding.' Surely only an Ewe or Ga, or Asante or Kusassi or Dagomba who understands his own past and respects his own cultural heritage as the woman in my friend Okot p'Bitek's *Song of Lawino* does, can develop confidence in himself and look at members of the other groups of the state in the face. Moreover, a good knowledge of our past and cultures will enable us to sift the relevant from the irrelevant, the progressive elements from the stagnant or retrogressive ones, the genuine from the phoney, the solid from the mumbo jumbo, which should jointly constitute the yarns that should be used in the weaving of new nations in Africa. Like Blyden, that great pioneer of African personality and Pan-Africanism, I believe that 'Every race . . . has a soul, and the soul of the race finds expression in its institutions, and to kill those institutions is to kill the soul – a terrible homicide. No people can profit by or be helped under institutions which are not the outcome of their own character'. Or as Solanke, that great Nigerian nationalist of the 1920s put it, 'How is the spirit of a people to be formed and animated and cheered but out of the store house of its historical recollections'.

Finally, History will also, to quote Rivkin, reveal to us a glorious past 'which can be invoked as a goal to recapture, as a birthright, the enjoyment of which was interrupted by the colonialists, and now ripe for restoration, or as a colonialist act of "balkanization" which must be politically corrected as part of the emergence of the African personality'. It will also enable us, I should quickly add, to avoid some of the mistakes, blunders and follies of our own predecessors and past regimes, civil and military alike. Indeed, the editorial of the *Gold Coast People* written probably by that versatile scholar, lawyer and nationalist, John Mensah Sarbah, gives a more balanced account of the use of Clio in nation-building. Advancing reasons for the founding of the Collegiate School, the editorial said: 'In our opinion, a young man should learn what the constitution of his country really was and is, how the country had progressed into its present state, the people that had threatened it, the malignity that had attacked it, the courage that had fought for it, and the wisdom that had made it great. And it is because we believe an intelligent study of our own history will breathe into our youth a pure public taste and kindle the flame of patriotism in each native breast, that we hope great things for the country from the Collegiate School.' Incidentally, Mr Vice-Chancellor, I am happy and proud to say that I am a product of this Collegiate School, the school which after all manner of vicissitudes developed into the Mfantsipim School of today.

....

Finally, however, if African history is to be of really effective use in our task of nation-building, if it is to be a source of knowledge, provide the appropriate material out of which properly orientated textbooks can be written, then it should first and foremost be thoroughly historicized at the University and post-University levels. By the historicization of African history, I mean the conduct of research into, and the writing of, African history at these levels, in strict accordance with scientific and objective analysis of available data, and by the application of the most rigorous stand-ards and techniques of scholarship. We should not replace one set of myths and stereotypes concocted by Europeans and Americans with another set formulated by Africans. Myths are myths be they white or black and they should be avoided at all costs at the levels in question.

Besides historicizing African history, we should also decolonize, or to use a more positive term, Africanize African history. By the decolonization of African history I mean four main things: the use of other sources besides the documentary, the approach to research into African history from the African and not the European perspective, the interpretation of data against the African and not the European background, and finally the application of the same terminologies by historians the world over.

There are many European historians who believe, to quote one of them, Professor A.P. Newton, that 'History begins when men take to writing', and who therefore use only documentary sources in the reconstruction of the past. Indeed, so close is this identification of history with the use of written sources that some historians did arrive at the conclusion that since Africa had no writ-ing until the coming of Europeans, and since only the history of Europeans in Africa could be reconstructed from these European documentary sources, there was nothing like African history. It is gratifying to be able to assert here that the view that Africa has no history until the coming of Europeans is now being entertained only by a few eccentric professors such as Professor Trevor-Roper and in a few eccentric Universities such as Oxford, and I have neither the time nor even the inclination to flog dead or virtually dead horses here.

Suffice it to say that this view which once held almost universal sway was based on three assumptions which can all be readily refuted. The first was that writing was introduced into Africa only by Europeans from the fifteenth century onwards. This is palpably false since even ignoring the old African Meroitic and Axumite scripts, the former dating to as early as 300 B.C., writing was introduced into Africa by the Arabs in the eighth century A.D. following the rise of Islam and its meteoric spread into eastern, northern and western Africa.

The second assumption is that only the activities of Europeans can be reconstructed from the European records. Indeed as one of them, the controversial Regius Professor of History, Hugh Trevor-Roper, put it as recently as 1962: 'Nowadays, undergraduates demand that they should be taught the history of Black Africa. Perhaps in future, there will be some African history to teach. But at present there is none. There is only the history of Europeans in Africa. The rest is darkness . . . and darkness is not a subject of history.' But these historians forget that the Europeans in Africa paid attention not only to their ships and castles, their trade goods and balance sheets, their bibles and chapels but also to the attitudes and the circumstances of the Africans among whom they had taken up residence and with whom they had to deal. Moreover, trading and missionary activities were affected one way or the other by the state of politics, by inter-state wars, and by the state of the roads linking their castles and forts with the inland regions. Therefore there are accounts in these European sources of what was going on not only within the range of the guns of their forts and castles, but also in the inland regions from which the history of Black Africa, to borrow Trevor-Roper's term, can be written.

The third assumption referred to already and the one most relevant here is that African history can be reconstructed only from written sources. This assumption, I dare say, remained unchallenged until as recently as the late fifties, and African historiography was then characterized by the use exclusively of documentary and usually only European documentary sources. But this veteran and popular assumption is also false for African history can be constructed not only from documentary sources but also from such non-documentary sources as archaeology, social anthropology, musicology, ethno-botany, serology, linguistics, even eclipses and the last but by no means the least important, oral traditions and other traditional African sources. The contributions that archaeology has made to the study of history including that of Professor Trevor-Roper's own country are too well-known to be repeated here. The increasingly scientific study of African languages, music, art and blood-groups are proving invaluable in the identification of the cradles of various ethno-linguistic groups, of the routes of their migrations and of the nature of the contacts and borrowings between and among various African peoples, while ethno-botany is steadily illuminating the dark question of the origins of the neolithic revolution and the diffusion of various food crops in Africa.

However, the source whose enormous potentiality in the reconstruction of the African past is only now being realized is the oral traditions of African peoples. This source includes oral narratives, oaths, appellations of various stools and names and court poetry. It is indeed true that most members of the Colonial School of African historiography and even some well-meaning European and American scholars are exceedingly sceptical about this particular source. The famous American cultural anthropologist, Murdock, has described it as 'the one type of historical information that is virtually useless'. Now, since many Europeans cannot even remember the maiden names of their grandmothers, let alone those of their great-grandmothers, I can appreciate their scepticism. But from my own work, and from that of others in this field, I can positively testify to the crucial importance of this source. The way in which oral sources have enabled us to fill in some of the yawning gaps left by the documentary sources and to add flesh to the bare bones provided by the other sources have been truly amazing. Besides oral traditions, mention should also be made of other African traditional sources, such as musical sources, material or physical sources and institutional sources. The first include information derived from various orchestras, songs, chants, funeral dirges and horn, flute and drum music; the material or physical sources include the regalia, the emblems, the drums and the stools of the various states, and the institutional sources include various rituals, ceremonies and festivals as well as the constitution and the gods of the state.

By decolonization of African history, then, I mean first and foremost the use of a greater variety of sources other than the written or the documentary. The data provided by such disciplines as archaeology, linguistics, musicology, social and cultural anthropology, serology and above all by oral traditions and African traditional institutions, ceremonies and music must all be grist to the mill of the new African historiography. Indeed it is the application of such a diversity of sources, disciplines and techniques which has made the study and writing of African history since the 1950s such a fascinating and challenging intellectual activity.

The second step towards decolonizing African history is by approaching research into African history essentially from the African perspective, that is, asking questions and exploring themes of relevance to the African and not the European. The themes and questions that should concern us are, for instance, not so much why and how Europeans came to Africa but rather what they found and how they were received on their arrival; not what they did so much as the reaction of the Africans to these activities and how the activities affected the social and political institutions and beliefs of the African. We should be concerned not only with why Europe abolished the slave trade but also with how the slaves were obtained in Africa and the effects of the slave trade on African states and societies; we should deal not so much with why Europe partitioned Africa and the sort of economic and social policies that were pursued as with the picture of the African states on the eve of the partition, the nature of the resistance or collaboration the Africans displayed, and the impact of colonial rule on Africa.

But even in the new historiography we should not end here. Unlike the study of European and American history, that of Africa should not be confined only to trade and politics but it should be culturally and institutionally orientated. We should therefore include the study of such institutions as the traditional systems of government, traditional diplomacy and diplomatic techniques, traditional orchestras, traditional gods and their roles, some rituals, ceremonies and festivals and such cultural activities as weaving, art and dancing. Such a study will enable us to present as comprehensive a picture as possible of the evolution and development of our societies. Above all, we should not be on the defensive by simply proving that Africa does have a past, but assume the offensive by exploring what impact Africa has made on the New World as well as on Europe, and not only in the prehistoric period but even in the era of colonialism and independence. In other words, the classical themes of colonial African historiography – the coming of Europeans, exploration of Africa, missionary activities, the slave trade and its abolition, partition and colonial rule – should be set in their proper perspective. And of course, the approach to history in which Africans were, to quote the words of Sir Reginald Coupland, the Beit Professor of Colonial History at Oxford, 'a great black background to the comings and goings of brown men and white men' should be buried in silence and oblivion.

....

It is only when African history has been decolonized along the lines outlined above that the appropriate textbooks can be prepared and the knowledge and understanding needed for the nation-building process in Africa can be derived from it. The task of decolonizing, or, if you like, of Africanizing African history or donning Clio in a mammy cloth with a headgear to match should thus be one of the major preoccupations of our historians and research scholars.

We in Africa are facing a problem that the Jews faced three thousand years ago, that the Europeans faced between the fourteenth and nineteenth centuries, and that Mansa Musa, Agorkoli, Okai Koi, Agaja, Jakpa and Osei Tutu faced between the fourteenth and eighteenth centuries. It is, of course, the problem of nation-building. In grappling with this problem in Africa today, we ignore the lessons that Clio, especially in her mammy cloth and *dansinkran* or any other authentic African hairdo, holds for us at our own peril.

Marxism

The status of Marxism as 'political' history is ambiguous. Marx's own engagement with history stemmed from his revolutionary politics. He valued historical enquiry as a means of fleshing out his ambitious schema of material development, and as a way of determining when the time was right for a proletarian revolution. Since that day historians have been prominently represented in the ranks of the Communist Party intelligentsia. Christopher Hill was a member of the party until 1956; E.J. Hobsbawm has never left it. On the other hand, the explanatory power of the Marxist theory of history is such that many historians have been deeply influenced by it without identifying in any way with Communism. Hobsbawm himself is an acknowledged master among many social and economic historians of the nineteenth century, and Hill has had a parallel impact on the historiography of the English Revolution. Inevitably it is the politically committed Marxists who set out most clearly the essentials of the theory. Eugene Genovese is in a somewhat different category, having only briefly been a member of the American Communist Party as a student, but however critical he was of Marx's treatment of American society, Marxism remains central to his practice as a radical historian, in books like *Roll, Jordan, Roll: The World the Slaves Made* (1974).

10. Christopher Hill

[from 'Marxism and History', Modern Quarterly *3 (1948), pp. 55–8, 60–4]*

During the century which has passed since the publication of *The Communist Manifesto*, the influence of Marxism has been more obvious in history than in any other branch of knowledge. We can list six main ways in which the ideas of Marx and Engels have, directly or indirectly, transformed the study of history over the last hundred years.

(i) Of all developments during this period, the recognition of the crucial importance of economic history has been the most striking. All historians now have quite a different approach to the past from that employed by their predecessors a century ago. They recognise that the way in which the wealth of a community is produced and distributed must affect all aspects of the structure and life of that community. This is the most conspicuous advance of history towards being a science: and it derives ultimately from Marx and Engels.

(ii) Second only in significance to this great change has been the growing recognition of the role of economic classes in historical development. A pamphlet published by the Historical Association two years ago on *The Causes of the French Revolution* illustrates this point. The author surveys the interpretation of the French Revolution from Burke to Mathiez; from an explanation in terms of the goodness and badness, wisdom and folly of individuals to one in terms of social classes. The name of Marx is not mentioned in the pamphlet; but there can be no doubt that this has been the decisive influence.

It has really become impossible to write a serious history of the nineteenth century (at least) if you 'do not believe in the class struggle'. This has made nonsense of the Whig approach to history, although the English genius for eclecticism still enables historians as eminent as Professor Trevelyan to graft a little economic history on to the traditional political narrative. But the nineteenth century is too like the twentieth to be told in terms of great leaders 'convincing' a rational people: the Whig mythology breaks down as soon as it comes up against facts that we can test. It survives, however, as a powerful tradition. It is also fostered for consciously political purposes by a man like Professor Butterfield, who (one suspects) repented of his juvenile onslaught on the Whigs as soon as he saw that Marxism was the only alternative.[1]

(iii) Historians during the last century have also come to recognise the social origins of human thinking, of ideology. They no longer accept at their face value the characters about whom they write. R.H. Tawney's *Religion and the Rise of Capitalism* is an example of the new method in practice, and K. Mannheim's *Ideology and Utopia* attempts to state it theoretically in non-Marxist terms; but both writers have clearly been influenced, directly or indirectly, by Marxism. Marx has rightly been called 'the father of modern sociology'.[2]

(iv) Together with this has gone a new relativism in the approach of historians. The great nineteenth-century historians approached history with moral standards which they believed to be absolute, although they were in fact the product of nineteenth-century capitalism. Most modern historians recognise that moral standards change as society changes. Some despairingly abandon the attempt to retain any moral standards at all. The Regius Professor of Modern History at Oxford is not a Marxist, but most Marxists would agree with his way of putting it when, after stating that 'the basic assumptions of the Victorians are today at least as much in question as their "facts",' he added:

> Historians, at any rate, should realise that in so far as they abandon these old-fashioned judgments, they are not so much bringing Victorian history up to date as undermining its foundations. If these are rejected, it is up to the next generation to replace the old assumptions by a new philosophy of events.[3]

In this sphere, in fact, the negative influence of Marxism has so far been greater than its positive influence – as was indeed to be expected in our society, whose economy has ceased to expand, and whose traditional ideas have ceased to inspire even its own ideologists.

(v) During the past century there has been a revolution in the sources from which history is written. Where previously these sources were primarily *literary* – chronicles, memoirs, letters, diaries, newspapers – they are now primarily *documentary*: public records, parish registers, charters, inscriptions, etc., and even archaeological – actual old tools, machines, buildings and fields. It would not be correct to ascribe this transformation directly to the influence of Marx, but it is one thoroughly in keeping with his approach to history; and in his own writings (notably *Capital*) Marx himself uses blue books and other official documents with admirable effect. Whether he would share the modern idolatry of 'documents' is another matter: Marx always had a certain scepticism of official publications, however sanctified by time and dust. And Marx's use of Dante, Shakespeare and Goethe to illustrate points in *Capital*, his epigrammatic and imaginative style of writing in all his best historical works, mark him off from those modern 'scientific' historians whose works are written only too obviously without any view to being read.

(vi) Finally, because Marx established the ultimate priority of economic facts, to which all political and cultural activities of man can in the last resort be related, it is to Marx that we must look back for the modern sense of the unity of history. Textbooks on history are still published in which chapters on 'Literature', 'The Arts', 'Religion' are tacked on to the end of a political narrative like the tail on to a donkey. But good modern historians would recognise that history should not be thus chopped up into fragments, that man's activity in all its manifestations is *one*. To be valid, a history of (let us say) nineteenth-century Russia must tell us about the literature of the intelligentsia and the art of the peasantry, about the religious and national forms in which the class struggle was sometimes fought out, as well as telling us what the Tsar said in 1881. But if history is thus one, the historian himself must have a vision of society and the social process as a whole: he must have a philosophy. Whether he adopts the standpoint of Marxism or not, in so far as he is a good historian he will come more and more to feel the need which Marxism meets by explaining the interrelation and interaction of the countless facets of man's activity. Even on a rather lower practical level the same need for a unifying philosophy is felt. The sheer mass of material with which they have to deal is making all historians feel the need for greater co-operation between research workers if they are not to spend all their time on points of small and insignificant detail. But the *Cambridge Modern History* has shown that a co-operative work which is not integrated and inspired by a common outlook and purpose cannot live as a whole, however admirable some of its component parts.

....

In reaction against the facile liberalism of the nineteenth and early twentieth centuries, many modern philosophers and historians have relapsed into a bleak pessimism. So far from having progressed, man has got progressively worse. His increased control of nature has produced atomic bombs and a tabloid civilisation. Humanism, belief in man's capabilities, is an idle self-delusion: despair is rational, and God the only alternative to suicide.

This is partially true, if one-sided. But it is not new. Marx and Engels took over from Rousseau the conception that a moral decline of mankind accompanies the rise of civilisation. History for Engels is 'about the most cruel of all goddesses': her story is that of the loss of the rights and equality which man enjoyed in primitive society. But, important though this is, it is only one aspect of the dual process of history. Marx and Engels gave a new significance to Rousseau's intuition by showing how loss of equality was the price paid for economic advance. Loss of control over production by the majority in society, and its concentration in the hands of a privileged minority, produced the hypocritical pretence that the interests of the ruling class were the same as the interests of society as a whole.[4] Marx believed that he had shown scientifically how the historical process (if it did not produce catastrophe first) must ultimately lead on to a regaining of the lost rights of man in a classless society. This society will be based on an infinitely higher technique, the development of which has only become possible by the countless centuries of class rule, of human suffering, which have intervened since the rise of private property dissolved primitive communism. Loss and gain are two sides of the same process: fair is foul and foul is fair.

This profound view of the history of civilisation as a whole contains a consolation which is far removed from the vulgar optimism of the nineteenth-century bourgeois. History is a tragedy, but not a meaningless tragedy. Nor are we mere spectators: we have our parts in the action. Atomic energy is not in itself either bad or good: its effect on humanity depends on the use to which it is put, and that depends on the organisation of society. The organisation of society depends on the political struggle of you, me and millions of others. Our forefathers in the nineteenth century were duped by excessive optimism into accepting a political régime which gave full rein to human selfishness. If, faced with the inevitable consequences of capitalism, we now abandon hope, we in our turn will fail to struggle for advance towards a free and equal society. 'Therefore we dare not despair,' said a character in Bunyan's *Holy War*.

Marxism can help us to see the grain of truth in the old legend that good and evil both resulted from the fall of man from his primitive state; so we can balance optimism and pessimism. Marxism, and only Marxism, can also help contemporary historians to preserve a sense of proportion between social forces and the men through whom they work, between statistics and poetry, necessity and freedom.

For a Marxist historian, given sufficient accumulation of factual material, should be able to differentiate at any stage of a society's development between those elements making for change and those retarding it; and between 'progressive' societies in which the political and ideological superstructure is in harmony with the economic structure of society and allows its further development, and 'reactionary' societies in which an outmoded ruling class strives to stifle economic advance, to maintain its privileged position by political force and ideological fraud. On this basis the historian can – scientifically, not merely as a projection of his personal preferences – assess the position of the clashing forces in a given society. This is not a matter of labelling a Shakespeare 'progressive' or 'reactionary', for (so far as we know) he did not consciously relate himself to the rival forces of his day: in so far as he is a great artist he reflects something of both sides in the struggle. But it does mean that in the great conflicts of history the historian takes sides, and has standards by which he can justify his choice. Many devoted fathers and virtuous husbands fought for Charles I in the English Civil War: yet their victory would have led to economic stagnation, political repression, the censorship employed against a Milton or a Bunyan. Doubtless some criminal types 'stormed heaven' with the Paris Communards in 1870–1; but that cannot alter the historian's judgment of the fundamental justice of their cause. Defeat was not in this case history's final word, as the French working-class movement of today demonstrates.

So Marxists believe neither that history is made by great men nor that economic changes automatically produce political results. Ideas are borne in on people by their environment. Social groups become dimly aware of the needs of their position, feel where the shoe pinches them. The 'great man', the political or intellectual leader, formulates their inarticulate feelings in time of crisis. If Lenin had never existed, the Russian Revolution would no doubt have occurred, but its course would have been very different. The human mind is one of the factors causing change.

Engels can sum up:

Men make their history themselves, but not as yet with a collective will or according to a collective plan, or even in a definitely defined, given society. Their efforts clash, and for that very reason all such societies are governed by *necessity*, which is supplemented by and appears under the forms of *accident*. The necessity which here asserts itself amidst all accident is again ultimately economic necessity. This is where the so-called great men come in for treatment. That such and such a man and precisely that man arises at that particular time in that given country is of course pure accident. But cut him out and there will be a demand for a substitute, and this substitute will be found, good or bad, but in the long run he will be found. That Napoleon, just that particular Corsican, should have been the military dictator whom the French Republic, exhausted by its own war, had rendered necessary, was an accident; but that, if a Napoleon had been lacking, another would have filled the place, is proved by the fact that the man has always been found as soon as he became necessary: Caesar, Augustus, Cromwell, etc. While Marx discovered the materialist conception of history, Thierry, Mignet, Guizot and all the English historians up to 1850 are the proof that it was being striven for; and the discovery of the same conception by Morgan proves that the time was ripe for it and that indeed it had to be discovered.[5]

Marxism then has contributed very largely to the creation of modern scientific history. But in the hands of academics this scientific history becomes arid, barren, determinist. Some have felt this as a reason for abandoning scientific history. But the Marxist approach, whilst thoroughly scientific – more so indeed than that of the economic determinists – can preserve the poetic element in history and the historian's right to a standard of moral values; for only Marxism scientifically analyses the class struggle as the motive force in history and sees individuals in relation to this struggle. Freedom for the individual consists in recognition of necessity, conscious co-operation with a historic process which can work only through individual men and women. Milton understood freedom in this sense, though he spoke of God's providence rather than of the historic process: but he put the argument against passive fatalistic determinism finally for his generation when he said that even if unjust princes are to be left to God to punish, still there is no reason why God should not use the people as his instruments. People, social classes, are the instruments through which social change is effected: and people only act when they are convinced of the need for action. The famous 'paradox' of Karl Marx devoting his life in poverty to organising a revolutionary struggle to bring about a result which he had already shown to be historically necessary turns out not to be a paradox at all as soon as we realise that Marx was not a determinist.

The history of mankind is the history of the growth in freedom of moral judgment. Milton was freer and more morally responsible than most of his contemporaries, just because he had a clear conception of a historical trans-formation that he *must* fight for, even though he still thought of himself in mystifying terms as carrying out the will of God. A Marxist today is freer than Milton because his formulation of the relation of freedom and necessity, by eliminating God, has eliminated an arbitrary element and the compulsion of certain inescapable dogmas. But just because of this the Marxist today can see even more clearly than Milton what there is that still hampers full freedom; his study of history helps him to learn how to make society and himself freer. The past is not just a film to be run over before a passive audience: it is a laboratory in which experiments are carried out, theories tested, scientific knowledge amassed. We study it in order to fit ourselves for action.

'Men make their history themselves,' wrote Engels in the passage quoted above, 'but not *as yet* with a collective will or according to a collective plan. . . . Their efforts clash, and for that very reason all such societies are governed by *necessity*.' The next step is to remove the clash of efforts by ending the clash of classes, to bring to an end the class struggle the history of which, *The Communist Manifesto* proclaimed, was 'the history of all *hitherto existing* society'. Then the way will be open from the realm of necessity to the realm of freedom, when undivided humanity can plan rationally how it proposes to live. 'Mankind always sets itself only such tasks as it can solve; since, looking at the matter more closely, we will always find that the task itself arises only when the material conditions necessary for its solution already exist or at least are in the process of formation.'[6]

Notes

1   Compare his *Whig Interpretation of History* with his *The Englishman and His History* [see above, extract 7 – ED].
2   Isaiah Berlin, *Karl Marx*, Oxford University Press, 1939, p. 138.
3   V.H. Galbraith, 'Good kings and bad kings in Medieval English history', *History* 30 (1945), p. 132.
4   Friedrich Engels, *The Origin of the Family, Private Property and the State*, Penguin, 1985, Ch. 9.
5   Marx and Engels, *Selected Correspondence*, Progress Publishers, 1975, pp. 517–18.
6   Karl Marx, *A Contribution to the Critique of Political Economy*, Lawrence & Wishart, 1971, p. 21.

11. E.J. Hobsbawm

[from 'Marx and History', first published in New Left Review *143 (February 1984), reprinted in* On History, *Weidenfeld & Nicolson, 1997, pp. 207–13, 221–5]*

We are here to discuss themes and problems of the Marxist conception of history a hundred years after the death of Marx. This is not a ritual of centenary celebration, but it is important to begin by reminding ourselves of the unique role of Marx in historiography. I will simply do so by three illustrations. My first is autobiographical. When I was a student in Cambridge in the 1930s, many of the ablest young men and women joined the Communist Party. But as this was a very brilliant era in the history of a very distinguished university, many of them were profoundly influenced by the great names at whose feet we sat. Among the young communists there we used to joke: the communist philosophers were Wittgensteinians, the communist economists were Keynesians, the communist students of literature were disciples of F.R. Leavis. And the historians? They were Marxists, because there was no historian that we knew of at Cambridge or elsewhere – and we did hear and know of some great ones, such as Marc Bloch – who could compete with Marx, as a master and an inspiration. My second illustration is similar. Thirty years later, in 1969, Sir John Hicks, Nobel Laureate, published his *Theory of Economic History*. He wrote: 'Most of those [who wish to fit into place the general course of history] would use the Marxian categories, or some modified version of them, since there is so little in the way of an alternative version that is available. It does, nevertheless, remain extraordinary that one hundred years after *Das Kapital* . . . so little else should have emerged.'[1] My third illustration comes from Fernand Braudel's splendid *Capitalism and Material Life* – a work whose very title provides a link with Marx. In that noble work Marx is referred to more often than any other author, even than any *French* author. Such a tribute from a country not given to underestimate its national thinkers is impressive in itself.

This influence of Marx on the writing of history is not a self-evident development. For although the materialist conception of history is the core of Marxism, and although everything Marx wrote is impregnated with history, he himself did not write much history as historians understand it. In this respect Engels was more of a historian, writing more works which could be reasonably classified as 'history' in libraries. Of course Marx studied history and was extremely erudite. But he wrote no work with 'History' in the title except a series of polemical anti-Tsarist articles later published as *The Secret Diplomatic History of the Eighteenth Century*, which is one of the least valuable of his works. What we call Marx's historical writings consist almost exclusively of current political analysis and journalistic comment, combined with a degree of historical background. His current political analyses, such as *Class Struggles in France* and *The Eighteenth Brumaire of Louis Bonaparte*, are truly remarkable. His voluminous journalistic writings, though of uneven interest, contain analyses of the greatest interest – one thinks of his articles on India – and they are in any case examples of how Marx applied his method to concrete problems both of history and of a period which has since become history. But they were not written as history, as people who pursue the study of the past understand it. Finally, Marx's study of capitalism contains an enormous amount of historical material, historical illustration and other matter relevant to the historian.

The bulk of Marx's historical work is thus integrated into his theoretical and political writings. All these consider historical developments in a more or less long-term framework, involving the whole span of human development. They must be read together with his writings which focus on short periods or particular topics and problems, or on the detailed history of events. Nevertheless, no complete synthesis of the actual process of historical development can be found in Marx; nor can even *Capital* be treated as 'a history of capitalism until 1867'.

There are three reasons, two minor and one major, why this is so – and why Marxist historians are therefore not merely commenting on Marx but doing what he himself did not do. First, as we know, Marx had great difficulty in bringing his literary projects to completion. Second, his views continued to evolve until his death, though within a framework established in the middle of the 1840s. Third, and most important, in his mature works Marx deliberately studied history in reverse order, taking developed capitalism as his starting-point. 'Man' was the clue to the anatomy of the 'ape'. This is not, of course, an anti-historical procedure. It implies that the past cannot be understood exclusively or primarily in its own terms: not only because it is part of a historical process, but also because that historical process alone has enabled us to analyse and understand things about that process and the past.

Take the concept of *labour*, central to the materialist conception of history. Before capitalism – or before Adam Smith, as Marx says more specifically – the concept of labour-in-general, as distinct from particular kinds of labour which are qualitatively different and incomparable, was not available. Yet if we are to understand human history, in a global, long-term sense, as the progressively more effective utilization and transformation of nature by mankind, then the concept of social labour in general is essential. Marx's approach still remains debatable, in that it cannot tell us whether future analysis, on the basis of future historical development, will not make comparable analytical discoveries that enable thinkers to reinterpret human history in terms of some other central analytical concept. This is a potential gap in the analysis, even though we do not think that such a hypothetical future development is likely to abandon the centrality of Marx's analysis of labour, at least for certain obviously crucial aspects of human history. My point is not to call Marx into question, but simply to show that his approach must leave out, as not immediately relevant to his purpose, much of what historians are interested to know – for example, many aspects of the transition from feudalism to capitalism. These were left to later Marxists, although it is true that Friedrich Engels, always more interested in 'what actually happened', did concern himself more with such matters.

Marx's influence on historians, and not only Marxist historians, is nevertheless based both upon his general theory (the materialist conception of history), with its sketches of, or hints at, the general shape of human historical development from primitive communalism to capitalism, and upon his concrete observations relating to particular aspects, periods and problems of the past. I do not want to say much about the latter, even though they have been extremely influential and can still be enormously stimulating and illuminating. The first volume of *Capital* contains three or four fairly marginal references to Protestantism, yet the entire debate on the relationship between religion in general, and Protestantism in particular, and the capitalist mode of production derives from them. Similarly, *Capital* has one footnote on Descartes linking his views (animals as machines, real as opposed to speculative, philosophy as a means of mastering nature and perfecting human life) with the 'manufacturing period' and raising the question why the early economists preferred Hobbes and Bacon as their philosophers, and later ones Locke. (For his part, Dudley North believed that Descartes' method had 'begun to free political economy from its old superstitions'.)[2] In the 1890s this was already used by non-Marxists as an example of Marx's remarkable originality, and even today it would provide seminar material for at least a semester. However, nobody at this meeting will need to be convinced of Marx's genius or the range of his knowledge and interests; and it should be appreciated that much of his writing about particular aspects of the past inevitably reflects the historical knowledge available in his lifetime.

The materialist conception of history is worth discussing at greater length because it is today controverted or criticized not only by non-Marxists and anti-Marxists, but also within Marxism. For generations it was the least questioned part of Marxism and was regarded, rightly in my view, as its core. Developed in the course of Marx's and Engels' critique of German philosophy and ideology, it is essentially directed against the belief that 'ideas, thoughts, concepts produce, determine and dominate men, their material conditions and real life'.[3] From 1846 this conception remained essentially the same. It can be summarized in a single sentence, repeated with variations: 'It is not consciousness that determines life, but life that determines consciousness.'[4] It is already elaborated in *The German Ideology*:

> This conception of history thus relies on expounding the real process of production – starting from the material production of life itself – and comprehending the form of intercourse connected with and created by this mode of production, i.e., civil society in its various stages, as the basis of all history; describing it in its action as the state, and also explaining how all the different theoretical products and forms of consciousness, religion, philosophy, morality, etc., etc., arise from it, and tracing the process of their formation from that basis; thus the whole thing can, of course, be depicted in its totality (and therefore, too, the reciprocal action of these various aspects on one another).[5]

We should note in passing that for Marx and Engels the 'real process of production' is not simply the 'material production of life itself' but something broader. To use Eric Wolf's just formulation, it is 'the complex set of mutually dependent relations among nature, work, social labour and social organization'.[6] We should also note that humans produce with both hand and head.[7]

This conception is not history but a guide to history, a programme of research. To quote *The German Ideology* again:

> Where speculation ends, where real life starts, there consequently begins real, positive science, the expounding of the practical activity, of the practical process of human development. . . . When reality is described, self-sufficient philosophy [*die selbständige Philosophie*] loses its medium of existence. At the best its place can only be taken by a summing-up of the

most general results, abstractions which are derived from the observation of the historical development of men. These abstractions in themselves, divorced from real history, have no value whatsoever. They can only serve to facilitate the arrangement of historical material, to indicate the sequence of its separate strata. But they by no means afford a recipe or schema, as does philosophy, for neatly trimming the epochs of history.[8]

The fullest formulation comes in the 1859 Preface to *A Contribution to the Critique of Political Economy*. It has to be asked, of course, whether one can reject it and remain a Marxist. However, it is perfectly clear that this ultra-concise formulation requires elaboration: the ambiguity of its terms has aroused debate about what precisely are 'forces' and 'social relations' of production, what constitutes the 'economic base', the 'superstructure' and so on. It is also perfectly clear from the beginning that, since human beings have consciousness, the materialist conception of history is the *basis* of historical explanation but not historical explanation itself. History is not like ecology: human beings decide and think about what happens. It is not quite so clear whether it is determinist in the sense of allowing us to discover what will inevitably happen, as distinct from the general procedures of historical trans-formation. For it is only in retrospect that the question of historical inevitability can be firmly settled, and even then only as tautology: what happened was inevitable because nothing else happened; therefore, what else might have happened is academic.

....

Let me now return to the illustrations of Marx's unique significance for historians which I gave at the start of this talk. Marx remains the essential base of any adequate study of history, because – so far – he alone has attempted to formulate a methodological approach to history as a whole, and to envisage and explain the entire process of human social evolution. In this respect he is superior to Max Weber, his only real rival as a theoretical influence on historians, and in many respects an important supplement and corrective. A history based on Marx is conceivable without Weberian additions, but Weberian history is inconceivable except insofar as it takes Marx, or at least the Marxist *Fragestellung*, as its starting-point. To investigate the process of human social evolution means asking Marx's type of questions, if not accepting all his answers. The same is true if we wish to answer the second great question implicit in the first: that is, why this evolu-tion has not been even and unilinear, but extraordinarily uneven and com-bined. The only alternative answers which have been suggested are in terms of

biological evolution (for example sociobiology), but these are plainly inadequate. Marx did not say the last word – far from it – but he did say the first
word, and we are still obliged to continue the discourse he inaugurated.

The subject of this talk is Marx and history, and it is not my function here to
anticipate discussion on what the major themes are or ought to be for Marxist
historians today. But I would not wish to conclude without drawing attention
to two themes which seem to me to require urgent attention. The first I have
already mentioned: it is the mixed and combined nature of the development
of any society or social system, its interaction with other systems and with the
past. It is, if you wish, the elaboration of Marx's famous dictum that men make
their own history but not as they choose, 'under circumstances directly found,
given and transmitted from the past'. The second is class and class struggle.

We know that both concepts are essential to Marx, at least in the discussion
of the history of capitalism, but we also know that the concepts are poorly
defined in his writings and have led to much debate. A great deal of traditional
Marxist historiography has failed to think them out, and has therefore landed
in difficulties. Let me give just one example. What is a 'bourgeois revolution'?
Can we think of a 'bourgeois revolution' as being 'made' by a bourgeoisie, as
being the objective of a bourgeoisie's struggle for power against an old regime
or ruling class which stands in the way of the institution of a bourgeois society?
Or *when* can we think of it in this way? The present critique of Marxist interpretations of the English and French revolutions has been effective, largely
because it has shown that such a traditional image of the bourgeoisie and bourgeois revolution is inadequate. We should have known this. As Marxists, or
indeed as realistic observers of history, we will not follow the critics in denying
the existence of such revolutions, or in denying that the seventeenth-century
English revolutions and the French Revolution did mark fundamental changes
and 'bourgeois' reorientations of their societies. But we shall have to think
more precisely about what we mean.

How, then, can we summarize Marx's impact on the writing of history a
hundred years after his death? We may make four essential points.

(1) Marx's influence in non-socialist countries is undoubtedly greater
among historians today than ever before in my own lifetime – and my memory
goes back fifty years – and probably than ever before since his death. (The
situation in countries officially committed to his ideas is obviously not comparable.) This needs to be said, because at this moment there is a fairly
widespread move away from Marx among intellectuals, particularly in France
and Italy. The fact is that his influence may be seen not only in the number
of historians who claim to be Marxist, though this is very large, and in the
number who acknowledge his significance for history (such as Braudel in

France, the Bielefeld school in Germany), but also in the large number of ex-Marxist historians, often eminent, who keep Marx's name before the world (such as Postan). Furthermore, there are many elements which, fifty years ago, were stressed chiefly by Marxists and have now become parts of mainstream history. True, this has not only been due to Karl Marx, but Marxism probably has been the main influence in 'modernizing' the writing of history.

(2) As it is written and discussed today, at least in most countries, Marxist history takes Marx as its starting-point and not as its point of arrival. I do not mean that it necessarily disagrees with Marx's texts, although it is prepared to do so where these are factually wrong or obsolete. This is clearly so in the case of his views on Oriental societies and the 'Asiatic mode of production', brilliant and profound though his insights so often were, and also of his views on primitive societies and their evolution. As a recent book on Marxism and anthropology by a Marxist anthropologist has pointed out: 'Marx and Engels's knowledge of primitive societies was quite insufficient as a basis for modern anthropology.'[9] Nor do I mean that it necessarily wishes to revise or abandon the main lines of the materialist conception of history, although it is prepared to consider these critically where necessary. I, for one, do not want to abandon the materialist conception of history. But Marxist history, in its most fruitful versions, now uses his methods rather than commenting on his texts – except where these are clearly worth commenting on. We try to do what Marx himself did not as yet do.

(3) Marxist history is today plural. A single 'correct' interpretation of history is not a legacy that Marx left us: it became part of the heritage of Marxism, particularly from 1930 or thereabouts, but this is no longer accepted or acceptable, at least where people have a choice in the matter. This pluralism has its disadvantages. They are more obvious among people who theorize about history than among those who write it, but they are visible even among the latter. Nevertheless, whether we think these disadvantages are greater or smaller than the advantages, the pluralism of Marxist work today is an inescapable fact. Indeed, there is nothing wrong with it. Science is a dialogue between different views based upon a common method. It only ceases to be science when there is no method for deciding which of the contending views is wrong or less fruitful. Unfortunately this is often the case in history, but by no means only in Marxist history.

(4) Marxist history today is not, and cannot be, isolated from the remainder of historical thinking and research. This is a double-sided statement. On the one hand, Marxists no longer reject – except as the source of raw material for their work – the writings of historians who do not claim to be Marxists, or indeed who are anti-Marxist. If they are good history, they have to be taken

account of. This does not stop us, however, from criticizing and waging ideological battle against even good historians who act as ideologists. On the other hand, Marxism has so transformed the mainstream of history that it is today often impossible to tell whether a particular work has been written by a Marxist or a non-Marxist, unless the author advertises his or her ideological position. This is not a cause for regret. I would like to look forward to a time when nobody asks whether authors are Marxist or not, because Marxists could then be satisfied with the transformation of history achieved through Marx's ideas. But we are far from such a utopian condition: the ideological and political, class and liberation struggles of the twentieth century are such that it is even unthinkable. For the foreseeable future, we shall have to defend Marx and Marxism in and out of history, against those who attack them on political and ideological grounds. In doing so, we shall also defend history, and man's capacity to understand how the world has come to be what it is today, and how mankind can advance to a better future.

Notes

1 J.R. Hicks, *A Theory of Economic History*, Oxford University Press, 1969, p. 3.
2 Quoted from Karl Marx, *Capital*, Penguin, 1976, vol. I, p. 513.
3 Karl Marx and Friedrich Engels, *The German Ideology* in *Collected Works*, Lawrence & Wishart, 1976, p. 24 (translation modified).
4 Ibid., p. 37.
5 Ibid., p. 53.
6 Eric R. Wolf, *Europe and the People Without History*, California University Press, 1983, p. 74.
7 Ibid., p. 75.
8 Marx and Engels, *German Ideology*, p. 37.
9 Maurice Bloch, *Marxism and Anthropology*, Oxford University Press, 1983, p. 172.

12. Eugene Genovese

*[from 'Marxian Interpretations of the Slave South',
first published in 1968, reprinted in* In Red and Black,
Pantheon, 1971, pp. 315–25]

A merican Marxism has had a curious history; in a sense, it has not so much had a history as a series of aborted births. In the political realm the experience of the last half-century has been unpleasant: the large and promising Socialist party of the World War I era went to pieces and the impressive stirrings of the Communist party during the 1930s have culminated in the pathetic exhortations of a beleaguered sect kept alive by government persecution and a franchise from the slight remains of a world movement. The political record, however disappointing, constitutes a history; the same could only be said for the intellectual record if one were determined to display Christian charity. In the early period Marxian thought, typified perhaps in the historical writing of Algie M. Simons, rarely rose above the level of economic determinism. In the 1930s the economic determinism remained but was encased in the romanticization of the lower classes. The workers, farmers, and Negroes increasingly became the objects of affection and adulation. In both periods the political movement was on the upswing, and the prime function of theory, and especially of the interpretation of history, was assumed to be to provide a justification for the revolutionary cause by uncovering roots in American experience and to give the intellectuals and the masses a sense of a common and inevitably victorious destiny.

Most American Marxian historians of any reputation came out of the generation of the 1930s. The depression helped forge them as Communists, but the advance of fascism and the threat to the survival of the world's only socialist state in some ways had a more profound impact. The racist doctrines of the German fascists led Marxists, as well as others, to reaffirm their commitment to racial equality and to view with intense hostility any critical comment on

Jews, Negroes, or other peoples. The possibility of a fascist victory led them to seek allies in a defensive Popular Front, which despite rhetoric and appearance generally produced ideological as well as political capitulation to New Deal liberalism. The Communist party's search for an alliance with liberals, from Roosevelt to the Kennedys, has stressed the possibilities of working with the 'progressive' sections of the bourgeoisie against the 'reactionary' sections. In practice this policy has meant support for those who have been willing to accede to a modus vivendi with the U.S.S.R. in return for the sterilization of the revolutionary forces in the world generally and the underdeveloped countries in particular. For American Marxian historiography it has meant a lack of concern with class forces and the process of capitalist development in favor of the pseudo-radical division of historical categories into 'progressive' and 'reactionary', which has generally been translated into the glorification of the Jefferson–Jackson–Roosevelt liberal tradition and the denigration of the evil men of the Right. This parlor game, so reminiscent of liberals like Parrington and Josephson, spiced with leftist jargon and a few words about the masses and the revolutionary heritage, has passed for Marxism.

Popular Front liberalism has by no means been merely a product of the political exigencies of the 1930s; it has deep roots in the history of the American working class. From the beginning the working class has held full political rights within a bourgeois-democratic republic that has been one of the modern world's great success stories. Presided over by a powerful, confident bourgeoisie, which has had to face serious internal opposition only once in its life and which crushed that opposition during the war of 1861–1865, American capitalism has generally been able to divert, placate, and buy the potentially troublesome sections of its working class. Without much possibility of building a revolutionary working-class movement in the near future, more and more Marxists have turned in despair to an illusory 'people's movement' against entrenched privilege and have taken this alleged movement to be the principal manifestation of the class struggle in America. For the specific subject at hand – the slave South – the results were predictable. The slaveholders naturally and wonderfully qualify as reactionaries and defenders of an entrenched privilege, which of course they were, and important sections of the bourgeoisie qualify as candidates for membership in a progressive coalition, which they, in the same sense, also were. All that is missing from this viewpoint is an awareness of the process of capitalist development and of the metamorphosis of the bourgeoisie – that is, all that is missing is the essence of a Marxian analysis.

For Popular Front Marxists – that is, for liberals with radical pretensions – the slave South constitutes a nightmare. It is not so much that it conjures up the full horror of white supremacy and chattel slavery, although the emotional reaction to these has been both genuine and understandable; it is rather that the slaveholders presented the only politically powerful challenge to liberal capitalism to emanate from within the United States. It was they, especially in the brilliant polemics of George Fitzhugh but also in the writings of Calhoun, Holmes, Hughes, Hammond, Ruffin, and others, who questioned the assumptions of liberal society, denounced the hypocrisy and barbarism of the market-place, and advanced a vision of an organic society and a collective community. That their critique was self-serving and their alternative reactionary need not detain us. As in the European tradition of feudal socialism, the self-serving and reactionary can prove illuminating and, in the most profound sense, critical. The commitment of American Marxists to Popular Front liberalism has prevented them from taking the ideology of the slave South seriously. As a result, they have been unable to reconstruct the historical reality and have been unwilling to admit that certain elements of the slaveholders' ideology deserve the attention and respect of those who would build a socialist order. It is no accident that the one American socialist historian to glimpse these pos-sibilities, William Appleman Williams, is more of a Christian than a Marxist.

Even the strongest proponents of Marxism must admit that Marxian historical writing in the United States has been something less than a cause for rejoicing and that it has not approached the level attained by such English Marxists as Christopher Hill, Eric J. Hobsbawm, and E.P. Thompson. Marxian writing on the slave South and the origins of the secession crisis looks especially weak when ranked alongside work done on Brazilian slave society by such Marxists as Caio Prado Júnior, Octávio Ianni, and Fernando Henrique Cardoso. The record is so poor that we would be justified in ignoring it, if it had not become so curiously influential in traditional circles and if Marxism did not have so much to contribute to the interpretation of American history.

The paradoxical juxtaposition of ostensible Marxian influence and the low level of Marxian performance arises in part out of the widespread confusion of Marxism with economic determinism. American historians, especially the most harshly anti-Marxian, generally confuse the two and then, since eco-nomic determinism is easy to refute, dismiss Marxism as being of no value. This game would prove entertaining, were it not that these same historians so often retreat into banal economic explanations to suit their convenience. How often does one find discussions of the profitability of slavery embracing the assumption that one or another accounting result would explain the course of political events? Or that the idea of an irrepressible conflict between North and South has to stand on proof of an unnegotiable economic antagonism? Or that proof of natural limits to slavery expansion would constitute proof that the slave system, left to itself, would evolve into something else? These and even cruder notions run through the literature, and their equivalents infect much of American history. The fountainhead of this tendency has been the work of Charles Beard. When his line of thought has proven useful for conservative or liberal purposes, his arguments have been appropriated and his name more often than not dropped; when it has proven an obstacle, his name has been remembered and linked with Marxism in order to discredit him. Yet, a concern for 'economics', and more to the point, for 'classes', has been irresistible even for his most caustic critics. Marxism has both fed the stream of economic interpretation and been contaminated by it.

Of greater importance is what Marxism, shorn of its romanticism and superficial economic determinist trappings, might offer. That it has not accomplished more has been due to many things, not the least of which have been the periodic purges of Marxists from our universities and the venal treatment meted out by professional associations and learned journals. (It would be wonderful fun to list the respected and influential historians who have protected their jobs and their families by eschewing the Marxist label while writing from a Marxian viewpoint and even greater fun to recount the multitude of ways in which the profession has misunderstood what they are in fact doing and saying.) More fundamental, however, has been the misrepresentation of Marxism by our official Marxist historians – that is, by those who have written with the blessings of the more important, if also the most morally discredited, political organizations. These blessings have proven a double joy: to the writers in question, generally although by no means always men of little talent, they have provided high status in a limited but adoring circle; to the profession as a whole, ever anxious to identify Marxism with imbecility, they have provided the perfect straw men. They have converged – I almost said conspired – to present Marxism on the general level as economic determinism and on the level of specific analysis as some variation of moralistic fatalism. We may properly suspect that Herbert Aptheker's grand pronouncement would simultaneously have convulsed Marx with laughter and raised his temper to the boiling point: 'There is an immutable justice in history, and the law of dialectical development works its inexorable way.'[1] For the liberals, statements such as this prove Marxism's uselessness; for the illiterates among the political faithful of the Left, they offer consolation in a period of defeat. All they fail to do is to present Marxian thought seriously and therefore to provide the slightest genuine utility for a political movement that seeks to alter the existing order.

Perhaps the strongest indication of the power of Marxian analysis, even its more vulgar forms, has been the extent to which class analysis has intruded itself into American history despite the contempt poured out on 'Marxian economic determinism.' For this reason alone a careful review of Marxian interpretations of a defined portion of American history has its uses. If vulgar Marxism and simplistic economic interpretations have, as is generally conceded, somehow illuminated the subject, Marxism, purged of its adolescent cravings for neat packages and the easy way, ought to be able to do much more. The first task is to see clearly and specifically what has gone wrong.

Would it not be incongruous for Marxists to believe in original sin, we might trace our embarrassment to our fathers, for, in truth they are guilty; but it is incumbent upon us to be charitable, for their guilt is less than that of their descendants. Marx and Engels restricted themselves to journalistic pieces on the secession crisis and never attempted that kind of analysis of class dynamics which we have come to call Marxian. As political journalism their writings are of a high order and ought to give their admirers no cause to blush. As Professor Runkle, hardly a friendly critic, has shown, their writings display remarkable insight into a wide variety of political and military problems and still repay careful reading.[2] It is not their fault that later generations of epigoni have canonized them and insisted on the value of every word, have mistaken political commitment for historical analysis, and have done violence to Marxism by defending positions taken by Marx and Engels on matters to which they devoted little study. Marx and Engels probably had not read much more than Olmsted's travel accounts and J.E. Cairnes's *The Slave Power*, which is hardly unimpeachable even as a secondary source; their writings show little special acquaintanceship with Southern life and history. Political journalism, even at its best, often breathes passionate commitment, which rarely facilitates sober historical analysis. We need not side with those who would transform Marx into a nonpartisan sociologist – those who would draw his revolutionary teeth in the manner of the European Social Democrats – to recognize that his burning hatred of slavery and commitment to the Union cause interfered with his judgment. It need not have been so, for as Karl Kautsky observes, if the socialist movement genuinely believes that history is on its side, it can profit only from the truth, no matter how disadvantageous in the short run, and can only lose by politically expedient fabrications.[3] It was proper for Marx to hate slavery and to throw his efforts into organizing the European proletariat against it; it was neither proper nor necessary for him to permit his partisanship to lead to a gross underestimation of the slaveholding class and to an ambiguous assessment of the origins of the war.

It would be comfortable to account for the weakness in the performance of Marx and Engels wholly by reference to their political engagement and thereby, in a sense, to acquit them at the expense of their successors. There is, however, a deeper difficulty. The Marxian interpretation of history contains an undeniable ambiguity, which creates a dangerous tendency toward economic determinism – that vulgar and useless historical dogma. Even Marx's preface to *The Critique of Political Economy*, which remains the best brief statement of the Marxian viewpoint, may be reduced to economic determinism, not to mention such politically serviceable if historically simplistic notions as the unilinear theory of history.[4] As a general and preliminary statement, the preface[5] leaves little to be desired, but it does, by its necessarily schematic form, lend itself to economic, unilinear, and other deterministic interpretations. To be understood properly – I refer not to what Marx 'really meant' but to what is meaningful in his thought – passages such as this must be understood in the context of his life's work. The Hegelian and dialectical side of Marx's thought cannot be introduced and dropped at will; it constitutes an integral part of its core and renders, on principle, all forms of mechanism foreign to its nature.

Marx and Engels tell us that ideas grow out of social existence, but have a life of their own. A particular base (mode of production) will generate a corresponding superstructure (political system, complex of ideologies, culture, etc.), but that superstructure will develop according to its own logic as well as in response to the development of the base. If, for example, the crisis of ancient slave society produced the Christian religion, the development of its theology would still depend – and in fact has depended – significantly on its own internal logic and structure as well as on social changes. The staying power of such a religion would depend, therefore, on the flexibility of its leaders in overcoming unavoidable contradictions between internal and external lines of development.

If ideas, once called into being as a social force, have a life of their own, then it follows that no analysis of the base is possible without consideration of the superstructure it engenders since the development of that superstructure is determined only partially by its origins, and since any changes in the superstructure, including those generated by its inner logic, must modify the base itself. If, from the Marxian point of view, classes and class struggles are at the center of historical transformations, then economic determinism, in any of its forms, can have no place in Marxism. The confusion between Marxism and economic determinism arises from the Marxian definition of classes as groups, the members of which stand in a particular relationship to the means of production. This definition is essentially 'economic' but only in the broadest sense. Broad or narrow, there is no excuse for identifying the economic origins of a social class with the developing nature of that class, which necessarily embraces the full range of its human experience in its manifold political, social, economic, and cultural manifestations. That the economic interests of a particular class will necessarily prove more important to its specific behavior than, say, its religious values, is an ahistorical and therefore un-Marxian assumption. Since those values are conditioned only originally and broadly by the economy, and since they develop according to their own inner logic and in conflict with other such values, as well as according to social changes, an economic interpretation of religion can at best serve as a first approximation and might even prove largely useless.

On a more general level the distinction between 'objective' and 'subjective' forces in history, which so persistently fascinates dogmatic Marxists, ends by making a mockery of dialectical analysis. As the great Italian Marxist, Antonio Gramsci, observes after noting Marx's more sophisticated statements on the role of ideas: 'The analysis of these statements, I believe, reinforces the notion of "historical bloc", in which the material forces are the content and ideologies the form – merely an analytical distinction since material forces would be historically inconceivable without form and since ideologies would have to be considered individual dabbling without material forces.'[6] The decisive element in historical development, from a Marxian point of view, is class struggle, an understanding of which presupposes a specific historical analysis of the constituent classes. Such an analysis must recognize the sociological uniqueness of every social class as the product of a configuration of economic interests, a semi-autonomous culture, and a particular world outlook; and it must recognize the historical uniqueness of these classes as the product of the evolution of that culture and world outlook in relation to, but not wholly subordinate to, those economic interests. If certain kinds of economic threats sometimes shake a society more severely than do other kinds of threats, it is only because they ordinarily strike more closely at the existence of the ruling class. Most ruling classes have been wise enough to know, however, that particular ideological challenges can be quite as dangerous as economic ones, and that no challenge need be taken seriously unless it presents itself, at least potentially, on the terrain of politics.

If Marxism is misrepresented as economic determinism by friends as well as foes, Marx and Engels are partly responsible. As Gramsci observes, Karl Marx, 'the writer of *concrete* historical works', was not guilty of such naiveté,[7] but as the statement implies, Karl Marx, the journalist and essayist, cannot always be acquitted. With a tendency toward economic interpretation and an intellectually undisciplined political passion, Marx and Engels left us nothing close to a coherent and comprehensive critique of the slave South. In view of how hard our official Marxists have been working to conceal this fact, one would suppose they think Marxism too fragile to withstand the revelation.

Notes

1 Herbert Aptheker, *American Foreign Policy and the Cold War*, New Century, 1962, p. 291.
2 Gerald Runkle, 'Karl Marx and the American Civil War', *Comparative Studies in Society and History* 6 (1963–64), pp. 117–41.
3 Karl Kautsky, *The Foundations of Christianity*, International Publishers, 1925, Foreword.
4 For a discussion of this point, see E.J. Hobsbawm's introduction to Karl Marx, *Pre-Capitalist Economic Formations*, Lawrence & Wishart, 1964.
5 Karl Marx, *A Contribution to the Critique of Political Economy*, Lawrence & Wishart, 1971.
6 Antonio Gramsci, *Il materialismo stòrico e la filosofia di Benedetto Croce*, Turin, 1949, p. 49.
7 Quoted by John M. Cammett, *Antonio Gramsci and the Origins of Italian Communism*, Stanford University Press, 1967, p. 191.

Part Three

The New Radicalism

History from below

History from below, or 'People's History', is a broad umbrella embracing a number of populist reactions against the monopolisation of history-writing by elites. Even in the nineteenth century the 'high politics' approach to historiography was contested by writers committed to 'the people'. The 1960s saw a whole-hearted rejection of 'history from above' among many younger academics, and at the same time a certain impatience with the more abstract tendencies in Marxist scholarship. The outcome was an impressive set of writings committed to rescuing the experience of ordinary people in the past. The most influential work was E. P. Thompson's *The Making of the English Working Class* (1963).

Raphael Samuel was one of the central figures in History Workshop, a British movement of academics and worker-historians of the Left founded in 1967. His own interest in History from below extended from past movements of popular subversion to 'heritage' in its more demotic manifestations today. Here he charts the political affiliations of People's History – both Right and Left – and emphasises its special importance for British Marxists.

History from below has had the sharpest cutting edge when practised by ethnic minorities in highly polarised and unequal societies. In the United States, before the Civil Rights movement of the 1950s and the coming of Black Power in the 1960s, black people were virtually excluded from the national history. Vincent Harding was both political activist and historian, notably in *There is a River: The Black Struggle for Freedom in America* (1981). In the article reproduced here he explains how during the 1960s black history developed from a demand for inclusion in a white-defined America to an assertion of self-definition. The motivation was political, but the distortions of conventional historiography were so pronounced that black historians had a major educative role to perform.

History from below embraces not only Harding's polemical intensity but also a more dispassionate aspiration to reconstruct ordinary lives in the past. This was a significant aspect of History Workshop in its early years. It has been most systematically developed by the History of Everyday Life (*Alltagsgeschichte*) movement which began in West Germany in the 1970s and which shared History Workshop's somewhat selective approach to Marxism. The focus was on the material conditions of everyday life and the subjective experience of work, family and popular culture. Alf Lüdtke has been a leading figure in the History of Everyday Life. Here he sets out a considered case for its contribution to social history.

13. Raphael Samuel

[from 'People's History', in Raphael Samuel (ed.), People's History and Socialist Theory, *Routledge & Kegan Paul, 1981, pp. xv–xvi, xx–xxiii, xxx–xxxiii]*

The term 'people's history' has had a long career, and covers an ensemble of different writings. Some of them have been informed by the idea of progress, some by cultural pessimism, some by technological humanism, as in those histories of 'everyday things' which were so popular in 1930s Britain. The subject matter of 'people's history' varies too, even if the effort is always that of 'bringing the boundaries of history closer to those of people's lives'. In some cases the focus is on tools and technology, in others on social movements, in yet others on family life. 'People's history' has gone under a variety of different names – 'industrial history' in the 1900s and the years of the Plebs League, 'natural history' in those comparative ethnologies which arose in the wake of Darwin (Marx called Volume 1 of *Capital* a 'natural history' of capitalist production); 'Kulturgeschichte' (cultural history) in those late nineteenth-century studies of folkways to whose themes the 'new' social history has recently been returning. Today 'people's history' usually entails a subordination of the political to the cultural and the social. But in one of its earliest versions, splendidly represented in this country by John Baxter's *New and Impartial History of England* (1796) – the 830-page work of a radical Shoreditch artisan, dedicated to his friends in jail – it was concerned rather with the struggle for constitutional rights.

The term 'people's history' is one which could be applied, in the present day, to a whole series of cultural initiatives which are to be found mainly, though not exclusively, outside the institutions of higher education, or on their extra-mural fringes. It has been enthusiastically adopted by such community based publishing projects as the 'People's autobiography of Hackney', whose work is discussed in these pages by Ken Worpole, Jerry White and

Stephen Yeo. Here the emphasis – as in the History Workshop – has been on democratising the act of historical production, enlarging the constituency of historical writers, and bringing the experience of the present to bear upon the interpretation of the past. A good deal of oral history work falls within the same ambit. 'People's history' is also a term which might be retrospectively applied to those various attempts to write an archive-based 'history from below' which have played such a large part in the recent revival of English social history. As a movement, this began outside the universities. One of the key texts – *The Making of the English Working Class* (1963) – was generated in the WEA classes of the West Riding. 'History on the ground', the movement immediately preceding 'history from below' – represented by such fine books as Maurice Beresford's *Lost Villages of England* (1954) and Hoskins' *Making of the English Landscape* (1955) – found its natural constituency among those who were termed, in the 1950s, 'amateur historians'; much the same is true of that kindred recent enthusiasm, industrial archaeology. Nevertheless 'history from below' has found an increasing resonance in the research seminars, and one may note a gravitational shift in scholarly interest from the national to the local or regional study, from public institutions to domestic life, from the study of statecraft to that of popular culture. Parallel shifts of attention appear to be occurring in other countries in Europe, as a number of papers in the present volume suggest. In France, where there is a long-standing reading public for 'vie privée' and 'vie quotidienne' (i.e. the history of everyday things), and where social history has long enjoyed a far greater intellectual prestige than it does in England, the change is less apparent. Yet one may note, in the wake of the student revolt of 1968, a shift in the *Annales* school from a 'history without people' – a history built on the impersonal determinants of climate, soil, and centuries-long cycles of change – to the kind of ethno-history, dealing with individual experience at a particular time and place, represented by Le Roy Ladurie's *Montaillou* and *Carnival*; a new attention to outcast social groups (the 'marginal' and 'deviant'); and latterly (as Paul Thompson reports in the present volume), a strong, if somewhat belated, recognition of the claims of oral history.

··

People's history, whatever its particular subject matter, is shaped in the crucible of politics, and penetrated by the influence of ideology on all sides. In one version it is allied with Marxism, in another with democratic liberalism, in yet another with cultural nationalism, and it is difficult to dismiss these couplings as illegitimate even where they may be mutually exclusive. The main thrust of people's history has usually been radical, yet the Left can make no proprietorial claim to it. In our own time one might note the almost simultaneous appearance of E.P. Thompson's *Making of the English Working Class* (1963) and Peter Laslett's *World We Have Lost* (1965), the one a celebration of popular insurrection, the other a Betjemanesque lament for the vanished patriarchal family of old. Each, in its own way, represents a revolt from 'dry as dust' scholarship and an attempt to return history to its roots, yet the implicit politics in them could hardly be more opposed.

The 'people' of people's history have as many different shades of meaning as the term has usages. They are always majoritarian, but the connotations vary according to whether the pole of comparison is that of kings and commons (as it is in J.R. Green), rich and poor; or the 'educated' and those whom Michelet called the 'simples'. In one version of people's history – radical-democratic or Marxist – the people are constituted by relations of exploitation, in another (that of the folklorists) by cultural antinomies, in a third by political rule. The term also takes on quite different meanings within particular national traditions. In France, the nineteenth-century idea of the people was indelibly marked by the rhetoric of the Revolution, the term was inescapably associated with notions of class power. In England, with its long inheritance of popular constitutionalism, it was rather associated with the defence of political and social rights. In Germany, where folk-life studies ('Volkskunde') provided the chief idiom for people's history, in both its radical and conservative versions, the people were defined in terms of externality, as a folk community subject to alien influences and rule. For the folklorists 'the people' is fundamentally a peasantry, for sociologists it is the working class, while in democratic or cultural nationalism, it is coextensive with an ethnic stock.

The right-wing version of people's history is characteristically a history with the politics left out – as in Trevelyan's *English Social History* – a history devoid of struggle, devoid of ideas, but with a very strong sense of religion and of values. It is apt to idealise the family – 'a circle of loved, familiar faces' – and to interpret social relationships as reciprocal rather than exploitative. Class antagonisms may be admitted, but they are contained within a larger whole, and softened by cross-cutting ties. The characteristic location of right-wing people's history is in the 'organic' community of the past – the recent past in the case of Ronald Blythe's *Akenfield*, early modern England in Laslett's *World We Have Lost*, the free German peasants before the Carolingian conquest in Riehl's *Natural History of German Life*. The ideology is determinedly anti-modern, with urban life and capitalism as alien intrusions on the body politic, splintering the age-old solidarities of 'traditional' life. In the case of Riehl, the father of German ethnology, and the founder of 'Volkskunde' as an empirical science, the conservative implications are quite explicit. Writing in the aftermath of the failed revolution of 1848, he advocated decentralisation, a return to the system of feudal estates, and a revival of the traditional family 'in which the key virtues were authority, piety and simplicity'. G.K. Chesterton – a liberal populist turned Catholic – is more ambiguous: he had a keen sense of the dignity of the poor, and his *Short History of England* (1917) retains an anti-plutocratic edge: medieval England 'possessed many democratic ideals . . . it . . . was . . . moving towards a more really democratic progress'. But there is no doubt that he regarded 'Protestantism', 'Rationalism' and the 'Modern World' as enemies; he yearned for a return to the 'lovable localisms' of the past, and in his enthusiasm for it, he was apt to idealise medieval kingship – Edward I 'was never more truly representative . . . than in the fact that he expelled the Jews'; Richard II championed the cause of the peasants.

Despite their obvious differences, the left- and right-wing versions of people's history overlap at an uncomfortable number of points. Both may be said to share a common heritage of romantic primitivism, celebrating the natural, the naive and the spontaneous. Both share a common yearning for the vanished solidarities of the past, and a belief that modern life is inimical to them; but whereas for socialists the alienating force is capitalism, in the right-wing version of people's history it is characteristically such a-social forces as 'individualism', 'industrialism' or 'mass society'. There is a certain traffic of ideas between the right- and left-wing views. G.K. Chesterton's interpretation of medieval England leans heavily on Cobbett's *History of the Reformation* (1827), a proclaimedly radical work which anticipates some of the leading themes later developed, in a more socialist direction, by R.H. Tawney and Christopher Hill. Conversely, one could point to the indebtedness of contemporary Marxist and left-wing studies of 'mentalités collectives', to the anti-class sociology of Durkheim, the right-wing crowd theories of Le Bon, and even to such sinister inventions of turn-of-the-century social theory as the notion of the racial soul.

The liberal version of people's history is characteristically much more optimistic than either the socialist or the conservative, treating material progress as fundamentally benevolent in its effects. Capitalism, whether in the form of the growth of towns, the extension of commerce, or the rise of individualism, is very far from being a destructive force, but appears rather as the harbinger of moral and social advance, 'laying the foundations of that glorious and growing system which is destined, ere long, to sweep from the face of the land the last vestiges of feudal tyranny'. Modernisation is synonymous with the march of mind, the progress of civil liberty, and the extension of religious toleration. The people, far from representing the forces of traditionalism, may rather be seen as the subterranean source of change, 'a slow but always progressive influence upon the social life of the country'. Medievalism, by contrast, is equated with superstition and warfare. One of the major themes of liberal nineteenth-century history is the struggle of the medieval municipalities to achieve self-government (the subject of a massive appendix in Thierry's *Rise of the Third Estate*). Another is the emancipation of the peasantry from serfdom, while in the battle of ideas between science and religion, liberal history places itself firmly on the side of heresy and experimentalism against the sacerdotal authority of the church. The idea of nationality is pursued in a similar spirit – as a progressive assertion of liberty on the part of subject peoples.

....

For Marxists, to reject people's history would be, in Britain, to reject the major heritage of socialist historical work. The whole movement of 'history from below', and therefore, if only indirectly, the present flourishing state of English social history, was incubated in the Communist Party Historians' Group of the late 1940s and early 1950s, during the dark days of the Cold War. It was there – as Hans Medick indicates in his paper – that some of its major themes were rehearsed; that its most creative practitioners – Christopher Hill, Eric Hobsbawm and E.P. Thompson – did their early work; and that its most prestigious journal, *Past and Present*, was conceived, as also, if more obliquely, the Society for the Study of Labour History. In the case of the second folk song revival, and the 'discovery' of industrial song, the whole movement, from the Hootenannies of the early 1950s to the folk clubs of today, owes its inspiration (and much of its historical scholarship) to two Communist scholar-singers, A.L. Lloyd and Ewan MacColl. Socialists have also been very much to the fore in the recovery of popular art: one need only mention the pioneering role of the Marxist art critic Francis Klingender, whose *Art and the Industrial Revolution* (1947) was undertaken in collaboration with the Amalgamated Engineering Union, of John Gorman's *Banner Bright*, the work of a printer-historian who was making banners for the labour movement before he came to research them, or of Victor Neuberg and Louis James in the 'discovery' of popular literature. Community-based publications projects – such as Centerprise in Hackney, Queenspark in Brighton, Strong Words in Durham – usually turn out to have a nucleus of strongly committed socialists among both the writers and the co-ordinators. Women's history in Britain is to a striking extent in the hands of, or strongly influenced by, Marxist-feminists, and Sheila Rowbotham's work has given some of its themes a mass readership. It is right that such work should be submitted to theoretical interrogation, but to reject it on the grounds that it was tainted with populism or epistemologically impure, would leave us with little but such *histoire raisonnée* as Hindess and Hirst's *Pre-Capitalist Modes of Production* – a thin fare to offer the labour movement, and hardly the brightest ornament of either literary art or Marxist historical scholarship.

The notion of 'real life experience' is certainly in need of critical scrutiny; but whatever its ambiguities it is certainly not one which Marxists can afford to despise at a time when questions of subjectivity are so insistently on the socialist agenda. The attempt to recover the texture of everyday life may be associated with a 'neo-Romantic intellectual enterprise' – one of the charges levelled against it; but it is perfectly compatible – if that is to be the test of scientificity – with elaborate day-charts and passionless prose. Among Marxist and feminist historians it has arisen from a radical discontent with the use of categories which remain wholly external to the object they purport to account for. For the women's movement it is plainly a political decision; not a question of investigating trivia, but a way of challenging centuries of silence. It is unclear why a preoccupation with the material practices of everyday life – or for that matter the structure of popular belief – is either Utopian or undesirable from a Marxist point of view. Nor is there any reason to counterpose the personal and the familial with global, overall views. In most of the periods with which historians deal, the home has been the principal site of production, the family the vector of property and inheritance, the locality a universe of class. Hans Medick, in his work on 'proto-capitalism', has shown that it is only by reconstructing the life cycle of domestic workers, and the material deprivations under which they worked, that one can understand the base, in production, of primitive capitalist accumulation; and it seems possible that the work of Marxist-feminist historians, centring on the inter-relationship of family, work and home, will have a comparably radical effect on our understanding of class formation and class consciousness. It is of course possible for a preoccupation with the everyday to degenerate into a catalogue of inanimate objects. But work such as Ronald Fraser's *Blood of Spain*, or Luisa Passerini's article on Turin workers under fascism shows that, ambitiously handled, an understanding of subjective experience and everyday social relationships can be used to pose major questions in theory.

British Marxism is certainly in need of the kind of nourishment – or dialectical tension – which an encounter with people's history could provide. Too often, in theory as in political practice, its propositions have been impoverished by the fact that they have remained locked in their own conceptual world, as though designed to keep reality at bay rather than to engage with it.

A history of capitalism 'from the bottom up' might give us many more clues as to the sources of its continuing vitality than debates on the law of value, necessary and illuminating though these may be; a discussion of lordship or chivalry in the Middle Ages or of, say, the peasant roots of individualism might do more for our theoretical understanding of ideology and consciousness than any number of further 'interpellations' on the theme of 'relative autonomy'; and indeed it is unlikely that we shall ever be able effectively to combat bourgeois ideology until we can see how it arises in ourselves, until we explore the needs and desires it satisfies, and the whole substratum of fears on which it draws. Our understanding of socialism too might be less abstract, if we were to explore it historically 'from the bottom up', looking at its secret languages, its unarticulated passions, its cognitive unconscious and dissonances. Above all, the questions posed by feminism leave no category of Marxist historical analysis unscathed, and it is one of the strengths of people's history that it is proving a far more hospitable terrain for asking them than more abstract analytic planes. People's history also has the merit of raising a crucial question for both theoretical and political work – that of the production of knowledge, both the sources on which it draws and its ultimate point of address. It questions the existing intellectual division of labour and implicitly challenges the professionalised monopolies of knowledge. It makes democratic practice one of the yardsticks by which socialist thought is judged, and thus might encourage us not only to interpret the world, but to see how our work could change it.

On the other side of the coin, it is also true that people's history needs, or at any rate would benefit from, a more sustained encounter with Marxism. If it is to achieve the aim implicit in its title – that of creating an alternative, or oppositional history – then it has to link the particular to the general, the part to the whole, the individual moment to the *longue durée*. To write a history of the oppressed – one of its abiding inspirations – needs an understanding of the totality of social relations, while that of marginal social groups, one of its more recent preoccupations (e.g. bandits, outcasts, heretics), can only be understood in terms of centre–periphery relationships. Working lives – one of the major subjects of community-based people's history – need to be situated within the wider social and sexual division of labour and the ideologies clustering around the notion of (say) skill and masculinity; family reconstitution, if it is to do more than computerise nuclear households, must address itself to those questions of power, patriarchy and property relationships which Marxist-feminists have so insistently raised. Popular culture, if it is not to be cut up by students of 'leisure' and 'recreation', needs to be discussed in relation to those questions of symbolic order and non-verbal communication which structural linguistics have raised, as well as to that changing balance of the 'public' and the 'private' spheres which, in this volume, Catherine Hall discusses in relation to notions of femininity. Again, if we are to learn from life histories, whether in the form of oral history or written autobiography, we need a theoretically informed discussion of both language and oral tradition if we are to avoid misconstruing the words that we record. That is, that we have to ask ourselves theoretical questions about popular memory and historical consciousness, to take into account the double character of the spoken word – what it conceals as well as what it expresses – and to build our understanding from such dualities.

Left to itself, people's history can enclose itself in a locally defined totality where no alien forces intrude. It can serve as a kind of escapism, a flight from the uncertainties of the present to the apparent stabilities of the past. But it can also suggest a strenuous programme of work, an attempt to change our understanding of history as a whole. One major element of it is suggested by Brecht, in a poem which interestingly explains why Marxism and people's history – for all the theoretical differences between them – have so often had occasion to converge:

> Who built Thebes of the Seven Gates?
> In the books stand the names of Kings.
> Did they then drag up the rock-slabs?
> And Babylon, so often destroyed,
> Who kept rebuilding it?
> In which houses did the builders live
> In gold-glittering Lima?
> Where did the bricklayers go
> The evening the Great Wall of China was finished?
> Great Rome is full of triumphal arches.
> Over whom did the Caesars triumph?
> Were there only palaces for the inhabitants of much-sung Byzantium?
>
> Even in legendary Atlantis
> Didn't the drowning shout for their slaves
> As the ocean engulfed it?
> The young Alexander conquered India.
> He alone?
> Caesar beat the Gauls.
> Without even a cook?
> Philip of Spain wept when his fleet went down.
> Did no one else weep besides?
> Frederick the Great won the Seven Years' War.
> Who won it with him?

A victory on every page
Who cooked the victory feast?
A great man every ten years.
Who paid the costs?

So many reports.
So many questions.

14. Vincent Harding

[from 'Beyond chaos: black history and the search for the New Land', Amistad 1 (1970), pp. 267–71, 278–84]

When the poet Don L. Lee lately wrote of his commitment to a new integration 'between Negroes and Blacks', several things were already clear. One was that he spoke for a significant part of the black generation which has been coming to intellectual maturity since 1954. It was also evident that he dealt not in semantics, but in the hard, often jagged personal and political differences represented by those two words – Negro and Black. Finally, those who know him (and others young with him) realize that he spoke not as a provocateur but as a healer who had seen our wounds, and desired our wholeness.

For within the heart of the black community in America there exists today a set of agonies which apparently are part of the necessary inheritance of any community that has been engaged in prolonged struggles for radical change, true freedom and lasting justice. In the realm of academic affairs no less than in the arena of political action the extended nature of the struggle and the modern reality of telescoped generational change have created gaps in understanding and intensities of feeling which are too often marked by bitterness and hostility.

One of the most significant examples of this painful division can be found in the movement which has transformed the traditional approaches to Negro History into Black History and now burgeons into the search for Black Studies. Some of the hurt is necessary, for it grows at once out of the nature of the struggle and out of the natural tendency of the sons (especially with Westernized training) to seek to devour their fathers. (Indeed, this essay is itself an attempt to come to terms with the fathers and to understand the nature of the new paths we younger black historians have begun to walk. As such it is a tentative set of suggestions, a brooding over the past and present in search of meaning, form and possibly hope.) But some of the pain is unnecessary, and

part of the motivation for this work is the hope that it may enter into the healing process simply by suggesting briefly the larger historical perspective in
which we have moved from Negro History to Black History and now stretch
out into the yet undefined ground of Black Studies. For this is part of a larger
process extending over much of the world, for which no man here can claim
praise or take blame.

It is impossible, of course, to speak of the 'intellectual' pilgrimage toward
blackness without mentioning the political one – even in a sketchy way. As is
the case with the intellectuals of any hard-pressed and colonized people, black
intellectuals in America have had their inner lives inextricably bound up with
the life of the 'outer' struggles of our people.

The initial (and still overwhelming) struggles were, of course, for unim-
peded citizenship rights, for the recognition of our manhood and for the
opening of the American society to full participation by its black builders. But
a key to this struggle was found in the fact that it was, by and large, a battle in
which we sought to be accepted on the terms by which this nation defined
itself. This meant not only that the majority of us who struggled accepted the
idea that the myth of American democracy was a great truth – except for us –
but we also accepted on various levels of our consciousness the fact that only a
minority of us would actually make it into the mainstream. For only a minority
was 'ready' for integration at any given time, as the keepers of the society
defined 'readiness'.

Fortunately this view was always questioned by some black persons. In the
twentieth century their views began to be expressed most eloquently by
W.E.B. Du Bois, who compared black people to would-be passengers on
a train. Du Bois said that blacks were like passengers who had spent all of
their time and energies trying to prove to their fellow passengers and to the
conductor that they had a right to be on the American train. Indeed, he said
that we had given so much of our attention to this task that we had never
bothered to ask about the train's destination. Finally, said Du Bois, after a few
seats had been commandeered and some of the immediate attacks had died
down, a few black persons began to ask (and he was surely foremost among
them): 'Where, by the way, is this train going?' What is its destination? Most
often no one knew. When answers were supplied some of us began to wonder
if we really wanted to go, especially if our destination would always be determined by the people who had fought for centuries to keep us off, or confined
to the Negro car.

As important as anything else for the political story, however, was the
rising surge of anticolonialism throughout the nonwhite world. With it developed overwhelming movements toward self-definition, self-determination and

liberation. Those whose institutions had been controlled by the white West were demanding more autonomy than assimilation. This, too, was part of the development of a ground for American black-consciousness, and the ideology of the postwar mood was most clearly expressed for American blacks in the writings of Frantz Fanon.

At the same time significant numbers of middle-class young blacks were experiencing the levels of relationship with the white world for which their fathers had lived and sometimes died. This was especially so after 1963. In the midst of this encounter with white America they discovered an atmosphere that often suggested tiredness and death and dying. Often the newly arriving black people found that individual prejudices, institutional racism, and the colonialism of the society had not in any way abated simply because token blacks were present and accounted for. The desperate searches for new levels of black solidarity and for the 'integration' of Negroes and blacks came out of a host of such experiences. One of the young poets simply said: 'America, we've found you out.'

So a movement which began largely as a struggle for inclusion in America as America defined itself increasingly became a political struggle for the power of self-definition and self-determination and for the ability to make America 'ready' for the coming of black men. (Whether that can happen short of revolutionary changes remains to be seen.)

The movement from Negro History to Black History has amazing parallels to the political encounter, partly because they are both really a part of the larger issue.

We who write Black History cannot track our 'bleeding countrymen through the widely scattered documents of American history' and still believe in America. We cannot see luster when we must glimpse it through oceans of tears. We cannot – do not wish to – write with detachment from the agonies of our people. We are not satisfied to have our story accepted into the American saga. We deal in redefinitions, in taking over, in moving to set our own vision upon the blindness of American historiography.

Black History is that plunge which refuses to fall prey to the American dream, which is romanticism and childlike avoidance of tragedy and death. We have tasted too much of these, known too much chaos and uncertainty and struggle and survival and overcoming and prevailing to walk away from the gates of death.

Black History does not seek to highlight the outstanding contributions of special black people to the life and times of America. Rather our emphasis is on exposure, disclosure, on reinterpretation of the entire American past. We want to *know* America at its depths, now that invitations to its life are besieging us. And it is clear even now that the black past cannot be remade and clearly known without America's larger past being shaken at the foundations. While Negro History almost never questioned the basic goodness and greatness of American society, while it assumed its innate potential for improvement (provided it was ready to read additional volumes on Negro History), Black History has peeped a different card.

Black History suggests that the American past upon which so much hope has been built never really existed, and probably never will. We who have been forced to be both black and white in America have seen the society from the dark side, and are therefore dangerous, just as our street brothers are dangerous when they refuse to be absorbed into the corruption they have seen around them since childhood. We are dangerous because we suggest to the society that we are simply the vanguard of all those who must one day awake from the dream of America. What will happen when the dream opens into nothingness? (We are, of course, also dangerous to ourselves, for what can a man do when the goal for which he fought all his life becomes no goal, becomes antilife, becomes nothing worth having?)

As it moves into the chasm of the past, Black History is clearly more than the study of exclusively black things, for since the days of our slavery we could not be understood in an exclusively black light. So that Black History which seeks to deal with America begins with its European heritage, assesses the 'Rise of the West'. It asks how much of this ascendancy came at the expense of the death and degradation of our fathers and other nonwhite peoples of the globe. When it is clear that the 'greatness' of Europe was built under the shadow of our ancestors' deaths, how shall we view this Western world and its major child – America? Black History is the reassessment of an unrequited love affair. It is the exposure of the strange foundations of Western power. Therefore it might be an intimation of things to come.

Black History looks upon America with little of the affection and admiration which was obviously carried by our Negro History fathers. We look at the paradox of Black indentured-servitude/slavery being introduced into the colony of Virginia at the same time that the House of Burgesses came into being. So slavery and 'representative government' were planted together. We ask: Which defined the reality? Or did both? From the perspective of Black History, the greater freedom which was gained for local government in the English colonies actually turned out to be freedom to embed the slavery of our forefathers deep into freedom's soil. So we are forced to begin to ask whether it was ever freedom's soil.

Black History looks at the slave codes of the seventeenth and eighteenth centuries and it reminds a society obsessed by pseudo-law-and-order that the first law and order we knew was the law of our repression and our bondage, the order that comes naturally out of death. So the introduction of black men to American law was not auspicious. Black History bears long testimony to this.

Indeed, a black reading of America is weighted with testimony – and perhaps this is why our fathers avoided dwelling on certain matters; the burden was too much to bear – even against the original religious sense of mission of the first white settlers. For it suggests that if there were men who sensed a calling from God which was more than arrogance, a sense of being sent on an errand into a new land for an opportunity to encounter new righteousness, then those men and their mission were almost immediately corrupted upon contact with the new land. For blacks must read history with Indian eyes as well, and cannot fail to note that many of the New England 'fathers' participated not only in the forced migration and decimation of the original inhabitants, but gave full strength to that trade in men which brought other dark men to these shores. The treatment received by both blacks and Indians cannot fail to shape the black approach to New England history, a history which set in motion an American dream of 'Manifest Destiny' which may yet bring to the world its ultimate corruption.

Indeed Black History is forced to press on to ask about the meaning of America itself. (This raising of questions did not mark Negro History. Perhaps our fathers lived too close to the brutal experiences of black life to allow such a luxury.) When the spirit and institutions of the nation were so fully formed and defined by the leaders of Massachusetts and the rest of New England – slave traders on the one hand, slaveholders on the other – what indeed is the nation's meaning? Whose founding 'fathers' were they, and what does their creation mean for the children of their slaves?

Black History is not satisfied with telling how many black men fought in the Revolutionary War. We are not among those who lift the banner of Crispus Attucks, for we are caught in painful dilemmas. While we recognize their heroism, we recognize too that a revolution which ended with more than 700,000 persons still in slavery was perhaps no revolution at all, but essentially a war among colonialist powers. So the children of the slaves who fought might better mourn rather than rejoice and celebrate, for it is likely that our fathers were no different than the millions of nonwhite pawns who have been pushed about by the military leaders of the colonizers for centuries. (And we save our energies and our wits for the exposing of this delusion and the encouraging of the heirs of the slaves to refuse to be pawns any longer.) In this way the experiences of our forefathers and the developments of this generation coalesce into a totally different reading of America than is usually known.

By the stabbing light of Black History the Declaration of Independence becomes something close to mockery. For what is such a declaration signed by slaveholders, and what did it mean to their slaves – our forefathers? We know why the Declaration did not mention slavery. We know why the Constitution not only mentioned it, but protected it so carefully that it had to be exorcised from the heart of the nation by blood. Black History looks at the 'great historical documents' and realizes that we are a people of the future so far as 'official' America is concerned. For we cannot look back to the masters of our fathers for the 'wisdom' that our friends seem to find when they turn in the direction of the nation's founding documents. We can only mark the corruption written into the origins of the Republic and reflect on the comments of one of the few radicals of 1776, Thomas Paine:

> Now is the seed-time of continental union, faith and honor. The least fracture now will be like a name engraved with the point of a pin on the tender rind of a young oak; the wound would enlarge with the tree, and posterity would read it in full grown characters.

Black History suggests that we are the name (that nobody knew), we are the wound (that nobody saw – or saw and refused to heal), we are the letters of judgment growing fuller every moment. Black History is an attempt to read them clear.

Such a reading of America presses us to ask whether it was ever a democracy, demands to know whether it is possible for a democracy to exist where one quarter of the population of the land is either in slavery or being steadily driven off its ancient grounds. Black History is not simply 'soul food' and 'soul music' as some of its misinterpreters have suggested. Black History is the history of the Black Experience in America, which is the history of black and white – and Indian – inextricably, painfully, rarely joyfully, entwined. So Black History explores Henry Adams concerning the American nation at the beginning of the nineteenth century and hears him say that America in 1800 was a healthy organism. Then in the same work we read that the one major problem in America in 1800 was 'the cancer' of slavery. In that set of statements America is diagnosed for black eyes: Healthy – except for cancer.

Black History is the constant demand that the cancerous state of America be seen and known. Sometimes it hopes, as Martin King used to hope, to expose the sore and thus move to its healing. King (who would have fitted more easily among the Negro Historians for most of his life) was more optimistic than most of the generation just below his. For they are not sure that national cancer can be cured. So, listening to the historian Henry Adams, they shape their own political question: Who wants to integrate with cancer?

Black History cannot help but be politically oriented, for it tends toward the total redefinition of an experience which was highly political. Black History must be political, for it deals with the most political phenomenon of all – the struggle between the master and the slave, between the colonized and the colonizer, between the oppressed and the oppressor. And it recognizes that all histories of peoples participate in politics and are shaped by political and ideological views.

15. Alf Lüdtke

*[from 'What is the History of Everyday Life and Who Are Its
Practitioners?', in Alf Lüdtke (ed.),* The History of Everyday
Life: Reconstructing Historical Experiences and Ways of Life,
*trans. William Templer, Princeton University Press, 1995,
pp. 3–9]*

What *Alltagsgeschichte*—the history of everyday life—is and the uses it
serves remains a matter of spirited debate, not just among historians.
But the controversy itself has evidently helped to spark further interest in the
field. Recent years have witnessed a flood of new articles, books, glossy coffee-
table volumes, films, and television series all dealing with "historical everyday
life"—publications and productions that have found a welcome market, and
often stirred considerable attention.

It is not just the topic that is controversial—even the term *Alltagsgeschichte*
has been subject to criticism, and the label is indeed something of a less-than-
ideal solution, employed for want of a better name. Nonetheless, the designation retains its utility as a brief and succinct formulation, targeted polemically
against a tradition of historiography that has largely excluded "everyday life"
from its purview.

In sketching its essential contours, we are immediately struck by a characteristic feature of much research and most presentations that deal with the
history of everyday life: they center on the actions and sufferings of those
who are frequently labeled "everyday, ordinary people" (*kleine Leute*), a term as
suggestive as it is imprecise. What is foregrounded is their world of work and
nonwork. Descriptions detail housing and homelessness, clothing and naked-
ness, eating habits and hunger, people's loves and hates, their quarrels and
cooperation, memories, anxieties, hopes for the future. In doing the history of
everyday life, attention is focused not just on the deeds (and misdeeds) and
pageantry of the great, the masters of church and state. Rather, central to the

thrust of everyday historical analysis is the life and survival of those who have remained largely anonymous in history—the "nameless" multitudes in their workaday trials and tribulations, their occasional outbursts or *dépenses* (Georges Bataille).

In studies on the everyday toil and festive joys of men and women, the young and the old, individuals emerge as actors on the social stage. But this historiographic perspective also sharpens our sights for history's victims and the multiple contours of their suffering. One representative example is the case of the brutal torture and murder of tens of thousands of women, as well as many men and children, that accompanied the waves of witch-hunting hysteria which swept across the early modern era. That topic has become a major subject for research and representation, extending far beyond the narrow confines of the immediate professional discipline. In particular, feminists regard the memory of historical oppression as an indispensable ingredient in a process leading to a better understanding of how one's own individual identity has been shaped and constructed.

But in Germany, it is studies of *Alltag* in the Nazi period that have had truly reverberating implications—both for public debate and private discourse on one's own history. These investigations attempt to give (back) a human face to the victims of German fascism—the hounded, exploited, and murdered millions. For example, only the painstaking reconstruction of the "ordinary, run-of-the-mill" brand of contempt for the foreign forced laborers employed in such massive numbers in the Nazi war effort beginning in 1941–42 was able to shed crucial light on attitudes toward them: the way in which, at the grass roots, local level, feelings of national and "folk-racial" resentment commingled with an amalgam of fears and a sense of subservience conditioned and inculcated by one's biography—at least among the great majority of *Reichsdeutsche*.

Inquiry into the history of everyday life points up the extent to which most "average people" actually clung to the Nazi regime in their concern to survive. In the end, it was the "others" who bore the "costs" of that process—especially those whose exclusion seemed so "businesslike" in its methodical application: fellow human beings labeled as "subhuman creatures," "elements alien to the folk community" (*Gemeinschaftsfremde*), and "foreign workers" (*Fremdarbeiter*). Thus, research into everyday historical realities has also explored the "inner perspective" of the acquisition and exercise of power by the Nazi rulers. In the light of such inquiry, the gaping distance between rulers and ruled is reduced —a presumed gulf that has so often appeared to exonerate the majority of their guilt. A window is opened on that "shared . . . experience" (Raul Hilberg) that animated bureaucrats and others actively to contribute their skills to mass murder. Those who supposedly were only cogs in the machine, carrying out orders, became active accomplices.[1]

Insights such as these can no longer be ignored in the continuing controversy about the true contours of German history. This became amply evident in the much-discussed "historians' debate" of the mid-1980s. Referring to the experiences of those who had been directly affected by events, Andreas Hillgruber, for example, argued that historians should "identify with the concrete fate of the German people in the East" and the "desperate efforts" of the German armies in 1944–45, which "took such a heavy toll."[2] Findings from research into everyday life on the countless atrocities committed or defended by German functionaries, civil servants, police, and the military at the concrete, local level after 1933 or 1939 have become central in refuting such theses. These studies on "fascism's everyday face" have underscored the extent to which suffering among Germans toward the end of the war was associated in consciousness with the concatenation of terror and suffering *caused* by Germans themselves—and highlighted the fact that many Germans at the time also realized this connection. That is a key point in the historiography of everyday life: actions and experience cannot be separated from the *context* of their genesis and impact.

Investigations of the ways in which "most people" managed somehow to "get by" during the era of German fascism have been explosive in their impact, especially because they have tended to reveal the degree to which the preponderant majority of Nazi *Volksgenossen* were in fact themselves perpetrators or accomplices. Such research, of course, does not address itself solely to those who were contemporaries of these events. We younger generations can no longer feel safe simply by girding ourselves with theories and analytical concepts. Evidently, it is not enough simply to determine what the "situation and circumstances" were back then, and explore whether these have changed. It is obvious that the historical actors were (and are) more than mere blind puppets or helpless victims.

The "Repetitive" Character of Everyday Life—or Forms of (Re)appropriation?

Several key conceptual orientations and emphases of *alltagsgeschichte* should be specified more precisely.[3] Two principal foci can be distinguished.

The first stresses everyday activities in which an element of "repetitiveness" predominates.[4] This perspective, as elaborated by Peter Borscheid, asserts that via repetition, "everyday thinking and action become pragmatic," because routines function to "relieve" the individual of constant uncertainty or doubts. For social groups and institutions, routinization means "submission to authority" as a precondition of their "stability." This orientation, which takes its conceptual cues from the social thought of Arnold Gehlen, reflects the continuity of that older conceptualization of social history viewed as "structural history," where stress was placed on the "structure" of social forms and configurations. In keeping with such a static conception, its more recent variant, associated with the history of everyday life, presupposes a clear-cut separation between the spheres of everyday life and the noneveryday. At the same time, an explicit hierarchy is assumed: everyday life is the preschool, as it were, for the sphere of noneveryday eventfulness. But its crowning conception centers on the mechanisms of historical change: this view posits that nothing but a "select few personalities" are granted the privilege to "cross over" into the realm of the noneveryday. Yet these select few are the only ones "able to bring about further development in the quotidian basis . . . of everyday life." Such development necessitates action by persons "outside of the sphere of *Alltag*."

A second set of approaches, in themselves rather diverse, nonetheless represent a fundamentally different perspective. Certain shared orientations emerge, and these are also the crux of the essays gathered together in the present volume. In contrast with the nondynamic concept just sketched, the reference point is not static structure, what remains "eternally the same." On the contrary: the dynamism and contradictory character of radical historical change are linked with the "production and reproduction of real life" (F. Engels).[5] In this view, reconstructions in the history of everyday life involve more than situations recurrent in the daily struggle for survival (and momentary experiencing of workaday events). Rather, such reconstructions reveal in particular the way in which participants were—or could become— *simultaneously* both objects of history and its subjects.

From the perspective of the direction in social history known in Germany as "historical social science" (*historische Sozialwissenschaft*), the expansion of market relations, the implementation of wage labor and the increased division of labor, bureaucratization and "modern" forms of the central state, as well as the transition to what A.E. Imhof has termed a "lifetime in safety and security" —these constitute the central historical processes over recent centuries. By contrast, *alltagsgeschichte*—conceived as the history of everyday behavior and experience—does not try to raise fundamental secular change to a level detached from human agents, occurring behind their backs, as it were. Rather, historical change and continuity are understood as the outcome of action by concrete groups and individuals. Human *social practice* is shifted into the foreground of historical inquiry.[6]

Scrutiny is not focused on what Engels called the "average axis"[7] around which interests rotate. Instead, the multifaceted ways in which individuals and groups make known (or conceal), implement (or block) their considerations of cost and utility are foregrounded. The thrust here is to demonstrate how social impositions or stimuli are perceived and processed as interests and needs, anxieties and hopes; indeed, how they are generated in the very process. To phrase it differently: the focus is on the forms in which people have "appropriated"—while simultaneously transforming—"their" world.

From this vantage, conditions for action appear ambivalent in their complexity: though given, they are in equal measure a product. These conditions change and acquire nuance within such "reappropriations." Hence, historical subjects are not detached from the social "field-of-force" (E.P. Thompson).[8] Initially, what this implies is that they cannot be considered "autonomous" personalities. It is not a question of "ego strength" as a counterpole, pitted against social conditions for expression. Individuals and groups do not construct the profile of the modes in which they perceive and act in some sphere *removed and beyond* the web of social relations—no, such a profile is generated *in* and *through* that very web. Acts in which people distance themselves from social rules utilize (or refer) to socially understood languages, discourses and codes: the matrix of resistance also marks a social relation. Of course, that relation is created anew by the subjects in concrete situations, and in a manner specific *for them*.

Decentering and "Otherness"

Doing *alltagsgeschichte* involves more than striking out on a new approach to historical research and representation. This work is part of a more inclusive effort, namely, the attempt to forge a fundamentally new perspective on the way historians see the "achievements" of the modern era.

It is no longer merely a matter of broadening customary concepts by including calculations on the so-called costs of secular modernization since the sixteenth century. Instead, inquiry privileges crucial questions about the motivating factors underlying that complex of historical shifts and transformations subsumed under the term "modernism." Doubts now abound about any theses which posit "rationalization" as some sort of ineluctable process—one which supposedly provides the motive force for promoting the process of secular "emancipation" from uncomprehended (or "mythical") forces. Concepts linking "rationalization" with the progress of humankind have also lost much of their persuasiveness. There is another side, methodological and theoretical, to the coin of these doubts: does the image of the "grand contours" of historical life actually accord with the concrete *experience* of "the many"? It becomes necessary to historicize the very assumption of the "shaping power of supraindividual forces," that is, "societal structures and processes."[9] Are they not themselves the product of a society and culture that are decidedly "bourgeois" in character—a society in which a ruling elite, as disciplined as it was domineering, sought, through its explorers and entrepreneurs, to measure the rest of the world by its imperial yardstick?

The concept of "peoples devoid of history" (E. Wolf) that has gained a niche in thinking within the European metropolitan "centers" does not only refer to the colonized nations.[10] In these centers, the strange and alien element of "one's own Otherness" remains hidden and uncharted territory as well: the history of the dependent and dominated, largely mute to date, still beckons to be disclosed. What is at issue is the "other half" of a process encompassing all of society: the history of how the expansion of commodity production, the state, and bureaucracy was *experienced* by "the many." How was the uneven development of the *forces of production*, a process inseparable from the development of the *forces of destruction*, implemented in concrete terms? And in what way did these cataclysmic changes prove useful (or become at the very least tolerable) for the "masses" in the metropolitan centers?

Such a shift in perspective necessitates a double effort. It is imperative not only to describe historical processes but to explain them—though without succumbing to the temptations of an objectivizing view. Historians who prepare their specimen objects using categories providing the greatest selectivity proceed based on a principle akin to Bentham's all-seeing "panopticon": pervasive and encompassing insight, but only from one's own elevated top-down vantage point. Paradoxically, the further this view extends, the more it precludes any chance of being able to visualize how things look when seen from the bottom up.

Criticism of well-worn, fixed forms of scientific objectivizing does not substitute some mode of rapturous emotive comprehension or indiscriminate all-inclusive understanding in their stead. Rather, it is crucial to recognize that the distance between "us" and the "others" is not something self-evident and given, but problematical; it may be possible to bridge the gulf, but it cannot be eliminated. Above all else, this means that we must constantly strive to comprehend our own ideas about those "others"—peasants in the seventeenth century, workers in the nineteenth century, the educated middle class, civil servants— for what they really are: reconstructions after the fact. It becomes evident that these concepts, even when rendered more and more sophisticated (but not "sharper"!), remain nonetheless constructions; they are provisional and fragile.

A glance at one's own first fumbling attempts at understanding may be instructive: there is no way that unsuitable or shattered concepts can be quickly replaced or mended. Moreover, ambivalences cannot be resolved; instead, they have to be reckoned as fundamental to historical praxis and processes. Doing science can trigger the anxiety mechanism when confronted by such situations without the armor of concepts or theories. However, that very anxiety may generate one of those psychological self-blocks that tend to impede a productive approach to multiple meanings and fuzziness. To be sure, such shackled vision has a long tradition. After all, isn't one of the abiding illusions of a naive "enlightened" optimism (in both its non-Marxist and Marxist variants) that the negation of existing circumstances is always pregnant with something "better" to replace them? At this juncture, a stocktaking by the profession is urgently required, namely, the *historical* self-enlightenment of the seemingly ahistorical social sciences, insight into their historicity.

Notes

1 R. Hilberg, *The Destruction of the European Jews*, New York, 1985; M. Broszat and S. Friedlander, 'A controversy about the historicization of National Socialism', *Yad Vashem Studies* 19 (1988), pp. 1–47.

2 A. Hillgruber, *Zweierlei Untergang: Die Zerschlagung des deutschen Reiches und der Untergang des europäischen Judentums*, Berlin, 1986.

3 The multiplicity of conceptual approaches to 'everyday life' has been trenchantly treated in N. Elias, 'Zum Begriff des Alltags', in K. Hammerlich and M. Klein (eds), *Materialien zur Soziologie des Alltags*, Opladen, 1978, pp. 22–9.

4 P. Borscheid, 'Plädoyer für eine Geschichte des Alltäglichen', in P. Borscheid and H.J. Teutenberg (eds), *Ehe, Liebe, Tod: Zum Wandel der Familie, der Geschlechts und Generationsbeziehungen in der Neuzeit*, Münster, 1983, pp. 1–14.

5 F. Engels to J. Bloch, Sept. 21–22 1890, in *Marx-Engels-Werke*, vol. 37, Berlin [GDR], 1978, p. 463.

6 See especially Michel de Certeau, *The Practice of Everyday Life*, trans. Steven Rendall, Berkeley, 1984.

7 F. Engels to W. Borgius, Jan. 25 1894, in *Marx-Engels-Werke*, vol. 39, Berlin [GDR], 1968, p. 207.

8 E.P. Thompson, 'Eighteenth-century English society: class struggle without class?', *Social History* 3 (1978), p. 151.

9 H.-U. Wehler, 'Alltagsgeschichte—Konigsweg zu neuen Ufern oder Irrgarten der Illusionen?', in Wehler, *Deutsche Gesellschaftsgeschichte*, vol. 1, Munich, 1987, pp. 6–30.

10 Eric Wolf, *Europe and the People Without History*, Berkeley, 1982 (ED).

Gender

Beginning in the United States in the 1970s, women's history has probably done more than any other recent radical innovation to modify the shape of the discipline, enlarging its subject-matter and influencing its modes of explanation. Carroll Smith-Rosenberg well conveys the political atmosphere in which women's history got under way: 'we turned to our history to trace the origins of women's second-class status', she writes. 'Foremothers' were reclaimed, and the roots of sexual oppression were uncovered. Smith-Rosenberg describes how she came to focus on passionate relationships between women – one of the most neglected aspects of the historical record.

But women's history was always more than a way of raising political consciousness among women. It also aspired to change the way in which all history was written. The key concept in this endeavour was 'gender', which is now used to denote the distinctions of sex which are constitutive of all social relations. Joan Wallach Scott was one of the first to set out the theoretical implications of writing gender history. In this highly influential article (first published in 1986) she argued that gender was not only a crucial dimension of social stratification, but a form of identity and a culturally powerful means of signifying other forms of power. Gisela Bok takes up one of the most important implications of gender history, which is that it concerns men as well as women. This does not mean continuing to write the history of men in the traditional way, but understanding men within a gender order, and always in relation to women: that is what is understood by the relatively new field of the history of masculinity.

16. Carroll Smith-Rosenberg

[from 'Hearing Women's Words: a Feminist Reconstruction of History', in her Disorderly Conduct: Visions of Gender in Victorian America, *Oxford University Press, 1986, pp. 11–15, 17–19]*

Women's history bridges the scholarly and political, weaving their disparate visions into one. The political feminism of the 1960s and 1970s drew scholars and students to the field of women's history, informing the questions women's historians first addressed. Self-conscious feminism strengthened the resolve of those who insisted upon restructuring the scholarly canon to make the study of women's roles and visions, power and oppressions central to historical analysis. If the personal was the political, so too was the historical. Yet at the same time women's historians claimed Clio, muse of history, as their second mother. While a sense of personal oppression and revolt against marginality and invisibility shaped the questions women's historians first addressed, those questions in turn pushed the methodological approaches and conceptual framework of traditional history to new frontiers. They revolutionized historians' understanding of the family, of the processes of economic change, and of the distribution of power within both traditional and industrial societies. A vision of past cultures as multilayered composites of women's and men's experiences, rich in complexity and conflict, emerged from women's historians' merger of the political and the professional.

Revolutionaries are rarely trained for their roles. They come forward to answer unexpected challenges, at times when old paradigms prove obsolete and new visions are required. Certainly those of us who in the early 1970s responded to the feminist call to discover our collective past had been brought up in the assumptions and methods of conventional history. We were not trained to study women, nor had we thought to do so until the women's movement transformed our lives and our consciousness. Then, we struggled to master the skills necessary to reconstruct women's past. The vision and determination that characterized these early years of women's history – the excitement of our discoveries; the sense of a collective enterprise; the long debates as to the place of women's history within traditional scholarship; the ideological and practical need to develop new, cooperative, noncompetitive approaches to research; the dedication of those who founded the first feminist presses and journals, in their living rooms, during hours stolen from work and family – all are now largely lost to history. We have so quickly become part of the professional mainstream that it is easy to forget the spirit of those early years, the camaraderie with which we turned to each other.

Without question, our first inspiration was political. Aroused by feminist charges of economic and political discrimination, angered at the sexualization of women by contemporary society and at the psychological ramifications of that sexualization, we turned to our history to trace the origins of women's second-class status. Perhaps the most revolutionary aspect of contemporary women's history was our refusal to accept gender-role divisions as natural. Gender, we insisted, was man-made, the product of cultural definitions, not of biological forces. No universal femaleness or maleness existed. Rather, economic, demographic, and ideational factors came together within specific societies to determine which rights, powers, privileges, and personalities women and men would possess.

For us the search to determine what concatenation of factors had decreed the particular gender assumptions the Western world imposed on its women and its men was far from academic. These assumptions had shaped our own lives. The intricate relation between the construction of gender and the structure of power became our principal concern.

We began our investigation by examining the impact of industrialization upon the construction of gender roles in both the work force and the family. Certainly the gender division of labor, as Engels argued a hundred years ago, had predated capitalism. But why, feminist historians asked, had not industrialization undercut those distinctions and made new roles and economic opportunities available for women? Mechanization, by minimizing the importance of brawn to production, had opened up a host of new areas to the potential of female employment. Certainly it was to the economic advantage of the entrepreneurial class to expand the labor force. Why, then, did entrepreneurs bar women from most areas of manufacturing? Who profited from such discrimination? Did the fact that entrepreneurs structured the radically new labor force of an industrializing economy around traditional role divisions suggest that, at the very outset of industrialization, male capital and male labor shared a fundamental social and economic vision that cut across class lines and, in the face of violent economic change, reasserted male social cohesion? If this were true, we would have discovered one critical factor that had kept the emerging and uncertain world of nineteenth-century industrial capitalism from fragmenting. A key social function of women's economic oppression would then become clear, a function that presumably continues to play a vital role in its perpetuation. Historians of women began to examine the ramifications of economic discrimination against women, pointing to the ways it spread out in a ripple effect to alter virtually all forms of social relations. Low wages, the absence of upward mobility, depressing and unhealthy working conditions, all made marriage an attractive survival strategy for working-class women. Once married, women found the workplace closed even more firmly against them. A vicious cycle of economic and psychological dependency emerged, with few if any escape routes even for women of talent and ambition. Of course, feminist historians were not the first to uncover the social construction of women's domestic dependency. Theodore Dreiser had described Sister Carrie's horror when brought face to face with the barren drabness which both her married sister and the unmarried 'girls' in the sweatshops experienced. Anzia Yezierska's stories detail the blighted hopes and wasted lives of countless married and unmarried immigrant women.[1]

Within the bourgeois world, a confining ideology reinforced these pervasive patterns of economic discrimination. Erecting the nonproductive woman into a symbol of bourgeois class hegemony, the new bourgeois men of the 1820s, 1830s, and 1840s formulated the Cult of True Womanhood, which prescribed a female role bounded by kitchen and nursery, overlaid with piety and purity, and crowned with subservience.[2] The women who rejected these constraints, or who, pushed by poverty, entered the labor force, were viewed as unnatural. Intrigued by the proliferation of bourgeois literature that sought to reinforce these economic dictates, the new women's historians began to pore over advice books to young women and men, to young wives and husbands. We surveyed children's literature, school curricula, religious sermons, popular magazines, fiction, and poetry. We compared the presentation of gender by women and men writers. In short, we began to dissect the nineteenth century's construction of gender.[3]

The contemporary feminist movement, especially in its earliest years, had focused on the sexual objectivization of women, seeing in it the psychological roots of women's passivity. Choosing abortion as their premier issue, feminists of the 1960s and 1970s demanded that women assert control over their own bodies. Again, the focus of women's historians followed contemporary feminist concerns. We explored the clinical use of women's bodies by the nineteenth century's male-dominated medical profession. We discovered that, as male physicians transformed gynecology and obstetrics – traditional female mysteries – into male surgical specialties barred to women practitioners, they sought clinical subjects to use in expanding their medical and surgical knowledge. European laws regulating prostitution – requiring regular gynecological examination and hospitalization for venereal disease – provided one such group of subjects. In America, early nineteenth-century physicians had turned to Afro-American slaves and to almshouse inhabitants. Later in the century, they encouraged working-class women to frequent the lying-in hospitals and the outpatient clinics medical schools established to provide students with clinical training. In fact, beginning in the 1880s and extending into the twentieth century, the growing centrality of clinical training to medical education, the provision of inexpensive medical care for poor women, and the exclusion of all but the token woman from medical schools went hand in hand. Professionalization and male dominance within medicine became synonymous.

As political feminists and historians we searched history for political 'foremothers'. We retraced the development of the nineteenth-century suffrage movement. We reconstructed the ties that bound the early feminists to Garrisonian abolitionism and the political realities that severed those ties. We searched for the origins of the feminist movement in earlier British radical and utopian socialist movements – in the writings of Mary Wollstonecraft and the work of Fanny Wright, Robert Dale Owen, and others. We turned to women's religious enthusiasm, tracing the influence of millennial religion on women's reform activities and role expansion. Some women who held back from self-conscious feminism, we discovered, had nevertheless assumed innovative roles as urban philanthropists, public-health advocates, opponents of child labor. They had battled male power under the banner of the Women's Christian Temperance Union and waged a victorious war against the inhumanity of lynching. Women had actively forged a native American brand of socialism, encouraged their sisters to form trade unions, lobbied successfully for social legislation.

....

The daughter of political feminism, women's history played a critical role within the growing sophistication of contemporary social history. The New Social History popularized techniques developed by French historical demographers in the 1950s and 1960s that encouraged social historians to turn from a study of the notable and public to an analysis of the hitherto largely overlooked domestic world of the inarticulate, the black, the working class, the immigrant – and even of women within these groups. Innovative demographic techniques threw open the accumulated census, town, and church records of earlier centuries. Historians could now trace developments in family and household structure, birth and death rates, patterns of geographic or economic mobility. The new social historians borrowed analytic concepts and interpretive models from L'Ecole des Annales in France, from British and American behavioral scientists, and from the New Economists. They began to investigate child-rearing practices and their effect on later personality developments, generational relations within the family, sexual values. Institutions and processes central to women's lives emerged as central to the historical process. Women's historians adopted the new methods and analytic framework.

Women's history's relation to the New History was not one of dependency but of mutual enrichment. The history of women has significantly expanded the horizons of other social historians, broadening the questions they ask about *both* men and women, encouraging a far more complex view of social processes. For despite their focus upon institutions and events of greatest concern to women, the new historians of the family, religion, medicine, education, and the working class tended to ignore women. In doing so they often dealt superficially with a major segment of the population, and underestimated the complexity of institutional arrangements and of social processes. The new male historians expressed little enthusiasm for examining the ways gender informed economic and political decisions and channeled their impact, for the fact that women's and men's interests within the family and the workplace might be not only different but in conflict. Class, religious, and family structures, as seen by historians who looked only at the male experience, took on a more monolithic – at times static – appearance than they possessed. In contrast, women's historians self-consciously searched for that excluded Other. A far more heterogeneous and inharmonious view of the past characterized our analysis. We insisted that women and men experienced, used, and conceived of the family, religion, work, and public and private space differently. The factory imposed distinctive burdens and offered divergent opportunities for women and for men, as did religious piety.

Like male social historians, we borrowed analytical tools from anthropology, sociology, and psychology, but at the same time we remained critical of the insensitivity so many scholars in those disciplines had displayed toward women's experiences and perceptions. We saw rituals of cohesion not as constructive social dramas but as potentially repressive of legitimate female protest and supportive of male hegemony. We did not take as a statement of inevitability Lévi-Strauss's insight that families, and indeed civilization itself, are structured around male traffic in women, rather we transformed it into a fundamental criticism of social structures. We explored the complex ways language, transposed into myth, distorts reality, so that what is too conflicted to be spoken directly can nevertheless be said. In Roland Barthes's terminology, we became myth decipherers, skeptical of all institutions and processes that presented themselves as 'natural'.[4] In all of these ways we sought to compensate for perceived limitations in the assumptions of both conventional and social-science history. We have been constructive iconoclasts, or, rather, pioneers who helped open to scholarly analysis a new continent of experiences and relations.

In this sense women's history challenges traditional history in a far more basic way than do any of the other new subspecialties in conveniently labeled 'minority history'. Male historians have customarily linked women's history with black or ethnic history, or with the study of homosexuality. To the extent that women are an oppressed social category, a group whose economic and political exploitation finds parallels within a scholarly canon which discounts their significance, the analogy of women's history and minority history is appropriate. Both minority and women's history, moreover, constitute radically innovative and creative forms of historical analysis. Both challenge historical conventions. Both insist on new approaches and demand new answers. Furthermore, women comprise a central component within all minority history. But, at rock bottom, the essential difference distinguishing them is this: women are not a forgotten minority. Rather, women constitute the forgotten majority in virtually every society and within every social category. To ignore women is not simply to ignore a significant subgroup within the social structure. It is to misunderstand and distort the entire organization of that society. Incorporating women's experiences into our social analysis involves far more than adding another factor to our interpretation and thus correcting an admittedly glaring oversight. It forces us to reconsider our understanding of the most fundamental ordering of social relations, institutions and power arrangements within the society we study.

But how can we effectively integrate women into social analysis? By inverting the questions we customarily ask, Joan Scott argues. Feminist historians, concerned with the ways social arrangements and the distribution of power affected women, Scott continues, have ironically maintained the centrality of male decisions and institutions within their analytic schemas. They thus kept women as but one variable within a larger (male) picture. By asking, instead, what the particular conformation of gender in a society tells us about the society that so constructed gender, we will make women and gender central to social analysis.

Notes

1 Theodore Dreiser, *Sister Carrie*, University of Pennsylvania Press, 1981; Anzia Yezierska, *Bread Givers*, George Braziller, 1975.
2 Barbara Welter, 'The cult of True Womanhood, 1820–1860', *American Quarterly* 18 (1960).
3 See for example Nancy Cott, *The Bonds of Womanhood: 'Woman's Sphere' in New England, 1780–1835*, Yale University Press, 1977; Kathryn Kish Sklar, *Catherine Beecher: A Study in American Domesticity*, Yale University Press, 1973.
4 Roland Barthes, *Mythologies*, trans. Annette Lavers, Hill & Wang, 1972.

17. Joan Scott

[from 'Gender: a useful category of historical analysis', in her Gender and the Politics of History, *Columbia University Press, 1988, pp. 28–31, 41–6]*

Gender. n. a grammatical term only. To talk of persons or creatures of the masculine or feminine gender, meaning of the male or female sex, is either a jocularity (permissible or not according to context) or a blunder.

Fowler's *Dictionary of Modern English Usage*

Those who would codify the meanings of words fight a losing battle, for words, like the ideas and things they are meant to signify, have a history. Neither Oxford dons nor the Académie Française has been entirely able to stem the tide, to capture and fix meanings free of the play of human invention and imagination. Mary Wortley Montagu added bite to her witty denunciation 'of the fair sex' ('my only consolation for being of that gender has been the assurance of never being married to any one among them') by deliberately misusing the grammatical reference.[1] Through the ages, people have made figurative allusions by employing grammatical terms to evoke traits of character or sexuality. For example, the usage offered by the *Dictionnaire de la langue française* in 1876 was: 'On ne sait de quel genre il est, s'il est mâle ou femelle, se dit d'un homme très-caché, dont on ne connait pas les sentiments.'[2] And Gladstone made this distinction in 1878: 'Athene has nothing of sex except the gender, nothing of the woman except the form.'[3] Most recently – too recently to find its way into dictionaries or the *Encyclopedia of the Social Sciences* – feminists have in a more literal and serious vein begun to use 'gender' as a way of referring to the social organization of the relationship between the sexes. The connection to grammar is both explicit and full of unexamined possibilities. Explicit because the grammatical usage involves formal rules that follow from the masculine or feminine designation; full of unexamined possibilities because in many Indo-European languages there is a third category – unsexed or neuter. In grammar, gender is understood to be a way of classifying phenomena, a socially agreed upon system of distinctions rather than an objective description of inherent traits. In addition, classifications suggest a relationship among categories that makes distinctions or separate groupings possible.

In its most recent usage, 'gender' seems to have first appeared among American feminists who wanted to insist on the fundamentally social quality of distinctions based on sex. The word denoted a rejection of the biological determinism implicit in the use of such terms as 'sex' or 'sexual difference'. 'Gender' also stressed the relational aspect of normative definitions of femininity. Those who worried that women's studies scholarship focused too narrowly and separately on women used the term 'gender' to introduce a relational notion into our analytic vocabulary. According to this view, women and men were defined in terms of one another, and no understanding of either could be achieved by entirely separate study. Thus Natalie Davis suggested in 1975: 'It seems to me that we should be interested in the history of both women and men, that we should not be working only on the subjected sex any more than a historian of class can focus entirely on peasants. Our goal is to understand the significance of the *sexes*, of gender groups in the historical past. Our goal is to discover the range in sex roles and in sexual symbolism in different societies and periods, to find out what meaning they had and how they functioned to maintain the social order or to promote its change.'[4]

In addition, and perhaps most important, 'gender' was a term offered by those who claimed that women's scholarship would fundamentally transform disciplinary paradigms. Feminist scholars pointed out early on that the study of women would not only add new subject matter but would also force a critical reexamination of the premises and standards of existing scholarly work. 'We are learning,' wrote three feminist historians, 'that the writing of women into history necessarily involves redefining and enlarging traditional notions of historical significance, to encompass personal, subjective experience as well as public and political activities. It is not too much to suggest that however hesitant the actual beginnings, such a methodology implies not only a new history of women, but also a new history.'[5] The way in which this new history would both include and account for women's experience rested on the extent to which gender could be developed as a category of analysis. Here the analogies to class and race were explicit; indeed, the most politically inclusive of scholars of women's studies regularly invoked all three categories as crucial to the writing of a new history.[6] An interest in class, race, and gender signaled, first, a scholar's commitment to a history that included stories of the oppressed and an analysis of the meaning and nature of their oppression and, second, scholarly understanding that inequalities of power are organized along at least three axes.

The litany of class, race, and gender suggests a parity for each term, but, in fact, that is not at all the case. While 'class' most often rests on Marx's elaborate (and since elaborated) theory of economic determination and historical change, 'race' and 'gender' carry no such associations. No unanimity exists among those who employ concepts of class. Some scholars employ Weberian notions, others use class as a temporary heuristic device. Still, when we invoke class, we are working with or against a set of definitions that, in the case of Marxism, involve an idea of economic causality and a vision of the path along which history has moved dialectically. There is no such clarity or coherence for either race or gender. In the case of gender, the usage has involved a range of theoretical positions as well as simple descriptive references to the relationships between the sexes.

Feminist historians, trained as most historians are to be more comfortable with description than theory, have nonetheless increasingly looked for usable theoretical formulations. They have done so for at least two reasons. First, the proliferation of case studies in women's history seems to call for some synthesizing perspective that can explain continuities and discontinuities and account for persisting inequalities as well as radically different social experiences. Second, the discrepancy between the high quality of recent work in women's history and its continuing marginal status in the field as a whole (as measured by textbooks, syllabi, and monographic work) points up the limits of descriptive approaches that do not address dominant disciplinary concepts, or at least that do not address these concepts in terms that can shake their power and perhaps transform them. It has not been enough for historians of women to prove either that women had a history or that women participated in the major political upheavals of Western civilization. In the case of women's history, the response of most nonfeminist historians has been acknowledgment and then separation or dismissal ('women had a history separate from men's, therefore let feminists do women's history which need not concern us'; or 'women's history is about sex and the family and should be done separately from political and economic history'). In the case of women's participation, the response has been minimal interest at best ('my understanding of the French Revolution is not changed by knowing that women participated in it'). The challenge posed by these responses is, in the end, a theoretical one. It requires analysis not only of the relationship between male and female experience in the past but also of the connection between past history and current historical practice. How does gender work in human social relationships?

How does gender give meaning to the organization and perception of histor-ical knowledge? The answers depend on gender as an analytic category.

....

Concern with gender as an analytic category has emerged only in the late twentieth century. It is absent from the major bodies of social theory articulated from the eighteenth to the early twen-tieth century. To be sure, some of those theories built their logic on analogies to the opposition of male and female, others acknowledged a 'woman ques-tion', still others addressed the formation of subjective sexual identity, but gender as a way of talking about systems of social or sexual relations did not appear. This neglect may in part explain the difficulty that contemporary fem-inists have had incorporating the term 'gender' into existing bodies of theory and convincing adherents of one or another theoretical school that gender belongs in their vocabulary. The term 'gender' is part of the attempt by con-temporary feminists to stake claim to a certain definitional ground, to insist on the inadequacy of existing bodies of theory for explaining persistent inequalities between women and men. It seems to me significant that the use of the word 'gender' has emerged at a moment of great epistemological turmoil that takes the form, in some cases, of a shift from scientific to literary paradigms among social scientists (from an emphasis on cause to one on meaning, blurring genres of inquiry, in anthropologist Clifford Geertz's phrase)[7] and, in other cases, the form of debates about theory between those who assert the transparency of facts and those who insist that all reality is construed or constructed, between those who defend and those who question the idea that 'man' is the rational master of his own destiny. In the space opened by this debate and on the side of the critique of science developed by the humanities, and of empiricism and humanism by post-structuralists, feminists have begun to find not only a theor-etical voice of their own but scholarly and political allies as well. It is within this space that we must articulate gender as an analytic category.

What should be done by historians who, after all, have seen their discipline dismissed by some recent theorists as a relic of humanist thought? I do not think we should quit the archives or abandon the study of the past, but we do have to change some of the ways we've gone about working, some of the ques-tions we have asked. We need to scrutinize our methods of analysis, clarify our operative assumptions, and explain how we think change occurs. Instead of a search for single origins, we have to conceive of processes so interconnected that they cannot be disentangled. Of course, we identify problems to study, and these constitute beginnings or points of entry into complex processes. But it is the processes we must continually keep in mind. We must ask more often how things happened in order to find out why they happened; in anthropologist

Michelle Rosaldo's formulation, we must pursue not universal, general causality but meaningful explanation: 'It now appears to me that women's place in human social life is not in any direct sense a product of the things she does, but of the meaning her activities acquire through concrete social interaction.'[8] To pursue meaning, we need to deal with the individual subject as well as social organization and to articulate the nature of their interrelationships, for both are crucial to understanding how gender works, how change occurs. Finally, we need to replace the notion that social power is unified, coherent, and centralized with something like Michel Foucault's concept of power as dispersed constellations of unequal relationships, discursively constituted in social 'fields of force'.[9] Within these processes and structures, there is room for a concept of human agency as the attempt (at least partially rational) to construct an identity, a life, a set of relationships, a society within certain limits and with language – conceptual language that at once sets boundaries and contains the possibility for negation, resistance, reinterpretation, the play of metaphoric invention and imagination.

My definition of gender has two parts and several subsets. They are interrelated but must be analytically distinct. The core of the definition rests on an integral connection between two propositions: gender is a constitutive element of social relationships based on perceived differences between the sexes, and gender is a primary way of signifying relationships of power. Changes in the organization of social relationships always correspond to changes in representations of power, but the direction of change is not necessarily one way. As a constitutive element of social relationships based on perceived differences between the sexes, gender involves four interrelated elements: first, culturally available symbols that evoke multiple (and often contradictory) representations – Eve and Mary as symbols of woman, for example, in the Western Christian tradition – but also, myths of light and dark, purification and pollution, innocence and corruption. For historians, the interesting questions are, Which symbolic representations are invoked, how, and in what contexts? Second, normative concepts that set forth interpretations of the meanings of the symbols, that attempt to limit and contain their metaphoric possibilities. These concepts are expressed in religious, educational, scientific, legal, and political doctrines and typically take the form of a fixed binary opposition, categorically and unequivocally asserting the meaning of male and female, masculine and feminine. In fact, these normative statements depend on the refusal or repression of alternative possibilities, and sometimes overt contests about them take place (at what moments and under what circumstances ought to be a concern of historians). The position that emerges as dominant, however, is stated as the only possible one. Subsequent history is written as if these normative positions were the product of social consensus rather than of conflict. An example of this kind of history is the treatment of the Victorian ideology of domesticity as if it were created whole and only afterwards reacted to instead of being the constant subject of great differences of opinion. Another kind of example comes from contemporary fundamentalist religious groups that have forcibly linked their practice to a restoration of women's supposedly more authentic 'traditional' role, when, in fact, there is little historical precedent for the unquestioned performance of such a role. The point of new historical investigation is to disrupt the notion of fixity, to discover the nature of the debate or repression that leads to the appearance of timeless permanence in binary gender representation. This kind of analysis must include a notion of politics and reference to social institutions and organizations – the third aspect of gender relationships.

Some scholars, notably anthropologists, have restricted the use of gender to the kinship system (focusing on household and family as the basis for social organization). We need a broader view that includes not only kinship but also (especially for complex modern societies) the labor market (a sex-segregated labor market is a part of the process of gender construction), education (all-male, single-sex, or coeducational institutions are part of the same process), and the polity (universal male suffrage is part of the process of gender construction). It makes little sense to force these institutions back to functional utility in the kinship system, or to argue that contemporary relationships between men and women are artifacts of older kinship systems based on the exchange of women. Gender is constructed through kinship, but not exclusively; it is constructed as well in the economy and the polity, which, in our society at least, now operate largely independently of kinship.

The fourth aspect of gender is subjective identity. I agree with anthropologist Gayle Rubin's formulation that psychoanalysis offers an important theory about the reproduction of gender, a description of the 'transformation of the biological sexuality of individuals as they are enculturated'.[10] But the universal claim of psychoanalysis gives me pause. Even though Lacanian theory may be helpful for thinking about the construction of gendered identity, historians need to work in a more historical way. If gender identity is based only and universally on fear of castration, the point of historical inquiry is denied. Moreover, real men and women do not always or literally fulfill the terms either of their society's prescriptions or of our analytic categories. Historians need instead to examine the ways in which gendered identities are substantively constructed and relate their findings to a range of activities, social organizations, and historically specific cultural representations.

The first part of my definition of gender consists, then, of all four of these elements, and no one of them operates without the others. Yet they do not operate simultaneously, with one simply reflecting the others. A question for historical research is, in fact, what the relationships among the four aspects are. The sketch I have offered of the process of constructing gender relationships could be used to discuss class, race, ethnicity, or, for that matter, any social process. My point was to clarify and specify how one needs to think about the effect of gender in social and institutional relationships, because this thinking is often not done precisely or systematically. The theorizing of gender, however, is developed in my second proposition: gender is a primary way of signifying relationships of power. It might be better to say, gender is a primary field within which or by means of which power is articulated. Gender is not the only field, but it seems to have been a persistent and recurrent way of enabling the signification of power in the West, in the Judeo-Christian as well as the Islamic tradition. As such, this part of the definition might seem to belong in the normative section of the argument, yet it does not, for concepts of power, though they may build on gender, are not always literally about gender itself. French sociologist Pierre Bourdieu has written about how the 'di-vision du monde', based on references to 'biological differences and notably those that refer to the division of the labor of procreation and reproduction', operates as 'the best founded of collective illusions'. Established as an objective set of references, concepts of gender structure perception and the concrete and symbolic organization of all social life.[11] To the extent that these references establish distributions of power (differential control over or access to material and symbolic resources), gender becomes implicated in the conception and construction of power itself. The French anthropologist Maurice Godelier has put it this way: 'It is not sexuality which haunts society, but society which haunts the body's sexuality. Sex-related differences between bodies are continually summoned as testimony to social relations and phenomena that have nothing to do with sexuality. Not only as testimony to, but also testimony for – in other words, as legitimation.'[12]

The legitimizing function of gender works in many ways. Bourdieu, for example, showed how, in certain cultures, agricultural exploitation was organized according to concepts of time and season that rested on specific definitions of the opposition between masculine and feminine. Gayatri Spivak has done a pointed analysis of the uses of gender and colonialism in certain texts of British and American women writers.[13] Natalie Davis has shown how concepts of masculine and feminine related to understandings and criticisms of the rules of social order in early modern France.[14] Historian Caroline Bynum has thrown new light on medieval spirituality through her attention to the relationships between concepts of masculine and feminine and religious behavior. Her work gives us important insight into the ways in which these concepts informed the politics of monastic institutions as well as of individual believers.[15] Art historians have opened a new territory by reading social implications from literal depictions of women and men. These interpretations are based on the idea that conceptual languages employ differentiation to establish meaning and that sexual difference is a primary way of signifying differentiation. Gender, then, provides a way to decode meaning and to understand the complex connections among various forms of human interaction. When historians look for the ways in which the concept of gender legitimizes and constructs social relationships, they develop insight into the reciprocal nature of gender and society and into the particular and contextually specific ways in which politics constructs gender and gender constructs politics.

Notes

1 *Oxford English Dictionary*, 1961, p. 4.
2 E. Littre, *Dictionnaire de la langue française*, Paris, 1876.
3 Raymond Williams, *Keywords*, Oxford University Press, 1983, p. 285.
4 Natalie Zemon Davis, 'Women's history in transition: the European case', *Feminist Studies* 3 (1975–6), p. 90.
5 Ann D. Gordon, Mari Jo Buhle and Nancy Shrom Dye, 'The problem of women's history', in Berenice Carroll (ed.), *Liberating Women's History*, Illinois University Press, 1976, p. 89.
6 The best example is Joan Kelly, 'The doubled vision of feminist theory', in her *Women, History and Theory*, Chicago University Press, 1984, pp. 51–64.
7 Clifford Geertz, 'Blurred genres', *American Scholar* 49 (1980), pp. 165–79.
8 Michelle Zimbalist Rosaldo, 'The uses and abuses of anthropology: reflections on feminism and cross-cultural understanding', *Signs* 5 (1980), p. 400.
9 Michel Foucault, *The History of Sexuality*, vol. 1, Vintage, 1980; idem, *Power/Knowledge: Selected Interviews and Other Writings. 1972–1977*, Pantheon, 1980.
10 Gayle Rubin, 'The traffic in women: notes on the political economy of sex', in Rayna R. Reiter (ed.), *Towards an Anthropology of Women*, Monthly Review Press, 1975.
11 Pierre Bourdieu, *Le sens pratique*, Paris, 1980.

12 Maurice Godelier, 'The origins of male domination', *New Left Review* 127 (1981), p. 17.

13 Gayatri Chakravorty Spivak, 'Three women's texts and a critique of imperialism', *Critical Inquiry* 12 (1985), pp. 243–6.

14 Natalie Zemon Davis, 'Women on top', in her *Society and Culture in Early Modern France*, Stanford University Press, 1975, pp. 124–51.

15 Caroline Walker Bynum, *Jesus as Mother: Studies in the Spirituality of the High Middle Ages*, University of California Press, 1982.

18. Gisela Bok

*[from 'Women's history and gender history: aspects of
an international debate',* Gender & History 1 (1989),
pp. 10–11, 15–18]

Gender as a Social, Cultural, Historical Category

In studying women's past, one important point of departure has been the
observation that women are half of humankind and in some countries and
times, even more than half; indeed, an important and influential contribution
bears the title *The Majority Finds Its Past.*[1] In conceptual terms, this observation implies the following principle: it is no less problematic to separate the
history of women from history in general than to separate the history of men –
and even more so, truly general history – from the history of women. Women's
history concerns not merely half of humankind, but all of it.

The most important step in efforts to link the history of one half to the other
half, and both to history in general, has been to conceptualize women as a
sociocultural group, i.e. as a sex. As a result, men also become visible as sexual
beings, so that the new perspective turns out to be not just about women and
women's issues but about all historical issues. Since the mid-1970s, gender
(*Geschlecht, genere, genre, geslacht*) has been introduced as a fundamental
category of social, cultural and historical reality, perception and study, even
though the new terminology, which in some languages indicates a shift from a
grammatical concept to a broader sociocultural one, has different linguistic
and cultural connotations in different tongues. One of the major reasons
for the introduction of the term 'gender' in this broader sense as well as for its
relatively rapid diffusion in place of the word 'sex' (at least in English), has
been the insistence that the 'woman question', women's history and women's
studies, cannot be reduced solely to sex in the sense of sexuality, but must
embrace all areas of society including the structures of that society. Hence the

concept gender implies that history in general must also be seen as the history of the sexes: as gender history (*Geschlechtergeschichte, storia di genere* or *storia sessuata, histoire sexuée*).

To the same extent that the need to study gender has for many people become self-evident, gender or the sexes are no longer perceived as something self-evident: neither as an obvious matter nor as an *a priori* given. It is now clear that the concepts, the underlying assumptions and the consequences of historical research in gender terms, must be created, conceived and investigated anew, since they have not been part of the historiographic vocabulary. Thus, for instance, in the important multi-volume *Geschichtliche Grundbegriffe* (Fundamental Historical Concepts), the entry *Geschlecht* does not appear alongside such other terms as 'work', 'race' or 'revolution', nor does 'woman', let alone 'man'. Despite centuries of philosophical speculation about the sexes, *Geschlecht* likewise fails to appear in the *Historisches Wörterbuch der Philosophie* (Historical Dictionary of Philosophy), and under the entry *Geschlechtlichkeit* (sexuality) we find cell plasma, genes, and hormones.[2]

But gender history rejects both these approaches: the omission of gender and its reduction to an object of apparently natural science. We have learned to see that, on the one hand, all known societies have gender-based spaces, behaviours, activities and that gender-based differentiation exists everywhere. On the other hand, the concrete manifestations of gender difference are not the same in all societies; they are not universal, and the variations within the status of the female sex are just as manifold as those within the status of the male sex. Secondly, we have learned to separate the question of gender-based difference from the question of gender-based hierarchies, i.e. the power relations between men and women. The differentiation and the hierarchies are not always necessarily connected with one another nor are they identical: for instance, a sexual division of labour does not necessarily imply a sexual division of social rewards and of power. Thirdly, it has become clear that the perception of male and female scholars, most of whom are West Europeans or North Americans, is often profoundly shaped by the gender relations of their own culture, by widespread ethno- or Euro-centrism, and by differing assumptions about the status and the emancipation of women. The current perceptions of the sexes and the terms used to describe them are to a large extent a product of the history of culture, science and of gender relations themselves, particularly since the eighteenth century. Therefore, the sexes and their relations must be perceived as social, political and cultural entities. They cannot be reduced to factors outside of history, and still less to a single and simple, uniform, primal or inherent cause or origin.

When we speak of gender as a 'category' in this context, the term refers to an intellectual construct, a way of perceiving and studying people, an analytic tool that helps us to discover neglected areas of history. It is a conceptual form of sociocultural inquiry that challenges the sex-blindness of traditional historiography. It is important to stress that the category gender is, and must be perceived as, context-specific and context-dependent. While it does offer fundamental possibilities for a more profound understanding of virtually all historical phenomena, it should not be used as a static pattern, a myth of origins for explaining the panorama of historical events. Its power is not one of elimination – by reducing history to a model – but of illumination, as a means to explore historical variety and variability. Gender is a 'category', not in the sense of a universal statement but, as the Greek origin of the word suggests, in the sense of public objection and indictment, of debate, protest, process and trial.

Gender as Social, Cultural, Historical Relations

Gender or the sexes refer neither to an object, nor to various objects; rather, they refer to a complex set of relations and processes. 'Thinking in relations'[3] is needed in order to understand gender as an analytical category as well as a cultural reality, in the past as well as in the present. Such a vision of gender has implications for all forms of history as they are now practiced:

Women's History as Gender History

Perceiving gender as a complex and sociocultural relation implies that the search for women in history is not simply a search for some object which has previously been neglected. Instead, it is a question of previously neglected relations between human beings and human groups. In the words of the late anthropologist Michelle Zimbalist Rosaldo, 'Women must be understood . . . in terms of relationship – with other women and with men – (not) of difference and apartness'.[4] Rosaldo pointed to an important and often ignored dimension which goes beyond the now obvious insistence that women's history be integrated into general history through the study of relations between women and men. Not only must we study the relations *between* the sexes, but also the relations *within* the sexes, not only those of women to men, and of men to women, but also relations among women and among men.

Many relations among men have been the focus of historical writing, those emerging in the political, military, economic and cultural realms, and those between kin and friends, but rarely have they been studied as intra-gender relations or as to their impact on women. On the other hand, it is also vital to look at women's relationships with each other: between housewives and female servants, between mothers and daughters, between mothers, wet-nurses and midwives, between social workers and poor women, between female missionaries and the women of colonized peoples, among women in the professions and in politics, and to be aware of relations of conflict as well as solidarity. The history of female kin, friendship and love between women has become an important area of research. Such studies have usually focused strongly on intra-gender relations as well as on their significance to men.

Insisting on the importance of studying the relations within the sexes and particularly between women becomes all the more crucial in the 1980s as the concept of *gender*, *Geschlecht*, *genere*, *genre* threatens to become high fashion, which seeks to soften the challenge of women's history by developing a kind of gender-neutral discourse on gender. But if it is forgotten that the discovery of the social, cultural and historical relations between and within the sexes was the result of women studying women and men, we have fallen far short of our goal: not a gender-neutral but a gender-encompassing approach to general history. Women's history is gender history *par excellence*.

The fact that it is still not evident for scholars to view gender history, par-ticularly in respect to women, also as a history within the sexes was recently shown by the eminent British historian Lawrence Stone. Expert on, among other areas, *Family, Sex and Marriage*, he has studied a field where gender relations are of conspicuous importance and where women are half of the group to be examined. In his article, 'Only Women', he set himself up as a historians' god and handed down 'Ten Commandments' for the writing of women's history which – surprising for a historian – were to apply: 'at any time and in any place'. The first of them: 'Thou shalt not write about women except in relation to men and children'. Whereas the author correctly recognized that the new approaches deal essentially with relations and their history, he failed to see that women are not conditioned solely by their relations to men, that the relations of women to other women are just as important as those of women to men, that children are not genderless beings, and that the history of men should also include their relations to women.[5]

Gender History as Men's History

Examining men's relations to women means viewing what previously counted as an object of 'history in general' in gender-conscious and thus 'male-specific' terms: the history of men as men. Questions about gender have mainly focused on the female sex, on 'the woman question'. Men appear to exist beyond gender relations to the same degree that they dominate them. While the imperative that women's history always be related to men's has become commonplace, up to now the reverse has hardly been true.

Military history and the history of warfare are a case in point. They have dealt exclusively with men – and for good reason, since warfare in the Western world (at least within Europe) has generally been a form of direct confrontation between groups of men. Nonetheless, explicitly male-specific issues have not been raised in this field, for example its connection with the history of masculinity. Furthermore, wars have had an enormous significance for women and for the relations between and within the sexes. We need only think of the strongly gender-based and sexual war symbols and language in wars of liberation as well as in civil wars, in aggressive as well as in defensive wars, of women camp followers in the early modern armies, of the women's peace movement before, during and after the First World War or of the new forms of prostitution which appear in the First and Second World Wars.

The past few years have seen a rise of 'men's studies', mainly carried out by men, which deal with the relations between men and women, and among men. Some authors have examined the relation between war and the social construction of masculinity, and they have underlined that the latter should not be understood as a 'biological given'. What women's studies have shown is now being confirmed by men's studies: gender norms and gender realities are not identical and they are subject to historical change. According to a French historian, masculinity meant not only power but also grief and suffering for nineteenth century men. Fatherhood has also become a focus of interest for historians. Some of these studies – those being done by men – draw inspiration from a current call for male participation in female experiences and work ('Pregnant Fathers: How Fathers can Enjoy and Share the Experiences of Pregnancy and Childbirth') or for 'men's rights', a tendency not merely corresponding to feminist demands for women's rights, but – as might be expected – also at odds with them. Although these men's studies have illuminated some topics, much remains to be done, particularly in the field of history.

An issue which is still often considered as 'women's history', namely the ways in which famous – that is, male – philosophers and other thinkers have thought about women, the sexes, sexuality and the family, must in fact be viewed as men's history. It is men's, not women's history for reasons which have been discussed in various contexts, i.e. the fact that these writings present primarily men's views on women, that their image of the sexes is rarely descriptive but normative and proscriptive, and that the norms for women are usually not only different from the norms for men, but also from the realities of women's lives. The study of men's thinking on gender has come to be very diversified and it has brought to light many and unexpected complexities and contradictions, between different philosophers as well as within individual men's thought.

Such studies have also promoted the awareness of a specifically historical question of method: the problematic character of a historiography which limits itself to the presentation and repetition of the misogynous pronouncements which were said and written by men over the centuries. This often leads from outrage and denunciation to a kind of fascination. It risks becoming anachronistic as it neglects the analysis of such texts against the background of their historical context and significance, of their role within the complete works of an author and how they were judged by their female contemporaries.

Studies in intellectual history which turn to the fewer and often less known female philosophers or to the thought and judgements of other women regarding gender as well as other relations, often uncover important differences from male thinking. Here one might consider Hannah Arendt's central concept of political thought, 'natality' – the principle and capacity of human beings to act in new ways, beyond whatever happened in history, by virtue of their being born – and her notion of human plurality which she saw symbolized in the plurality of the sexes, or in the case of Carol Gilligan's insights into women's 'different voice' in moral judgements.[6] Thus, intellectual history also demonstrates that the history of men as men becomes visible only when seen in relation to women's history and women's thought and hence in a perspective of gender history.

Notes

1 Gerda Lerner, *The Majority Finds its Past: Placing Women in History*, Oxford University Press, 1979.
2 Otto Brunner, Werner Conze and Reinhardt Koselleck (eds), *Geschichtliche Grundbegriffe*, Klett Verlag, 5 vols, 1972–84; Joachim Ritter (ed.), *Historisches Wörterbuch der Philosophie*, Wissenschaftliche Buchgesellschaft, 1974, p. 443.
3 Jane Flax, 'Gender as a Problem: In and for feminist theory', *American Studies* 31 (1986), p. 199; Joan W. Scott, 'Gender: a useful category of historical analysis' (see previous excerpt, ED).
4 Michelle Z. Rosaldo, 'The use and abuse of anthropology', *Signs* 5 (1980), p. 409.
5 Lawrence Stone, 'Only women', *New York Review of Books*, 11 April 1986, p. 21.
6 Carol Gilligan, *In A Different Voice*, Harvard University Press, 1982.

Postcolonialism

Postcolonialism refers to the intellectual position which regards the relationship between the former coloniser and the colonised as funda-mental to the world today and long overdue for critical scrutiny. In particular it seeks to show how Western knowledge and culture have consistently misrepresented the peoples of the Third World in order to disempower them and lock them into continuing dependence on the West.

In Postcolonial writing a key term is the *subaltern*. It denotes the majority of people in colonised societies who were excluded from power and from the culture of the westernized elite. The historian Ranajit Guha took the lead in setting up the Indian journal, *Subaltern Studies*, in 1981. The aim was to take back the representation of the Indian past from Western scholars – and Indian scholars trained in their likeness. In this piece Guha attacks the tradition of writing the history of Indian nationalism with sole reference to the indigenous elite and the British administration: 'the people *on their own*' made a vital contribution.

Dipesh Chakrabarty takes the metaphor of subalternity a stage further. In countries like India, history-writing itself is in a cadet position: historians are expected to be familiar with European history, while their Western counterparts work in complete ignorance of Asian or African history. Indian history is pressed into a mould already formed by the master-narrative of Western history. Chakrabarty calls for the balance to be restored by the 'provincialising' of Western history – the theme of his later book, *Provincialising Europe: Postcolonial Thought and Historical Difference* (2000).

In fact the historical implications of postcolonialism are as unsettling for the metropolis as they are for the periphery. Catherine Hall here outlines an ambitious programme, much of which she has since fulfilled in her *Civilising Subjects* (2002). If Britain is a postcolonial country, then full weight must be given to the many ways in which the empire penetrated the country's social and cultural experience over a period of 500 years. The historical presence of black people in Britain is only one aspect, though it has important implications for today's cultural politics. Hall's analysis rests on the thoroughly postcolonial proposition that neither metropole nor periphery can be understood apart from the other.

19. Ranajit Guha

['On Some Aspects of the Historiography of Colonial India',
Subaltern Studies *I, Oxford University Press (New Delhi), 1981,*
pp. 1–8]

The historiography of Indian nationalism has for a long time been dominated by elitism – colonialist elitism and bourgeois-nationalist elitism.
Both originated as the ideological product of British rule in India, but have
survived the transfer of power and been assimilated to neo-colonialist and
neo-nationalist forms of discourse in Britain and India respectively. Elitist
historiography of the colonialist or neo-colonialist type counts British writers
and institutions among its principal protagonists, but has its imitators in
India and other countries too. Elitist historiography of the nationalist or neo-
nationalist type is primarily an Indian practice but not without imitators in the
ranks of liberal historians in Britain and elsewhere.

Both these varieties of elitism share the prejudice that the making of the
Indian nation and the development of the consciousness – nationalism
– which informed this process were exclusively or predominantly elite
achievements. In the colonialist and neo-colonialist historiographies these
achievements are credited to British colonial rulers, administrators, policies,
institutions and culture; in the nationalist and neo-nationalist writings – to
Indian elite personalities, institutions, activities and ideas.

The first of these two historiographies defines Indian nationalism primarily as a function of stimulus and response. Based on a narrowly behaviouristic
approach this represents nationalism as the sum of the activities and ideas by
which the Indian elite responded to the institutions, opportunities, resources,
etc. generated by colonialism. There are several versions of this historiography, but the central modality common to them is to describe Indian nationalism as a sort of 'learning process' through which the native elite became
involved in politics by trying to negotiate the maze of institutions and the

corresponding cultural complex introduced by the colonial authorities in order to govern the country. What made the elite go through this process was, according to this historiography, no lofty idealism addressed to the general good of the nation but simply the expectation of rewards in the form of a share in the wealth, power and prestige created by and associated with colonial rule; and it was the drive for such rewards with all its concomitant play of collaboration and competition between the ruling power and the native elite as well as between various elements among the latter themselves, which, we are told, was what constituted Indian nationalism.

The general orientation of the other kind of elitist historiography is to represent Indian nationalism as primarily an idealist venture in which the indigenous elite led the people from subjugation to freedom. There are several versions of this historiography which differ from each other in the degree of their emphasis on the role of individual leaders or elite organizations and institutions as the main or motivating force in this venture. However, the modality common to them all is to uphold Indian nationalism as a phenomenal expression of the goodness of the native elite with the antagonistic aspect of their relation to the colonial regime made, against all evidence, to look larger than its collaborationist aspect, their role as promoters of the cause of the people than that as exploiters and oppressors, their altruism and self-abnegation than their scramble for the modicum of power and privilege granted by the rulers in order to make sure of their support for the Raj. The history of Indian nationalism is thus written up as a sort of spiritual biography of the Indian elite.

Elitist historiography is of course not without its uses. It helps us to know more about the structure of the colonial state, the operation of its various organs in certain historical circumstances, the nature of the alignment of classes which sustained it; some aspects of the ideology of the elite as the dominant ideology of the period; about the contradictions between the two elites and the complexities of their mutual oppositions and coalitions; about the role of some of the more important British and Indian personalities and elite organizations. Above all it helps us to understand the ideological character of historiography itself.

What, however, historical writing of this kind cannot do is to explain Indian nationalism for us. For it fails to acknowledge, far less interpret, the contribution made by the people *on their own*, that is, *independently of the elite* to the making and development of this nationalism. In this particular respect the poverty of this historiography is demonstrated beyond doubt by its failure to understand and assess the mass articulation of this nationalism except, negatively, as a law and order problem, and positively, if at all, either as a response to the charisma of certain elite leaders or in the currently more fashionable terms of vertical mobilization by the manipulation of factions. The involvement of the Indian people in vast numbers, sometimes in hundreds of thousands or even millions, in nationalist activities and ideas is thus represented as a diversion from a supposedly 'real' political process, that is, the grinding away of the wheels of the state apparatus and of elite institutions geared to it, or it is simply credited, as an act of ideological appropriation, to the influence and initiative of the elite themselves. The bankruptcy of this historiography is clearly exposed when it is called upon to explain such phenomena as the anti-Rowlatt upsurge of 1919 and the Quit India movement of 1942 – to name only two of numerous instances of popular initiative asserting itself in the course of nationalist campaigns in defiance or absence of elite control. How can such one-sided and blinkered historiography help us to understand the profound displacements, well below the surface of elite politics, which made Chauri-Chaura or the militant demonstrations of solidarity with the RIN mutineers possible?

This inadequacy of elitist historiography follows directly from the narrow and partial view of politics to which it is committed by virtue of its class outlook. In all writings of this kind the parameters of Indian politics are assumed to be or enunciated as exclusively or primarily those of the institutions introduced by the British for the government of the country and the corresponding sets of laws, policies, attitudes and other elements of the superstructure. Inevitably, therefore, a historiography hamstrung by such a definition can do no more than to equate politics with the aggregation of activities and ideas of those who were directly involved in operating these institutions, that is, the colonial rulers and their *élèves* – the dominant groups in native society – to the extent that their mutual transactions were thought to be all there was to Indian nationalism, the domain of the latter is regarded as coincident with that of politics.

What clearly is left out of this un-historical historiography is the *politics of the people*. For parallel to the domain of elite politics there existed throughout the colonial period another domain of Indian politics in which the principal actors were not the dominant groups of the indigenous society or the colonial authorities but the subaltern classes and groups constituting the mass of the labouring population and the intermediate strata in town and country – that is, the people. This was an *autonomous* domain, for it neither originated from elite politics nor did its existence depend on the latter. It was traditional only in so far as its roots could be traced back to pre-colonial times, but it was by no means archaic in the sense of being outmoded. Far from being destroyed or rendered virtually ineffective, as was elite politics of the traditional type by the intrusion of colonialism, it continued to operate vigorously in spite of the latter, adjusting itself to the conditions prevailing under the Raj and in many respects developing entirely new strains in both form and content. As modern as indigenous elite politics, it was distinguished by its relatively greater depth in time as well as in structure.

One of the more important features of this politics related precisely to those aspects of mobilization which are so little explained by elitist historiography. Mobilization in the domain of elite politics was achieved vertically whereas in that of subaltern politics this was achieved horizontally. The instrumentation of the former was characterized by a relatively greater reliance on the colonial adaptations of British parliamentary institutions and the residua of semi-feudal political institutions of the pre-colonial period; that of the latter relied rather more on the traditional organization of kinship and territoriality or on class associations depending on the level of the consciousness of the people involved. Elite mobilization tended to be relatively more legalistic and con-stitutionalist in orientation, subaltern mobilization relatively more violent. The former was, on the whole, more cautious and controlled, the latter more spontaneous. Popular mobilization in the colonial period was realized in its most comprehensive form in peasant uprisings. However, in many historic instances involving large masses of the working people and petty bourgeoisie in the urban areas too the figure of mobilization derived directly from the paradigm of peasant insurgency.

The ideology operative in this domain, taken as a whole, reflected the diversity of its social composition with the outlook of its leading elements dominating that of the others at any particular time and within any particular event. However, in spite of such diversity one of its invariant features was a notion of resistance to elite domination. This followed from the subalternity common to all the social constituents of this domain and as such distinguished it sharply from that of elite politics. This ideological element was of course not uniform in quality or density in all instances. In the best of cases it enhanced the concreteness, focus and tension of subaltern political action. However, there were occasions when its emphasis on sectional interests disequilibrated popular movements in such a way as to create economistic diversions and sectarian splits, and generally to undermine horizontal alliances.

Yet another set of the distinctive features of this politics derived from the conditions of exploitation to which the subaltern classes were subjected in varying degrees as well as from its relation to the productive labour of the majority of its protagonists, that is, workers and peasants, and to the manual and intellectual labour respectively of the non-industrial urban poor and the lower sections of the petty bourgeoisie. The experience of exploitation and labour endowed this politics with many idioms, norms and values which put it in a category apart from elite politics.

These and other distinctive features (the list is by no means exhaustive) of the politics of the people did not of course appear always in the pure state described in the last three paragraphs. The impact of living contradictions modified them in the course of their actualization in history. However, with all such modifications they still helped to demarcate the domain of subaltern politics from that of elite politics. The co-existence of these two domains or streams, which can be sensed by intuition and proved by demonstration as well, was the index of an important historical truth, that is, the *failure of the Indian bourgeoisie to speak for the nation*. There were vast areas in the life and consciousness of the people which were never integrated into their hegemony. The *structural dichotomy* that arose from this is a datum of Indian history of the colonial period, which no one who sets out to interpret it can ignore without falling into error.

Such dichotomy did not, however, mean that these two domains were hermetically sealed off from each other and there was no contact between them. On the contrary, there was a great deal of overlap arising precisely from the effort made from time to time by the more advanced elements among the indigenous elite, especially the bourgeoisie, to integrate them. Such effort when linked to struggles which had more or less clearly defined anti-imperialist objectives and were consistently waged, produced some splendid results. Linked, on other occasions, to movements which either had no firm anti-imperialist objectives at all or had lost them in the course of their development and deviated into legalist, constitutionalist or some other kind of compromise with the colonial government, they produced some spectacular retreats and nasty reversions in the form of sectarian strife. In either case the braiding together of the two strands of elite and subaltern politics led invariably to explosive situations indicating that the masses mobilized by the elite to fight for their own objectives managed to break away from their control and put the characteristic imprint of popular politics on campaigns initiated by the upper classes.

However, the initiatives which originated from the domain of subaltern politics were not, on their part, powerful enough to develop the nationalist movement into a full-fledged struggle for national liberation. The working class was still not sufficiently mature in the objective conditions of its social being and in its consciousness as a class-for-itself, nor was it firmly allied yet with the peasantry. As a result it could do nothing to take over and complete the mission which the bourgeoisie had failed to realize. The outcome of it all was that the numerous peasant uprisings of the period, some of them massive in scope and rich in anti-colonialist consciousness, waited in vain for a leadership to raise them above localism and generalize them into a nationwide anti-imperialist campaign. In the event, much of the sectional struggle of workers, peasants and the urban petty bourgeoisie either got entangled in economism or, wherever politicized, remained, for want of a revolutionary leadership, far too fragmented to form effectively into anything like a national liberation movement.

It is the study of this *historic failure of the nation to come to its own*, a failure due to the inadequacy of the bourgeoisie as well as of the working class to lead it into a decisive victory over colonialism and a bourgeois-democratic revolution of either the classic nineteenth-century type under the hegemony of the bourgeoisie or a more modern type under the hegemony of workers and peasants, that is, a 'new democracy' – *it is the study of this failure which constitutes the central problematic of the historiography of colonial India*. There is no one given way of investigating this problematic. Let a hundred flowers blossom and we don't mind even the weeds. Indeed we believe that in the practice of historiography even the elitists have a part to play if only by way of teaching by negative examples. But we are also convinced that elitist historiography should be resolutely fought by developing an alternative discourse based on the rejection of the spurious and un-historical monism characteristic of its view of Indian nationalism and on the recognition of the co-existence and interaction of the elite and subaltern domains of politics.

We are sure that we are not alone in our concern about the present state of the political historiography of colonial India and in seeking a way out. The elitism of modern Indian historiography is an oppressive fact resented by many others, students, teachers and writers like ourselves. They may not all subscribe to what has been said above on this subject in exactly the way in which we have said it. However, we have no doubt that many other historiographical points of view and practices are likely to converge close to where we stand. Our purpose in making our own views known is to promote such a convergence. We claim no more than to try and indicate an orientation and hope to demonstrate in practice that this is feasible. In any discussion which may ensue we expect to learn a great deal not only from the agreement of those who think like us but also from the criticism of those who don't.

A note on the terms 'elite', 'people', 'subaltern', etc. as used above

The term 'elite' has been used in this statement to signify *dominant* groups, foreign as well as indigenous. The *dominant foreign* groups included all the non-Indian, that is, mainly British officials of the colonial state and foreign industrialists, merchants, financiers, planters, landlords and missionaries.

The *dominant indigenous* groups included classes and interests operating at two levels. At the *all-India level* they included the biggest feudal magnates, the most important representatives of the industrial and mercantile bourgeoisie and native recruits to the uppermost levels of the bureaucracy.

At the *regional and local levels* they represented such classes and other elements as were *either* members of the dominant all-India groups included in the previous category *or* if belonging to social strata hierarchically inferior to those of the dominant all-India groups still *acted in the interests of the latter and not in conformity to interests corresponding truly to their own social being.*

Taken as a whole and in the abstract this last category of the elite was *heterogeneous* in its composition and thanks to the uneven character of regional economic and social developments, *differed from area to area.* The same class or element which was dominant in one area according to the definition given above, could be among the dominated in another. This could and did create many ambiguities and contradictions in attitudes and alliances, especially among the lowest strata of the rural gentry, impoverished landlords, rich peasants and upper-middle peasants all of whom belonged, *ideally speaking,* to the category of 'people' or 'subaltern classes', as defined below. It is the task of research to investigate, identify and measure the *specific* nature and degree of the *deviation* of these elements from the ideal and situate it historically.

The terms 'people' and 'subaltern classes' have been used as synonymous throughout this note. The social groups and elements included in this category represent *the demographic difference between the total Indian population and all those whom we have described as the 'elite'.* Some of these classes and groups such as the lesser rural gentry, impoverished landlords, rich peasants and upper-middle peasants who 'naturally' ranked among the 'people' and the 'subaltern', could under certain circumstances act for the 'elite', as explained above, and therefore be classified as such in some local or regional situations – an ambiguity which it is up to the historian to sort out on the basis of a close and judicious reading of his evidence.

20. Dipesh Chakrabarty

[from 'Postcoloniality and the Artifice of History: Who Speaks for "Indian" Pasts?', Representations 37 (1992), pp. 1–3, 19–21, 22–3]

It has recently been said in praise of the postcolonial project of *Subaltern Studies* that it demonstrates, "perhaps for the first time since colonization," that "Indians are showing sustained signs of reappropriating the capacity to represent themselves [within the discipline of history]."[1] As a historian who is a member of the *Subaltern Studies* collective, I find the congratulation contained in this remark gratifying but premature. The purpose of this article is to problematize the idea of "Indians" "representing themselves in history." Let us put aside for the moment the messy problems of identity inherent in a transnational enterprise such as *Subaltern Studies*, where passports and commitments blur the distinctions of ethnicity in a manner that some would regard as characteristically postmodern. I have a more perverse proposition to argue. It is that insofar as the academic discourse of history—that is, "history" as a discourse produced at the institutional site of the university—is concerned, "Europe" remains the sovereign, theoretical subject of all histories, including the ones we call "Indian," "Chinese," "Kenyan," and so on. There is a peculiar way in which all these other histories tend to become variations on a master narrative that could be called "the history of Europe." In this sense, "Indian" history itself is in a position of subalternity; one can only articulate subaltern subject positions in the name of this history.

While the rest of this article will elaborate on this proposition, let me enter a few qualifications. "Europe" and "India" are treated here as hyperreal terms in that they refer to certain figures of imagination whose geographical referents remain somewhat indeterminate.[2] As figures of the imaginary they are, of course, subject to contestation, but for the moment I shall treat them as though they were given, reified categories, opposites paired in a structure of domination and subordination. I realize that in treating them thus I leave myself open to the charge of nativism, nationalism, or worse, the sin of sins, nostalgia. Liberal-minded scholars would immediately protest that any idea of a homogeneous, uncontested "Europe" dissolves under analysis. True, but just as the phenomenon of orientalism does not disappear simply because some of us have now attained a critical awareness of it, similarly a certain version of "Europe," reified and celebrated in the phenomenal world of everyday relationships of power as the scene of the birth of the modern, continues to dominate the discourse of history. Analysis does not make it go away.

That Europe works as a silent referent in historical knowledge itself becomes obvious in a highly ordinary way. There are at least two everyday symptoms of the subalternity of non-Western, third-world histories. Third-world historians feel a need to refer to works in European history; historians of Europe do not feel any need to reciprocate. Whether it is an Edward Thompson, a Le Roy Ladurie, a Georges Duby, a Carlo Ginzberg, a Lawrence Stone, a Robert Darnton, or a Natalie Davis—to take but a few names at random from our contemporary world—the "greats" and the models of the historian's enterprise are always at least culturally "European." "They" produce their work in relative ignorance of non-Western histories, and this does not seem to affect the quality of their work. This is a gesture, however, that "we" cannot return. We cannot even afford an equality or symmetry of ignorance at this level without taking the risk of appearing "old-fashioned" or "outdated."

The problem, I may add in parenthesis, is not particular to historians. An unselfconscious but nevertheless blatant example of this "inequality of ignorance" in literary studies, for example, is the following sentence on Salman Rushdie from a recent text on postmodernism: "Though Saleem Sinai [of *Midnight's Children*] narrates in English . . . his intertexts for both writing history and writing fiction are doubled: they are, on the one hand, from Indian legends, films, and literature and, on the other, from the West—*The Tin Drum, Tristram Shandy, One Hundred Years of Solitude*, and so on."[3] It is interesting to note how this sentence teases out only those references that are from "the West." The author is under no obligation here to be able to name with any authority and specificity the "Indian" allusions that make Rushdie's intertexuality "doubled." This ignorance, shared and unstated, is part of the assumed compact that makes it "easy" to include Rushdie in English department offerings on postcolonialism.

This problem of asymmetric ignorance is not simply a matter of "cultural cringe" (to let my Australian self speak) on our part or of cultural arrogance on the part of the European historian. These problems exist but can be relatively easily addressed. Nor do I mean to take anything away from the achievements of the historians I mentioned. Our footnotes bear rich testimony to the insights we have derived from their knowledge and creativity. The dominance of "Europe" as the subject of all histories is a part of a much more profound theoretical condition under which historical knowledge is produced in the third world. This condition ordinarily expresses itself in a paradoxical manner. It is this paradox that I shall describe as the second everyday symptom of our subalternity, and it refers to the very nature of social science pronouncements themselves.

For generations now, philosophers and thinkers shaping the nature of social science have produced theories embracing the entirety of humanity. As we well know, these statements have been produced in relative, and sometimes absolute, ignorance of the majority of humankind—i.e., those living in non-Western cultures. This in itself is not paradoxical, for the more self-conscious of European philosophers have always sought theoretically to justify this stance. The everyday paradox of third-world social science is that *we* find these theories, in spite of their inherent ignorance of "us," eminently useful in understanding our societies. What allowed the modern European sages to develop such clairvoyance with regard to societies of which they were empirically ignorant? Why cannot we, once again, return the gaze?

....

So long as one operates within the discourse of "history" produced at the institutional site of the university, it is not possible simply to walk out of the deep collusion between "history" and the modernizing narrative(s) of citizenship, bourgeois public and private, and the nation state. "History" as a knowledge system is firmly embedded in institutional practices that invoke the nation state at every step—witness the organization and politics of teaching, recruitment, promotions, and publication in history departments, politics that survive the occasional brave and heroic attempts by individual historians to liberate "history" from the meta-narrative of the nation state. One only has to ask, for instance: Why is history a compulsory part of education of the modern person in all countries today including those that did quite comfortably without it until as late as the eighteenth century? Why should children all over the world today have to come to terms with a subject called "history" when we know that this compulsion is neither natural nor ancient?[4] It does not take much imagination to see that the reason for this lies in what European imperialism and third-world nationalisms have achieved together: the universalization of the nation state as the most desirable form of political community. Nation states have the capacity to enforce their truth games, and universities, their critical distance notwithstanding, are part of the battery of institutions complicit in this process. "Economics" and "history" are the knowledge forms that correspond to the two major institutions that the rise (and later universalization) of the bourgeois order has given to the world—the capitalist mode of production and the nation state ("history" speaking to the figure of the citizen). A critical historian has no choice but to negotiate this knowledge. She or he therefore needs to understand the state on its own terms, i.e., in terms of its self-justificatory narratives of citizenship and modernity. Since these themes will always take us back to the universalist propositions of "modern" (European) political philosophy—even the "practical" science of economics that now seems "natural" to our constructions of world systems is (theoretically) rooted in the ideas of ethics in eighteenth-century Europe[5]—a third-world historian is condemned to knowing "Europe" as the original home of the "modern," whereas the "European" historian does not share a comparable predicament with regard to the pasts of the majority of humankind. Thus follows the everyday subalternity of non-Western histories with which I began this paper.

Yet the understanding that "we" all do "European" history with our different and often non-European archives opens up the possibility of a politics and project of alliance between the dominant metropolitan histories and the subaltern peripheral pasts. Let us call this the project of provincializing "Europe," the "Europe" that modern imperialism and (third-world) nationalism have, by their collaborative venture and violence, made universal. Philosophically, this project must ground itself in a radical critique and transcendence of liberalism (i.e., of the bureaucratic constructions of citizenship, modern state, and bourgeois privacy that classical political philosophy has produced), a ground that late Marx shares with certain moments in both poststructuralist thought and feminist philosophy. In particular, I am emboldened by Carole Pateman's courageous declaration—in her remarkable book *The Sexual Contract*—that the very conception of the modern individual belongs to patriarchal categories of thought.[6]

The project of provincializing "Europe" refers to a history that does not yet exist; I can therefore only speak of it in a programmatic manner. To forestall misunderstanding, however, I must spell out what it is *not* while outlining what it could be.

To begin with, it does not call for a simplistic, out-of-hand rejection of modernity, liberal values, universals, science, reason, grand narratives, totalizing explanations, and so on. Frederic Jameson has recently reminded us that the easy equation often made between "a philosophical conception of totality"

and "a political practice of totalitarianism" is "baleful."[7] What intervenes
between the two is history—contradictory, plural, and heterogeneous struggles whose outcomes are never predictable, even retrospectively, in accordance with schemas that seek to naturalize and domesticate this heterogeneity.
These struggles include coercion (both on behalf of and against modernity)
—physical, institutional, and symbolic violence, often dispensed with
dreamy-eyed idealism—and it is this violence that plays a decisive role in the
establishment of meaning, in the creation of truth regimes, in deciding, as
it were, whose and which "universal" wins. As intellectuals operating in
academia, we are not neutral to these struggles and cannot pretend to situate
ourselves outside of the knowledge procedures of our institutions.

The project of provincializing "Europe" therefore cannot be a project
of "cultural relativism." It cannot originate from the stance that the reason/
science/universals which help define Europe as the modern are simply
"culture-specific" and therefore only belong to the European cultures. For
the point is not that Enlightenment rationalism is always unreasonable in
itself but rather a matter of documenting how—through what historical
process—its "reason," which was not always self-evident to everyone, has
been made to look "obvious" far beyond the ground where it originated. If a
language, as has been said, is but a dialect backed up by an army, the same
could be said of the narratives of "modernity" that, almost universally today,
point to a certain "Europe" as the primary habitus of the modern.

This Europe, like "the West," is demonstrably an imaginary entity, but the
demonstration as such does not lessen its appeal or power. The project of
provincializing "Europe" has to include certain other additional moves: 1) the
recognition that Europe's acquisition of the adjective *modern* for itself is a
piece of global history of which an integral part is the story of European imperialism; and 2) the understanding that this equating of a certain version of
Europe with "modernity" is not the work of Europeans alone; third-world
nationalisms, as modernizing ideologies *par excellence*, have been equal partners in the process. I do not mean to overlook the anti-imperial moments in the
careers of these nationalisms; I only underscore the point that the project of
provincializing "Europe" cannot be a nationalist, nativist, or atavistic project.
In unraveling the necessary entanglement of history—a disciplined and institutionally regulated form of collective memory—with the grand narratives of
"rights," "citizenship," the nation state, "public" and "private" spheres, one
cannot but problematize "India" at the same time as one dismantles "Europe."

The idea is to write into the history of modernity the ambivalences, contradictions, the use of force, and the tragedies and the ironies that attend it. That

the rhetoric and the claims of (bourgeois) equality, of citizens' rights, of self-determination through a sovereign nation state have in many circumstances empowered marginal social groups in their struggles is undeniable—this recognition is indispensable to the project of *Subaltern Studies*. What effectively is played down, however, in histories that either implicitly or explicitly celebrate the advent of the modern state and the idea of citizenship is the repression and violence that are as instrumental in the victory of the modern as is the persuasive power of its rhetorical strategies.

....

And, finally—since "Europe" cannot after all be provincialized within the institutional site of the university whose knowledge protocols will always take us back to the terrain where all contours follow that of my hyperreal Europe—the project of provincializing Europe must realize within itself its own impossibility. It therefore looks to a history that embodies this politics of despair. It will have been clear by now that this is not a call for cultural relativism or for atavistic, nativist histories. Nor is this a program for a simple rejection of modernity, which would be, in many situations, politically suicidal. I ask for a history that deliberately makes visible, within the very structure of its narrative forms, its own repressive strategies and practices, the part it plays in collusion with the narratives of citizenships in assimilating to the projects of the modern state all other possibilities of human solidarity. The politics of despair will require of such history that it lays bare to its readers the reasons why such a predicament is necessarily inescapable. This is a history that will attempt the impossible: to look toward its own death by tracing that which resists and escapes the best human effort at translation across cultural and other semiotic systems, so that the world may once again be imagined as radically heterogeneous. This, as I have said, is impossible within the knowledge protocols of academic history, for the globality of academia is not independent of the globality that the European modern has created. To attempt to provincialize this "Europe" is to see the modern as inevitably contested, to write over the given and privileged narratives of citizenship other narratives of human connections that draw sustenance from dreamed-up pasts and futures where collectivities are defined neither by the rituals of citizenship nor by the nightmare of "tradition" that "modernity" creates. There are of course no (infra)structural sites where such dreams could lodge themselves. Yet they will recur so long as the themes of citizenship and the nation state dominate our narratives of historical transition, for these dreams are what the modern represses in order to be.

Notes

1 Ranajit Guha and Gayatri Chakravorty Spivak (eds), *Selected Subaltern Studies*, New Delhi, 1988; Ronald Inden, 'Orientalist constructions of India', *Modern Asian Studies* 20 (1986), p. 445.

2 For the term *hyperreal* see Jean Baudrillard, *Simulations*, New York, 1983.

3 Linda Hutcheon, *The Politics of Postmodernism*, Routledge, 1989, p. 65.

4 On the close connection between imperialist ideologies and the teaching of history in colonial India, see Ranajit Guha, *An Indian Historiography of India: A Nineteenth-Century Agenda and its Implications*, Calcutta, 1988.

5 See Amartya Kumar Sen, *Of Ethics and Economics*, Oxford University Press, 1987.

6 Carole Pateman, *The Sexual Contract*, Polity, 1989, p. 184.

7 Frederic Jameson, 'Cognitive mapping', in Cary Nelson and Lawrence Grossberg (eds), *Marxism and the Interpretation of Culture*, Urbana, 1988, p. 354.

21. Catherine Hall

[from 'Histories, empires and the post-colonial moment', in Iain Chambers and Lidia Curti (eds), The Post-Colonial Question: Common Skies, Divided Horizons, *Routledge, 1996, pp. 65–70, 76]*

In the late twentieth century questions about cultural identity seem to have become critical everywhere. 'Who are we?' 'Where do we come from?' 'Which "we" are we talking about when we talk about "we"?' Such questions are always there, intimately connected to but distinct from the insistent questions of origin that engage every child, but they have a new salience in the contemporary moment. The global changes of the last fifty years have involved the movements of peoples on an unprecedented scale, the break-up of empires and decolonisation, the creation of the New Europe and other new power blocs, the destruction of old nations and the re-formation of new ones. Such shifts, taking place on such a scale, are profoundly destabilising. They provide the context for the contradictory tendencies which surround us – globalism alongside localism, new nationalisms and ethnic identities alongside the international communication highways. Questions as to roots and origins haunt the imaginations of disparate peoples across national and inter-continental boundaries.

Such questions raise critical issues for historians. Eric Hobsbawm in a recent lecture at the Central European University reflected on the role of historians in the contemporary world. Until 1989 Hobsbawm was a confident believer in the emancipatory purpose of history, but in the post-communist world he takes a more sombre and pessimistic stance. 'History', he argues:

> is the raw material for nationalist or ethnic or fundamentalist ideologies, as poppies are the raw material for heroin addiction. The past is an essential element, perhaps *the* essential element in these ideologies. If there is no

suitable past, it can always be invented . . . I used to think that the profession of history, unlike that of, say, nuclear physics, could at least do no harm.
Now I know it can. Our studies can turn into bomb factories. This state of
affairs affects us in two ways. We have a responsibility to historical facts
in general, and for criticising the politico-ideological abuse of history in
particular.[1]

Hobsbawm goes on to argue that it is the historian's responsibility to stand
aside from 'the passions of identity politics', a politics associated for him with
the women's movement and the gay movement, movements which he sees as
incapable of transforming societies unlike the communist politics with which
he was engaged. For Hobsbawm a belief in historical truth and reason provides one way to resist the barbarism which he sees around him and to have
a sense of history may be one way of dealing with the present. Historians
must separate themselves from inventions of the past, insist on the difference
between fact and fiction, stand aside from national narratives or rituals, distinguish between myths and history. I am sceptical about such distinctions,
distinctions which post-structuralism has profoundly disrupted. If we are
interested in the ways in which history is lived, how it offers answers to the
questions as to who we are and where we came from, if we want to know how
we are produced as modern subjects, what narratives from the past enable us
to construct identities, how historical memories and the shadows and ghosts
of memories are internalised in our lives, then 'the passions of identity politics'
may drive us to ask new questions of old and new sources, fiction may give us
necessary tools, the construction of new myths may be part of our work.

George Steiner, in a very different mood, has discussed the ancient power
of myth and wondered whether the 'New Europe' could provide us with a new
myth that will enable us to face our past and, therefore, our future.[2] The past
that was on his mind was the Holocaust. But there are other European pasts
that have also been repressed, in particular imperial pasts, which, to the mind of
many in the present, are best remembered only through the mists of nostalgia.
Many Europeans, concerned to forget that past, look to a future which focuses
on Europe and discards the uncomfortable memories of colonialism. Perhaps
before we can embark on the construction of new myths we need to do some
'memory work' on the legacy of Empire. Memory, as we know, is an active
process which involves at one and the same time forgetting and remembering.
Toni Morrison's *Beloved* powerfully evokes a past which African-Americans
as well as white Americans have found too painful to remember but which
needs to be recovered through what she calls 're-memory' if that society is to
reorient itself in such a way that it can come to terms with its own raced history.

If such memories are not 're-membered' then they will haunt the social imagination and disrupt the present.[3]

In Britain the traces of those imperial histories appear everywhere – in the naming of streets, the sugar in tea, the coffee and cocoa that are drunk, the mango chutney that is served, the memorials in cemeteries, the public monuments in parks and squares. Such traces are frequently left unexplored, or are refracted through a golden glow of better days, days when Britons led the world. If it is to be possible to construct myths which could bind Europeans together in ways that are inclusive not exclusive, not reminiscent of 'Fortress Europe' with its boundaries firmly in place against brown, black and yellow migrants, then we need to begin the work of remembering empires differently. Such a project might begin from the recognition of inter-connection and inter-dependence, albeit structured through power, rather than a notion of hierarchy with the 'centre' firmly in place and the 'peripheries' marginalised.

The legacy of the British Empire is immediately visible in contemporary Britain, where 6.3% of the population are now classified as ethnic minorities. In urban areas such as London and Birmingham, where ethnic minorities make up over 20 per cent of the population, African-Caribbean and South-Asian people constitute the majority groupings. The decolonised peoples of Jamaica, Trinidad, Barbados, Guyana, India, Pakistan, Bangladesh and other once colonies of the Empire who have made their home in Britain, together with their children and their children's children, act as a perpetual reminder of the ways in which the once metropolis is intimately connected to its 'peripheries'. Both colonisers and colonised are linked through their histories, histories which are forgotten in the desire to throw off the embarrassing reminders of Empire, to focus instead on the European future.

In Britain questions about cultural identity have been at the forefront of the national imagination since it became clear that Britain no longer had an Empire and had become, in a very particular sense of the term, a post-colonial nation. For centuries white identities in Britain have been rooted in a sense of superiority derived from the power exercised over racialised others. The loss of that power, the recognition that Britain was only a minor player in the great affairs of the globe, has been a long-drawn-out and difficult affair. Since the 1960s the right of the Tory party has been central to the articulation of Britain as a white nation, its black population only acceptable on the basis that they become culturally British, or indeed English.[4] English, because while Britain has always been a multi-ethnic nation the hegemony of England has signified the historic marginalisation of the 'Celtic fringes'. With a well-established discourse of 'race' and nation articulated by the Tories, the Labour party has been singularly weak on these issues. Nervous of being identified with black people, or the Irish and the 'Celtic fringes' (despite its dependence on their votes), the Labour party has clung to its conviction that it must respond to the right's agenda on the nation, rather than imagining a different kind of future. At best it has a weak multicultural position and is certainly not in the business of envisioning Britain as what might be described as a 'post-nation': a society that has discarded the notion of a homogeneous nation state with singular forms of belonging. In this context Islamic cultural nationalisms flourish, as do some elements of black cultural nationalism: responses in part to the difficulties associated with articulating an identity that is both black and British.

A re-thinking of the British imperial legacy needs input from the 'peripheries' for it would be very limited to re-think that history only from the 'centre'. Australia and Jamaica, in very different ways, provide my counterpoints which allow me to begin to re-map the history of Empire. Australia was a white settler colony where it was widely assumed in the nineteenth century that the Aboriginal population would die out. Jamaica was colonised by the British in the seventeenth century, when its indigenous peoples had already been wiped out by the Spanish, and was populated mainly by enslaved Africans and white settlers. In Australia it is quite as difficult to be black and Australian, despite a very different history from that of Britain. In Australia debates about cultural identity have been focused by particular moments. First the bicentenary in 1988, when two hundred years of settlement were celebrated by some in the face of considerable Aboriginal outrage. More recently, 2001, the centenary of Australian federation, has provided the site for a national debate about the future of Australia as a republic, with the associated threatened demise of the monarchy. At play in those debates are definitions of citizenship, of nation, of community. While some long for a safe return to the old white nation and some Aboriginal people are turning to forms of separatist nationalism, there is a felt need amongst others to pioneer 'a "post-nationalist" political concept of citizenship free from ethnocentric notions of political identity'.[5]

Prime Minister Keating's new notion of citizenship is one that is dependent on the notion of mix, one that refuses ethnic purity and that argues for a national 'act of recognition', recognition of the wrongs done to Aboriginal peoples in the seizure of their land, the destruction of their cultures. Rejecting the idea of an Australia composed, as in the moment of Federation, by European peoples with Aboriginal peoples denied citizenship, he calls attention to the waves of immigration of the twentieth century and the impact of the Asian presence on this society perched on the Pacific rim. Australia, as a popular postcard proclaims, is no longer 'down under', for mapping from a different perspective places Australia differently in the global frame. As Ann Curthoys and Stephen Muecke argue, while the earlier nationalism of the Australia of Federation was based on the unity of 'race', the exclusion of others (particularly Aboriginal people) and white exploitation of the land, one dream is that the post-nationalist new settlement should be predicated on difference (both internal and external), inclusion (that would not be confined to Europeans but would be multicultural) and Aboriginal sovereignty over land.[6]

In Jamaica, another 'periphery' of the erstwhile British Empire, cultural identity is a critical issue too. The Caribbean, as Stuart Hall has argued, has something to offer in terms of the movement which has been possible towards what Rushdie might call, in an intentionally provocative term, the mongrel, post-colonial society.[7] In the Caribbean almost all the indigenous population was destroyed in the first wave of colonisation. Consequently almost everyone who lives there has come from somewhere else, whether through slavery, the enforced movement of peoples from Africa, the semi-enforced movement represented by indentured labour from one part of the British Empire to another (South Asians to Trinidad and Guyana in particular), or by persecution, as in the case of Portuguese Jews. Then there were the colonisers – the British, the Spanish, the French, the Dutch, who stayed and became the white creole presence. But 'the stamp of historical violence and rupture' is central to any Caribbean narrative.

Fanon has been crucial to our understanding of the internal traumas of identity which are associated with colonisation and enslavement. For colonisation is never only about the external processes and pressures of exploitation. It is always also about the ways in which colonised subjects internally collude with the objectification of the self produced by the coloniser.[8] The search for independence and the struggle for decolonisation, therefore, had to be premised on new identities. In the Caribbean the reinvention of Africa was crucial to this process as was a re-worked and syncretised Christianity. The Christianity of the missionaries was re-invented by slaves and emancipated peoples, utilising the story of the Exodus and the journey to freedom. From the mayalism of the late eighteenth and nineteenth centuries to the Rastafarianism of the 1960s and after, black people in Jamaica decolonised their minds with the tools of the colonisers turned to new uses. As Stuart Hall puts it,

> What they felt was I have no voice, I have no history, I have come from a place to which I cannot go back and I have never seen. I used to speak a language which I can no longer speak, I had ancestors whom I cannot find, they worshipped gods whose names I do not know. Against this sense of profound rupture, the metaphors of a new kind of imposed religion can be reworked, can become a language in which a certain kind of history is

retold, in which aspirations of liberation and freedom can be for the first time expressed, in which what I would call the imagined community of Africans can be symbolically reconstructed.[9]

So out of the traditions and myths which were available new fictions and new histories were constructed, telling stories of new identities for men and women, enabling Caribbean peoples to recognise themselves as Africans and diasporised, as Indians and diasporised, imaginatively connected in complex ways to the histories of slavery and indenture, as well as colonisers who were also diasporised: all having made new identities in societies with no easy myth of origins, no simple way of defining who belonged and who did not, who was included, who excluded.

At a time when some are insisting that nations must only comprise one ethnicity, that they must be exclusive and racially pure, there is a vital alternative project which developments both in the Caribbean and Australia might help us to think through. That is to imagine a British 'post-nation' which is not ethnically pure, which is inclusive and culturally diverse. This necessarily involves a re-working of the history of Empire for the Empire has been central to the ways in which British national identities have been imagined and lived. It matters, therefore, how the Empire is remembered and what kind of historical work is done. A re-read, re-imagined imperial history, focusing on inter-dependence and mutuality as well as on the patterns of domination and subordination which are always inscribed in the relations between coloniser and colonised, might provide some resources from which new notions of twenty-first century British cultural identities might be drawn. For cultural identities are always a construction, are never fixed or essential and new identities could draw on new repertoires.

There is an important task here for feminist and left historians. Some male left historians have found it difficult to establish new languages with the certainties of Marxism gone and with the impact of feminism and post-structuralism. They have lost their sense of the laws of history, the truth of their narratives, the conviction that class provides the key, 'the motor of history'. Feminist historians have been much less traumatised by these changes. They have been more open to theory, and necessarily had less investment in established narratives for their narratives have been built on critique. Yet neither group has been at the forefront of 'imperial history' in the last twenty years. Marxist historians combined a commitment to internationalism with a relatively benign view of the nation. So, for example, E.P. Thompson celebrated English traditions with all their in-built ethnocentrism.[10] Feminist historians have been too preoccupied with rewriting histories through gender or recovering women's worlds and have been very slow to respond to the black feminist critique which has insisted on the interconnections between the power relations of 'race' and gender and the implications of imperial history. But histories and historians have always been central to the project of constructing cultural and national identities. We need now to re-think what this agenda might be in the context of the end of Empire, decolonisation, and new patterns of migration and settlement.

....

The post-colonial moment in Britain is the moment after Empire, when British identities have to be imagined anew, when 'we' are no longer the centre. A moment of potential, when 'we' could come to terms with the myth of homogeneity, when 'we' could recognise the inequalities associated with the different raced and gendered ways of belonging to the British nation/state, when 'we' could build a different kind of future which was inclusive rather than exclusive, when whiteness would not be a condition of belonging. History and memory are central to that process. Unpicking imperial histories, grasping the raced and gendered ways in which inter-connections and inter-dependencies have been played out, developing a more differentiated notion of power than that which focuses simply on coloniser and colonised, can have emancipatory potential. It is a history which involves recognition and the re-working of memory. A history which shows how fantasised constructions of homogeneous nations are constructed and the other possibilities which are always there. A history which is about difference, not homogeneity. In re-imagining the past and re-evaluating the relations of Empire 'we' can begin to understand the ties which bind the different peoples of contemporary Britain in a web of connections which have been mediated through power, the power of coloniser over colonised, that have never moved only from 'centre' to 'periphery', but rather have criss-crossed the globe.

Notes

1 E.J. Hobsbawm, 'The new threat to history', *New York Review*, 15 December 1993.
2 George Steiner, 'The ancient power of myth', *The Guardian*, 6 August 1994.
3 Toni Morrison, *Beloved*, Picador, 1988.

4 Paul Gilroy, *There Ain't No Black in the Union Jack*, Hutchinson, 1987.
5 Wayne Hudson and David Carter (eds), *The Republicanism Debate*, New South Wales University Press, 1993, p. 3.
6 Ibid.
7 Stuart Hall, 'Myths of Caribbean identity', Walter Rodney Memorial Lecture, University of Warwick, 1991.
8 Frantz Fanon, *Black Skins, White Masks*, Pluto Press, 1986.
9 Hall, 'Myths of Caribbean identity', p. 10.
10 E.P. Thompson, *The Making of the English Working Class*, Penguin, 1967.

Part Four

Learning from Historical Perspective

Persistence and change

A ccustomed to the charge that they impose lessons on the past rather than derive insights from it, historians have developed a number of arguments which suggest that socially useful knowledge can be drawn from the study of history. One of the most convincing of these arguments is that historical perspective tells us which of our social arrangements are of recent origin – and thus quite possibly transient – and which have endured over a long time.

Marc Bloch was co-founder of the influential *Annales* school of historians in the 1920s. His reflections on the nature of history, published after his death at the hands of the Nazis, are now his most widely read work. As a specialist in early Medieval social history, Bloch was in a strong position to indicate those aspects of French life which had persisted through hundreds of years, and which were therefore unlikely to change overnight. Peter Laslett stresses even more the practical relevance of this perspective. He was a pioneer of demographic approaches to the history of the family in Britain, and in his classic *The World We Have Lost* (1965) he presented his findings in a way which addressed topical concerns. Contrasting 'our' social arrangements with 'theirs', Laslett maintained, enables us to distinguish what is recurrent about our predicament from what is new, and to devise policies accordingly.

22. Marc Bloch

[from The Historian's Craft, *Manchester University Press, 1954, pp. 35–43]*

The Boundaries between Past and Present

Must we believe, because the past does not entirely account for the present, that it is utterly useless for its interpretation? The curious thing is that we should be able to ask the question today.

Not so very long ago, the answer was almost unanimously predetermined. 'He who would confine his thought to present time will not understand present reality.' So Michelet expressed it at the beginning of his *Peuple* – a fine book, but infected with the fever of the age in which it was written. And Leibniz before him ranked among those benefits which attend the study of history 'the origins of things present which are to be found in things past; for a reality is never better understood than through its causes'.

But since Leibniz, and since Michelet, a great change has taken place. Successive technological revolutions have immeasurably widened the psychological gap between generations. With some reason, perhaps, the man of the age of electricity and of the airplane feels himself far removed from his ancestors. With less wisdom, he has been disposed to conclude that they have ceased to influence him. There is also a modernist twist inherent in the engineering mind. Is a mastery of old Volta's ideas about galvanism necessary to run or repair a dynamo? By what is unquestionably a lame analogy, but one which readily imposes itself upon more than one machine-dominated mentality, it is easy to think that an analysis of their antecedents is just as useless for the understanding and solving of the great human problems of the moment. Without fully recognizing it, the historians, too, are caught in this modernist climate. Why then should they not feel that, within their province, there has also been a shift in the line which separates the new from the old? What, for example, of the system of stabilized currency and the gold standard which, only yesterday, would have figured as the very norm of up-to-dateness in every manual of political economy? To the modern economist, do they belong to the present, or to a history already reeking with mold?

Behind these confused impressions, it is possible to discover a number of more consistent ideas, whose simplicity, at least on the surface, has captivated certain minds.

One short period seems somehow set apart from the vast sweep of time. Its beginning was relatively recent, and its end overlaps our own day. Nothing in it – neither its outstanding social and political characteristics, nor its physical equipment, nor its cultural tone – presents any important contrasts with our own world. It appears, in a word, to assume a very marked degree of 'contemporaneousness' with us. And, from this, it derives the virtue or defect of being distinct from the rest of the past. A high-school teacher, who was very old when I was very young, once told us: 'Since 1830, there has been no more history. It is all politics.' One would no longer say 'since 1830' – the July Days have grown old in their turn. Nor would one say: 'It is all politics.' Rather, with a respectful air: 'It is all sociology.' Or, with less respect: 'It is all journalism.' Nevertheless, there are many who would gladly repeat that since 1914, or since 1940, there has been no more history. Yet they would not agree very well in other respects as to the reasons for this ostracism.

Some, who consider that the most recent events are unsuitable for all really objective research just because they are recent, wish only to spare Clio's chastity from the profanation of present controversy. Such, I believe, was the thought of my old teacher. This is to rate our self-control rather low. It also quite overlooks that, once an emotional chord has been struck, the line between present and past is no longer strictly regulated by a mathematically measurable chronology. In the Languedoc high school where I served my first term as a teacher, my good headmaster issued a warning in a voice befitting a captain of education. 'Here, with the nineteenth century, there is little danger; but when you touch on the religious wars, you must take great care!' In truth, whoever lacks the strength, while seated at his desk, to rid his mind of the virus of the present may readily permit its poison to infiltrate even a commentary on the *Iliad* or the *Ramayana*.

There are other savants who consider, quite to the contrary and with reason, that contemporary society is perfectly susceptible of scientific investigation. But they admit this only to reserve its study for branches of learning quite distinct from that which has the past for its object. They analyze, and they claim, for example, to understand the contemporary economic system on the basis of observations limited to a few decades. In a word, they consider the epoch in which we live as separated from its predecessors by contrasts so clear as to be self-explanatory. Such is also the instinctive attitude of a great many of the merely curious. The history of the remoter periods attracts them only as an innocuous intellectual luxury. On one hand, a small group of antiquarians taking a ghoulish delight in unwrapping the winding-sheets of the dead gods; on the other, sociologists, economists, and publicists, the only explorers of the living.

Understanding the Present by the Past

Under close scrutiny the prerogative of self-intelligibility thus attributed to present time is found to be based upon a set of strange postulates.

In the first place, it supposes that, within a generation or two, human affairs have undergone a change which is not merely rapid, but total, so that no institution of long standing, no traditional form of conduct, could have escaped the revolutions of the laboratory and the factory. It overlooks the force of inertia peculiar to so many social creations.

Man spends his time devising techniques of which he afterwards remains a more or less willing prisoner. What traveler in northern France has not been struck by the strange pattern of the fields? For centuries, changes in ownership have modified the original design; yet, even today, the sight of these inordinately long and narrow strips, dividing the arable land into a prodigious number of pieces, is something which baffles the scientific agriculturalist. The waste of effort which such a disposition entails and the problems which it imposes upon the cultivators are undeniable. How are we to account for it? Certain impatient publicists have replied: 'By the Civil Code and its inevitable effects. Change the laws on inheritance and the evil will be removed.' Had they known history better, or had they further questioned a peasant mentality shaped by centuries of experience, they would not have thought the cure so simple. Indeed, this pattern dates back to origins so distant that no scholar has yet succeeded in accounting for it satisfactorily. The settlers in the era of the dolmens have more to do with it than the lawyers of the First Empire. Perpetuating itself, as it were, of necessity, for want of correction, this ignorance of the past not only confuses contemporary science, but confounds contemporary action.

A society that could be completely molded by its immediately preceding period would have to have a structure so malleable as to be virtually invertebrate. It would also have to be a society in which communication between generations was conducted, so to speak, in 'Indian file' – the children having contact with their ancestors only through the mediation of their parents.

Now, this is not true. It is not true even when the communication is purely oral. Take our villages, for example. Because working conditions keep the mother and father away almost all day, the young children are brought up chiefly by their grandparents. Consequently, with the molding of each new mind, there is a backward step, joining the most malleable to the most inflexible mentality, while skipping that generation which is the sponsor of change. There is small room for doubt that this is the source of that traditionalism inherent in so many peasant societies. The instance is particularly clear, but it is far from unique. Because the natural antagonism between age groups is always intensified between neighboring generations, more than one youth has learned at least as much from the aged as from those in their prime.

Still more strongly, between even widely scattered generations, the written word vastly facilitates those transfers of thought which supply the true continuity of a civilization. Take Luther, Calvin, Loyola, certainly men from another time – from the sixteenth century, in fact. The first duty of the historian who would understand and explain them will be to return them to their milieu, where they are immersed in the mental climate of their time and faced by problems of conscience rather different from our own. But who would dare to say that the understanding of the Protestant or the Catholic Reformation, several centuries removed, is not far more important for a proper grasp of the world today than a great many other movements of thought or feeling, which are certainly more recent, yet more ephemeral?

In a word, the fallacy is clear, and it is only necessary to formulate it in order to destroy it. It represents the course of human evolution as a series of short, violent jerks, no one of which exceeds the space of a few lifetimes. Observation proves, on the contrary, that the mighty convulsions of that vast, continuing development are perfectly capable of extending from the beginning of time to the present. What would we think of a geophysicist who, satisfied with having computed their remoteness to a fraction of an inch, would then conclude that the influence of the moon upon the earth is far greater than that of the sun? Neither in outer space, nor in time, can the potency of a force be measured by the single dimension of distance.

Finally, what of those things past which seem to have lost all authority over the present – faiths which have vanished without a trace, social forms which have miscarried, techniques which have perished? Would anyone think that, even among these, there is nothing useful for his understanding? That would be to forget that there is no true understanding without a certain range of comparison; provided, of course, that that comparison is based upon differing and, at the same time, related realities. One could scarcely deny that such is here the case.

Certainly, we no longer consider today, as Machiavelli wrote, and as Hume or Bonald thought, that there is, in time, 'at least something which is change-less: that is man'. We have learned that man, too, has changed a great deal in his mind and, no less certainly, in the most delicate organs of his body. How should it be otherwise? His mental climate has been greatly altered; and to no less an extent, so, too, have his hygiene and his diet. However, there must be a permanent foundation in human nature and in human society, or the very names of man or society become meaningless. How, then, are we to believe that we understand these men, if we study them only in their reactions to circumstances peculiar to a moment? It would be an inadequate test of them, even for that particular moment. A great many potentialities, which might at any instant emerge from concealment, a great many more or less unconscious drives behind individual or collective attitudes, would remain in the shadows. In a unique case the specific elements cannot be differentiated; hence an interpretation cannot be made.

23. Peter Laslett

[from The World We Have Lost, *Methuen, 1965,*
pp. 242–4, 248–50]

Since we can only properly understand ourselves and our world, here and now, if we have something to contrast it with, the historians must provide that something. It is true that people and nations and cultures vary in the extent to which they wish to understand themselves in time in this way, but to claim that there has ever been a generation anywhere with no sense of history is to go too far. From this point of view therefore all historical knowledge is knowledge with a view to ourselves as we are here and now. But, and here is our second consideration, historical knowledge is also interesting in itself, objectively, 'scientifically' once more. It is in fact almost always of greater intrinsic interest than Jupiter's moons, or the wingspan of fly populations, because it is knowledge about people with whom we can identify ourselves.

Historical knowledge then, and the activity of the historian, need no apology. Without such knowledge we could not understand ourselves in contrast with our ancestors, and possessing it we also satisfy a spontaneous interest in the world around us and in the people who have been within it. Taken together, though with the emphasis on the first source of our interest, history often provides useful knowledge which we could not have in any other way. In order to know how to change and improve the National Health Service in our country, for example, it is necessary to know what it actually consists of and knowing that almost always means getting to know its history. So it is that the politician and administrator finds himself going through the story in chronological order; how before 1911 everyone in England had to pay for medical attention, although in New Zealand and in Germany health insurance was already in force; how in 1911 Mr Lloyd George got the first National Health Insurance act passed and how various acts succeeded it as the century went on, until in 1948 Mr Bevan and the Attlee government . . . and so on, and so on. The same sort of chronological explanation is necessary, along with some considerations about geography and economics of course, to understand why Jugoslavia will not fit into the Communist Bloc, or why it is that the Elgin marbles are in the British Museum and no longer on the site of the Parthenon.

Historical knowledge for use might perhaps be regarded as distinct from historical knowledge acquired to understand ourselves in time and to satisfy our curiosity about our past. But these distinctions need be pressed no further for our present purposes, and we must recognize that the functions of the historian which are implied by these elementary considerations scarcely make it likely that this subject will be a progressive one. If this is what the historian has to do, it is not to be expected that what he is doing in England today should be very different from what he has always been doing, here and elsewhere. There cannot be a 'new history' in quite the sense that Einstein founded a 'new physics' nor indeed a new branch of historical study of quite the type of radio astronomy, which is a new and very recent branch of physics as a whole in virtue of its subject matter. Nevertheless the shift of interest towards inquiries of the sort which are reported with such brevity and sketchiness in this book, ought perhaps to be called a new branch of history.

The phrase 'sociological history' has been occasionally used here as its title, but it might almost be better to use 'Social structural history' instead. This new title is required first and foremost to register a distinction in subject matter, for confessedly historical writing has not previously concerned itself with births, marriages and deaths as such, nor has it dwelt so exclusively on the shape and development of social structure. But the outlook is novel as well as the material, at least in its emphasis. Perhaps the distinctive feature of the attitude is the frank acceptance of the truth that all historical knowledge, from one point of view, and that an important and legitimate one, is knowledge about ourselves, and the insistence on understanding by contrast.

From this flows an irreverent impatience with established conventions of the subject as it has been traditionally studied in our country. The search for contrasts in social arrangements leads one to demand that English society shall not be seen for itself alone, but alongside French, German, Spanish, Dutch, Italian, Scandinavian society, as one variation on the Western European pattern. But even this cannot be wide enough. Russian and Eastern European societies, Asian, African and Oceanic societies too, are relevant to the study of our own, if contrast is what we are in need of. The object of the English historian of his own country may remain to get to know his own society, but now as one amongst others.

The search for contrast does not end even here. It is not simply geographical. We all know (and an exasperatingly imprecise thing it is to know) that in England and in Western Europe we live in an 'advanced' industrial society, to be further described as a 'capitalist' as opposed to a 'socialist' industrial society. There are in the contemporary world societies which are not industrial at all in the sense given to the word here. These are the primitive societies, as we somewhat patronizingly call them, of Africa, Asia, Australia, South America and Oceania. But what is 'industrialization', what are 'socialist' and 'capitalist' economies, what indeed is 'society' and what is objectively known and knowable about the constitution of societies and the ways in which they cohere, change, evolve, solve their conflicts and fight them out?

....

The evidence about the household as it was in England before the industrial process began has been referred to on various occasions throughout this essay, though not presented in a systematic way. It seems to make impossible any belief that the independent, nuclear family-household of man, wife and children is an exclusive characteristic of industrialized society. When all allowance has been made for the very different assumptions about the household which then obtained, and the very different kinship relationships too, it remains the case that there ordinarily slept together under each roof in 1600 only the nuclear family, with the addition of servants when necessary. Therefore in that vital respect our ancestors were not different from ourselves. They were the same.

The assumption seems to have been that the contrary was true, an assumption made not so much by historians, too preoccupied with traditional activities, but by the sociologists themselves. Much of the alienation discussion of our time seems to suppose that the horror of industrialization was in part the result of separating the nuclear family from the kin group and the kin group was usually conceived of in terms of joint or extended households.

There is more to this than a faulty account of how things have changed. Our whole view of ourselves is altered if we cease to believe that we have lost some more humane, much more *natural* pattern of relationships than industrial society can offer. When we inquire, for example, what we are trying to do for the lonely old people who are becoming so lamentably common as the twentieth-century decades go by, we find ourselves assuming that they must be restored to the family, where they belong. Perhaps none of those who write so urgently about these problems have a very clear notion of the situation which they are trying to restore. But few of them can have realized

how inappropriate it is to think of restoration at all, in the sense of returning
to the historical past. We have already talked of the identical error in relation
to broken homes and the criminal tendency of our young people and shown
that the problem of our ancestors in this regard may well have been worse,
not better, than our own.

In fact, in tending to look backwards in this way, in diagnosing the difficulties as the outcome of something which has indeed been lost to our society,
those concerned with social welfare are suffering from a false understanding of
ourselves in time. Not completely false, of course; if that were so it would make
nonsense of our general title. We have seen that in the traditional world the
family did fulfil many functions which are left to very different institutions in
our day, or which are not fulfilled at all.

But was it more 'natural' that this should have been so? Was *The World
we have lost* a more appropriate one for human beings to dwell in? These are
very vague and general questions, unlikely to be worth trying to answer in this
book. But the point of importance to our argument is to have got into a position where such questions must arise. To recognize their urgency is also to
begin to take a different view of our own place in time, and more than this. It
may, perhaps ought to, change our view of what we should be trying to do. We
can only begin to get into this position if we admit that historical knowledge is
knowledge to do with ourselves, now.

Beyond stereotypes

S tereotypes are socially harmful because they lead to rigid thinking and blinkered action. Given the huge variety of the recorded past – even in a single country over a few generations – history potentially offers a powerful antidote to stereotyped thinking. Historians can fairly claim that those who are completely immersed in the present day are much less likely to question received views or to recognise the full complexity of the world in which they live. This applies particularly to the view we take of other countries: a couple of standard adjectives – often pejorative or condescending – so often take the place of real understanding. Michael Howard, an authority on military history and international relations, took up this theme in his inaugural lecture of 1981 in relation to British foreign policy between the wars. An informed historical understanding of central Europe would have given the policy-makers some insight into the mentality of the Nazi leadership; their ignorance led them to make glib assessments which cost their country dear.

The American radical historian, Howard Zinn, makes fundamentally the same point with regard to national consensus. A consensus may minimise conflict, but it also reflects a passive acceptance of stereotypic ideas, which allows little room for a sense of positive alternatives and a readiness to entertain other values. Zinn advocates a history which opens our eyes to the experience of other, less privileged groups, and which discloses some of the possibilities that might lie before us – a history to 'pull us out of lethargy'.

24. Michael Howard

[from The Lessons of History, *Oxford University Press, 1989, pp. 12–20]*

I am very well aware that the argument that historians have a social function – indeed a social obligation – is likely to be no more welcome among scholars today than it was when the first holder of this Chair was appointed over two and a half centuries ago. Professor Galbraith himself sounded from this very rostrum a trumpet blast against the conversion of the study of history to 'mere propaganda, resting on a narrow basis of civic usefulness', and we know what he meant. 'Socially useful' or 'relevant' history, whether consciously or unconsciously selected or tailored to meet contemporary social or political needs, has no place in a university or anywhere else. But there is a danger that this is the kind of history that almost automatically would get taught, or at least learned, if the historical profession did not exist to prevent it. For all societies have *some* view of the past; one that shapes and is shaped by their collective consciousness, that both reflects and reinforces the value-systems which guide their actions and judgements; and if professional historians do not provide this, others less scrupulous or less well qualified will. Far more than poets can historians claim to be the unacknowledged legislators of mankind; for all we believe about the present depends on what we believe about the past.

Certainly the historian cannot escape from the present. The more ambitious he is in attempting to create great comprehensive patterns of historical development, as did Marx, or Toynbee, or Spengler, or Sorokhin, the more evidently will he betray the moods and preoccupations of his own day. But he can, even within the limits imposed by his own cultural environment, ensure that our view of the past is not distorted by fraud, by evident prejudice or by simple error. Our primary professional responsibility is to keep clear and untainted those springs of knowledge that ultimately feed the great public reservoirs of popular histories and school text books and are now piped to every household in the country through the television screens. It is not an indifferent matter, or one of purely scholarly interest, to choose examples from recent history, if it is widely believed that Adolf Hitler had no special responsibility for the Second World War; or that 120,000 people were killed in the Allied bombing of Dresden; or that Churchill connived in the murder of General Sikorski, or deliberately allowed Coventry to be bombed in order to protect the ULTRA secret; or that the United States deliberately destroyed Hiroshima and Nagasaki, not in order to forward their military operations against Japan, but as a demonstration intended to overawe the Soviet Union. Such beliefs about the past, however indirectly, shape attitudes and guide judgement for the present. It is important to be sure that they are correct.

So the first lesson that historians are entitled to teach is the austere one: not to generalize from false premises based on inadequate evidence. The second is no more comforting: the past is a foreign country; there is very little we can say about it until we have learned its language and understood its assumptions; and in deriving conclusions about the processes which occurred in it and applying them to our own day we must be very careful indeed. The *understanding* of the past, particularly of the beliefs and assumptions that held societies together and determined those activities on the level of high politics that are normally regarded as 'history', is the most rewarding, as it is the most difficult, of the historian's tasks. And it is here that he needs that quality of imagination so properly called for by my predecessor in his valedictory lecture. Yet it is a quality best used, not in creating alternative 'scenarios' of the past, but in recreating the structure of beliefs that determined action and perhaps made some actions more likely than others. It would indeed be fascinating and not illegitimate to ask what would have happened if Hitler had shown more interest in sea power; or had spared more resources for the Mediterranean theatre; or had above all shown more knowledge and understanding of the United States. But perhaps it is more useful to understand the prejudices and the order of priorities likely to exist in the mind of an autodidact whose formative years were spent in Vienna, where the great issues of the day related not to the rivalry of distant seaborne Empires but to the clash between Teuton and Slav, between German and Czech, between Western and Russian power and – with horrible implications for the future – between Gentile and Jew.

For this quality of historical imagination is needed as much in dealing with the recent as it is with the more remote past. No one can be under any illusions about the difficulties of comprehending the world of Charlemagne, or of Frederick Barbarossa or even of Napoleon Bonaparte. But is it really any easier for us today to understand the world of High Victorian Imperialism or of Edwardian England? And how many historians can claim to have comprehended, not so much the motives and intentions of Adolf Hitler, over which so much ink has been spilled, but the world-outlook and the value-systems that held the Third Reich together and kept the entire German people working and fighting until the very framework of their society had been destroyed over their heads? It is only if we have achieved such an understanding that we can plausibly answer such hypothetical questions as, whether the Second World War could have been averted or curtailed if we had 'stood up to' Hitler sooner; or if we had given greater encouragement to the clandestine opposition within Germany; or if we had not demanded unconditional surrender. What was the *society* that we were dealing with, and how could it have reacted to these events?

If it is difficult for historians in retrospect, with all the wisdom of hindsight and all the time in the world, to comprehend the complex processes that went to the creation of the Third Reich and the nature of the society to which it gave political expression, we should not be too quick to condemn those contemporary British statesmen who so tragically misunderstood the phenomenon in their own day. For their perceptions were also constrained by their cultural framework. Neville Chamberlain and his closest colleagues had been brought up in the England of Queen Victoria and were middle-aged when the First World War began. Their world was that of the British Empire. The problems posed by the Congress Party in India, by the Wafd movement in Egypt, and by the relations of Briton and Boer in South Africa were more immediate to them, more real, more urgent, than were the racial antagonisms of Central Europe. How could they be expected to see the significance of that populist nationalism, fuelled invariably by anti-Semitism, that was seeping up everywhere in the Continent like so much sewage through the cracks in the old order; the *anomie* that ravaged societies where traditional values had been destroyed by war and revolution? The works on European history on which they had been brought up had been written before the turn of the century in a spirit of optimistic liberalism, seeing in the unification of Germany and of Italy the happy climax to a long struggle for freedom and self-expression and taking little account of anything that had happened after that. Even those of their Foreign Office advisers who saw the dangers of National Socialism saw them in traditional terms: the revival of the power and the pretensions of the German, indeed the *Prussian* state, which they had known in their youth. Few if any comprehended the full challenge posed by the 'Revolution of Nihilism' which enabled the Nazis to find willing collaborators in every country they conquered; and made of Nazism a popular, indeed a *populist* movement, of a kind that both liberal and Marxist historians have found difficult to explain away.

When we consider the insularity of our attitude to our continental neighbours after 1945, the patronizing aloofness displayed by so many British statesmen and senior civil servants towards the birth of the European Community, their reluctance to give that lead in the remaking of Europe which was for so many years ours for the asking, we may wonder how far this attitude was rooted in a historical consciousness nurtured by university history teachers who for generations had seen the Continent as an area of concern for specialists, the study of whose problems was an interesting option but no more. It is significant that in the Oxford history syllabus in the 1920s there was only one special subject available in modern continental history – that on Congress diplomacy between 1815 and 1822. Others available included British rule in India, the development of Canada and the revolt of the American colonies. Admirable as it was that the horizons of undergraduates should have been extended to the other side of the Atlantic, the contribution that the Oxford History School made to our understanding of our nearest neighbours was, for that generation, notably small.

And this perhaps indicates that the value of history as a training of the judgement and of the imagination is very limited if it is exercised only in recreating our own past, with little reference to the total context within which our society developed and, more particularly, the often very divergent structures of other societies whose development may have been of yet greater importance to the making of the world in which we live today. If it is, indeed, one of the major functions of the historian to explain the present by deepening our understanding of the past, then a study simply of our own society will not get us very far. Our awareness of the world and our capacity to deal intelligently with its problems are shaped not only by the history we know but by what we do *not* know. Ignorance, especially the ignorance of educated men, can be a more powerful force than knowledge. Ethnocentrism in historical studies, whatever its advantages in scholarly training, is likely to feed parochialism in the societies which those historians serve; and such parochialism can have pretty disastrous results.

Am I now suggesting that the history taught in universities and schools should, in spite of all I said a few moments ago, be 'relevant', and guided by some criterion of civic usefulness? In a sense I must admit that I am. But we must distinguish between *how* history is studied by the professional historians and *what* history is taught to the laity. The range of the historical profession must be universal, and universities exist to make possible that universality. In the eyes of the scholar, as in the eyes of God, all ages are of equal significance. It is as important to understand Byzantium as it is to understand the Soviet Union (and unless one understands Byzantium how can one understand the

Soviet Union?). It is as important to understand the pre Columbian societies of Central America as it is to understand Moghul dynastic rule in India, or the system of land tenure in fifteenth-century Franconia, or the development of municipal government in Leeds. The past is a vast chain, every link of which must be kept in good repair. The links that lie chronologically or geographically near us can claim no special priority from the professional historian, and one of the things we have to teach the laity is that this is so.

But if our object in teaching history to the laity is to enable them to understand the present by explaining the past, and we have only three years in which to do this, then we cannot avoid making hard decisions about what we are going to select from the illimitable range offered by the past; what aspects of it we allocate for the compulsory and what for optional study. If a valid definition can be given to the term 'Modern History' – and I sometimes doubt whether it can – then it must be the history concerned with the world in which we live today and with the processes that have gone to form it. We are therefore justified in asking how far the subjects we prescribe for study will enhance that understanding, and in giving some priority to those for which a case can most easily be made. Of course it is true that for a full understanding of the contemporary world it is as important to understand the causes of the decline of the Roman Empire as those for the rise and fall of the Third Reich. The academic snobbery that disdains the history of the recent past precisely because it relates so obviously to the present is as indefensible as the lay impatience with a remote past because on the face of it it does not. But the layman has every right to ask the historian, not how his own reseaches contribute to our understanding of the contemporary world, but how do the studies that he, the layman, is required to pursue? And there is a certain obligation on our part to provide a convincing answer.

In the eighteenth century the world of classical antiquity provided a model whose 'relevance' to contemporary issues was unquestioned, or only just beginning to be questioned. In the nineteenth century the historian was expected to show only how his society had reached its existing state of perfection or – for the less easily satisfied – might be expected to progress to a future state of perfection. But the demands of our own tumultuous century have been more complex. To explain 'the modern world', the historian has to involve himself and his pupils in the study of societies sometimes very different from his own. And he may find himself forced to adopt a standpoint, from which the history of his own society will appear to be of secondary importance.

The range of the Oxford History School has been commendably extended since the Second World War. Special Subjects and Further Subjects have splendidly proliferated, bringing every corner of the world within the purview of any student who wants to take advantage of them. But the Anglocentric core remains – and I use the prefix 'Anglo' advisedly. The Irish dimension is still peripheral, studied only in so far as it affects the fortunes of the political parties in Westminster; and again one may wonder how far its absence has contributed to the neglect shown by the British public and the incompetence displayed by successive British administrations in dealing with the Irish problem over so many years. It is still possible here to study nothing that has happened beyond these shores save for a period of 'General History' covering a couple of centuries; which effectively means the history of Europe and of Western Europe at that; and woe betide the naive examiner who demands any broader knowledge from the candidates who take this paper! As for the history of the United States, a society which more than any other is likely to shape our lives if not our deaths, that is regarded as a matter for specialist study, and the great bulk of undergraduates leave the Oxford History School as ignorant of it as they were when they arrived.

If we are properly to educate the laity it is not enough to awaken an interest in the past to provide them with an agreeable leisure occupation. It is not enough to provide for them scholarly exercise in the handling of evidence on which they can sharpen their wits. We have to teach them how to step outside their own cultural skins and enter the minds of others; the minds not only of our own forebears, enormously valuable though this is, but of those of our contemporaries who have inherited a different experience from the past. And important as is the contribution of our colleagues the geographers and anthropologists, on whose insights we increasingly draw, the study of history alone can teach how to do this; history and the subject so properly associated with it when this Chair was founded: modern languages. As Burckhardt said, we cannot know too many languages. We need them not so much in order to make ourselves understood but in order to understand. Without knowing the languages that shape and express their thought our comprehension of other cultural communities will be dim and unreliable, however great in the abstract may be our knowledge of their past. Lord Dacre, in his farewell to his colleagues, congratulated us on having resisted up till now the general decline into 'monoglot illiteracy'. If we do not continue to resist it, and more, if we do not fight hard to reverse it, we shall find our range not being extended but narrowed, and our contribution to the understanding of both the past and present reduced to the level of parochial trivia.

And this is the third 'lesson' that historians must teach: the importance of comprehending cultural diversity and equipping oneself to cope with it. Much has properly been made of Neville Chamberlain's failure to understand Hitler, as of Roosevelt's failure to understand Stalin; but these disastrous misunderstandings are often depicted as cases of honest men being outwitted by crooks. Alas, the misunderstanding was at a far deeper level than that, and it is one that is constantly recurring as new elites, almost boastfully ignorant of their knowledge of any world save their own, acquire authority in some of the most powerful states in the world. We have seen so much of this since the Second World War: people often of masterful intelligence, trained usually in law or economics or perhaps in political science, who have led their governments into disastrous decisions and miscalculations because they have no awareness whatever of the historical background, the cultural universe, of the foreign societies with which they have to deal. It is an awareness for which no amount of strategic or economic analysis, no techniques of crisis-management or conflict-resolution and certainly no professed understanding of the 'objective historical process of the international class struggle' can provide a substitute. Such miscalculations are always dangerous. In our own day they may be lethal on a very large scale indeed.

This brings me to the last and most sombre 'lesson' that the study of history has to impart; and that is, how vulnerable may be the social framework which permits the historian to ply his trade at all. I am not referring to the fact of which we are all uncomfortably aware, or should be; that if the statesmen of the world do not conduct their affairs with prudence, I might well be the last occupant of this Chair. Our own generation knows from experience that no society has a dispensation from catastrophe, and that history provides no sure formula for avoiding one. This knowledge is in itself the beginning of wisdom. But there are other, more subtle, dangers to which societies have succumbed; dangers which, by destroying the insights that historical studies can provide, could make catastrophe more likely. Sir Maurice Powicke, one of the most learned and humane scholars ever to hold this Chair, once proclaimed confidently, 'Nobody can abolish the past'. Today if he attended many International Historical Congresses, he might be less sure. There are countries in the world where it is precisely the duty of historians to abolish the past, and their own professional survival depends on their success in keeping it abolished and erecting in its place a socially convenient myth which it is their function to defend, embellish and generally keep up to date.

Such a role is nothing new for historians. In most societies, in most eras, they have received official countenance only on condition they subscribed to and reinforced the reigning dogmas. The emergence of bourgeois liberal societies in which historians are free to publish what *had* 'really happened' in the past, at whatever embarrassment to the authorities of the present, to demolish myths rather than create them, is only a few centuries old. Such 'bourgeois objectivism' does not flourish in totalitarian societies, nor is it very helpful to the nation-building élites in the Third World. The freedom of historians to teach, study and publish as their scholarly instincts dictate, and to treat professors intruded by the Crown with the genial tolerance they deserve, is itself the result of historical circumstances which historians themselves should understand very well; as they can understand how fragile and fortuitous these circumstances can be. And this is a matter of which no historian can afford to be simply a dispassionate chronicler and analyst. However great his intellectual and moral detachment, in the last resort he is committed to the values, and to the society, that enables him to remain so detached. He is a member of the polis and cannot watch its destruction without himself being destroyed. However impatient the historian may be of lay requirements for guidance, however diffident he may be in claiming a wisdom he knows he does not possess, this is the one thing he *should* know. This is the one 'lesson of history' he must never allow himself to forget.

25. Howard Zinn

[from The Politics of History, *Beacon Press, 1970,
pp. 35–9, 41, 47–8, 54–5]*

What is radical history?

Historical writing always has some effect on us. It may reinforce our passivity; it may activate us. In any case, the historian cannot choose to be neutral; he writes on a moving train.

Sometimes, what he tells may change a person's life. In May 1968 I heard a Catholic priest, on trial in Milwaukee for burning the records of a draft board, tell (I am paraphrasing) how he came to that act:

> I was trained in Rome. I was quite conservative, never broke a rule in seminary. Then I read a book by Gordon Zahn, called *German Catholics and Hitler's Wars*. It told how the Catholic Church carried on its normal activities while Hitler carried on his. It told how SS men went to mass, then went out to round up Jews. That book changed my life. I decided the church must never behave again as it did in the past; and that I must not.

This is unusually clear. In most cases, where people turn in new directions, the causes are so complex, so subtle, that they are impossible to trace. Nevertheless, we all are aware of how, in one degree or another, things we read or heard changed our view of the world, or how we must behave. We know there have been many people who themselves did not experience evil, but who became persuaded that it existed, and that they must oppose it. What makes us human is our capacity to reach with our mind beyond our immediate sensory capacities, to feel in some degree what others feel totally, and then perhaps to act on such feelings.

I start, therefore, from the idea of writing history in such a way as to extend human sensibilities, not out of this book into other books, but into the going conflict over how people shall live, and whether they shall live.

I am urging value-laden historiography. For those who still rebel at this – despite my argument that this does not determine answers, only questions; despite my plea that aesthetic work, done for pleasure, should always have its place; despite my insistence that our work is value-laden whether we choose or not – let me point to one area of American education where my idea has been accepted. I am speaking of 'Black Studies', which, starting about 1969, began to be adopted with great speed in the nation's universities.

These multiplying Black Studies programs do not pretend to just intro-duce another subject for academic inquiry. They have the specific intention of so affecting the consciousness of black and white people in this country as to diminish for both groups the pervasive American belief in black inferiority.

This deliberate attempt to foster racial equality should be joined, I am suggesting, by similar efforts for national and class equality. This will prob-ably come, as the Black Studies programs, not by a gradual acceptance of the appropriate arguments, but by a crisis so dangerous as to *demand* quick changes in attitude. Scholarly exhortation is, therefore, not likely to initiate a new emphasis in historical writing, but perhaps it can support and ease it.

What kind of awareness moves people in humanistic directions, and how can historical writing create such awareness, such movement? I can think of five ways in which history can be useful. That is only a rough beginning. I don't want to lay down formulas. There will be useful histories written that do not fit into preconceived categories. I want only to sharpen the focus for myself and others who would rather have their writing guided by human aspiration than by professional habit.

We can intensify, expand, sharpen our perception of how bad things are, for the victims of the world. This becomes less and less a philanthropic act as all of us, regardless of race, geography, or class, become potential victims of a burned, irradiated planet. But even our own victimization is separated from us by time and the fragility of our imagination, as that of others is separated from us because most of us are white, prosperous, and within the walls of a country so over-armed it is much more likely to be an aggressor than a victim.

History can try to overcome both kinds of separation. The fascinating pro-gression of a past historical event can have greater effect on us than some cool, logical discourse on the dangerous possibilities of present trends – if only for one reason, because we learn the end of that story. True, there is a chill in the contemplation of nuclear war, but it is still a contemplation whose most hor-rible possibilities we cannot bring ourselves to accept. It is a portent that for full effect needs buttressing by another story whose conclusion is known. Surely, in this nuclear age our concern over the proliferation of H-bombs is powerfully magnified as we read Barbara Tuchman's account of the coming of the First World War:

> War pressed against every frontier. Suddenly dismayed, governments struggled and twisted to fend it off. It was no use. Agents at frontiers were reporting every cavalry patrol as a deployment to beat the mobilization gun. General staffs, goaded by their relentless timetables, were pounding the table for the signal to move lest their opponents gain an hour's head start. Appalled upon the brink, the chiefs of state who would be ultimately responsible for their country's fate attempted to back away but the pull of military schedules dragged them forward.[1]

There it is, *us*. In another time, of course. But unmistakably us.

Other kinds of separation, from the deprived and harried people of the world – the black, the poor, the prisoners – are sometimes easier to overcome across time than across space: hence the value of historical recollection. Both the *Autobiography of Malcolm X* and the *Autobiography of Frederick Douglass* are history, one more recent than the other. Both assault our complacency. So do the photos on television of blacks burning buildings in the ghetto today, but the autobiographies do something special: they let us look closely, carefully, personally behind the impersonality of those blacks on the screen. They invade our homes, as the blacks in the ghetto have not yet done; and our minds, which we tend to harden against the demands of *now*. They tell us, in some small degree, what it is like to be black, in a way that all the liberal clichés about the downtrodden Negro could never match. And thus they insist that we act; they explain why blacks are acting. They prepare us, if not to initiate, to respond.

Slavery is over, but its degradation now takes other forms, at the bottom of which is the unspoken belief that the black person is not quite a human being. The recollection of what slavery is like, what slaves are like, helps to attack that belief. Take the letter Frederick Douglass wrote his former master in 1848, on the tenth anniversary of his flight to freedom:

> I have selected this day to address you because it is the anniversary of my emancipation . . . Just ten years ago this beautiful September morning yon bright sun beheld me a slave – a poor, degraded chattel – trembling at the sound of your voice, lamenting that I was a man . . .
>
> When yet but a child about six years old I imbibed the determination to run away. The very first mental effort that I now remember on my part, was

an attempt to solve the mystery, Why am I a slave . . . When I saw a slave driver whip a slave woman . . . and heard her piteous cries, I went away into the corner of the fence, wept and pondered over the mystery . . . I resolved that I would someday run away.

The morality of the act, I dispose as follows: I am myself; you are yourself; we are two distinct persons. What you are, I am. I am not by nature bound to you nor you to me. . . . In leaving you I took nothing but what belonged to me . . .[2]

Why do we need to reach into the past, into the days of slavery? Isn't the experience of Malcolm X, in our own time enough? I see two values in going back. One is that dealing with the past, our guard is down, because we start off thinking it is over and we have nothing to fear by taking it all in. We turn out to be wrong, because its immediacy strikes us, affects us before we know it; when we have recognized this, it is too late – we have been moved. Another reason is that time adds depth and intensity to a problem which otherwise might seem a passing one, susceptible to being brushed away. To know that long continuity, across the centuries, of the degradation that stalked both Frederick Douglass and Malcolm X (between whose lives stretched that of W.E.B. DuBois, recorded in *The Souls of Black Folk* and *Dusk of Dawn*) is to reveal how infuriatingly long has been this black ordeal in white America. If nothing else, it would make us understand in that black mood of today what we might otherwise see as impatience, and what history tells us is overlong endurance.

....

There is no need to hide the data which show that some Negroes are climbing the traditional American ladder faster than before, that the ladder is more crowded than before. But there is a need – coming from the determination to represent those still wanting the necessities of existence (food, shelter, dignity, freedom) – to emphasize the lives of those who cannot even get near the ladder. The latest report of the Census Bureau is as 'true', in some abstract sense, as the reports of Malcolm X and Eldridge Cleaver on their lives. But the radical historian will, without hiding the former (there are already many interests at work to tell us that, anyway) emphasize those facts we are most likely to ignore – and these are the facts as seen by the victims.

Thus, a history of slavery drawn from the narratives of fugitive slaves is especially important. It cannot monopolize the historiography in any case, because the histories we already have are those from the standpoint of the slaveholder (Ulrich Phillip's account, based on plantation diaries, for instance), or from the standpoint of the cool observer (the liberal historian, chastising slavery but without the passion appropriate to a call for action). A slave-oriented history simply fills out the picture in such a way as to pull us out of lethargy.

....

We can recapture those few moments in the past which show the possibility of a better way of life than that which has dominated the earth thus far. To move men to act it is not enough to enhance their sense of what is wrong, to show that the men in power are untrustworthy, to reveal that our very way of thinking is limited, distorted, corrupted. One must also show that something else is possible, that changes can take place. Otherwise, people retreat into privacy, cynicism, despair, or even collaboration with the mighty.

History cannot provide confirmation that something better is inevitable; but it can uncover evidence that it is conceivable. It can point to moments when human beings cooperated with one another (the organization of the underground railroad by black and white, the French Resistance to Hitler, the anarchist achievements in Catalonia during the Spanish Civil War). It can find times when governments were capable of a bit of genuine concern (the creation of the Tennessee Valley Authority, the free medical care in socialist countries, the equal-wages principle of the Paris Commune). It can disclose men and women acting as heroes rather than culprits or fools (the story of Thoreau or Wendell Phillips or Eugene Debs, or Martin Luther King or Rosa Luxemburg). It can remind us that apparently powerless groups have won against overwhelming odds (the abolitionists and the Thirteenth Amendment, the CIO and the sit-down strikes, the Vietminh and the Algerians against the French).

Historical evidence has special functions. It lends weight and depth to evidence which, if culled only from contemporary life, might seem frail. And, by portraying the movements of men over time, it shows the possibility of change. Even if the actual change has been so small as to leave us still desperate today, we need, to spur us on, the faith that change is possible. Thus, while taking proper note of how much remains to be done, it is important to compare the consciousness of white Americans about black people in the 1930s and in the 1960s to see how a period of creative conflict can change people's minds and behavior. Also, while noting how much remains to be done in China, it is important to see with what incredible speed the Chinese Communists have been able to mobilize seven hundred million people against famine and disease. We need to know, in the face of terrifying power behind the accusing shouts against us who rebel, that we are not mad; that men in the past, whom we know, in the perspective of time, to have been great, felt as we do. At moments when we are tempted to go along with the general condemnation of revolution, we need to refresh ourselves with Thomas Jefferson and Tom Paine. At times when we are about to surrender to the glorification of law, Thoreau and Tolstoi can revive our conviction that justice supersedes law.

That is why, for instance, Staughton Lynd's book, *Intellectual Origins of American Radicalism*, is useful history. It recalls an eighteenth-century Anglo-American tradition declaring:

> . . . that the proper foundation for government is a universal law of right and wrong self-evident to the intuitive common sense of every man; that freedom is a power of personal self-direction which no man can delegate to another; that the purpose of society is not the protection of property but fulfillment of the needs of living human beings; that good citizens have the right and duty, not only to overthrow incurable oppressive governments, but before that point is reached to break particular oppressive laws; and that we owe our ultimate allegiance, not to this or that nation, but to the whole family of man.[3]

In a time when that tradition has been befogged by cries on all sides for 'law and order' and 'patriotism' (a word playing on the ambiguity between concern for one's government and concern for one's fellows) we need to remind ourselves of the *depth* of the humanistic, revolutionary impulse. The reach across the centuries conveys that depth.

....

History is not inevitably useful. It can bind us or free us. It can destroy compassion by showing us the world through the eyes of the comfortable ('the slaves are happy, just listen to them' – leading to 'the poor are content, just look at them'). It can oppress any resolve to act by mountains of trivia, by diverting us into intellectual games, by pretentious 'interpretations' which spur contemplation rather than action, by limiting our vision to an endless story of disaster and thus promoting cynical withdrawal, by befogging us with the encyclopedic eclecticism of the standard textbook.

But history can untie our minds, our bodies, our disposition to move – to engage life rather than contemplating it as an outsider. It can do this by widening our view to include the silent voices of the past, so that we look behind the silence of the present. It can illustrate the foolishness of depending on others to solve the problems of the world – whether the state, the church, or other self-proclaimed benefactors. It can reveal how ideas are stuffed into us by the powers of our time, and so lead us to stretch our minds beyond what is given.

It can inspire us by recalling those few moments in the past when men did behave like human beings, to prove it is *possible*. And it can sharpen our critical faculties so that even while we act, we think about the dangers created by our own desperation.

These criteria I have discussed are not conclusive. They are a rough guide. I assume that history is not a well-ordered city (despite the neat stacks of the library) but a jungle. I would be foolish to claim my guidance is infallible. The only thing I am really sure of is that we who plunge into the jungle need to think about what we are doing, because there *is* somewhere we want to go.

Notes

1 Barbara Tuchman, *The Guns of August*, Macmillan, 1962, p. 72.
2 Quoted in H. Aptheker, *A Documentary History of the Negro People*, Citadel, 1951, p. 2.
3 Staughton Lynd, *Intellectual Origins of American Radicalism*, Pantheon, 1968, p. vi.

Qualified predictions

Historians are uncomfortable with the idea of prediction because it usually rests on an assumption of repetition, and this raises the question of whether any historical phenomenon can happen twice. Repetition does occur in the superficial sense that economic slumps and political revolutions, for example, continue to happen. But given the nature of historical change the circumstances must be different in each case, and this crucially affects the meaning of the event. Any prediction must be based on the proviso 'other things being equal', and they never are: the complex and contingent circumstances which seem to point to a particular eventuality are just what will unravel through the process of time.

The two authors excerpted here both explore this issue in relation to twentieth-century history. H.R. Trevor-Roper is in the unusual position of having published extensively on both seventeenth-century England and the Third Reich. Despite his penchant for the bird's-eye view and the grand historical sweep, he concludes that only 'conditional prophecy' is possible – and then only if the conditions are clearly understood. Alan Bullock, biographer of Hitler and Ernest Bevin, acknowledges that accurate prediction is usually frustrated by the incongruous combination of continuity and change. But he makes a virtue of this: if we face up to the fact that the future is not predetermined, we may be able to play some role in shaping it.

26. H.R. Trevor-Roper

[from 'The Past and the Present: History and Sociology',
Past and Present *42 (1969), pp. 4–6, 10–12, 15–17]*

I venture to suggest that, whether it is entertaining or not, the study of the past is, or can be, useful. Perhaps I would go further and maintain that it is necessary. To those who would say, with Marx, that it is more important to change than to understand the world, I would reply that, even so, without understanding we cannot rationally change it. To those who see the past as an incubus from which we must set ourselves free, I would reply, with Freud, that obsessions are purged only by understanding, not by repudiation. We cannot profitably look forward without also looking back.

Of course we must not be too ambitious. We must not expect too much from the study of history. The historical lens is not exact, and whether we look forward or backward through it, the image is quickly blurred, so that fine detail is often missed and precise parallels cannot be drawn. We cannot compare history with the exact sciences, like mathematics or engineering. Marxists indeed speak of 'scientific history', and they have sometimes adjusted the recalcitrant details to fit the rules of their science. But I do not agree with them in this. If the phenomena do not obey the rules, I believe it is better to relax the rules in favour of the phenomena. History, I believe, has its rules, but they are not 'scientific': they are tentative and conditional, like the rules of life. There is an excellent historical periodical entitled, like this lecture, *Past and Present*. It began under Marxist control. The date of its escape from that control can be easily determined: it is the date (1950) when the sub-title was changed from 'a journal of scientific history' to 'a journal of historical studies'.

But if the lessons of history elude easy formulation, they are none the less real, and they provide the reasons for its serious study. What then are these reasons?

First of all, I would suggest, there is a general reason: to avoid parochialism. We all agree that parochialism is a fault. By this we generally mean parochialism in space. But there is also parochialism in time. To understand our own country, we need to see it in its wider context of space, among other countries. Equally, to understand our own age, we need to see it in its wider context of time, among other ages. To study only our own time may seem, at first sight, proof of our modernity: it is a sign that we are concentrating on the real world. But in fact such concentration may easily be very superficial. It removes a whole dimension of thought, and so deprives us of the means of comparison. So much of our own contemporary history is hidden from us that we cannot hope to see it in full. It is so close to us that we cannot see it in correct proportion. It is not yet over, so that we cannot judge it by the result. Familiarity with the past can supply some of those defects. It can provide a standard of comparison. It can point to a known issue. By so doing, it can chasten our parochial arrogance.

Of course, to speak thus is to speak in generalities. To define is more difficult. Perhaps we can best define by opposition. In order to discover the advantages of studying history, we may consider the dangers of neglecting history. For both nations and individuals have sometimes made a virtue of neglecting history; and history has taken its revenge on them.

One instance of such historical revenge is the rise of nationalism in the nineteenth century. In many ways nationalism is the revolt of historically minded peoples against rulers who have thought in non-historical terms. In eighteenth-century Europe most enlightened men were cosmopolitan, international. They looked back at history and saw a 'gothic' past from which they had emerged into the full light and freedom of the present; and they regarded 'patriotism', national loyalty, national pride, as a vulgar relic of tribalism. How condescendingly the 'enlightened' French Encyclopaedists looked at the literature of the past, of which one of them, D'Alembert, would have made a periodic bonfire! How contemptuously they dismissed the atavistic, irrational complaints of the bigoted, unenlightened Poles who squealed and squirmed in a most undignified fashion when their country was carved up and absorbed by the Enlightened Despots of Prussia, Russia and Austria! How impatiently, a generation later, the Bonapartist *afrancesados* of Spain looked down on the obscurantist bigots who resisted their rational reforms! But this triumph of Reason did not last. In the next century the nations revolted; and their revolt was nourished, everywhere, by history. It was the 'historic nations', the nations which were conscious of their history – the Poles, Italians, Germans – which led the revolt; and all the nations in revolt began by discovering, or inventing, their history. No doubt the history which they discovered was not very good: the cosmopolitan historians of the eighteenth century were probably better as historians; but there was a large area of history which those historians had dangerously ignored and which now took its revenge.

....

When people ask me whether historians should not be able, ideally, to prophesy the future, I ask them a simple question. Let them place themselves at any date in past history and say honestly whether any man could rationally have prophesied the course of the next fifty years. In 1900? Who could conceivably have forecast the convulsions of Europe or foreseen the total dissolution of the recently united German Reich? In 1950? Who would have supposed that America, the liberator of Europe, with its inherited cult of isolation and its public hatred of imperialism, would become the very type of imperialist power, fighting a long and bitter war in the Far East, and that a Democratic President would be denounced in Asia, however unjustly, as 'the new Hitler'? I do not believe that any such prophecy would have been possible. If it had been made, it would have been not scientific but an inspired guess.

On the other hand conditional prophecy is always possible, if the conditions are clearly understood, and the more we study history, and the more scientific its content becomes, and the more we respect its limits, the better we can prophesy. Jacob Burckhardt's prophecy, in the 1870s and 1880s, that the old monarchies would be pushed aside and a new race of *Gewaltmenschen* would rule as terrible dictators, beginning perhaps in Germany, was a rational, limited prophecy based on historical understanding: he saw that the new industrial power, if it became political, would be quite different from the old, and that it was most likely to take root where industry was heaviest and old 'liberal' forms weakest.[1] Similarly Sir Halford Mackinder's prophecy, before the first World War, that the struggle for mastery in the world would centre on Eastern Europe and that Tsarist Russia would be the great power of the future, was not invalidated by the total ruin of Tsarist Russia, first in war, then in revolution.[2] Nor would it have been invalidated if Hitler had won his war. The essential condition was the control of the 'Heartland'. In fact, it was for that Heartland that Hitler and Stalin fought, and it was an ideological war, fought to the death, because both belligerents know that the winner, whichever he was, would be the arbiter of Europe.

There are numerous such conditional laws of history: empirical rules which can be taken from a wide range of historical experience. Any of them may be applicable to the present, none of them provides a certain formula for the present. For one safe rule of history is that historical situations never exactly repeat themselves: there are too many variable ingredients in each situation for identical recurrence. Even if they should do so, the mere fact of repetition is a new ingredient which may alter the mixture.

I have often been asked, in the last twenty years, whether I could forecast an effective revival of nazism in Germany. I have always answered, no; because I have never believed that the old doctrines could revive in the old form. They might survive, as a kind of dead deposit, in ageing minds. Elements of them would recur, here and there, in new situations: for some of the elements are permanent features of German history, and some are predictable responses to recurrent social pressures. But the fusion of all these elements in a particular dynamic pattern was caused, in the past, by the particular unrepeatable experience of one generation, and even if all the same circumstances should recur, in the same order (which is inconceivable) the emotional content would not be communicable, unchanged, to another generation: for the identical pattern of pressures and the same intellectual climate would not recur. For this reason, the new fascism, when it occurs, will occur with radical differences. Indeed, with such differences, it has already occurred. The arrogant cult of youth, the nihilism, the intolerance of dissent, the rejection of rational argument, the deliberate invocation of force to justify counter-force – all these have recently been resumed. But they have been resumed in classes and circumstances very different from those of the 1920s and 1930s; and although a knowledge of the original fascism may help us to understand the new phenomenon, the precise form in which they have been resumed could not, I think, have been predicted.

....

Once, in 1950, I had a provocative experience. I was at a Congress in Berlin. It was the time of the outbreak of the Korean War, and feelings in that vulnerable, isolated city, were running high. The Congress was run by the American C.I.A. As I sat there, one distinguished speaker after another rose to speak. All of them were Marxist social scientists in their original intellectual formation, though by now they had put their convictions into reverse. They now declared that communist society and western society were immutable models, absolutely incompatible with each other, and that one must destroy the other: there was no alternative. Therefore, he who was not for us was necessarily against us in the holy war. As I listened to those remorseless speeches, historical analogies coursed through my head, and I saw, in past history, a very different lesson. I saw a succession of supposedly incompatible forms of society, sometimes indeed engaged in mutually destructive crusades, but sometimes also, behind their heavily fortified frontiers, competing with each other in less violent manner:

out-manoeuvring each other, borrowing from each other, learning from each other, changing by contact with each other, until, with a change of generations, the crusading spirit (which was the product of a particular conjuncture) had evaporated, and the crusade itself, having been happily avoided, now seemed unnecessary. In order to expound my theme, I made several attempts to catch the chairman's eye, but somehow my attempts were never noticed; so I came home and wrote a short historical article which today, I hope, reads slightly better than those crusading speeches. It was an article on the co-existence of Christendom and the Turkish Empire;[3] but it could equally have been on other such ideological confrontations.

I believe that there are at least two golden rules which Macaulay himself would sometimes have been well advised to follow.

First, we must not force the pace of history or seek to extract from it more precise lessons than it will yield. The very value of history lies in its general lessons, its complexity, its suggestions and analogies, and the highly conditional nature of its parallels, not in concrete lessons or dogmatic conclusions. I know that people want such conclusions, and when historians will not give them such conclusions, they sometimes, in their disappointment, turn aside to the more positive (but not necessarily more helpful) assurances of the social scientists. But I insist that such precise conclusions are not warrantable, or valuable. All the greatest historians have refused to produce them, and those who have complied with the public demand by producing them, are quickly out of date. The great historians – Thucydides, Gibbon, Ranke – do not press an interpretation. The concessions that they make to the public are in form only: in style, in lucidity, in readability. They do not spell out crude lessons which can be neatly tabulated for busy readers by obliging epitomists. Therefore they are not always popular with those hasty students who wish to have their historical philosophy served up to them in a nutshell. The philosophy of the greatest historians cannot be quickly summarized. It is not crude. It is subtle; and in a long work it must be allowed gradually to emerge.

Secondly, we must, I believe, respect the independence of the past. All of us, living in our own time, tend to see the past on our own terms. We like to recognize, in past centuries, familiar problems, familiar faces: to see men looking towards us, not away from us. But this tendency, though natural, contains great dangers. It is right, I believe, to look for lessons in the past, to see its relevance to our own time, to observe the signs of continuity, connection and process. The past is not to be studied for its own sake. That is mere antiquarianism. But it is anachronistic, distorting, to judge the past as if it were subject to the present, as if the men of the eighteenth or the sixteenth or the tenth century had no right to be independent of the twentieth. We exist in and for our own time: why should we judge our predecessors as if they were less self-sufficient: as if they existed for us and should be judged by us? Every age has its own social context, its own intellectual climate, and takes it for granted, as we take ours. Because it was taken for granted, it is not explicitly expressed in the documents of the time: it has to be deduced and reconstructed. It also deserves respect. This is what the greatest of nineteenth-century historians, Leopold von Ranke, meant when he wrote that every age was 'immediate to God', and implicitly blamed Macaulay for arraigning past ages before the tribunal of the present – the brief present of the mid-nineteenth century, which has now passed and may seem to us, in retrospect, a very partial tribunal.[4] To discern the intellectual climate of the past is one of the most difficult tasks of the historian, but it is also one of the most necessary. To neglect it – to use terms like 'rational', 'superstitious', 'progressive', 'reactionary', as if only that was rational which obeyed our rules of reason, only that progressive which pointed to us – is worse than wrong: it is vulgar.

Finally, in studying history, I believe that while we must always appreciate its extent and variety, we must always study one part of it in detail. To study on too narrow a front deprives us of the chance of analogy; but to study too generally is not study at all. We cannot penetrate below the surface all the time, or we shall never come up for air, never rise above the subject to survey and compare. But if we do not, at some point, penetrate below the surface, we shall fall into the opposite error. We shall be obliged to take all our evidence at second-hand and shall end by believing, without testing, the fashionable orthodoxy of our time or place. Every age has its orthodoxy and no orthodoxy is ever right. It is changed, in due course, by those who approach the subject, whatever it is, with a certain humility and, above all, independence of mind. But those intellectual gifts need material on which to work, and that material, in history, must be raw material. In other words, the historian is amphibious: he must live some part of his time below the surface in order that, on emerging, he can usefully survey it from above. The historian who has specialized all his life may end as an antiquarian. The historian who has never specialized at all will end as a mere blower of froth. The antiquarian at least is useful to others.

I would have all historians specialize, for however short a space, on some part of their own history – for there they are at home: they can read the sources in their own language. This will prevent them from too easy generalization by showing upon what uncertain and controversial foundations received opinions are often based. But having done this, I would have them read the history of other countries, knowing that they will then do so with a double advantage. From their specialist study of their own history they will know how to reserve judgment on general history where they have not penetrated so deeply; and from their general study of foreign history, thus qualified, they will learn that comparative method which will prevent them from too readily accepting one formula of historical causation: from assuming (for instance) that parliamentary democracy, or trades unions, or liberal catchwords, or any catchwords, are the only way of salvation. By this double process they may make the study of the past not only interesting but useful. It will not prove to be a science. It will produce no ready-made answers. It will not enable them to prophesy. But it will enlarge their views. It may bring independence of judgment. And so it may enable them to understand, and by understanding to improve, the present.

Notes

1 See Jacob Burckhardt, *Briefe*, Leipzig, 1935, esp. pp. 348–9, 355–6, 484–7.
2 Halford Mackinder, *Democratic Ideas and Reality*, Constable, 1919.
3 Hugh Trevor-Roper, 'A case of co-existence: Christendom and the Turks', in his *Historical Essays*, Macmillan, 1957, pp. 173–8.
4 Ranke's implied criticism of Macaulay appears in his *History of England*, English trans., Oxford University Press, 1875, vol. 4, p. 364.

27. Alan Bullock

[from 'Has History ceased to be relevant?', The Historian 43 (1994), pp. 16–19]

There has been much debate in my lifetime about the question whether or not history in its traditional form – narrative, political history, history from above – has ceased to be relevant and should be replaced by a new model: social and economic history, history from below, closely allied to the social sciences, economics, sociology and anthropology. I shall return to this debate later, but the question I want to ask is more fundamental: whether any form of historical study has a future, whether the past itself has not ceased to be relevant.

There are many people – perhaps a majority – who would say not only that this has happened, but that it is to be welcomed or at least accepted as inevitable. There are at least three obvious reasons for taking such a view.

The first is the continuous and constantly accelerating pace of change. Between 1500 and 1800, that is, between the Renaissance and the French Revolution, change in the conditions of human life was sufficiently slow as to be easily assimilated and the continuity between past and present to be obvious and taken for granted. This is no longer the case. The distance that separates the present from the past – not just from 1800 or even 1900, but from the world of the 1950s and 1960s – is immense and constantly increasing.

The second is because this extraordinary acceleration of the rate of change has been accompanied by an equally dramatic increase in scale. The population of the world increased threefold between the birth of Christ (say, 250 million) and 1800 (say, 750 million). In 1825 when the Reverend Thomas Malthus (now restored to fame) was making the final revision of his *Essay on Population*, the figure had reached one billion. In the following 100 years the world's population doubled to two billion, in the following half century (1925–1975) doubled again to four, and in the following quarter century, i.e. by the year

2000, is calculated to pass the six billion mark. This is a change not of degree but of kind. One illustration will make clear what I mean. As late as 1800 the great majority of the world's population lived in villages or small towns. Only two cities, Canton and London, are believed to have had a population of more than a million. Today there are 134 cities with a population of one million; seven of them with a population of ten millions, another nine with six millions.

The third reason is that those who have to foresee and deal with the problems of the future towards which we are rushing at accelerated speed, have become convinced that they must rely on the unique success of scientific discovery and technological innovation in comparison with all other human activities, and that it is a waste of time to look for answers in the past. In a civilization increasingly oriented towards the future, a knowledge of history, along with literature and the arts, may be valued for its own sake or, in Francis Bacon's stinging phrase, as an 'ornament of discourse', but history is unlikely to be seen as having anything to contribute to the serious business of life.

The case for history's relevance

Is there anything to be said on the other side? Let me begin with the peoples of Eastern Europe from Poland, Slovakia and Yugoslavia to Rumania, the Ukraine and the Caucasus, Georgia, Azerbaijan and Armenia. Their historic identities were a major source of strength in maintaining their resistance to the Communist process of homogenization. But, with the Communist pressure removed, the same historic identities and the conflicting claims to territory which are part of them have become the greatest obstacle to their ever achieving peace and stability. True, in many cases, these conflicts are being manipulated by former Communist bosses, and the claims are often based on historical myths or highly selected versions of history. But this does not alter the fact that throughout Eastern Europe the most intractable element, an ever-present threat even where it has not yet led to open hostilities, is the past.

Turn to the countries of Western Europe. The logic of geography and economics points to the creation of some form of closer association, and will in the end, I hope, bring it about. A major obstacle, however, standing in its way and holding us back, is again the past. The same is true of the Middle East – what has to be overcome is the past in the shape of the conflicting claims of Israelis and Arabs, the conflicts and distrust between rival Moslem powers following the break up of the Ottoman empire. The same is true of many parts of Africa, and nearer home in Northern Ireland and Quebec.

Let me make clear that this is not an argument in favour of historical determinism: the future, as always, remains unpredictable. Who would ever have predicted that the two nations which suffered such overwhelming defeat in World War II, the Germans and the Japanese, would, in the 45 years after the war, have achieved a greater measure of economic success and political stability than any other people? Who would have dared to predict that the Soviet Union, far from coming to the rescue of its satellite regimes in Eastern Europe, would abandon the whole of its sphere of influence occupied after the war and withdraw its massive forces without a shot being fired; and, most startling of all, that the peoples of South Africa, and the Israelis and Palestinians would make their present bold attempt to break with the past? But the past, however much we may rebel against and seek to repudiate it, is not easily exorcised. The history of this century provides two striking examples of attempts to do just that, to abolish the past and make a new start.

The first was the Bolshevik Revolution of 1917 in Russia, the second the Communist revolution in China culminating in the establishment of the People's Republic of 1949. Each was made at an incalculable cost in human suffering, not only in the initial seizure of power, and civil war, but in the second revolutions – Stalin's collectivization of agriculture and purges in the 1930s, Mao's Cultural Revolution and purges in the 1960s. The Communist leaders had foreseen that there would be resistance to the changes they sought to impose on the Russian and Chinese peoples. They had made up their minds to use the most ruthless means to suppress it and to make the break with the past decisive. But the result was the opposite of what they wanted. Instead of liberating the masses and energizing them to create a new world, they cowed and alienated them. The methods they used had no less destructive an effect on the Communist leadership itself, corrupting and distorting the revolution to a degree from which neither party was able to free itself. Far from abolishing the past, an ostensibly revolutionary regime – in practice, highly conservative – added an additional layer of history which made the task of adapting to change much more difficult.

In the reform period, the 1980s, when I first visited China, President Li Xiannian (like Deng Xiao Ping, a veteran of Mao's Long March) told a group of us in private conversation that the mistake they had made was 'working against the grain of Chinese history'. In future, he added, they would work with it. In the ten years since, however, this is precisely what the Chinese Communist leadership, more and more isolated from the Chinese people, has shown itself incapable of doing – in contrast to the pragmatic and dynamic development of a potential rival alternative, the free enterprise version of the Chinese future in the southern province of Guangdong.

The point I am making is not limited to revolutions carried out in the name of a left-wing ideology. It can be illustrated equally well from the case of Iran, where the Shah and his advisers, bent upon the modernization of the country in a single generation, ignored the strength of the Islamic traditions of Iran's past and were destroyed by the head-on collision that resulted, fastening the hold of the past more firmly than ever on the Iranian people.

The assimilation of change

Do not misunderstand me. I am not seeking to use the past as an argument against change or in favour of the status quo. On the contrary, I believe that change has to come, but that we need to recognize that it will create resistance and instead of determining to crush this, seek to understand first why this should be so, and then look for ways of making the assimilation of change easier.

Men and women, the individuals who are called upon to adapt themselves to change, are born into societies each of which derives its identity from its past – for example in the language its members learn to speak. Language, the fundamental human faculty of communication, deeply rooted in the history of the particular group who inherit it, is an example of constant adaptation to new needs – you have only to think of the way in which the Anglo-Saxon spoken in pre-Norman days evolved into the English which has become the international language of today.

Nineteenth-century Japan provides another striking example of what I mean. The most successful revolution of modern times I believe to be the drastic changes that converted Japan between 1868 and 1900 from an isolated, feudal society into the first Asian nation capable of meeting Western countries on equal terms, whether in war, industry or trade. It was deliberately disguised, however, to appear not as a revolution – which it most certainly was – but as a restoration, the restoration of the Emperor's powers which had been delegated to the powerful feudal family of the Tokugawa as Shoguns (Mayors of the Palace) since the early seventeenth century. The restoration was a fiction, but it was one that enabled the reformers to avoid repudiating the past and to combine the changes they introduced with some of the most important traditions they had inherited from pre-modern Japan. Thus by the end of the nineteenth century the Japanese had effectively carried out the modernization of one of the most remote and feudal societies in the world, a process which the Chinese have been struggling to accomplish since 1911 and which the peoples of the Soviet Union are having to begin all over again.

A third example, of a different kind, is Spain, especially interesting for us today because it suffered from a bitter civil war in 1936–39. When Franco died there was a natural anxiety lest quarrels and hatreds might flare up again. Happily, Spain avoided this by restoring the monarchy in place of the former fascist regime, with a king who had learned a great deal from the past and so was able to provide the guarantee of stability which made possible the peaceful election of a social democratic government – an outcome no one had foreseen.

'The sense of the otherwise'

I have been writing so far about the past as a constraint upon change. But the past can also be seen as one of the sources of man's freedom.

Here I come to a paradox. I have argued that, if you want to predict the future you are forced to take the past into account. But it is also the study of history – the study of what happened to past predictions which provides overwhelming evidence that the future cannot be foretold with confidence.

I hazard a guess that the future will continue to be marked by the same ill-assorted, illogical mixture of predictable elements (survivors from the past or, in the case of technology, extrapolations from it) and the unpredictable. It is this incongruous combination of the two, of continuity and change, which produces an overall result that no one expects.

Most of us, I suspect, find it difficult to think of the future except as a con-tinuation of the present – or at least as an extrapolation of developments already visible. By reminding us how different the present has turned out to be from what was expected – even a generation ago – a sense of the past can break the tyranny of the present and thereby help to develop 'a sense of the other-wise' (Daniel Boorstin's phrase), of how different the course of history might have been. This stimulates the imagination to conceive of a future which may be as different from the present as the present is from the past.

This is a faculty which can be made to serve very different purposes. An obvious example in our time has been the use the Communists made, in stak-ing out a unique claim to shape the future, of the Marxist version of history, leading inevitably – 'History on our side', that was the claim – to the triumph of revolutionary socialism in the industrialized world and of the Marxist-led liberation movements in the Third World. If the future is not to be discovered but created, we need to recognize the power of such historical myths in help-ing to project a picture of the future which will rouse the enthusiasm or anger of the masses and sustain the faith or fanaticism of the elite. As the American historian Carl Becker put it: 'The past is a kind of screen upon which each generation projects its vision of the future'.

Culture and continuity

Let me now extend my argument to a cultural context. The Harvard socio-logist Daniel Bell has defined human culture as a construction by men, whether conscious or not, to maintain continuity, to express their sense of a continuing humanity through their shared experience, defying individual mortality and bridging generations by means of myth, symbols, art and ritual. Any culture that loses the power to grow and to add to itself, becoming wholly oriented toward the past, soon dies. But I suggest it is equally true that any culture that dissociates itself from the past and has only the shallow soil of the present from which to draw nourishment will soon wither too.

Fortunately, the past has ways of re-establishing continuity. The Modern Movement in the Arts and Literature which flourished between the 1890s and the Second World War provides a striking example. This was one of the great episodes in the cultural history of the West, a remarkable burst of creativity in which Picasso and Matisse, Kandinsky and Klee, Frank Lloyd Wright and Le Corbusier, Stravinsky and Schönberg, Proust and Joyce, Kafka and Strindberg, Freud and Wittgenstein and their contemporaries transformed our ways of looking at the world and ourselves. So rich and tumultuous a period of innovation cannot be captured in any formula or generalization – except one. Whereas earlier movements – movements such as the Renaissance and the Romantic Movement had turned for inspiration to the past – even if it was a past which they themselves created – the Modern Movement either consciously turned its back on the past or ignored it.

And what has happened? The Modern Movement in its turn has itself become a part of history. The past has flowed round and absorbed it, elevating its most radical innovators to the status of classics. What was heralded as an irreparable break with cultural traditions of the West is now seen as an extension and enlargement of it. How can the past become irrelevant when it is constantly renewed and extended in this way by the absorption of yesterday's futures, and the future itself remains as elusive as ever, always receding and only capable of definition when it becomes part of the past? If one wants to know what is to be the future of history, one may well begin by studying the history of past futures.

The barrier of uniqueness

Let me underline what I have already said, that a culture or society oriented towards the past and refusing to look for and identify the new elements of experience in the future will first stagnate and then disintegrate. But a culture or society that turns its back on the past falls into a cultural and historical amnesia which weakens its sense of identity. For collectively as well as individually, our sense of our own identity is bound up with *memory*.

More than that, a culture or society that turns its back on the past also cuts itself off from the most obvious source of values, and this is true, once again, of societies as well as individuals. If you are not going to seek the source of values in divine authority, what other source is there than human experience? But why limit this to our own? Of course, values based upon past experience have to be tested against and modified in the light of the new experience of each generation. But to ignore or throw them overboard, so that each generation starts again from scratch, in the belief that no other has ever faced similar questions, and that nothing is to be learned from them, appears not only a form of arrogance but a wilful act of self-mutilation.

The stumbling block to accepting this is the belief that *our* experience is unique, and that we confront unique difficulties. Of course, this is true. But we are not unique in feeling this, in feeling that *we* are unique. It has certainly been felt by many preceding generations in the past 200 years, from the time of the French Revolution and the start of industrialization, when the rate of change began to quicken. In 1789, in 1848, the year of revolutions, in 1851, the year of the first Great Exhibition in London, in 1900–1901, with the birth of the twentieth century, at the time of the Russian Revolution of 1917, at the end of the First World War, at the end of the Second, people have expressed with fervent conviction the belief – sometimes in an optimistic, sometimes in a pessimistic mood, sometimes in both at the same time – that they were entering a new era. And they were right: it *was* a new era at the time, the impact of the new appeared to wipe out the past and to disrupt continuity. But, looking back, one can see that in each generation there is always the same incongruous mixture of the new and the old. The mixture is never the same; history does not repeat itself; the new *is* new. But the old persists alongside it and in time the new is grafted on to the old and continuity with the past – continuity, not identity – is not disrupted but restored.

The German dramatist, Berthold Brecht, put it in half a dozen lines:

New Ages don't begin all at once.
My grandfather lived in the new age.
My grandson will still live in the old.
New meat is eaten with old forks . . .
From the new antennae come the old stupidities.
Wisdom is passed from mouth to mouth.

I have always remembered another quotation, from the American critic Harry Levin: 'No form of provinciality is more confining than ignorance of other times than our own; no intellectual exercise can be more liberating than the attempt to look before and after the limits of contemporaneity'. It is surely a remarkable fact that, thanks to the continuity of human experience, we can reach back across the centuries to understand and enter into the thoughts and feelings of a Plato, a Euripides or Aristophanes, an Augustine or Erasmus, Shakespeare or Goethe – or when the historian can recover for us the thoughts and feelings of ordinary men and women in their everyday lives.

I know of no more telling example of the latter than the study by the French historian Le Roy Ladurie of one particular French mountain village, Montaillou, in the Pyrenees, in the period 1294–1324. It was a small community of no more than 250 persons of no special interest if it had not been the subject of an extraordinarily detailed inquisition by Jacques Fournier, the Bishop of Pamiers and later one of the Avignon popes. Fournier conducted his investigation with a remorseless and inexhaustible interest, not only into heresy, with which the village was riddled, but into every detail of the lives, customs, relationships and beliefs of these men and women. Their depositions and replies over no less than 370 days of interrogation, recorded verbatim and now recovered from the Vatican archives, provide a vivid and penetrating insight into what it was like to live in France and be a heretic 650 years ago. Le Roy Ladurie's study, in my view, represents a form of knowledge that illuminates and complements any number of generalizations about French medieval history. Equally interesting for my argument is the fact that in the year it was published, it became the best-selling book in France, outselling novels and biographies as well as other history books and immediately acquiring the status of a classic.

How is this understanding possible, in face of all the great changes that have taken place between the material circumstances in which they lived and those of the world of the late twentieth century? The answer, I believe, is this: it is because the existential questions – what is the meaning of life, how one meets death, what, if anything lies beyond it, how one accounts for evil and suffering, what words like justice, law, obligation, equality and freedom mean, how we are to interpret our feelings of love and sympathy, how we are to live with our divided nature and its contradictory impulses – these questions are both universal and recurrent, confronting individuals and societies across the ages.

As Daniel Bell puts it:

> The answers vary – and this is the *history* of human culture, the variations in myth, philosophy, symbols, and styles. But the questions always recur, and it is this that makes it possible for different cultures to understand each other because they arise in response to the common human predicament.

I do not say that if you turn to the past you will necessarily find answers to these questions – any answers, in my view, have always to be taken as an act of faith, acting 'as if' they are true – but you will certainly find a range of experience and richness of speculation far beyond anything a single human being or even a single generation can achieve in the short time they are alive. For my part, to be shut out from such intercourse with the past, from the world of antiquity to that of the earlier years of the twentieth century, would be to reduce myself to that 'one-dimensional man' of whom we so often hear, to foreshorten the historical perspective in which my own life is lived. To me the knowledge that men and women like myself, with whom I can recognize a common humanity across the gap of years, have been here before me, the crises and fears they faced and somehow mastered, the courage they managed to find in face of loneliness and disaster, the fear and even the fact of seeing their world collapse – this is a source of encouragement to me, nourishing my confidence that if they could get through, so perhaps can I, and that the future is always open, never predetermined, and that we can have a part in shaping it.

Part Five

History as Social Science

New questions, new concepts

Over the twentieth century the writing of history has owed more to the influence of the social sciences than to any other discipline. If only a minority of historians now work on institutional politics, this is because their sense of the significant questions in history has been transformed by the concerns of economists, sociologists and political scientists. There had been periodic calls for this enlargement of scope since the beginning of the century (notably from the early protagonists of the *Annales* School in the 1930s). Richard Hofstadter's essay, written in the 1950s, articulated a major shift in American historiography, with economics, sociology and demography assuming a higher profile over the next two decades. Hofstadter's acknowledgement of the conceptual richness of the social sciences was all the more telling since his own best-known work was in the field of intellectual history (notably *The Progressive Historians*, 1968).

Philip Abrams produced distinguished work in both history and sociology. His book *Historical Sociology* (1982) was intended primarily to convince his colleagues in sociology of the necessity of a historical approach, on the grounds that only work in a time perspective could illumine the relationship between human agency and social structure. But equally, he believed that historians stood in need of a theoretical approach to structure if they were to avoid exaggerating the scope of agency and piling up atmospheric detail. History must, according to this prescription, draw closer to sociology.

28. Richard Hofstadter

[from 'History and the social sciences' (1956), in Fritz Stern (ed.), Varieties of History, *2nd edn, Macmillan, 1970, pp. 359–68]*

The professional academic historian suffers in these times from a persistent uncertainty about precisely what he is. Two traditions govern his training and his work. On one side there is the familiar historical narrative, a form of literature for which there is always much demand. On the other is the historical monograph, ideally supposed to approximate a scientific inquiry, which the historian is professionally trained to write. Authors of narrative histories rarely hesitate to retell a story that is already substantially known, adding perhaps some new information but seldom in a systematic fashion or with a clear analytical purpose. Authors of monographs, on the other hand, take it upon themselves to add new information to the fund of knowledge, or to analyze in a new way the meaning of a given sequence of historical events. Many historians, especially the great ones, have combined in single works both sides of this dual tradition, but in the profession as a whole the double function of the historian has been an important cause of the uncertain value of much historical writing. Many a historian feels that it is unsatisfactory merely to repeat with minor modifications what we already know of the past; but many a monograph, though intended to overcome this limitation, leaves its readers, and perhaps even its author, with misgivings as to whether that part of it which is new is truly significant.

This duality is reinforced by the demands made upon the historian. Society and special interests in society call upon him to provide them with memory. The kind of memory that is too often desired is not very different from what we all provide for ourselves – that is, memory that knows how to forget, memory that will rearrange, distort, and omit so much as is needed to make our historical self-images agreeable. In a liberal society the historian is free to try to dissociate myths from reality, but that same impulse to myth-making that moves his fellow men is also at work in him. Society has another, more instrumental task for the historian: to analyze its experience in such a way as to put into its hands workable tools for the performance of certain tasks. In this spirit the military services ask historians to compile the records of previous wars in the hope that such information will be useful in future wars. In the same spirit the Japanese government called upon Charles A. Beard to help with the problems arising out of the Tokyo earthquake of 1923, and wired him: 'Bring your knowledge of disaster'.

Both advantages and disadvantages arise from this duality of tradition and of function. They bring certain confusions to the historian's role: understandably he may wonder whether he is a writer or a technician, a scientist or a prophet. But there are compensations. The same ambiguities that present him with his problems of method and even of identity give him an opportunity to have valuable interchanges with many kinds of intellectual and practical activity, with politics and public affairs, with journalism and mass media, with literature and criticism, with science, philosophy, and art, and with the social sciences.

I speak of the historian as having contacts with the social sciences rather than as being a social scientist for reasons which I hope to make clear. Although each of the disciplines that study human culture has characteristics that in one way or another set it off from the rest, history is in a still further degree set off from the others by its special constellation of problems, methods, limitations, and possibilities. But the historian's contact with the social sciences is clearly of more importance to the present generation of historians than it has been at any time in the past. Perhaps this closer relationship is in some part attributable to a more receptive frame of mind among historians to inter-disciplinary work; it is more largely due to the fact that in the past quarter century the achievements of the social sciences have been impressive. My interest here is not in the ultimate nature of history or the social sciences or the relations between them, but in the progress of inter-disciplinary work, which I should like to illustrate by reference to some of my own intellectual experiences. What I hope to do, then, is not to deal with philosophical issues but in some measure to clarify an attitude which is becoming fairly widespread among contemporary historians.

Despite what is surely no more than a fragmentary and random acquaintance with the literature of the social sciences, I have found that my interest and gratification in my own discipline have been enormously intensified by what I have been able to take for it from the other disciplines. That I am unable to systematize or formalize what it is that I owe, as a historian, to the social sciences I find puzzling. But I feel sure that in a general way what the social sciences have helped to do is to suggest a new resolution – not a solution, for such problems are never solved – to the problems created by the duality of the historian's role. In brief what they offer him is a host of new insights and new creative possibilities.

When I was first attracted to history as a vocation, it was by a two-fold interest: I was attracted both by what might be called orthodox political history and also by the history of ideas. At first these two seemed parallel rather than converging. Not only did I not have a very clear idea of how the two might be put together, but I had little interest in doing so. As time went on I realized that what I most wanted to write about were things marginal to both political historians and to practitioners of the history of ideas who stem, say, from the severe tradition in which Arthur O. Lovejoy has done such impressive work. My interests lay between the two fields, at the intersection of their perimeters.

I belong to the generation that came of age during the middle thirties. This was a period, of course, of tremendous conflict on a world scale and of intense and lively controversy in American domestic politics. A battle of ideologies roughly similar to that which took place in a world-wide theatre of action could be seen at home as well. For many of us an interest in studying the formation and development of ideologies was a natural intellectual response to the conflict raging around us. But to a detached observer these ideologies were far more interesting for their extraordinary appeal to various types of individuals than they were for their rational or philosophic content. I found myself, therefore, becoming interested in individual and social character types, in social mythologies and styles of thought as they reveal and affect character, and in politics as a sphere of behavior into which personal and private motives are projected.

....

It is here that the social sciences may become particularly valuable to any historian who shares these concerns. The monograph has been unsatisfactory, most commonly as literature but often even in the very analytical functions it was designed to perform. The narrative, while it is sometimes good literature, has too often disappointed our desire for new understanding. What his use of the social sciences promises to the historian is a special kind of opportunity to join these two parts of his tradition in a more effective way. That the social sciences, with their striking methodological self-consciousness, should have something to contribute to the analytical dimension of the historian's work will not surprise us. But our attention may well be arrested by the likelihood that the literary possibilities of his work will also be enhanced, that the monograph, without in the least losing its analytical quality, may take on more of the literary significance that was previously preeminent in the historical narrative. The monograph, in short, may yet cease to be a poor imitation of science and may flourish as a kind of exploratory essay which will be a fuller consummation of the mind and spirit of the historian. We may well ask how this could be possible; how the social sciences, whose characteristic practitioners have not usually aspired to distinguish themselves through literary expression, should be able to help to quicken history as a literary art. The answer, I believe, lies largely in this: that it is the achievement of those forms of literature that are most like history that they deal significantly with the problems of human character. History too aspires to deal under-standingly with character, and the means for the formal understanding of character have grown enormously in the past half century. Perhaps the most important function which the social sciences can perform for the historian is that they provide means, in some cases indispensable means, by which he can be brought into working relationship with certain aspects of the modern intel-lectual climate. They bring to him a fresh store of ideas with which to disturb the excessively settled routines of his thought; but they also serve a catalytic function for him: they show him how he may adapt for his own purposes certain modern insights into human behavior and character which he cannot, on his own, immediately and directly appropriate.

The next generation may see the development of a somewhat new histor-ical genre, which will be a mixture of traditional history and the social sciences. It will differ from the narrative history of the past in that its primary purpose will be analytical. It will differ from the typical historical monograph of the past in that it will be more consciously designed as a literary form and will focus on types of problems that the monograph has all too often failed to raise. It will be informed by the insights of the social sciences and at some points will make use of methods they have originated. Without pretending to be scientific, it may well command more reciprocal interest and provide more stimulation for social scientists than a great deal of the history that is now being written. In this genre the work of the historian can best be described as a sort of literary anthropology. His aim will be a kind of portraiture of the life of nations and individuals, classes and groups of men; his approach to every system of culture and sub-culture will be that sympathetic and yet some-what alien and detached appreciation of basic emotional commitments that anthropologists bring to simpler peoples.

Most discussions of inter-disciplinary work with which I am familiar begin with the assumption that its value rests chiefly upon the exchange or cross-fertilization of methods. For the historian this means that he can acquire new methods with which to tackle his old problems. There are indubitable advantages for the historian in such techniques as panel studies, career-line analysis, content analysis, the comparative method, more sophisticated sampling, an increased use, where it is possible and appropriate, of measurement – all of them methods in which the social sciences have gone far ahead of him.

But to me it is not the formal methods of the social sciences, useful as they may be, that are of central significance, but rather their substantive findings, their intellectual concerns, and their professional perspectives. Taken in this way, their value paradoxically rests not in their ability to bring new methods to bear upon old problems but in their ability to open new problems which the historian has usually ignored. Prompted by the social sciences, the historian begins to realize that matters of central concern to other disciplines force him to enlarge his conception of his task. Questions associated with social status, social mobility, differences and conflicts between generations, child-rearing in its relation to culture, the sociology of knowledge and of the professions, are questions which he might properly take upon himself, and which are interwoven with his traditional concerns. It seems inevitable, too, that some of the discoveries made by modern social research about current mass political behavior and political influence will revise some of the historian's assumptions about political behavior in the past. In short, the other disciplines ask questions about society which the historian has not commonly asked, and collect data which have a bearing, at least by inference and analogy, upon his problems. Even though the historian cannot always answer these questions with the evidence available to him they remain significant for his work.

But it is not necessarily a scientific use that the historian makes of his conceptual borrowings. I have never thought, when approaching a historical problem from a perspective which I imagine to be rather like that of a sociologist or of an anthropologist, that I would therefore be able to answer my questions with greater definiteness and rigor. For me the fundamental value of these perspectives is in their addition to the speculative richness of history. The more the historian learns from the social sciences, the more variables he is likely to take account of, the more complex his task becomes. The result may be that his conclusions become more tenuous and tentative, but this is a result to be welcomed. The closer the historian comes, with whatever aids, to the full texture of historical reality, the more deeply is he engulfed in a complex web of relationships which he can hope to understand only in a limited and partial way. While he may acquire some usable methods from the social sciences, I doubt that the new techniques that he may acquire will outweigh the new problems that he will take on. His task has not been simplified; it has been enlarged. His work has not greater certainty, but greater range and depth.

Thus far I have spoken only about the value of the social sciences for the historian. While I should prefer to hear a sociologist speak on the other side of this relationship, I would not be fair to my own discipline if I did not say that history has much to offer in return. It is one of the characteristics of our present-minded and journalistically-minded culture that our sense of history is very thin. Oddly enough, while our age pays considerable deference to historians, our capacity to use history to enlarge our understanding is not impressive. Contemporary discussion of mass culture, for instance, is often carried on as though no previous age had ever presented problems to specialized intelligence and cultivated sensibility; because the media of mass communications are new, it is assumed that the past can teach us nothing about the relationship of artists and intellectuals to the public. Historians themselves are by no means immune to the general failing of which this is an example; the failing is also widespread among social scientists, not least among social psychologists and sociologists who need history very much.

While it is the primary business of these disciplines to analyze the relations among special abstracted factors in cultural situations, it is the distinctive business of the historian to define the actual situations in which these factors come into play, and to set the problems of social inquiry in their temporal relations and as nearly in their totality as it is given to the human mind to be able to do. However impartial and imperfect the achievement of these objects, it is history's primary gift to the other cultural disciplines. The historian tries to remind his fellow inquirers that, in the words of Michelet, 'He who would confine his thoughts to present time will not understand present reality'.

Most inquiries in sociology or social psychology are of necessity planned in a flat time-dimension. The character of a social-psychological experiment, or of most of the fruitful empirical work that has recently been done in mass communications, political behavior, and market research, demands that this be so. But in the long run and when it deals with the large questions, inquiry into human affairs must be historical in character, for the real development of human affairs cannot be sliced out of time in order to appease our curiosity. The transhistorical generalizations that are made by other disciplines that seek for a general theory of action – that is, generalizations about human behavior of such applicability that they cover more than one historical situation or one culture – have an operational meaning that is different from historical generalizations, in the sense that the non-historical generalizations are not intended to shed light upon any historical events, but rather to answer questions about certain abstracted factors of behavior. Social scientists, concerned as they are with the dynamics of behavior, are like the engineers who can tell us about the dynamics of flight. Historians are concerned with such questions as why a particular scheduled flight has ended in a crash.

It is difficult to show in the abstract how history and the social sciences complement each other. But when we get away from abstract discussions of the character and methods of the disciplines to focus our attentions upon actual problems of common concern, their mutual interaction and their value to each other emerge unmistakably. Not long ago a small group of social scientists and historians met to discuss the resurgence over the past five or six years of extreme right-wing politics in this country. We began by talking about the movement in terms set by the study of *The Authoritarian Personality* by T.W. Adorno and his co-workers; but as we got deeper into the problem, one of the most interesting aspects of the discussion was the way in which we found ourselves moving quite spontaneously back and forth between social-psychological categories and historical events, because neither approach was for long entirely adequate. There was no need for the historians to take the initiative in pushing the line of argument into the historical frame of reference; for since we were analyzing a problem that had been posed, so to speak, by historical events themselves and were not trying to work out a general theory of behavior, the relevance and mutual helpfulness of both the historical and the social-psychological approaches were immediately apparent to everyone.

There are important and increasingly numerous links between history and the social sciences, but the two are also held apart by real differences. Some of these differences arise out of problems of communication or out of institutional arrangements. Others have intellectual substance and among these probably none is so important as a difference over the scientific ideal, by which I mean the belief that the closer social science gets to the methods of the natural sciences, the more perfect it becomes. The prominence of this commitment to science is expressed in our terminology, for when we grow dissatisfied with 'social sciences' we speak of 'policy sciences' or 'behavioral sciences' – retaining the noun as clear testimony to an enduring ideal.

For many historians the scientific ideal has been a moving faith, since the days when Buckle asserted that he hoped to follow the example of natural science in his *History of Civilization in England.* But in our own time the scientific ideal no longer has quite the same plausibility for historians as it did for their predecessors in the Darwinian age, or as it now has for their colleagues in the social sciences. Most historians continue to feel that they deal with events which, though in some sense comparable, are essentially unique; and that this differentiates history from most branches of natural science, as well as from those branches of social science in which statistical generalization prevails and even some statistical prediction is possible. Formidable criticisms have been written of the familiar distinction between the nomothetic sciences (which can make general laws about repeatable events) and the ideographic sciences (which seek to understand unique and nonrecurrent events). I am here more concerned with the prevalent state of mind among historians than with the substance of this philosophic issue; and such criticisms, however impressive as forays in logical analysis, do not succeed in spreading among historians the conviction that what historians do is in any very satisfactory sense of the term scientific; and, perhaps what is still more important, do not affect profoundly the way they go about their tasks.

Unlike the philosopher of history or the philosopher of science, the working historian is not nearly so much interested in whether history can, after all, be logically classed with the natural sciences as he is in how far his mode of procedure is in fact a scientific one or could be changed to resemble it. Certainly, in the broad sense that he operates from a basis in fact, aspires to make warrantable assertions, and works in a self-critical discipline, the historian can see that he has something in common with science. But if the term science has any special meaning, he sees equally important differences. Since in his work quantification plays so limited a role, and since he cannot conduct experiments, or, strictly speaking, make predictions, he naturally feels that the difference between his methods and results and those prevailing in most branches of the natural sciences are of central importance. I do not forget that there are branches of natural science which are themselves historical. Perhaps the most notable of these is evolutionary biology; and yet the experience of some nineteenth-century historians in modelling their conceptions upon this type of scientific work is not such as to inspire historians today to follow their example. If history falls short of science, it may help to classify history as a *Wissenschaft* – no word in English quite conveys this distinction – that is, as a learned discipline with a firm cognitive element, based upon verifiable facts and yielding valid knowledge.

29. Philip Abrams

[from Historical Sociology, *Cornell University Press, 1982, pp. ix–xv]*

The chapters in this book try to do two things. They argue that many of the most serious problems faced by sociologists need to be solved historically. And they suggest that many of the supposed differences between sociology and history as disciplines do not really stand in the way of such solutions. Taken as a whole they propose that there might be much to be gained by reconstituting history and sociology as historical sociology. I am not talking about the need to give historical work more 'social context', nor about the need to give sociological work more 'historical background', nor even about the desirability of each field of work being 'informed' by work in the other. What I have in mind is a more radical recasting of problems, a deeper and subtler modification of styles of analysis, a more open and thorough-going recognition of the extent to which in some fundamental respects the two disciplines are trying to do the same thing and are employing the same logic of explanation to do so. The argument rests on the claim that at the heart of both disciplines is a common project: a sustained, diverse attempt to deal with what I shall call the problematic of structuring.

In the past thirty years the gap between history and sociology appears to have narrowed dramatically. The rise of quantitative history; a shift of interest among sociologists to problems of social transition; a growing concern among historians to understand the 'mentalities' of past societies and to explore the history of such unconventional matters as oppression, class-formation, lunacy, crime, magic, domestic social relations and generally, people in the mass; the publication of a series of very ambitious and ostensibly sociological works dealing with the processes involved in the formation of twentieth-century democracy and dictatorship, the great modern revolutions and even 'the modern world system'; a profound crisis in marxist thought over the nature of historical materialism and the passages between modes of production; a widespread borrowing of categories between the disciplines; all this has served to make earlier efforts to maintain strict distinctions and boundaries between history and sociology seem increasingly quaint, contrived and unnecessary. A few diehards on either side have held out for the old separations. Some radical critics have deplored the rather ill-considered and opportunistic nature of much of the recent convergence. Yet as Stedman Jones has noted the general consensus is plain enough: sociology as a theoretical discipline and history as an empirical discipline have been happily drifting towards one another for several years; a fruitful and contented marriage may now be envisaged.[1]

With Stedman Jones I am not altogether happy about this image of confluence. But whereas his reservations have to do with the poverty of the theory he sees sociology as likely to bring to history – history needs theory but not sociological theory – mine relate to the whole conception of the disciplines as somehow different in principle in the first place. My argument in this book is that in important ways the conventional debate on the relationship between history and sociology, both on the side of those who welcome convergence and on the side of those who deplore it, is essentially misconceived. In my understanding of history and sociology there can be no relationship *between* them because, in terms of their fundamental preoccupations, history and sociology are and always have been the same thing. Both seek to understand the puzzle of human agency and both seek to do so in terms of the process of social structuring. Both are impelled to conceive of that process chronologically; at the end of the debate the diachrony–synchrony distinction is absurd. Sociology must be concerned with eventuation, because that is how structuring happens. History must be theoretical, because that is how structuring is apprehended. History has no privileged access to the empirical evidence relevant to the common explanatory project. And sociology has no privileged theoretical access. Moreover it is the task that commands attention not the disciplines. That, in any event, is what I shall be arguing.

There have, undeniably, been many digressions, deviations, fantasies and false starts. Much of the inter-disciplinary flag-waving and territorial wrangling between historians and sociologists has been focused on these lapses rather than on the central concerns of the disciplines as such. Admittedly, boundary disputes still persist. But I shall suggest that many of them rest on a confusion between principle and practice, a failure to distinguish clearly between what history and sociology require historians and sociologists to do and what for a variety of fortuitous reasons some historians and sociologists actually do, a failure to separate the logic of explanation from the rhetoric of academic interests. Indeed, much of the claimed difference between the disciplines is hardly more than a series of attempts by the authors concerned to appropriate the sort of work they happen to do for the discipline they happen to profess. Conversely, to the extent that one directs attention to problems rather than to practices, and the more single-mindedly one does so, the harder it proves to establish credible boundaries. If one attends seriously to the problematic of structuring as a way of formulating fundamental issues of social analysis all the proposed boundaries seem to me to collapse.

Some familiar contributions to the debate by Edward Thompson may serve briefly to illustrate my argument at this point. On a number of occasions and in a number of widely-quoted statements Edward Thompson has sought to advance the claim that class is to be understood as a relationship and not as a thing; specifically, as an historical relationship, an event not a structure or object. Sociologists in general and some marxists in particular are singled-out by him as typical purveyors of the contrary view. Mistaken marxists, Thompson has argued, try to discover class as a thing; sociologists, equally mistaken, claim that class does not exist because they cannot discover it as a thing. Against both versions of the heresy Thompson maintains the thesis that 'the notion of class entails the notion of historical relationship'. And so, like any relationship, 'it is a fluency which evades analysis if we attempt to stop it dead at any given moment and anatomise its structure'. Hence, 'the finest-meshed sociological net cannot give us a pure specimen of class . . . the relationship must always be embodied in real people and in a real context'.[2] Many sociologists might have to be forgiven for being puzzled to know just what Thompson expects them to find controversial in such a statement. But let us leave them puzzling for a moment and consider the fuller and more famous version of his argument. Here again the 'placing' of sociology is achieved in quite blanket terms, as a gracious condescension:

> Sociologists who have stopped the time-machine and, with a good deal of conceptual huffing and puffing, have gone down to the engine-room to look, tell us that nowhere at all have they been able to locate and classify a class. They can find only a multitude of people with different occupations, incomes, status-hierarchies, and the rest. Of course they are right, since class is not this or that part of the machine, but *the way the machine works* once it is set in motion – not this interest and that interest, but the friction of interests – the movement itself, the heat, the thundering noise. Class is a social and cultural formation (often finding institutional expression) which cannot be defined abstractly or in isolation, but only in terms of relationship with other classes; and ultimately the definition can only be made in the medium of time – that is, action and reaction, change and conflict . . . class itself is not a thing, it is a happening.[3]

In his main argument here Thompson is of course also quite right – and I would extend his argument from class to most other supposed social entities. But it is not an argument which divides sociologists from historians in any generic way. Some sociologists, but also some historians, have indeed tried to treat class as a bit of the machine (and despite Thompson some of them have actually emerged from the engine-room waving what they claimed was the relevant bit). And some sociologists, as well as some historians, have insisted that as a social relationship class must be understood historically, in action. Weber's analysis, elaborated by Parkin, of the transparency and closure of classes is just such a treatment as Thompson favours.[4] So surely is the work done by Lockwood in *The Black-Coated Worker* (1958), by Willis in *Learning to Labour* (1977), by Mallet in *The New Working Class* (1975), by Sennett and Cobb in *The Hidden Injuries of Class* (1977), Westergaard and Resler in *Class in a Capitalist Society* (1975); by Barrington Moore Jnr. in *Injustice* (1978), by Wolf in *Peasant Wars of the Twentieth Century* (1971) and of course, triumphantly by Marx in *The 18th Brumaire of Louis Bonaparte* (1962). Appreciation of the historicity of class, of class as a relationship enacted in time (with equal stress on all four of those words) is simply not a form of wisdom private to the historian. Nor are the larger insights that time exists in motion and that society is the time-machine working. Sociologists and historians *alike* need to understand how that maddeningly non-mechanical machine works if the puzzle of human agency is to be resolved.

The paradox of human agency is hardly a new discovery, although from Hobbes onwards many people have unveiled it as solemnly as though it were. In effect it is the empirical common denominator of a vast body of social analysis which has always obstinately refused to be relegated or confined to any single formal academic discipline. We find it at the very origins of historical materialism in the work of Vico, pervasively in the writings of Marx and Engels. It is Schiller's problem of alienation, Hegel's problem of estrangement and Lukacs' problem of reification. It is celebrated as the intellectual pivot of sociology by Herbert Spencer. It is a recurrent nightmare in the work of Max Weber.

....

The problem of agency is the problem of finding a way of accounting for human experience which recognises simultaneously and in equal measure that history and society are made by constant and more or less purposeful individual action *and* that individual action, however purposeful, is made by history and society. How do we, as active subjects make a world of objects which then, as it were, become subjects making us their objects? It is the problem of individual and society, consciousness and being, action and structure; a problem to which the voices of everyday life speak as loudly as those of scholars. It is easily and endlessly formulated but, it seems, stupefyingly difficult to resolve. People make their own history – but only under definite circumstances and conditions: we act through a world of rules which our action creates, breaks and renews – we are creatures of rules, the rules are our creations: we make our own world – the world confronts us as an implacable and autonomous system of social facts. The variations on the theme are innumerable; and the failure of the human sciences to work the theme to a satisfactory conclusion is inscribed on page after page of the literature of each of those sciences, as it is in the babbling echoes of the theme constantly thrown up from our ordinary experience of ordinary social relations. The estranged symbiosis of action and structure is both a commonplace of everyday life and the unbudgeable fulcrum of social analysis.

In sociology the distinctive product of the puzzle of agency is 'the two sociologies', the coexistence of a sociology of action and a sociology of social system which never manage to meet to settle their residual problems of system and action. More especially, as Dawe has stressed, the history of sociology is a history of repeated attempts to give the idea of action a central and active place in interpretations of the relationship of individual and society which repeatedly end up negating themselves and producing a sociology in which action is subordinated to system. Just as in the practice of life action succumbs to powers and constraints which are themselves the products of action, so in sociology attempts to theorise the patterning of experience from the perspective of action have ended up as theories in which the explanation of agency succumbs to the logic of social system. By many devious routes sociology seems to have spent its time rediscovering the dismal paradox Dawe ascribes to Weber, 'human agency becomes human bondage because of the very nature of human agency'.[5]

Insofar as the dilemma of agency is a practical dilemma of individuals in society we should not expect it to be resolved by the human sciences. Marx was surely right when he maintained that practical dilemmas of that sort, the contrived dualities of consciousness and being, are to be resolved, if at all, in practice and not in thought. What thought, or at least knowledge, can do, however, is to help us to understand the terms and conditions of our dilemmas by filling-out their form and content. And the most promising move I can envisage from that point of view so far as the dilemma of human agency is concerned is to insist on the need to conceive of that dilemma historically: to insist on the ways in which and the extent to which the relationship of action and structure is to be understood as a matter of process in time. I would almost say that it is a question of trying to build a sociology of process as an alternative to our tried, worn and inadequate sociologies of action and system. And that is where the problematic of structuring comes in. It re-unites sociology with the other human sciences, especially history. And it does so, not by way of a casual marriage of defective theory to an unprincipled empiricism, but through the re-discovery of an authentic and fundamental common interest. Whatever the apparent pre-occupations of historians and sociologists, whatever excesses of self-indulgent fact-grubbing or zealous theory-construction may have distracted them, it is the common and inescapable problematic of structuring which gives their work its final seriousness.

Notes

1 Gareth Stedman Jones, 'From historical sociology to theoretic history', *British Journal of Sociology* 27 (1976), pp. 295–305.
2 E.P. Thompson, *The Making of the English Working Class*, Gollancz, 1963, p. 9.
3 E.P. Thompson, 'Peculiarities of the English', in R. Miliband and J. Saville (eds), *The Socialist Register, 1965*, Merlin Press, 1965, p. 357.
4 F. Parkin, 'Strategies of social closure in class formation', in F. Parkin (ed.), *The Social Analysis of Class Structure*, Tavistock, 1974.
5 A. Dawe, 'Theories of social action', in T. Bottomore and R. Nisbet (eds), *A History of Sociological Analysis*, Heinemann, 1979, p. 398.

The authority of numbers

Quantification lies at the heart of the claim by subjects like economics and sociology to be sciences. Partly this is a matter of precision: statements about collectivities or aggregates of people are more informative if they are expressed in precise figures, rather than impressionistically. But the method of the social sciences is also rooted in the use of explicit models of human behaviour, in which the relationship between the variables is expressed in statistical terms. As the leading *annaliste* Emmanuel Le Roy Ladurie explains, quantification was pioneered by historians of long-term economic trends; 'serial' history aimed to place the periodisation of the European economy on a more reliable footing. Ladurie himself employed quantification in an important socio-economic case-study, *The Peasants of Languedoc* (1966).

The champions of quantitative history in America called it 'cliometrics' (i.e. the measurement of history) and claimed that a scientific history was within their grasp. Robert William Fogel was at the forefront of this movement. In *Time on the Cross* (1974), co-authored with Stanley Engerman, he sought to demonstrate quantitatively that slaves in the American South were well treated, and that their owners behaved as a humane capitalist class. His argument in this extract is that cliometrics offers a methodologically superior approach, but one which still conforms to the fundamental assumptions of historicism.

30. Emmanuel Le Roy Ladurie

[from The Territory of the Historian, *Harvester, 1979,
pp. 7–15]*

Specialists in French economic history have always worked with figures
since the days of Levasseur, Hauser and Mantoux: they could hardly
do otherwise. But it was only after about 1932, with the publication of the
major works of Simiand and Labrousse that the systematic use of measurement became virtually obligatory among historians. Of course our procedures have remained simple, primitive even, by the sophisticated standards
of the econometricians and 'historio-metricians' of the USA. Even so, the
quantitative revolution has completely transformed the craft of the historian
in France.

   In retrospect, it appears to have been articulated around several key concepts. Originally developed in the context of considerations about price-
changes, it has led in more recent years to a study of economic growth analysed
by means of the factors of supply and demand – population, production and
incomes.

   The grand old man of prices in the 1930s was François Simiand – the
inspiration, directly or indirectly, of a whole generation of historians. The
central concept in his work is the long-term perspective of price movements,
which he took to be indicators of the first importance. If over the long term
(30 years or more) prices rise, usually under the impact of imported gold and
silver, they necessarily carry with them, according to Simiand, both profits and
eventually production, in the same upward movement towards prosperity.
This is the *A phase*. But if, by contrast, they should, following a 'monetary
famine', move downwards over several decades (the *B phase*) the result is
depression, collapse, unemployment and subsequently a decline in gross
product. *A phases* (rising prices and economic prosperity) alternate over the
centuries with *B phases* (falling prices, hence recession and a series of lean and

hungry years). The combination of A and B phases forms the very web and substance of economic history and sometimes of all history: what may be termed the *conjoncture*.

Simiand's ideas, which I have oversimplified in summary, were often schematic and sometimes one-dimensional. Even so, they were nevertheless illuminating. They acted as a stimulus to research at a time when the collapse of the market, and the American and world depression of the 1930s, had understandably impressed a generation of historians. A number of important books and articles set out to resurrect and reconstruct whole areas of the economic past, the years of plenty along with the years of starvation. Postan and Abel, whose direct or indirect influence on French medievalists was immense, contrasted the triumphs of the Gothic age and the thirteenth century with the long periods of depression which lay so heavy on the rural areas of the West, stifling them with price collapses between the crisis of 1310–1320 and the beginning of the Renaissance. The Hundred Years War, the disastrous reign of Charles the Mad, the massacres by the Armagnacs and the burning of Joan of Arc ceased to be thought of by the new generation of French medievalists as symptoms of a tragedy peculiar to France during the terrible years of the fifteenth century. Despite these troubles, France under Charles VII, for all its agony, when viewed through the dispassionate eyes of the quantitative historian now seems to have been merely a particularly hard-pressed area within a Europe itself on the rack, a Europe everywhere suffering from the rural crisis of the *Trecento* and *Quattrocento*.

And then, in the wake of these misfortunes, came the brilliant compensations of the Golden Age: Hamilton in 1936, and Braudel in 1949 pointed out the material foundations of the Renaissance, to be seen in the sudden rise in prices and the more than proportionate increases in rent and capital gains (realized on the backs of wage-earners) between 1500 and 1600. The 'price revolution', according to these historians, was the result of heightened demand, itself caused by a population increase and by the influx of precious metals from the mines of Mexico and Potosi.

With the seventeenth century, as the young (and not so young) researchers of the 1940s and 1950s discovered, we were once more in a B phase: prices had levelled off by about 1630 or 1660; the so-called *Grand Siècle* of Louis XIV was in fact caught in an interminable rut of economic depression. Seen against the unflattering background of the downward price curves, Colbert turns out not to be the history-book figure we all learnt about in school: no longer is he the great administrator from whose hands the manufactures of France sprang fully armed. Rather he is the grim agent of deflation. After his death, matters went from bad to worse. True, inflation returned after 1690, but in the form of such violent price rises that they put bread far beyond the purse of the poor, many of whom were thus sent to their graves.

This miserable seventeenth-century reality, which is described without embellishment in the work of Meuvret and Goubert, was not entirely over until after 1730. After this date, if we apply Simiand's still-useful model, the horizon seemed to brighten again, with the new splendours of an A phase which has been depicted in great detail in many works by Ernest Labrousse and later writers. Mexican silver and Brazilian gold, mined in large quantities during the Age of Enlightenment, helped to get the wheels of the economy moving again. While currency remained stable – as it was to do, apart from the brief interval of the *assignats*, from 1726 to 1914 – prices, profits, rents and production began to move up once more. An unprecedented wave of prosperity swept over the bourgeoisie, the Atlantic shores of France and colonial trade. All this only came to an end, and then briefly, in about 1780, when wine and grain prices collapsed, spreading crisis, overproduction, unsold surpluses and poverty, the breeding-ground for the popular discontents which were to explode in 1789 and thereafter.

To summarize in this way is of course to misrepresent. The thought of such men as Labrousse, Braudel, Meuvret and Goubert goes far beyond the narrow confines of a study of price movements. It can take the historian, depending on his interests, towards social history, Marxism, perhaps geography or the study of civilization, demography, etc. But it would not perhaps be entirely misleading to say that, apart from a general wish to go beyond the history of events, the common denominator in the work of these four historians is a concern to study the *conjoncture*, for which, at the time when they were writing, the price records offered the surest signposts. The conceptual framework proposed by Simiand over thirty-six years ago has had at all events the unquestionable merit of providing, for a while at least, a coherent theory of periodization covering more than five centuries: a considerable achievement in itself. But this approach was gradually and logically bound to transcend its own terms; it would have to look to more complex indicators than prices if it was not to collapse under the pressure of the new data being unearthed every day, the cumulative weight of relentless facts which were gradually making cracks everywhere in the structure. Already the nineteenth century was looking like a glaring counter illustration of Simiand's ideas. The period from 1820 to 1850 – a B phase if ever there was one – was characterized by a long period of price stagnation. But this sluggishness of the market, far from paralyzing the economy, was on the contrary accompanied by a fantastic increase in gross production. The B phase of price recession was not, in the particular example of France under Louis-Philippe, the mother of depression, but on the contrary the daughter of prosperity. The source of this B phase was the steadily growing supply of goods produced, which kept prices down and prevented them from rising. Simiand's model was in this case caught in flagrant contradiction to the real world. Something else would have to be found.

The 'something else' though turned out to be more than simply the consequence of disproving a theory, as in the case just mentioned. What has happened, since 1960, is that quantitative history has been granted a new lease of life. This revival can be attributed to the new theories of economic growth introduced quite recently to France. The general tenor of these theories has been popularized, thanks to the instructive, though somewhat oversimplified, concept of *economic take-off*. Economic historians and historical economists now generally distinguish between stable, traditional types of society – before take-off (for example rural Europe in the seventeenth century); and growth societies, after take-off: those in which the gross disposable per capita product grows steadily and slowly but surely. In the years 1960–1965, historians such as Bachrel, Chaunu, Delumeau, Vilar, and in particular Marczewski, centred their work on this new kind of data, systematically setting alongside the price indicator the indices of trade and production in the form of total or per capita income.

Nowadays the concept of growth (or in more traditional societies, non-growth) has won its place in historiography. When applied, it considerably modifies the notions we once had of French modernization in the nineteenth century. The concepts of 'industrial' and 'technological revolution' which were so popular for so long, have now been pushed into the background. The economic expansion which was so marked in this country during the first two-thirds of the nineteenth century was in fact very largely fuelled by the traditional sectors of the economy (agriculture, building, international trade in agricultural products) which were not modified by technological innovations of any importance for a very long time. On this issue (though with some reservations) French historians are at one with their 'historio-metric' colleagues in the United States, of whom Fogel is one of the leading representatives. Fogel has tried for instance to establish the truth about the famous legend of the railroads, which is still a powerful force in popular imagery, as addicts of westerns will know. By the use of figures and what he calls 'counterfactual hypotheses', he claims to demonstrate that, even if there had been no railroads at all, the impressive expansion of the American economy during the first eighty years of the nineteenth century would still have taken place in very much the same way. It was not the steam engine or the locomotive, he says, that created the wealth of America in the last century, but the efforts of the farmer and the ancient institution of slavery (which remained profitable right to its last gasp). If we can rely on Fogel's concepts and equations – which are possibly too ingenious to be totally convincing – the battle for the frontier had nothing to do with the epic of the railroads: it was an expansion of a traditional type – not so very different in certain respects from that of rural Europe in the eleventh century. Whether this is the case or not, the new quantitative studies of growth certainly emphasize the role of traditional elements in the apparently revolutionary take-off of the economy in the nineteenth century. At the same time by way of contrast, they are mapping the features of societies without growth as these once functioned in the west.

One such society was the French countryside from approximately 1330 to 1730. Many writers, from Marc Bloch to Poitrineau, have made us familiar with it. In some respects it deserves the name of a stable society. True, the stability was very relative: rural society in the past was constantly subject to immense, slow-moving fluctuations; and was also from time to time beset by alarming convulsions. It was nevertheless distinguished by its unwillingness to change – or, to put it another way, its incredible capacity for recovery. Even when disturbed or seriously damaged, this type of society has a powerful tendency to rebuild itself, to heal the wounds, along the lines of the original archetype. Fourquin and Tulippe have convincingly demonstrated this apropos of the Hundred Years War. The last trooper and the last Englishman had hardly left before the peasants of the Ile-de-France were beginning to reconstruct their parishes, their landscape and their population, in an exact replica of the time-honoured patterns which had flourished a century and a half before. In the reigns of Louis XII and François I, these country people were quite unapologetically reviving the age of Philip the Fair.

What statistical studies have recently brought to light about these *ancien régime* societies is the presence of a number of insuperable barriers and limitations. The most evident type of barrier (finding concrete expression in the shape of famine) concerned the production of subsistence foodstuffs and more particularly agricultural productivity which stubbornly refused to grow. A recent debate between the historians Slicher von Bath and Morineau has shed much light on this question: Morineau and several others have demonstrated, with the aid of documents and accounts, that the wheat yield per hectare – even on the richest of French soils – did not rise by so much as a quintal between the age of Saint Louis and that of Louis XV – or even that of Louis-Philippe. The study of tithes, those venerable and much-challenged measures of overall production, as recently undertaken by Goy and several other historians, leads towards similar conclusions: for long periods, between the fifteenth century and the early years of the eighteenth, grain production, measured by the tithe, failed to increase, thus imposing certain insurmountable limits on the expansion of the society as a whole. This does not mean of course that dynamic islands of growth did not exist within that society; but such islands were, under these conditions, long to remain exceptional or altogether insignificant.

Similar obstructions can be found at various levels, paralyzing the entire social body. Wage-rates for example, even in Paris, a city of rapid growth, were held down extremely rigidly between the fifteenth and the eighteenth centuries. Micheline Baulant has quantified them: between 1470 and 1750, wages kept falling: then at the very lowest point on the graph there was a long period of wage stagnation, which persisted heartbreakingly throughout the classical period. Marx saw the pauperization of the workers as the baptismal act of capitalism; in fact it seems to have been above all the distinctive mark of a blocked society, one incapable of raising productivity and hence the living standards of the lower classes.

Other blocks and barriers in traditional societies were the result of authoritarian or parasitical levies demanded from above in rent, tithes or taxes. Every time the royal administration, for example, tried to increase its share of the national cake, in the form of taxes, while the cake in question remained the same size or grew only very slowly, it triggered off as if by reflex action a number of violent disturbances. Richelieu was to find this to his cost: having turned the fiscal screw rather sharply, and without warning, in the period 1625–1630, he automatically received in reply the series of popular revolts which have received much recent attention following the work of Porchnev and Mousnier. And under the next cardinal, the response was – the Fronde.

In this context, the notion of fluctuation takes on a rather different meaning from that given it by Simiand. Price movements in particular, while certainly not negligible, are no longer accorded such predominant and exclusive importance: the historian is becoming increasingly aware that these occur (before 1700) within a primitive economy in which many products are bartered or consumed on the spot, without ever entering the market economy with its prices. So price changes during A and B phases cannot be regarded as explaining everything. Besides, to the extent that they nevertheless remain important, they necessarily refer the historian elsewhere, since they are located at the intersection of supply and demand. Demand was generally elastic: expressed in varying conditions by a fluctuating population; while supply was on the whole inelastic: consisting of subsistence production.

It is this basic contradiction – demand–supply, population–subsistence, population growth–gross product – which has, for the time being, provided the economic history of rural regions with a model of periodization in so far as it can be approximately mapped by quantified indicators. In general terms (if I can trust my own experience which is certainly very partial and localized) I see two great multisecular cycles, separated by the falling blade of the Black

Death. First the medieval cycle, with its topical contradictions on the one hand: rising demand, which might or might not be backed by the ability to pay, and a rising population, between the eleventh and the early fourteenth centuries; and then the counterpart to this upward movement, the growing inadequacy of subsistence production, leading to famines between 1310 and 1340 and finally culminating in a wave of epidemics and disasters which relieved demographic pressure tragically between 1348 and 1480. Once this apocalyptic time of plague and misery is over, towards the end of the fifteenth century, the second great cycle begins. This moves through various phases from the time of Louis XII to Louis XIV. It is characterized by a demographic recovery, a new rise in the population rate and, once more, saturation point in the Malthusian sense is reached in land, subsistence and employment, because of this human overload. The only way out of this dilemma and the harsh depressions that inevitably followed would be through growth, which eventually got under way, gradually, during the Age of Enlightenment. And for this growth it seems that the non-agricultural sector was initially responsible.

I have restricted myself in this survey to the area of economic history, where quantitative research is both essential and, nowadays, recognized as such. Statistical or 'serial' history as it is sometimes called, has nevertheless spread to other fields of enquiry: former patterns of religious observance and the history of attitudes have both been the subject of statistical studies (see the work of P. Pérouas and that of François Furet and his collaborators on *Livre et société au XVIIIe Siècle (Books and society in the eighteenth century)*). But certain pioneering and promising disciplines (for instance the field of historical psychology) remain resolutely qualitative, and very properly refuse to be quantified. They are still at the stage of conceptualizing their approach, seeking to build coherent and operational models, in short acquiring their credentials which must always, in any area, be a necessary preliminary for statistical analysis. Without such preliminary precautions, the numerical approach might run the risk of becoming platitudinous or ridiculous. But in the long run, even in the more esoteric branches of history, it must surely be the case that there will always come a moment when the historian, having worked out a solid conceptual basis, will need to start counting: to record frequencies, significant repetitions, or percentages. For only calculations of this kind, however tedious and even elementary they may seem, can in the end validate the data that has been collected and show whether this goes beyond the anecdotal to the typical or representative. To put it in its most extreme form (and it is an extreme so remote and in some cases so beyond the scope of present research as to be perhaps only imaginary), history that is not quantifiable cannot claim to be scientific.

31. Robert William Fogel

[from ' "Scientific" history and traditional history', in R. W. Fogel and G.R. Elton, Which Road to the Past?, *Yale University Press, 1983, pp. 23–34]*

The new brand of 'scientific' history, which I will call 'cliometrics', entered the historical lists during the 1950s. Although cliometricians are sometimes referred to as a 'school', the term is somewhat misleading since cliometrics encompasses many different subjects, viewpoints, and methodologies. The common characteristic of cliometricians is that they apply the quantitative methods and behavioral models of the social sciences to the study of history. The cliometric approach was first given systematic development in economic history, but like a contagion it rapidly spread to such diverse fields as population and family history, urban history, parliamentary history, electoral history, and ethnic history.

Cliometricians want the study of history to be based on explicit models of human behavior. They believe that historians do not really have a choice of using or not using behavioral models since all attempts to explain historical behavior – to relate the elemental facts of history to each other – whether called *ideengeschichte*, 'historical imagination', or 'behavioral modeling', involve some sort of model. The real choice is whether these models will be implicit, vague, incomplete, and internally inconsistent, as cliometricians contend is frequently the case in traditional historical research, or whether the models will be explicit, with all the relevant assumptions clearly stated, and formulated in such a manner as to be subject to rigorous empirical verification. The approach sometimes leads cliometricians to represent historical behavior by mathematical equations and then to seek evidence, usually quantitative, capable of verifying the applicability of these equations or of contradicting them. The behavior that cliometricians have dealt with so far has generally been represented by single equations or by simple simultaneous-equation models with relatively few variables. These equations are usually linear in form or involve linear or other low-order approximations.

Such mathematics might be thought to be too simple to be useful as a characterization of complex human behavior. Nevertheless, actual practice has shown that this simple mathematics is often a powerful instrument in advancing knowledge of the past. First, by making the assumed behavioral relationships explicit, these models lay the basis for a considered discussion of the circumstances under which linear or other lower-order approximations of more complex relationships are adequate or inadequate. Quite often the narratives of traditional historians, when dealing with relationships between variables, implicitly assume the most simple of all functions – strict proportionality between the variables. It has been shown that when this severe restriction is relaxed and a more realistic functional relationship is introduced, the interpretations of some historical events are greatly altered. Much of the work of the cliometricians has been directed to spelling out and formalizing the models implicit in traditional historical narratives and to considering the empirical validity of those models.

Second, the mathematical characterization of historical behavior has helped to identify the critical parameters in historical narratives. Because of incompleteness of data, historians frequently have widely different beliefs about the values of the parameters that implicitly or explicitly enter into their analyses. Translating such arguments into mathematical form makes it possible to engage in 'sensitivity analysis' – that is, to examine the sensitivity of the conclusions of an argument to alternative estimates of particular parameters. This procedure has eliminated many unnecessary wrangles by demonstrating that the absence of exact information on particular points is at times inconsequential. For quite often a measurement which is logically necessary for a given analysis may be such that any plausible number, even though it may deviate greatly from reality, is permissible and serves to close the logical system on which the analysis is based. Albert Fishlow, for example, employed this device in his reconstruction of the U.S. pattern of interregional trade before the Civil War by guessing at the share of southern imports that were re-exported and then demonstrating that no plausible error in his guess could alter his results by more than a few percentage points.[1] While such techniques do not eliminate all error or banish all needless wrangles, they reduce them by providing criteria that facilitate the identification of error and the resolution of issues.

It is not analysis but description that occupies most of the time of cliometricians. In this respect, cliometricians conform to Ranke's admonition that historians should devote themselves to the task of determining what actually happened. Just as the nineteenth- and early-twentieth-century followers of Ranke scoured the public archives for diplomatic and ministerial documents that would reveal what actually happened in government policy, so cliometricians have been scouring archives anew, this time searching for quantitative evidence bearing on what actually happened in social behavior.

And so we arrive at the crux of the difference between traditional history and cliometrics. Many traditional historians tend to be highly focused on specific individuals, on particular institutions, on particular ideas, and on nonrepetitive occurrences; those who attempt to explain collective phenomena generally make only limited use of explicit behavioral models and usually rely principally on literary evidence. Cliometricians tend to be highly focused on collections of individuals, on categories of institutions, and on repetitive occurrences; their explanations often involve explicit behavioral models and they rely heavily on quantitative evidence. A traditional historian, for example, might want to explain why John Keats died at the time, in the place, and under the particular circumstances that he did. But to a social-scientific historian attempting to explain the course of mortality among the English, the particular circumstances of Keats's death might be less interesting than those circumstances that contribute to an understanding of why deaths due to tuberculosis were so frequent during the first half of the nineteenth century. Of course these approaches are neither mutually exclusive nor in any sense antagonistic, although partisans of the two approaches often behave as if they were.

Some scholars treat quantification as *the* characteristic that identifies cliometricians. Quantification is more commonly encountered in cliometric work than the explicit mathematical modeling of behavior, but it is not a universal characteristic of such work. The term 'cliometrician' embraces scholars who, although they rarely use numbers or mathematical notation, nevertheless base their research on explicit social science models. For reasons already suggested, and more fully discussed in the next section of this paper, no single characteristic can be used to distinguish between traditional and 'scientific' historians, although a scholar's attitude toward the autonomy of history may go further in that direction than any other particular characteristic. 'Scientific' historians generally view history as a field of applied social science, contending that the analytical and statistical methods of these fields are as relevant to the study of the past as they are to contemporary problems. Traditional historians often and vigorously dispute that judgment. Handlin, J.H. Hexter, and Elton, among others, argue that history is a distinct branch of knowledge which (although it draws on the social and natural sciences, on literature and the other humanities, and on law) has a mode of thought that is quite distinct from those prevailing in other disciplines.[2]

Some scholars believe that the hallmark of cliometrics is the use of social science theories to interpret history. Yet long before the cliometricians appeared on the scene many traditional historians (especially those identified with the movement for 'total history') had turned to the social sciences for generalizations that could be used to order their evidence. When Elton criticized certain colleagues for imposing extraneous theories on history, his principal target was not the cliometricians but such traditional historians as Stone and Braudel, who have repeatedly drawn on sociological, anthropological, and economic theories for their synthesizing principles and interpretive frameworks. Cliometricians differ from these social-scientific traditionalists in their manner of employing social science theories rather than in a greater willingness to do so. Social-scientific traditionalists generally use theory, Elton points out, as 'a form of analogical argument'. For example, 'nineteenth century Bantus and Polynesians' have been used to explain 'pre-Columbian America and German forest tribes', comparisons so farfetched, according to Elton, that their value, 'even their capacity to suggest new questions and insights', is 'very problematical'.[3] Historians who use social science theories in this informal way rarely test the applicability of the theories to the particular historical situations on which they are imposed. Many contend that formal tests of theories have no place in history and deny that significant historical questions can be answered by the quantitative tests that are common in cliometric work. The formulation of social science theories in a manner that leads to rigorous testing of their applicability to specific historical circumstances, and the execution of such tests, distinguishes cliometricians from traditional historians.

Methods of authenticating evidence also serve to distinguish the two groups. The methods that traditional historians have developed for authenticating evidence were geared more to specific events involving specific individuals than to repetitive events involving large groups of individuals. Of what use is the criterion that an historian must seek two corroborating opinions, if the point at issue is whether the standard of living of the English working class declined during the Industrial Revolution? There were scores of different opinions on this question and even a fairly unresourceful historian would have no difficulty in discovering two or even several witnesses who shared a particular view. But such a limited degree of accord could also be established for directly opposed views.[4]

Indeed, the very concept of decline in the standard of living is much different for a group than for an individual. Even in the worst depressions, when the economic circumstances of most individuals are deteriorating, there are some individuals whose economic circumstances are improving. Methods of analysis that are appropriate for determining whether George Washington's income declined during the postrevolutionary years may not do for the determination of whether or not the income of American slaveowners as a class declined.

Simple transposition of techniques that work quite well for the analysis of individual behavior may do more to distort than to clarify collective behavior. An individual who had so politically split a personality that he simultaneously embraced the policies of a revolutionary party and their most ardent opponents would be classified as psychotic. Yet such split behavior is normal in the case of nations, churches, classes, and other substantial social, political, and economic formations. Whatever the qualities that give individuals a group identity, one never encounters such uniformity in their positions, attitudes, and responses that they can be treated as having an identical personality. Explaining the outcome of parliamentary struggles involving a large number of individuals thus frequently poses problems that are quite different from the explanation of the behavior of an absolute monarch, of a prime minister of a democratic government, or of a few of the leaders in a parliament.

This point is recognized by both traditional and 'scientific' historians, and both groups have sought to come to grips with the problems of studying collective behavior in their own ways. In dealing with parliaments, traditional historians have tended to rely on the opinions of individuals who were at the center of parliamentary struggles, and so were in a position to know what was going on, or who, although just observers, were of such keen mind that they were likely to have grasped the essence of the situations. Scientific historians have tended to concentrate on the analysis of roll calls and on quantifiable characteristics of legislators or their constituencies. They have sought statistical methods which are capable of squeezing from such evidence information on the existence of blocs in parliaments and parties, the intensity of adherence to various positions, the underlying factors which give unity to (or threaten to destroy) coalitions, and the mind set of particular legislators or categories of legislators.[5]

The cliometric approach would be of some interest even if it merely confirmed what had already been discovered by traditional historiographic methods. In virtually every field to which it has been applied, however, the cliometric approach has not only yielded substantive findings that are strikingly different from the findings of the older research but has also called attention to important processes that previously had escaped notice.

Notes

1 Albert Fishlow, 'Antebellum interregional trade reconsidered', *American Economic Review* 54 (1964), pp. 352–64 and appendix.
2 Oscar Handlin, *Truth in History*, Harvard University Press, 1979, Ch. 10; J.H. Hexter, 'History: the rhetoric of history', in *International Encyclopedia of the Social Sciences*, vol. 6, Macmillan, 1968, pp. 368–94; G.R. Elton, *The Practice of History*, Fontana, 1969, esp. pp. 20–4, 36–56.
3 Elton, *Practice of History*, pp. 46–7.
4 See Arthur J. Taylor (ed.), *The Standard of Living in Britain in the Industrial Revolution*, Methuen, 1975, for a survey and assessment of this debate to 1975.
5 The scope and methods of cliometric work in political history are indicated in, for example, William O. Aydelotte (ed.), *The History of Parliamentary Behavior*, Princeton University Press, 1977.

Reactions

G iven the ambitious and sometimes exclusive claims made by social science history, sharp reactions in defence of a more traditional approach were to be expected. Some historians were interested in a genuine engagement between the humanities and the social sciences; others turned their back on the new developments entirely. Fernand Braudel, doyen of the Annales School, may seem a surprising inclusion here, since he was a noted advocate of a structural approach to history, as in his *Capitalism and Material Life, 1400–1800* (1973). His quarrel with the social sciences was that they had no means of bringing together the surface event (*l'histoire événementielle*) and the scarcely moving time of long-term economic and cultural configurations (the *longue durée*); for this historical time was indispensable.

Lawrence Stone's critique went much further. He was a prolific social historian of early modern England and had been very receptive towards the agenda of the social sciences. But in this influential article he identified – and partly endorsed – a 'revival of narrative'. Structural and analytical history had gone too far; quantification had delivered much less than it had promised. What was needed was a creative adaptation of the historian's traditional technique of narrative to the new requirements of social history.

One of the more radical sceptics is Theodore Zeldin. His own interest in the study of past mentalities – notably in his *France, 1848–1945* (2 vols, 1973/1977) – has led him to advocate what he calls a 'personal' or 'individual' history. Here the focus is on past individuals and their emotions, and this will require a more subjective engagement on the part of the writer than anything allowed for in classical historicism. On this view, historical work requires self-knowledge as well as knowledge of the sources and critical procedures; generalisation and large-scale explanation are renounced.

32. Fernand Braudel

[from 'History and the social sciences: the longue durée*', in his*
On History, *trans. Sarah Matthews, University of Chicago Press,*
1980, pp. 26–7, 35–8, 47–9]

The other social sciences are fairly ill informed as to the crisis which our discipline has gone through in the past twenty or thirty years, and they tend to misunderstand not only the work of historians, but also that aspect of social reality for which history has always been a faithful servant, if not always a good salesman: social time, the multifarious, contradictory times of the life of men, which not only make up the past, but also the social life of the present. Yet history, or rather the dialectic of duration as it arises in the exercise of our profession, from our repeated observations, is important in the coming debate among all the human sciences. For nothing is more important, nothing comes closer to the crux of social reality than this living, intimate, infinitely repeated opposition between the instant of time and that time which flows only slowly. Whether it is a question of the past or of the present, a clear awareness of this plurality of social time is indispensable to the communal methodology of the human sciences.

So I propose to deal at length with history, and with time in history. Less for the sake of present readers of this journal, who are already specialists in our field, than for that of those who work in the neighboring human sciences: economists, ethnographers, ethnologists (or anthropologists), sociologists, psychologists, linguists, demographers, geographers, even social mathematicians or statisticians – all neighbors of ours whose experiments and whose researches we have been following for these many years because it seemed to us (and seems so still) that we would thus see history itself in a new light. And perhaps we in our turn have something to offer them. From the recent experiments and efforts of history, an increasingly clear idea has emerged – whether consciously or not, whether excepted or not – of the multiplicity of time, and of the exceptional value of the long time span. It is this last idea which even more than history itself – history of a hundred aspects – should engage the attention and interest of our neighbors, the social sciences.

All historical work is concerned with breaking down time past, choosing among its chronological realities according to more or less conscious preferences and exclusions. Traditional history, with its concern for the short time span, for the individual and the event, has long accustomed us to the headlong, dramatic, breathless rush of its narrative.

The new economic and social history puts cyclical movement in the forefront of its research and is committed to that time span: it has been captivated by the mirage and the reality of the cyclical rise and fall of prices. So today, side by side with traditional narrative history, there is an account of conjunctures which lays open large sections of the past, ten, twenty, fifty years at a stretch ready for examination.

Far beyond this second account we find a history capable of traversing even greater distances, a history to be measured in centuries this time: the history of the long, even of the very long time span, of the *longue durée*. This is a phrase which I have become accustomed to for good or ill, in order to distinguish the opposite of what François Simiand, not long after Paul Lacombe, christened '*l'histoire événementielle*', the history of events. The phrases matter little; what matters is the fact that our discussion will move between these two poles of time, the instant and the *longue durée*.

....

Nonetheless, the social sciences seem little tempted by such remembrance of things past. Not that one can draw up any firm accusation against them and declare them to be consistently guilty of not accepting history or duration as dimensions necessary to their studies. The 'diachronic' examination which reintroduces history is never absent from their theoretical deliberations.

Despite this sort of distant acknowledgment, though, it must be admitted that the social sciences, by taste, by deep-seated instinct, perhaps by training, have a constant tendency to evade historical explanation. They evade it in two almost contradictory ways: by concentrating overmuch on the 'current event' in social studies, thanks to a brand of empirical sociology which, disdainful of all history, confines itself to the facts of the short term and investigations into 'real life'; by transcending time altogether and conjuring up a mathematical formulation of more or less timeless structures under the name of 'communications science'. This last and newest way is clearly the only one which can be of any substantial interest to us. But there are enough devotees of the current event to justify examining both aspects of the question.

We have already stated our mistrust of a history occupied solely with events. To be fair, though, if there is a sin in being overconcerned with events, then history, though the most obvious culprit, is not the only guilty one. All the social sciences have shared in this error. Economists, demographers, geographers are all balanced (and badly balanced) between the demands of yesterday and of today. In order to be right they would need to maintain a constant balance – easy enough, and indeed obligatory, for the demographer, and almost a matter of course for geographers (particularly ours, reared in the Vidalian school) – but rare for economists, held fast to the most short lived of current events, hardly looking back beyond 1945 or forecasting further in advance than a few months, or at most a few years. I would maintain that all economic thinking is trapped by these temporal restrictions. It is up to historians, so economists say, to go back further than 1945, in search of old economies. Economists thus voluntarily rob themselves of a marvelous field of observation, although without denying its value. They have fallen into the habit of putting themselves at the disposal of current events and of governments.

The position of ethnographers and ethnologists is neither so clear nor so alarming. Some of them have taken great pains to underline the impossibility (but intellectuals are always fascinated by the impossible) and the uselessness of applying history within their profession. Such an authoritarian denial of history would hardly have served Malinowski and his disciples. Indeed, how could anthropology possibly not have an interest in history? History and anthropology both spring from the same impulse, as Claude Lévi-Strauss[1] delights in saying. There is no society, however primitive, which does not bear the 'scars of events', nor any society in which history has sunk completely without trace. This is something there is no need to complain about or to insist on further.

On the other hand, where sociology is concerned, our quarrel along the frontiers of the short term must necessarily be a rather bitter one. Sociological investigations into the contemporary scene seem to run in a thousand different directions, from sociology to psychology to economics, and to proliferate among us as they do abroad. They are, in their own way, a bet on the irreplaceable value of the present moment, with its 'volcanic' heat, its abundant wealth. What good would be served by turning back toward historical time: impoverished, simplified, devastated by silence, reconstructed – above all, let us say it again, *reconstructed*. Is it really as dead, as reconstructed, as they would have us believe, though? Doubtless a historian can only too easily isolate the crucial factor from some past age. To put it in Henri Pirenne's words, he can distinguish without difficulty the 'important events', which means 'those which bore consequences'. An obvious and dangerous oversimplification. But what would the explorer of the present-day not give to have this perspective (or this sort of ability to go forward in time), making it possible to unmask and simplify our present life, in all its confusion – hardly comprehensible now because so overburdened with trivial acts and portents? Claude Lévi-Strauss claims that one hour's talk with a contemporary of Plato's would tell him more than all our classical treatises on the coherence or incoherence of ancient Greek civilization. I quite agree. But this is because for years he has heard a hundred Greek voices rescued from silence. The historian has prepared his way. One hour in modern Greece would tell him nothing, or hardly anything, about contemporary Greek coherence or incoherence.

Even more to the point, the researcher occupied with the present can make out the 'fine' lines of a structure only by himself engaging in *reconstruction*, putting forward theories and explanations, not getting embroiled in reality as it appears, but truncating it, transcending it. Such maneuvers allow him to get away from the given situation the better to control it, but they are all acts of reconstruction. I would seriously question whether sociological photography of the present time is any more 'true' than the historical portrayal of the past, more particularly the more it tries to get any further away from the *reconstructed*.

Philippe Ariès[2] has emphasized the importance of the unfamiliar, of surprise in historical explanation: you are in the sixteenth century, and you stumble upon some peculiarity, something which seems peculiar to you as a man of the twentieth century. Why this difference? That is the question which one then has to set about answering. But I would claim that such surprise, such unfamiliarity, such distancing – these great highways to knowledge – are no less necessary to an understanding of all that surrounds us and which we are so close to that we cannot see clearly. Live in London for a year and you will not know much about England. But by contrast, in light of what has surprised you, you will suddenly have come to understand some of the most deep-seated and characteristic aspects of France, things which you did not know before because you knew them too well. With regard to the present, the past too is a way of distancing yourself.

In this way historians and social scientists could go on forever batting the ball back and forth between dead documents and all-too-living evidence, the distant past and the too-close present. But I do not believe that this is a crucial problem. Past and present illuminate each other reciprocally. And in exclusively observing the narrow confines of the present, the attention will irresistibly be drawn toward whatever moves quickly, burns with a true or a false flame, or has just changed, or makes a noise, or is easy to see. There is a whole web of events, as wearisome as any in the historical sciences, which lies in wait for the observer in a hurry, the ethnographer dwelling for three months with some Polynesian tribe, the industrial sociologist delivering all the clichés of his latest investigation, or who truly believes that he can thoroughly pin down some social mechanism with cunningly phrased questionnaires and combinations of punched cards. Social questions are more cunning game than that.

In fact, what possible interest can we take, we the human sciences, in the movements of a young girl between her home in the sixteenth arrondissement, her music teacher, and the Ecole des Sciences-Po, discussed in a sound and wide-ranging study of the Paris area?[3] They make up a fine-looking map. But if she had studied agronomy or gone in for water-skiing, the whole pattern of her triangular journeys would have been altered. It is nice to see on a map the distribution of all domiciles belonging to employees in a large concern. But if I do not have an earlier map, if the lapse of time between the two maps is not sufficient to allow the tracing of a genuine movement, then precisely where is the problem without which any inquiry is simply a waste of effort? Any interest in inquiries for inquiry's sake is limited to the collection of data at best. But even then these data will not all be *ipso facto* useful for future work. We must beware of art for art's sake.

In the same way I would question whether any study of a town, no matter which, could be the object of a sociological inquiry in the way that Auxerre was, or Vienne in the Dauphiné, without being set in its historical context. Any town, as an extended social entity with all its crises, dislocations, breakdowns, and necessary calculations, must be seen in relation to the whole complex of districts surrounding it, as well as in relation to those archipelagos of neighboring towns which Richard Häpke, the historian, was one of the first to discuss. Similarly, it must also be considered in relation to the movement, more or less distant in time, sometimes extremely distant, which directs this whole complex. It cannot be of no interest, it must rather surely be crucial to note down particular urban/rural exchanges, particular industrial or mercantile competition, to know whether you are dealing with a movement in the full flush of its youth, or at the end of its run, with the beginnings of a resurgence or a monotonous repetition.

One last remark: Lucien Febvre, during the last ten years of his life, is said to have repeated: 'History, science of the past, science of the present'. Is not history, the dialectic of time spans, in its own way an explanation of society in all its reality? and thus of contemporary society? And here its role would be to caution us against the event: do not think only of the short time span, do not believe that only the actors which make the most noise are the most authentic – there are other, quieter ones too. As if anybody did not know that already!

··

In truth, the historian can never get away from the question of time in history: time sticks to his thinking like soil to a gardener's spade. He may well dream of getting away from it, of course. Spurred on by the anguish of 1940, Gaston Roupnel[4] wrote words on this subject that will make any true historian suffer. Similar is the classic remark made by Paul Lacombe who was also a historian of the grand school: 'Time is nothing in itself, objectively, it is only an idea we have.'[5] But do these remarks really provide a way out? I myself, during a rather gloomy captivity, struggled a good deal to get away from a chronicle of those difficult years (1940–45). Rejecting events and the time in which events take place was a way of placing oneself to one side, sheltered, so as to get some sort of perspective, to be able to evaluate them better, and not wholly to believe in them. To go from the short time span, to one less short, and then to the long view (which, if it exists, must surely be the wise man's time span); and having got there, to think about everything afresh and to reconstruct everything around one: a historian could hardly not be tempted by such a prospect.

But these successive flights cannot put the historian definitively beyond the bounds of the world's time, beyond historical time, so imperious because it is irreversible, and because it flows at the very rhythm of the earth's rotation. In fact, these different time spans which we can discern are all interdependent: it is not so much time which is the creation of our own minds, as the way in which we break it up. These fragments are reunited at the end of all our labors. The *longue durée*, the conjuncture, the event all fit into each other neatly and without difficulty, for they are all measured on the same scale. Equally, to be able to achieve an imaginative understanding of one of these time spans is to be able to understand them all. The philosopher, taken up with the subjective aspect of things, interior to any notion of time, never senses this weight of historical time, of a concrete, universal time, such as the time of conjuncture that Ernest Labrousse[6] depicts at the beginning of his book like a traveler who is constantly the same and who travels the world imposing the same set of values, no matter the country in which he has disembarked, nor what the social order with which it is invested.

For the historian everything begins and ends with time, a mathematical, godlike time, a notion easily mocked, time external to men, 'exogenous', as economists would say, pushing men, forcing them, and painting their own individual times the same color: it is, indeed, the imperious time of the world.

Sociologists, of course, will not entertain this oversimplified notion. They are much closer to the *dialectique de la durée* as put forward by Gaston Bachelard.[7] Social time is but one dimension of the social reality under consideration. It is within this reality just as it is within a given individual, one sign of particularity among others. The sociologist is in no way hampered by this accommodating sort of time, which can be cut, frozen, set in motion entirely at will. Historical time, I must repeat, lends itself less easily to the supple double action of synchrony and diachrony: it cannot envisage life as a mechanism that can be stopped at leisure in order to reveal a frozen image.

This is a more profound rift than is at first apparent: sociologists' time cannot be ours. The fundamental structure of our profession revolts against it. Our time, like economists' time, is one of measure. When a sociologist tells us that a structure breaks down only in order to build itself up afresh, we are happy to accept an explanation which historical observation would confirm anyway. But we would wish to know the precise time span of these movements, whether positive or negative, situated along the usual axis. An economic cycle, the ebb and flow of material life, can be measured. A structural social crisis should be equally possible to locate in time, and through it. We should be able to place it exactly, both in itself and even more in relation to the movement of associated structures. What is profoundly interesting to the historian is the way these movements cross one another, and how they interact, and how they break up: all things which can be recorded only in relation to the uniform time of historians, which can stand as a general measure of all these phenomena, and not in relation to the multiform time of social reality, which can stand only as the individual measure of each of these phenomena separately.

Notes

1 Claude Lévi-Strauss, *Structural Anthropology*, Allen Lane, 1968, p. 23.
2 Philippe Ariès, *Les temps de l'histoire*, Paris, 1954, esp. p. 298ff.
3 P. Chombart de Lauwe, *Paris et l'agglomération parisienne*, Paris, 1952, vol. 1, p. 106.
4 Gaston Roupnel, *Histoire et destin*, Paris, 1943, p. 169 and passim.
5 Paul Lacombe, in *Revue de synthèse historique*, 1900, p. 32.
6 Ernest Labrousse, *La crise économique française à la veille de la Révolution française*, Paris, 1944, Introduction.
7 Gaston Bachelard, *Dialectique de la durée*, 2nd edn, Paris, 1950.

33. Lawrence Stone

*[from 'The revival of narrative: reflections on a new old history',
Past and Present 85 (1979), pp. 3–4, 8–13, 21–4]*

Historians have always told stories. From Thucydides and Tacitus to Gibbon and Macaulay the composition of narrative in lively and elegant prose was always accounted their highest ambition. History was regarded as a branch of rhetoric. For the last fifty years, however, this story-telling function has fallen into ill repute among those who have regarded themselves as in the vanguard of the profession, the practitioners of the so-called 'new history' of the post-Second-World-War era. In France story-telling was dismissed as 'l'histoire événementielle'. Now, however, I detect evidence of an under-current which is sucking many prominent 'new historians' back again into some form of narrative.

Before embarking upon an examination of the evidence for such a shift and upon some speculations about what may have caused it, a number of things had better be made clear. The first is what is meant here by 'narrative'. Narrative is taken to mean the organization of material in a chronologically sequential order and the focusing of the content into a single coherent story, albeit with sub-plots. The two essential ways in which narrative history differs from structural history is that its arrangement is descriptive rather than ana-lytical and that its central focus is on man not circumstances. It therefore deals with the particular and specific rather than the collective and statistical. Narrative is a mode of historical writing, but it is a mode which also affects and is affected by the content and the method.

The kind of narrative which I have in mind is not that of the simple anti-quarian reporter or annalist. It is narrative directed by some 'pregnant prin-ciple', and which possesses a theme and an argument. Thucydides's theme was the Peloponnesian wars and their disastrous effects upon Greek society and politics; Gibbon's the decline and fall of the Roman empire; Macaulay's the rise of a liberal participatory constitution in the stresses of revolutionary politics. Biographers tell the story of a life, from birth to death. No narrative historians, as I have defined them, avoid analysis altogether, but this is not the skeletal framework around which their work is constructed. And finally, they are deeply concerned with the rhetorical aspects of their presentation. Whether successful or not in the attempt, they certainly aspire to stylistic elegance, wit and aphorism. They are not content to throw words down on a page and let them lie there, with the view that, since history is a science, it needs no art to help it along.

The trends here identified should not be taken to apply to the great mass of historians. All that is being attempted is to point to a noticeable shift of content, method and style among a very tiny, but disproportionately prominent, section of the historical profession as a whole. History has always had many mansions, and must continue to do so if it is to flourish in the future. The triumph of any one genre or school eventually always leads to narrow sectarianism, narcissism and self-adulation, contempt or tyranny towards outsiders, and other disagreeable and self-defeating characteristics. We can all think of cases where this has happened. In some countries and institutions it has been unhealthy that the 'new historians' have had things so much their own way in the last thirty years; and it will be equally unhealthy if the new trend, if trend it be, achieves similar domination here and there.

It is also essential to establish once and for all that this essay is trying to chart observed changes in historical fashion, not to make value judgements about what are good, and what are less good, modes of historical writing. Value judgements are hard to avoid in any historiographical study, but this essay is not trying to raise a banner or start a revolution. No one is being urged to throw away his calculator and tell a story.

The first cause of the current revival of narrative is a widespread disillusionment with the economic determinist model of historical explanation and this three-tiered hierarchical arrangement to which it gave rise. The split between social history on the one hand and intellectual history on the other has the most unfortunate consequences. Both have become isolated, inward-looking, and narrow. In America intellectual history, which had once been the flagship of the profession, fell upon hard times and for a while lost confidence in itself; social history has flourished as never before, but its pride in its isolated achievements was but the harbinger of an eventual decline in vitality, when faith in purely economic and social explanations began to ebb. The historical record has now obliged many of us to admit that there is an extraordinarily complex two-way flow of interactions between facts of population, food supply, climate, bullion supply, prices, on the one hand, and values, ideas and customs on the other. Along with social relationships of status or class, they form a single web of meaning.

Many historians now believe that the culture of the group, and even the will of the individual, are potentially at least as important causal agents of change as the impersonal forces of material output and demographic growth. There is no theoretical reason why the latter should always dictate the former, rather than vice versa, and indeed evidence is piling up of examples to the contrary.[1] Contraception, for example, is clearly as much a product of a state of mind as it is of economic circumstances. The proof of this contention can be found in the wide diffusion of this practice throughout France, long before industrialization, without much population pressure except on small farms, and nearly a century before any other western country. We also now know that the nuclear family antedated industrial society, and that concepts of privacy, love and individualism similarly emerged among some of the most traditional sectors of a traditional society in late seventeenth- and early eighteenth-century England, rather than as a result of later modernizing economic and social processes. The Puritan ethic was a by-product of an unworldly religious movement which took root in the Anglo-Saxon societies of England and New England centuries before routine work-patterns were necessary or the first factory was built. On the other hand there is an inverse correlation, at any rate in nineteenth-century France, between literacy and urbanization and industrialization. Levels of literacy turn out to be a poor guide to 'modern' attitudes of mind or 'modern' occupations.[2] Thus the linkages between culture and society are clearly very complex indeed, and seem to vary from time to time and from place to place.

It is hard not to suspect that the decline of ideological commitment among western intellectuals has also played its part. If one looks at three of the most passionate and hard-fought historical battles of the 1950s and 1960s – about the rise or decline of the gentry in seventeenth-century England, about the rise or fall of working-class real income in the early stages of industrialization, and about the causes, nature and consequences of American slavery – all were at bottom debates fired by current ideological concerns. It seemed desperately important at the time to know whether or not the Marxist interpretation was right, and therefore these historical questions mattered and were exciting. The muting of ideological controversy caused by the intellectual decline of Marxism and the adoption of mixed economies in the west has coincided with a decline in the thrust of historical research to ask the big *why* questions, and it is plausible to suggest that there is some relationship between the two trends.

Economic and demographic determinism has not only been undermined by a recognition of ideas, culture and even individual will as independent variables. It has also been sapped by a revived recognition that political and military power, the use of brute force, has very frequently dictated the structure of the society, the distribution of wealth, the agrarian system, and even the culture of the élite. Classic examples are the Norman conquest of England in 1066, and probably also the divergent economic and social paths taken by eastern Europe, north-western Europe and England in the sixteenth and seventeenth centuries.[3] Future historians will undoubtedly severely criticize the 'new historians' of the 1950s and 1960s for their failure to take sufficient account of power: of political organization and decision-making and the vagaries of military battle and siege, destruction and conquest. Civilizations have risen and fallen due to fluctuations in political authority and shifts in the fortunes of war, and it is extraordinary that these matters should have been neglected for so long by those who regarded themselves as in the forefront of the historical profession. In practice the bulk of the profession continued to concern itself with political history, just as it had always done, but this is not where the cutting edge of the profession was generally thought to be. A belated recognition of the importance of power, of personal political decisions by individuals, of the chances of battle, have forced historians back to the narrative mode, whether they like it or not. To use Machiavelli's terms, neither *virtu* nor *fortuna* can be dealt with except by a narrative, or even an anecdote, since the first is an individual attribute and the second a happy or unhappy accident.

The third development which has dealt a serious blow to structural and analytical history is the mixed record to date in the use of what has been its most characteristic methodology – namely quantification. Quantification has undoubtedly matured and has now established itself as an essential methodology in many areas of historical inquiry, especially demographic history, the history of social structure and social mobility, economic history, and the history of voting patterns and voting behaviour in democratic political systems. Its use has greatly improved the general quality of historical discourse, by demanding the citation of precise numbers instead of the previous loose use of words. Historians can no longer get away with saying 'more', 'less', 'growing', 'declining', all of which logically imply numerical comparisons, without ever stating explicitly the statistical basis for their assertions. It has also made argument exclusively by example seem somewhat disreputable. Critics now demand supporting statistical evidence to show that the examples are typical, and not exceptions to the rule. These procedures have undoubtedly improved the logical power and persuasiveness of historical argument. Nor is there any disagreement that whenever it is appropriate, fruitful and possible from the surviving records, the historian should count.

There is, however, a difference in kind between the artisan quantification done by a single researcher totting up figures on a hand-calculator and producing simple tables and percentages, and the work of the cliometricians. The latter specialize in the assembling of vast quantities of data by teams of assistants, the use of the electronic computer to process it all, and the application of highly sophisticated mathematical procedures to the results obtained. Doubts have been cast on all stages of this procedure. Many question whether historical data are ever sufficiently reliable to warrant such procedures; whether teams of assistants can be trusted to apply uniform coding procedures to large quantities of often widely diverse and even ambiguous documents; whether much crucial detail is not lost in the coding procedure; if it is ever possible to be confident that all coding and programming errors have been eliminated; and whether the sophistication of the mathematical and algebraic formulae are not ultimately self-defeating since they baffle most historians. Finally, many are disturbed by the virtual impossibility of checking up on the reliability of the final results, since they must depend not on published footnotes but on privately owned computer-tapes, in turn the result of thousands of privately owned code-sheets, in turn abstracted from the raw data.

These questions are real and will not go away. We all know of doctoral dissertations or printed papers or monographs which have used the most sophisticated techniques either to prove the obvious or to claim to prove the implausible, using formulae and language which render the methodology unverifiable to the ordinary historian. The results sometimes combine the vices of unreadability and triviality. We all know of the doctoral dissertations which languish unfinished since the researcher has been unable to keep under intellectual control the sheer volume of print-out spewed out by the computer, or has spent so much effort preparing the data for the machine that his time, patience and money have run out. One clear conclusion is surely that, whenever possible, sampling by hand is preferable and quicker than, and just as reliable as, running the whole universe through a machine. We all know of projects in which a logical flaw in the argument or a failure to use plain common sense has vitiated or cast in doubt many of the conclusions. We all know of other projects in which the failure to record one piece of information at the coding stage has led to the loss of an important result. We all know of others where the sources of information are themselves so unreliable that we can be sure that little confidence can be placed in the conclusions based on their quantitative manipulation. Parish registers are a classic example, upon which a gigantic amount of effort is currently being spent in many countries, only some of which is likely to produce worthwhile results.

Despite its unquestionable achievements it cannot be denied that quantification has not fulfilled the high hopes of twenty years ago. Most of the great problems of history remain as insoluble as ever, if not more so. Consensus on the causes of the English, French or American revolutions are as far away as ever, despite the enormous effort put into elucidating their social and economic origins. Thirty years of intensive research on demographic history has left us more rather than less bewildered. We do not know why the population ceased to grow in most areas of Europe between 1640 and 1740; we do not know why it began to grow again in 1740; or even whether the cause was rising fertility or declining mortality. Quantification has told us a lot about the *what* questions of historical demography, but relatively little so far about the *why*. The major questions about American slavery remain as elusive as ever, despite the application to them of one of the most massive and sophisticated studies ever mounted. The publication of its findings, far from solving most problems, merely raised the temperature of the debate.[4] It had the beneficial effect of focusing attention on important issues such as the diet, hygiene, health and family structure of American Negroes under slavery, but it also diverted attention from the equally or even more important psychological effects of slavery upon both masters and slaves, simply because these matters could not be measured by a computer. Urban histories are cluttered with statistics, but mobility trends still remain obscure. Today no one is quite sure whether English society was more open and mobile than the French in the seventeenth and eighteenth centuries, or even whether the gentry or aristocracy was rising or falling in England before the Civil War. We are no better off now in these respects than were James Harrington in the seventeenth century or Tocqueville in the nineteenth.

It is just those projects that have been the most lavishly funded, the most ambitious in the assembly of vast quantities of data by armies of paid researchers, the most scientifically processed by the very latest in computer technology, the most mathematically sophisticated in presentation, which have so far turned out to be the most disappointing. Today, two decades and millions of dollars, pounds and francs later, there are only rather modest results to show for the expenditure of so much time, effort and money. There are huge piles of greenish print-out gathering dust in scholars' offices; there are many turgid and excruciatingly dull tomes full of tables of figures, abstruse algebraic equations and percentages given to two decimal places. There are also many valuable new findings and a few major contributions to the relatively small corpus of historical works of permanent value. But in general the sophistication of the methodology has tended to exceed the reliability of the data, while the usefulness of the results seems – up to a point – to be in inverse correlation to the mathematical complexity of the methodology and the grandiose scale of data-collection.

On any cost-benefit analysis the rewards of large-scale computerized history have so far only occasionally justified the input of time and money and this has led historians to cast around for other methods of investigating the past, which will shed more light with less trouble. In 1968 Le Roy Ladurie prophesied that by the 1980s 'the historian will be a programmer or he will be nothing'.[5] The prophecy has not been fulfilled, least of all by the prophet himself.

Historians are therefore forced back upon the principle of indeterminacy, a recognition that the variables are so numerous that at best only middle-range generalizations are possible in history, as Robert Merton long ago suggested. The macro-economic model is a pipe-dream, and 'scientific history' a myth. Monocausal explanations simply do not work. The use of feed-back models of explanation built around Weberian 'elective affinities' seems to provide better tools for revealing something of the elusive truth about historical causation, especially if we abandon any claim that this methodology is in any sense scientific.

Disillusionment with economic or demographic monocausal determinism and with quantification has led historians to start asking a quite new set of questions, many of which were previously blocked from view by the preoccupation with a specific methodology, structural, collective and statistical. More and more of the 'new historians' are now trying to discover what was going on inside people's heads in the past, and what it was like to live in the past, questions which inevitably lead back to the use of narrative.

....

The fundamental reason for the shift among the 'new historians' from the analytical to the descriptive mode is a major change in attitude about what is the central subject-matter of history. And this in turn depends on prior philosophical assumptions about the role of human free will in its interaction with the forces of nature. The contrasting poles of thought are best revealed by quotations, one on one side and two on the other. In 1973 Emmanuel Le Roy Ladurie entitled a section of a volume of his essays 'History without People'.[6] By contrast half a century ago Lucien Febvre announced, 'My quarry is man', and a quarter of a century ago Hugh Trevor-Roper, in his inaugural lecture, urged upon historians 'the study not of circumstances but of man in circumstances'.[7] Today Febvre's ideal of history is catching on in many circles, at the same time as analytical structural studies of impersonal forces continue to pour out from the presses. Historians are therefore now dividing into four groups: the old narrative historians, primarily political historians and biographers; the cliometricians who continue to act like statistical junkies; the hard-nosed social historians still busy analysing impersonal structures; and the historians of *mentalité*, now chasing ideals, values, mind-sets, and patterns of intimate personal behaviour – the more intimate the better.

The adoption by the historians of *mentalité* of minute descriptive narrative or individual biography is not, however, without its problems. The trouble is the old one, that argument by selective example is philosophically unpersuasive, a rhetorical device not a scientific proof. The basic historiographical trap in which we are ensnared has recently been well set out by Carlo Ginzburg: 'The quantitative and anti-anthropocentric approach of the sciences of nature from Galileo onwards has placed human sciences in an unpleasant dilemma: they must either adopt a weak scientific standard so as to be able to attain significant results, or adopt a strong scientific standard to attain results of no great importance.'[8] Disappointment with the second approach is causing a drift back to the first. As a result what is now taking place is an expansion of the selective example – now often a detailed unique example – into one of the fashionable modes of historical writing. In one sense this is only a logical extension of the enormous success of local history studies, which have taken as their subject not a whole society but only a segment – a province, a town, even a village. Total history only seems possible if one takes a microcosm, and the results have often done more to illuminate and explain the past than all the earlier or concurrent studies based on the archives of the central government. In another sense, however, the new trend is the antithesis of local history studies, since it abandons the total history of a society, however small, as an impossibility, and settles for the story of a single cell.

The second problem which arises from the use of the detailed example to illustrate *mentalité* is how to distinguish the normal from the eccentric. Since man is now our quarry, the narration of a very detailed story of a single incident or personality can make both good reading and good sense. But this will be so only if the stories do not merely tell a striking but fundamentally irrelevant tale of some dramatic episode of riot or rape, or the life of some eccentric rogue or villain or mystic, but are selected for the light they can throw upon certain aspects of a past culture. This means that they must be typical, and yet the wide use of records of litigation makes this question of typicality very difficult to resolve. People hauled into court are almost by definition atypical, but the world that is so nakedly exposed in the testimony of witnesses need not be so. Safety therefore lies in examining the documents not so much for their evidence about the eccentric behaviour of the accused as for the light they shed on the life and opinions of those who happened to get involved in the incident in question.

The third problem concerns interpretation, and is even harder to resolve. Provided the historian remains aware of the hazards involved, story-telling is perhaps as good a way as any to obtain an intimate glimpse of man in the past, to try to get inside his head. The trouble is that if he succeeds in getting there, the narrator will need all the skill and experience and knowledge acquired in the practice of analytical history of society, economy and culture, if he is to provide a plausible explanation of some of the very strange things he is liable to find. He may also need a little amateur psychology to help him along, but amateur psychology is extremely tricky material to handle successfully – and some would argue that it is impossible.

Another obvious danger is that the revival of narrative may lead to a return to pure antiquarianism, to story-telling for its own sake. Yet another is that it will focus attention upon the sensational and so obscure the dullness and drabness of the lives of the vast majority. Both Trevor-Roper and Richard Cobb are enormous fun to read, but they are wide open to criticism on both counts. Many practitioners of the new mode, including Cobb, Hobsbawm, Thompson, Le Roy Ladurie and Trevor-Roper (and myself) are clearly fascinated by stories of violence and sex, which appeal to the voyeuristic instincts in us all. On the other hand it can be argued that sex and violence are integral parts of all human experience, and that it is therefore as reasonable and defensible to explore their impact on individuals in the past as it is to expect to see such material in contemporary films and television.

The trend to narrative raises unsolved problems about how we are to train our graduate students in the future – assuming that there are any to train. In the ancient arts of rhetoric? In textual criticism? In semiotics? In symbolic anthropology? In psychology? Or in the techniques of analysis of social and economic structures which we have been practising for a generation? It therefore remains an open question whether this unexpected resurrection of the narrative mode by so many leading practitioners of the 'new history' will turn out to be a good or a bad thing for the future of the profession.

In 1972 Le Roy Ladurie wrote confidently: 'Present-day historiography, with its preference for the quantifiable, the statistical and the structural, has been obliged to suppress in order to survive. In the last decades it has virtually condemned to death the narrative history of events and the individual biography.'[9] It is far too early to pronounce a funeral oration over the decaying corpse of analytical, structural, quantitative history, which continues to flourish, and even to grow if the trend in American doctoral dissertations is any guide. Nevertheless in this, the third decade, narrative history and individual biography are showing evident signs of rising again from the dead. Neither look quite the same as they used to do before their alleged demise, but they are easily identifiable as variants of the same genus.

It is clear that a single word like 'narrative', especially one with such a complicated history behind it, is inadequate to describe what is in fact a broad cluster of changes in the nature of historical discourse. There are signs of change with regard to the central issue in history, from the circumstances surrounding man, to man in circumstances; in the problems studied, from the economic and demographic to the cultural and emotional; in the prime sources of influence, from sociology, economics and demography to anthropology and psychology; in the subject-matter, from the group to the individual; in the explanatory models of historical change, from the stratified and monocausal to the interconnected and multicausal; in the methodology, from group quantification to individual example; in the organization, from the analytical to the descriptive; and in the conceptualization of the historian's function, from the scientific to the literary. These many-faceted changes in content, objective, method, and style of historical writing, which are all happening at once, have clear elective affinities with one another: they all fit neatly together. No single word is adequate to sum them all up, and so, for the time being, 'narrative' will have to serve as a shorthand code-word for all that is going on.

Notes

1 M. Zuckerman, 'Dreams that men dare to dream: the role of ideas in Western modernization', *Social Science History* 2 (1978).
2 F. Furet and J. Ozouf, *Lire et écrire*, Paris, 1977.
3 I refer to the debate triggered off by Robert Brenner, 'Agrarian class structure and economic development in pre-industrial Europe', *Past and Present* 70 (1976), pp. 30–75.
4 R.W. Fogel and S. Engerman, *Time on the Cross*, 2 vols, Little, Brown, 1974; Paul A. David *et al.*, *Reckoning with Slavery*, Oxford University Press, 1976; Herbert G. Gutman, *Slavery and the Numbers Game*, University of Illinois Press, 1975.
5 Emmanuel Le Roy Ladurie, *Le territoire de l'historien*, vol. 1, Paris, 1973, p. 14 (translation by Lawrence Stone).
6 Emmanuel Le Roy Ladurie, *The Territory of the Historian*, Harvester, 1979, p. 285.
7 H.R. Trevor-Roper, *History: Professional and Lay*, Oxford University Press, 1957, p. 21.
8 Carlo Ginzburg, 'Roots of a scientific paradigm', *Theory and Society* 7 (1979), p. 276.
9 Ladurie, *Territory of the Historian*, p. 111.

34. Theodore Zeldin

[from 'Personal history and the history of the emotions',
Journal of Social History *15: 3 (Spring 1982), pp. 339–43]*

'I wish I *dared* write a book like yours.' The professor of Paris University who rather surprisingly said this to me is, in private conversation, witty, whimsical and modest; he regularly makes fun of the deadly serious, tough, argumentative and erudite monographs which he publishes and which have made him the leading expert in his field. He knows about many more subjects than he teaches, but he will never write on them. He is completely different in his public capacity from the man his family and friends know. Professors, particularly American professors, are no longer aloof towards their students, but they still generally keep a distance between themselves and their publications: you cannot normally tell what kind of man an author of a learned work is. That may imply that many professors still deliberately or unconsciously conform to a model of 'rigorous' style, as though the shadow of the stereotypic 19th century German Herr Professor Doktor still hovers over academia, to ensure that the rules are obeyed. Pomposity certainly provides a convenient mask, but why must historians wear masks when they sit at their typewriters? Is it that they worry about what the neighbours will say? The great difference between learned and imaginative literature is that the former has to convince the experts, even if it challenges them, while the latter can be a rejection of traditional forms of expression and an assertion of individual personality.

The distinction or barrier between these two forms of writing has been raised in the name of professionalism, but it has become constricting, and it is due for demolition. The humanisation of academia can extend to the learned monograph also; publications need not be so predictable a ritual for everybody. The main obstacle in the way of change is the rigidity of opinion about the form in which scholarly work should be presented. Pictorial art has allowed a vast range of experiment: a portrait can be painted in almost any colour now, in an infinite variety of shapes, styles and poses. Why are historians so indissolubly attached to a single classical style? I began my career as a historian by publishing one article in each of the major learned journals, and each demanded some changes. The price of publication is conformity to the opinions of the editor. A journal does more than exude a particular odour to determine the expectations of the reader. When I wrote for an American encyclopaedia that calls itself British, my style was radically altered to harmonise with its standard, even though my name appeared at the end. Publishers conspire to maintain traditional patterns of writing also; desperate to increase their sales, they try to mould books to look like textbooks and to fit into established courses; most authors will recall how they haggled about the titles of their books, in vain attempts to reconcile commercial, academic and personal considerations. Of course, when you have shown you can play the game their way, you sometimes do obtain the privilege or the confidence to write in your own way without any kind of pressure. It is the established author who is allowed most freedom, which is a pity, because it is the new author who is most in need of freedom and most likely to have something new to say.

Perhaps what is needed is a special variety of history which deliberately rejects such constraints. If I were asked what kind of history I enjoy writing most, I would answer personal or individual history. I do not like simple labels, but this one at least has the compensation that it has two faces, since it simultaneously hints at another aspiration of equal importance. On the one hand it suggests a form of writing which openly expresses the personality of individual historians, in the same way as paintings and novels do. The ideal of scientific history arose from the prestige of scientific discoveries in the 19th century; the growth of individualism must inevitably give rise to an individualistic kind of history. A profession begins by guaranteeing uniform standards: when it matures it is more able to admit, tolerate, even encourage pluralism. But personal history is not just a method: it also invites a different subject matter, a concern for the role of the individual in the past. I happen to believe that a reaction is needed against the priority given to the study of classes, nations, movements and abstract forces. Personal history appeals to historians who want to understand themselves through their work (as opposed to finding escape in their work) and who consider that a better understanding of the individual needs to be the next broad goal of historical research. It thus hopes to use the growth of self-consciousness and of interest in emotional states to advance knowledge of both past and present. It regards the individual as the atom of history, and thinks it is time historians tried to split their atom, studying its constituent parts more carefully. Nuclear scientists have transformed our notion of what matter is; things are no longer what they appear to be; it is possible to recombine molecules to create new materials; within limits man can manipulate his surroundings. Historians, by contrast, cannot go on repeating that human nature is always the same, refusing to reexamine this and many similar old adages which they take for granted, or to investigate whether human emotions are in fact permanent, immutable constants. The combination of these two broad aims indicates that personal history does not try to supersede other forms of history, or claim to be better than they: it represents a personal point of view, and no more. It applauds the fact that there are other kinds of history, because it values a variety of perspectives as an essential part of the historical art. It is not a substitute for the study of collective behaviour, institutions and communities, but a counterpart to it.

It might however perhaps stimulate a minor historians' liberation movement, in that it requires a new kind of relationship with the social sciences. Historians have been travelling on the bandwagon of interdisciplinary studies for some time now, and have derived much excitement and benefit from the ride. Their alliance with the social sciences has indeed often blossomed into a love affair and a more or less official marriage: there are historians who have changed their name and call themselves social scientists. The marriage was contracted in the hope that it would bring a broadening of horizons, which it has done, but the experience has now lapsed into a fairly predictable routine. In practice most historians have come to accept the dominant influence of sociology and economics, or if they do not like that, they have adopted psychoanalytic theories. To be a psycho-historian, you need to undergo psychoanalytic training. To be an economic historian, you need to be something of a mathematician. A great deal of what is considered most interesting in historical writing is based on the application of ideas and theories from other disciplines. Increasingly the implication is that historians can no longer perform their tasks except in so far as they master the theories and methods evolved by other sciences. Even those erstwhile pioneers, the Annales School, who once gave a new pride to historians, now say without a hint of complaint that historians are camp-followers, trailing behind other sciences which carry out the real advances in knowledge. So there is a vague parallel with the feeling some women have that their marriage deprives them of their identity. The historian's identity, the peculiar nature of the historical approach may be difficult to define, but the question is worth posing, whether history has no message, no value, independently of its partners.

The answer of course is that historians do not agree, which is why interdisciplinary studies are so convenient. But there probably is quite a large body of opinion among historians which might admit to cherishing three specific characteristics. In what other discipline would they be allowed an ineradicable fascination for the particular individual case, for its own sake, irrespective of the general conclusions that might be drawn? Secondly, which of the social sciences places quite as much emphasis as historians do on literary style, so that writing becomes almost as important as analysis? This is a relic perhaps from the days when historians were above all storytellers; ideally, they want the reader not only to feel wiser but also to be moved by a history book; the great historians of the past have always been great writers. And thirdly, do historians quite accept that they are simply specialists, and not also in some sense generalists, in that everything that has been done or thought falls within their domain? They have as much in common with novelists (who are not expected to prove anything) and with philosophers (who reflect on other disciplines) as with social scientists. Historians who think like this need to be able to use their maiden name sometimes and not try to be social scientists all the time, with the only differentiation that they exclude the present from their concerns. They need a haven for at least occasional use, where they can give free rein to aspects of their outlook and temperament which their partners do not satisfy, where they can set aside rigid frameworks or accepted styles, where they can adopt an attitude of independence towards fashionable theories, where they can admit they cannot explain everything and that there are unfathomable mysteries and random behaviour, where they can experiment in artistic creation.

Historians are in any case being liberated whether they like it or not, because the grand general theories which dominated social science over the last generation are collapsing, and a new age of pluralism is beginning. To borrow and test other people's concepts and hypotheses used to be fashionable: to invent one's own may be more so in the future. Interdisciplinary studies meant a sharing of ideas among experts: there may be a reaction against experts, and counterdisciplinary studies, protesting against the esoteric tendencies of experts, may be the next fashion. Women's studies, for example, conceived in the age of interdisciplinary studies, have so far used the same methods as everybody else, only limiting themselves to half the human species; having established their academic respectability, they may well be led by the new viewpoints and emphases they are revealing to develop really different methods. The snag about borrowing ideas from other disciplines is that one tends to borrow them rather late, often just as they have ceased to be believed by the pioneers in that subject. All academic disciplines are in turmoil now, subtly shifting their ground, and that calls for greater vigilance against complacency in established patterns of thought.

Imagination is moreover as important to historians as new documents. New documents are an easy way to give oneself an illusion of originality. It is much harder to think freshly about the known facts. The age of the Ph.D. dissertation will not last forever. As the available material grows so enormous that it becomes impossible to master, the premium will be on those who can reflect on it rather than add to it. So humane qualities, the capacity for sympathy and sensitivity will be increasingly valued as historians are expected to reinterpret and recreate the past, and not just add to knowledge. The explosion in research of the last decades must inevitably be balanced now by a period of digestion and reflection, and also by more confrontation of the research with present day experience. So the historian who can discover the links between his own life and what has happened in past centuries, who can express in a new way how the past is alive, or who can give it a new colouring through the sieve of his own idiosyncrasies, will no longer be idiosyncratic. The inequalities which bedevil the historical profession may well be attenuated as a result. Those who get research grants to visit archives, or who live in major cities with superior facilities, will no longer be able to give an inferiority complex to the teacher in the small town, or the family man who cannot get away. The quality of a historian's personal experience is ultimately decisive in determining the quality of his writings. And there is no real reason why historical study should necessarily manifest itself only through books or articles. The mania for publications at all costs is the result of administrative convenience and the search for promotion and tenure, not the needs of the subject. Philosophers have established their right to be philosophers simply by thinking and conversing. Philosophy can be treated as an experience. History can be a way of life too. Everybody recognises that there are excellent historians who never publish much but whose insights, dropped casually in conversation, can be more enlightening than a whole stack of monographs. Writing is only one way of working out what one thinks and only one way of communicating. Undoubtedly in the future film will be used to convey historical information and ideas. It may well be that the most influential historians of the next century will express themselves through visual means. This will pose entirely new problems, for film and history combine as a meeting of two arts. There is no ready made formula for their cooperation, which makes it all the more challenging.

The focusing on the individual as the central figure in history means more than the multiplication of biographies (though that is part of it); it means also an expansion of the ambitions of biography. Academic biography is usually subordinated to history, in the sense that it is expected to contribute to the solution of general problems about the subject's times. Thus when I wrote a biography myself twenty years ago, I excused myself in my preface with the statement that I was not writing an ordinary biography, because my main aim was to throw light on the constitutional evolution of Napoleon III's regime. I was reacting against the idea that popular biography is a mere string of anecdotes; at that time I was interested in my main character as much in his capacity as a politician as in his personal life. If I were rewriting the book now, I would be tempted to add to the chapters on the various political problems I dealt with others on egoism, loyalty, obstinacy and grief, that is to say, I would not take it for granted that his political career was the most important thing about him; I would try to develop other perspectives created by his peculiar experience. Biographers today can do not only more than biographers did in the past, but they can also go beyond applying the theories of other disciplines to biography. Thus it was fashionable to apply the theories of Freud or Erikson to explain past behaviour: this has enormously expanded our knowledge, of childhood and the family in particular. But there are now psychologists who are actively challenging the idea that events in infancy have a decisive effect on future conduct, or even that character is consistent through life: as more attention is devoted to the different stages of life, and particularly gerontology, man's capacity to change is being asserted.[1] Biography moreover is no longer a monopoly of historians. There is an emerging school of life-span psychology.[2] There is a revival and development of the biographical sociology sponsored by the Chicago School, culminating in the masterpieces of Oscar Lewis; there is even a new Paris 'group for the biographical approach in sociology'. All this indicates a new emphasis on individual experience, but a distinctly pluralist one. The conclusion today is not that historians must change their models and apply these new approaches to biography (stimulating though they can be), but that they need to develop approaches of their own.

Notes

1 Orville G. Brim, Jr and Jerome Kagan, *Constancy and Change in Human Development*, Harvard University Press, 1980.
2 Ibid. For historical applications see Glen H. Elder, Jr, *Children of the Great Depression*, Chicago University Press, 1977, and Tamara K. Hareven (ed.), *Transitions: The Family and the Life Course in Historical Perspective*, Academic Press, 1978.

Part Six

The Cultural Turn

The impact of Postmodernism

Whereas the 1960s and 1970s saw the credentials of the discipline being widely challenged by historians aligned with the social sciences, during the 1980s and 1990s the area of creative tension lay within the humanities – and specifically in the relativism associated with new approaches to textual study. Postmodernism is antithetical to conventional historiography on a wide front. The extracts here focus on its critique of the historical subject and of historical narrative, through the lens of first class, then gender.

Patrick Joyce has reflected at some length on the journey from Marxism to Postmodernism which he and other social historians have made since the mid-1980s. Modernity is ironically distanced as a 'grand narrative', and the formerly sovereign importance given to class is renounced as a piece of essentialism. Instead Joyce advocates a 'history of the social', in which 'the social' is taken to be not a material reality, but a discursive construct. His own work, notably *Democratic Subjects* (1994), goes some way to implement this programme.

Joan Scott has made a comparable intellectual journey, from a *marxisant* feminism in the 1970s, to a Postmodern feminism in the 1990s (see also extract 17). Whereas she previously studied the patriarchal structures which entrenched sexual inequality in industrial societies, she now directs attention at 'signification', that is the process whereby gendered meanings are constructed and contested. Linguistic and psycho-analytic theories of 'difference' lie at the centre of this enterprise.

The impact of such manifestos is to be seen in more measured accounts of Postmodernism, which criticise its tendency to extremes, while recognising the new insights which it makes possible. In that sense Postmodernism is where the cutting edge of the discipline lies. Joyce Appleby, Lynn Hunt and Margaret Jacob argue that 'Postmodern history' is a contradiction in terms, since Postmodernists espouse a relativism at odds with all notion of knowledge of the past. But they concede that Postmodernism has led to a fruitful focus on cultural history and a more sophisticated handling of certain types of historical text; these influences can readily be detected in Hunt's own work, for example *The Family Romance in the French Revolution* (1992).

35. Patrick Joyce

[from 'The end of social history?', Social History 20 (1995), pp. 81–6, 89–91]

As a contribution to finding a way out of the current impasse of social history I would like to propose the outlines of a history of the social, as well as some very brief and preliminary points concerning the question of 'social structure', a concept that has of course been of great importance for social history. The importance of post-modernist thought for social history can be described in terms of a challenge, or a series of challenges. These I will describe in terms of the understandings of identity, of modernity and of structure. New understandings in these three areas involve a challenge to, and critique of the founding categories of social history, above all class and the social.

In regard to identity, post-structuralist conceptions have been of crucial importance, especially feminist appropriations of them. Feminist theory has offered a new subject for analysis, and new conceptions of identity for our understanding, in the shape of gender. More than simply offering a new category, to contradict or complement old ones, such as class, feminist theory has helped problematize the whole question of what identity is. Gender identities are seen as historically and culturally formed. They are not the product of an external 'referent' which confers meaning on them. Identity is seen as a product of conflicting cultural forces, and viewed as relational, composed of systems of difference. The debt to post-structuralist theory is apparent, and its conception of language not as the mirror of a world external to it, but as a conventional and arbitrary structure of relations of difference, the eventual shape of which is produced through cultural and power relations.

The implications for understandings of class will be apparent: if gender cannot be derived from an external referent, then the same follows for class. It cannot be referred to an external 'social' referent which is its foundation or cause. This referent, the 'social', is itself a 'discursive' product of history.

The relevant questions then become, 'how have the links between language and its object – the wrongly assumed social referent – become established, and how have the conventional operations of discourse been produced?' These, eminently historical, questions produce a rather different agenda from more orthodox understandings of the social and of class. The search now is for how meanings have been produced by relations of power, rather than for 'external' or 'objective' class 'structures', or other 'social' referents. It also follows that if identity is composed through the relations of systems of difference, then it is marked by conflict, and is plural, diverse and volatile. The view of identity is one in which many 'identities' press in and react with one another (we are men and women, parents and children, members of classes and nations, modernists and post modernists, and so on). It is a view rather at odds with many accounts of class, which tend to deal in fairly uniform and coherent identities (the very idea of a class having a consciousness of itself puts a high premium on this view of identity as stable and uniform). 'Class' is indeed regularly stacked up with other, similarly stable identities (race, nation, gender, and so on). Out of these rough-hewn blocks sociologies and histories continue to be made. Perhaps it is time for a more credible notion of identity, one which considers the systems by which relations of difference work, including those means by which differences are composed into unities, however conditional these unities may sometimes be.

Let me move next from identity to the question of modernity. Considerations of identity involve notions of the human subject itself, and ultimately of modernity. Instead of a human subject conceived as the centre and organizing principle of multiple identities, human subjectivity is itself an historical creation. As Foucault has argued, the idea of a 'centred', controlling human subject is a product of the 'classical age', particularly the eighteenth century when the emergence of 'man' in his true grandeur becomes evident. In this argument the western subject has been constructed as an 'individual'. However, inseparable from this creation, and simultaneous with it, was the construction of 'the social'. The individual's rights, obligations and conduct were measured in terms of a 'social' that both guaranteed their integrity and policed their excesses. Strategies for the implementation of the individual – such as the constitution of the 'private sphere' – were inseparable from strategies implementing the social – such as the constitution of the 'public sphere' and 'civil society'. Thus it is the case that the radical questioning of identity and subjectivity indicated here poses further fundamental problems for the concept of class: that concept is one of the consequences of the implementation of 'the social' considered here. 'Society' is the ground upon which the figures of class have been placed, figures that in some readings of class have become not only social 'facts' but collective actors on the historical stage. It is necessary to go back and look at the history of this ground if the figures that are its consequence are to be understood.

The implementation of the human subject and of society may be seen as the implementation of 'modernity'. From this point of view 'modernity' describes a subject and a society which, though while eminently real in their consequences, are in fact themselves elements in a project. The project of modernity disguises the fact that 'individual' and 'society' are not real, 'objective' entities, but historical and normative creations, designed to handle the exigencies of political power and political order. This perspective on modernity, one of critique, can be understood as the perspective of post modernity, though many of those involved in the critique would not describe themselves thus. From a post-modern viewpoint, 'class', alongside categories like 'society' and 'economy', but also 'reason', 'the self', and so on, are all seen as exemplifications of a modernity that, as we have seen, takes them to be the 'foundations' of knowledge. Modernism is therefore conceived of as writing the 'grand narratives' of history in which these various essences play leading roles, for instance the narratives of science and progress, and of liberalism, socialism and conservatism.

If modernity is a project in these senses then sociology, and social theory more widely, can be said to be implicated directly in it, at once its progenitors and its products. Post-modern sociologies have increasingly asked whether the terms of nineteenth-century sociology are really satisfactory in describing the nature of twentieth- and twenty-first-century society. This suggests the possibility of a radical rethinking of the founding propositions of sociology, and social theory more generally, 'society' and 'class' among them. There is a further, and equally searching question to be asked of nineteenth-century sociology: if it does not describe present reality, can we be so sure it describes the reality of the times in which it grew up? The work of Bauman and Touraine, for example, offers categories of analysis which they regard as better able to interpret present reality than existing ones, class among them. Aiming to describe a world moving beyond the modern phase of society, they find the tools of a 'modernist' sociology inadequate.[1] The new tools they offer involve the attempt to transcend the old dualism of structure and agency (the emphasis, as will be seen, is broadly processual, 'society' in Bauman being replaced by 'sociality' for instance).[2] However, it is distinctly possible that such tools may help us understand the past as well as the present, especially as the old ones – among them class – are indeed seen to be part of a normative, historically situated 'project'. Both writers see the ideas of sociology, and the idea of society, to be modelled on the nation state, and in this mode conceived of as a system or a totality. The notion of society is also seen to be related to the problem of how political order might be secured in a period of what was held to be unparalleled change (a period described in the term 'progress', or the more neutral 'modern'). Classes were integral to this understanding of 'society' as a structure: they were the content of which it was the form, or – conceived more actively – they were the motors by which this structure was changed. This is not to say that the terms of classical sociology did not sometimes, indeed often, well describe the society that produced them, but the point, precisely, is that they were an historical product and not a neutral analytic. So, it is productive to think about a history of the social which conceives of this category as the product of modernity.

Finally, and briefly, the third challenge to orthodox accounts concerns the central problem of structure and agency, or structure and action (there are many terms for a dualism that has been a central concern of sociology and history). If these new sociologies are right it becomes very difficult to conceive of a structure of class relationships, or a structure of any set of 'social' variables (occupation, income, etc.), as lying objectively outside the agent or observer. This goes for the historical agent in the past, or the sociological one in the present, *and* for the observer who is employing a concept of structure in order to explain how society is organized or how people feel or behave. Agents in these accounts might usefully be seen as involved in creating or reproducing structure; observers as implicated in producing the knowledge they purport to be simply reporting on. Some of the more recent critiques of sociologized notions of structure will be considered later.

These various challenges to social history, and to the concepts of society and class, have many implications for historical work itself. Once these concepts are viewed as historically produced conventions it becomes necessary to trace their origins and development. And once a more credible notion of the formation of identity is forthcoming, in which we are led to examine the principles of unity and difference which compose personal and collective identity, it becomes possible to explore more productively the sources of identity and of different sorts of collective mobilization, political and otherwise. Here we are decidedly in the area of the operation of hegemonies: in social history the concept of hegemony has been very important, not least in the journal *Social History*, representing as it did in Gramsci and his powerful influence the attempt to square the traditional social-structural concerns of social history with a recognition of the indeterminacy of culture. The resulting intellectual gymnastics of the attempt to square this particular circle were never very convincing; the desire to ground culture in the structures of class resulted in the baroque complexities of 'hegemonic power blocks', 'elite ruling factions', and so on. Releasing the understanding of hegemony from class, as Curry has recently suggested, enables us to think more productively about the operations of power.[3]

How, then, do we trace the history of the discursivities of the social, including the ways in which they are produced by, and produce, power? The new history of class is of course one such way. Accounts of the operation of 'languages of class' have developed in the work of scholars like William H. Sewell, Gareth Stedman Jones, Joan W. Scott, Jacques Rancière and myself. The forthcoming work of Dror Wahrman is a further contribution to this,[4] and the approach can be extended in many ways. It promises to substantially rewrite the traditional narratives of social history, which still continue to be plotted in terms of classes as collective actors, and of the 'underlying' structural processes of capitalism. The language of class itself, as opposed to more populist forms, for instance, is in fact a good example of how one element in the discourse of the social has achieved hegemonic status: in Britain, until recently, the language of class was so firmly anchored in academic and popular common sense as to become naturalized, and invested with a spurious facticity it still retains today. In this process the presence of other collective subjects of the discourse of the social was forgotten, subjects such as 'the people', indeed 'people' and 'humanity' themselves, the absolutely central collective subjects of liberal democratic regimes.[5] These achieved hegemonic status in their own manner. Whatever the collective subjects involved, the 'linguistic turn', in looking at *how* such subjects are put in place, is pointing to the manner and mode in which hegemony is achieved: for instance, collective identity and political mobilization can be very valuably reinterpreted in terms of the narrative patterns that enunciated them. The example instanced earlier, drawn from the 'hybridized' operation of modernity in India, similarly points to new possibilities. Attention to the creation of subjectivity, to new 'social' subjects and to the manner in which subjectivity is produced, all suggest a new agenda for a reconfigured 'social history'.

However, there has been relatively little direct attention among mainstream historians to the history of the ground upon which these various subjects of the social may be said to move, namely 'society' and 'the social' themselves. Tracing the history (and hegemony) of the social directly has been left to other traditions, and is most notably evident in the work and influence of Foucault. The influence of Habermas has certainly been felt among historians concerned to write the history of 'civil society' and the 'public sphere', though this has tended to be simply grafted upon traditional approaches, and is in fact itself quite far removed from the perspective on the social developed here. While the influence of both men, and Elias, will no doubt continue to be productive, it seems to me that Foucault is the most suggestive figure, particularly in the form of the recent development of his work by a range of scholars working for the most part outside history.

Of these approaches, that of Habermas may be regarded as the most conventional. The argument against it, and of many of its appropriations by historians, would be that it posits as an explanation of the public sphere that which should in fact be the subject of an explanation (namely, the 'bourgeoisie'). From a 'languages of class' perspective, one could view the discourse and practice of the public sphere and civil society as that which enabled people to view themselves as 'bourgeois' in the first place (rather than a bourgeois class creating the public sphere). However, this might be to connect the public sphere too completely with the bourgeoisie: as Eley has recently pointed out, the public sphere was always gendered, and one can talk of many public spheres, not one, including a plebeian or 'working class' one (though this is open to the same counter-argument as above).[6]

It is Foucault's work that most emphatically releases us from the limits of traditional approaches to society and the social, the discourses and practices organized around conceptions of society becoming the means by which different groups, individuals and institutions identify and organize themselves, and handle power. It is Foucault's later work on the nature of rule that is the most apposite, where attention is given to its most expressly political forms, found, for example, in modes of 'governmentality' and in the role of the modern state. In this work, and its later extensions, liberalism is seen as a means, a 'technology', of rule. It is the mode of 'governmentality' that has marked the transition to the modern world in the west. The operation of 'the social', in the liberal mode of governmentality, is hence regarded as one of the major means by which identity and politics have historically evolved. Whereas Habermas, however critically, writes from within an ideology of liberalism, Foucault can be said to write outside one.

....

If we wish to retain the concept of structure in a reconfigured social history then it needs to be viewed in the light of new conceptions of structure evident in contemporary sociologies, and elsewhere. And surely some concept akin to structure needs to be retained if we are to discern what Giddens has termed the 'unconscious motivations' and 'unintended consequences' of action. Giddens's account of 'structuration' is one instance of a notion of 'structure' which, as was said earlier, involves the agent in its creation and reproduction,[7] which is to say that the agent is built into the reproduction of society and the social themselves. What the newer sociologies involve is precisely this sense of 'society' as constantly reproduced by its members, so that the emphasis, in Bauman for instance, is on 'sociality' rather than 'society', on 'processual' understandings of the social rather than structural or static ones. For instance, the conception of 'structuration' Giddens draws on is derived from language, in the sense of an 'absent totality' present only in its instantiation, rather than from static conceptions of 'presences', as in visual analogies of structure evident in ideas of the body or the building. As Giddens also puts it, arguing against the traditional dualism of action and structure and for what he calls a 'duality of structure', 'social structures are both constituted *by* human agency, and yet at the same time are the *medium* of this constitution'.

This emphasis on the processual nature of understandings of the social, where the social is seen as continually reproduced by the agents who make it up, has of course many sources, and cannot simply be termed post modern. The hermeneutic tradition, particularly in ethnomethodology, has been very important. There, emphatically anti-realist positions involve the argument that the action-structure dualism of the social sciences is something we simply impose on ourselves, unaware that it is a direct consequence of 'being-in-the-world', part of the more fundamental activity of comprehending social life in the first place. Post-Marxist traditions, evident for example in the relatively little discussed work of Cornelius Castoriadis,[8] insist on the irreducible reality of fantasy and the unconscious, and the creative role of the 'social imaginary' itself. The renaissance of interest in the work of Georg Simmel is also striking, and with it the emphasis on the self-constitution of the social world.[9] The sources are many, none the less they have been explored and developed most by self-consciously post-modernist sociologies, particularly the work of Bauman. There the whole emphasis is against understandings of society as a system or a totality, and upon self-constitution, randomness and the reflexivity of subjects.

If the accent is now upon the continuous recreation of society, then the means and manner of this recreation become very important. Attention shifts to this creative activity, which is always closely related to hermeneutic activity: to make the social is always to make meaning (in processes that may be conscious or not). Thus it is that the whole 'linguistic turn' in history, with its emphasis on representation, has an affinity with these more recent, post-modernist sociologies and the concepts in which they deal.

The latter certainly serve as a critique of the dualism of action and structure which still continues to mark sociology and social history, particularly in accounts of class. Yet the influence of not just new understandings of structure, but of a whole set of concepts drawn from anti-system forms of theorizing about the social, still remains to be considered within history, let alone worked out for historical practice. Nevertheless, a start has been made in developing more hermeneutically driven accounts of change, including accounts of 'structure' which build in access to and utilization of the recreative, representational activities of actors as they make the social world (one example would, again, be narrative itself, the concept of narrative, and who has access to what narratives, and to the means of communication themselves, serving to emphasize the centrality of hermeneutic activity for a reconfigured social history). The reproduction of the social world is seen to depend precisely on the processual activities which concepts like narrative give access to. And the same goes for all the categories employed by the 'new cultural history' in its turn to language as the model of culture, especially its turn to the analogy of the text itself. This 'aestheticization' of the social, what Hayden White calls 'the content of the form',[10] opens up many new questions. If the social world is at bottom a human construct, it is only by looking at the principles of its construction that headway will be made, and this applies to the history of the social, as well as to the theory of the social. The emerging history of the defining categories of western modernity described here, that of the discursive practices of the 'social', the 'economic', the 'cultural' and so on, itself invites new accounts of process and structure that will extend and criticize it.

Notes

1 Alain Touraine, 'Is sociology still the study of society?', *Thesis Eleven* 23 (1989); Zygmunt Bauman, *Intimations of Modernity*, Routledge, 1992, esp. Intro., Ch. 2, 4, 9.
2 Bauman, *Intimations*, pp. 190–1, 196, 204.
3 Patrick Curry, 'Towards a post-Marxist social history: Thompson, Clark and beyond', in Adrian Wilson (ed.), *Rethinking Social History: English Society 1570–1920 and its Interpretation*, Manchester University Press, 1993, pp. 167–72.
4 Dror Wahrman, *Imagining the Middle Class: The Political Representation of Class in Britain, c.1780–1840*, Cambridge University Press, 1995.
5 Patrick Joyce, *Democratic Subjects: The Self and the Social in Nineteenth-Century England*, Cambridge University Press, 1994; idem, *Visions of the People: Industrial England and the Question of Class 1840–1911*, Cambridge University Press, 1991.
6 Geoff Eley, 'Nations, publics and political cultures: placing Habermas in the nineteenth century', in Craig Calhoun (ed.), *Habermas and the Public Sphere*, MIT Press, 1993, pp. 303–4.
7 Anthony Giddens, *The Constitution of Society: Outline of the Theory of Structuration*, Cambridge University Press, 1984.

8   Cornelius Castoriadis, *The Imaginary Institution of Society*, Polity, 1987.

9   See, e.g., David Frisby, *Simmel and Since: Essays on Georg Simmel's Social Theory*, Routledge, 1992.

10 Hayden White, *The Content of the Form: Narrative Discourse and Historical Representation*, Johns Hopkins University Press, 1987.

36. Joan Scott

[from 'Women's history', in Peter Burke (ed.), New Perspectives on Historical Writing, *Polity, 1991, pp. 55–60]*

The goal of historians of women, even as they established the separate identity of women, was to integrate women into history. And the push for integration proceeded with funding from government and private foundations in the 1970s and early eighties. (These agencies were interested not only in history but also in the light historical studies could throw on contemporary policy about women.) Integration assumed not only that women could be fit into established histories, but that their presence was required to correct the story. Here the contradictory implications of the supplementary status of women's history were at work. Women's history – with its compilations of data about women in the past, with its insistence that accepted periodizations didn't work when women were taken into account, with its evidence that women influenced events and took part in public life, with its insistence that private life had a public, political dimension – implied a fundamental insufficiency: the subject of history was not a universal figure, and historians who wrote as if he were could no longer claim to tell the whole story. The project of integration made these implications explicit.

Undertaken with great enthusiasm and optimism, integration proved difficult to achieve. There seemed more to the resistance of historians than simple bias or prejudice, although that surely figured in the problem. Rather, historians of women themselves found it difficult to write women into history and the task of rewriting history called for reconceptualizations that they were not initially prepared or trained to undertake. What was needed was a way of thinking about difference and how its construction defined relations between individuals and social groups.

'Gender' was the term used to theorize the issue of sexual difference. In the United States, the term is borrowed both from grammar, with its implications about (man-made) conventions or rules of linguistic usage, and from sociology's studies of social roles assigned to women and men. Although sociological uses of 'gender' can carry with them functionalist or essentialist overtones, feminists chose to emphasize the social connotations of gender in contrast to the physical connotations of sex. They also stressed the relational aspect of gender: one could not conceive of women except as they were defined in relation to men, nor of men except as they were differentiated from women. In addition, since gender was defined as relative to social and cultural contexts, it was possible to think in terms of different gender systems and the relations of those to other categories such as race or class or ethnicity, as well as to take account of change.

The category of gender, used first to analyze differences between the sexes, was extended to the issue of differences within difference. The identity politics of the 1980s brought multiple allegiances into being that challenged the unitary meaning of the category of 'women'. Indeed, the term 'women' could hardly be used without modification: women of color, Jewish women, lesbian women, poor working women, single mothers were only some of the categories introduced. They all challenged the white middle class heterosexual hegemony of the term 'women', arguing that fundamental differences of experience made it impossible to claim a single identity. The fragmentation of a universal notion of 'women' by race, ethnicity, class, and sexuality was compounded by serious political differences within the women's movement on issues ranging from Palestine to pornography. The increasingly visible and vehement differences among women called into question the possibility for a unified politics and suggested that women's interests were not self-evident, but a matter of contest and debate. In effect, all the demands for recognition of the experiences and histories of diverse kinds of women, played out the logic of supplementarity, this time in relation to the universal category of women, to the sufficiency of any general women's history, and to the ability of any historian of women to cover all the ground.

The issue of differences within difference brought to the fore a debate about how and whether to articulate gender as a category of analysis. One of these articulations draws on work in the social sciences about gender systems or structures; it assumes a fixed opposition between men and women and separate identities (or roles) for the sexes, that operate consistently in all spheres of social life. It also assumes a direct correlation between the social categories male and female and the subject identities of men and women, and attributes their variation to other established social characteristics such as class or race. It extends the focus of women's history by attending to male/female relationships and to questions about how gender is perceived, what the processes are that establish gendered institutions, and to the differences that race, class, ethnicity and sexuality have made in the historical experiences of women. The social science approach to gender has pluralized the category of 'women' and produced a flourishing set of histories and collective identities; but it has also run into a seemingly intractable set of problems that follow from acknowledging differences among women. If there are so many differences of class, race, ethnicity and sexuality, what constitutes the common ground on which feminists can organize coherent collective action? What is the conceptual link for women's history or women's studies courses among what seems to be an infinite proliferation of different (women's) stories. (The two problems are linked: is there a common identity for women and is there a common history of them that we can write?)

Some feminists have tried to address these questions by analyzing gender with the literary and philosophical approaches that, as diverse as they are, are jointly grouped under the rubric of poststructuralism. Here the emphasis changes from documenting the binary opposition male versus female to asking how it is established, from assuming a pre-existing identity of 'women' to inquiring into the processes of its construction, from granting an inherent meaning for categories like 'men' and 'women' to analyzing how their meaning is secured. This analysis takes signification as its object, examining the practices and contexts within which the meanings of sexual difference are produced. It often uses psychoanalytic theory (particularly Lacanian readings of Freud) to discuss the complexity and instability of any subject identifications. Masculinity and femininity are taken to be subject positions not necessarily restricted to biological males or females.[1]

Most important have been the ways feminists have appropriated poststructuralism to think about difference. Difference lies at the heart of linguistic theories of signification. All meanings are said to be produced differentially, through contrasts and oppositions, and hierarchically, through the assignment of primacy to one term, subordination to another. The interconnectedness of the asymmetrical relationship is important to take into account because it suggests that change is more than a matter of the adjustment of social resources for a subordinated group, more than a question of distributive justice. If Man's definition rests on the subordination of Woman, then a change in the status of Woman requires (and brings about) change in our understanding of Man (a simple cumulative pluralism won't work). The radical threat posed by women's history lies exactly in this kind of challenge to established history; women can't just be added on without a fundamental recasting of the terms, standards and assumptions of what has passed for objective, neutral and universal history in the past because that view of history included in its very definition of itself the exclusion of women.

Those who draw on the teachings of poststructuralism argue that power must be understood in terms of the discursive processes which produce difference. How is knowledge of difference produced, legitimated and disseminated? How are identities constructed and in what terms? Feminist historians find answers to these questions in particular, contextual instances, but they do not simply produce separate stories. Rather the common ground, politically and academically, is one on which feminists produce analyses of difference and organize resistance to the exclusion, domination, or marginality that are the effects of systems of differentiation.

Unlike the social science approach which takes the identity and experience of women for granted, the poststructuralist approach relativizes identity and deprives it of its basis in an essentialized 'experience', both crucial elements, in most standard definitions of politics, for the mobilization of political movements. By problematizing the concepts of identity and experience, feminists using poststructuralist analyses have offered dynamic interpretations of gender that stress contest, ideological contradiction, and the complexities of changing power relationships. In many ways their work insists on greater historical variability and contextual specificity for the terms of gender itself than does the work of those relying on social scientific conceptualizations. But work influenced by poststructuralism runs into some of the same problems encountered by those who prefer social scientific approaches. If, as Denise Riley has argued, the category of 'women', and so women's identity and experience, are unstable because historically variable, what are the grounds for political mobilization? How to write coherent women's history without a fixed, shared notion of what women are? Riley answers, rightly I think, that it is possible to think about and organize politics with unstable categories, that indeed it has always been done, but exactly how is something that needs discussion. Ironically, however, rather than acknowledge the similarity of dilemmas confronted by feminist historians in the 1980s, dilemmas that stem from our need to think about politics in new terms, there has developed instead a polarized debate about the usefulness of poststructuralism for feminism that is cast as a contest between 'theory' and 'politics'.[2]

Feminists hostile to poststructuralism have generalized their critique as a denunciation of 'theory' and they have labelled it as abstract, elitist, and masculinist. They have, in contrast, insisted that their position is concrete, practical, and feminist, and so politically correct. Whatever is theoretical about feminism is renamed as 'politics' in this opposition because (according to one recent account) its insights come 'straight out of reflection on our own, that is, women's experience, out of the contradictions we felt between the different ways we were represented even to ourselves, out of the inequities we had long experienced in our situation'.[3] By casting the problem in terms of an intractable binary opposition, this formulation rules out the possibility of considering the usefulness of various theoretical approaches for feminist history and feminist politics, as well as the possibility of conceiving of theory and politics as inextricably linked.

I think the opposition between 'theory' and 'politics' is a false one that seeks to silence debates we must have about *which* theory is most useful for feminism by making only one theory acceptable as 'politics'. (In the language of those who use this dichotomy 'politics' really means good theory; 'theory' means bad politics.) The 'good' theory takes 'women' and their 'experience' as the self-evident facts that are the origin of collective identity and action. In effect (in a move that is the inverse of history's reaction to women's history) those who use this opposition establish 'politics' as the normative position, for some the ethical test of the validity of feminism and of women's history. And historians of women who reject 'theory' in the name of 'politics' are curiously allied with those traditional historians who find poststructuralism (and found women's history) antithetical to the tenets of their discipline. In both cases these historians are defending the concept of 'experience' by refusing to problematize it; by opposing 'theory' and politics' they remove 'experience' from critical scrutiny and protect it as the foundational and unproblematic ground of politics and historical explanation.

Yet the concept of experience has been rendered problematic for historians and needs to be critically discussed. Not only has poststructuralism questioned whether experience has a status outside linguistic convention (or cultural construction), but the work of women's historians, too, has pluralized and complicated the ways historians have conventionally appealed to experience. In addition, and most important for my argument here, the diverse world of the feminist political movement in the 1980s has made a single definition of women's experience impossible. As has always been the case, the questions posed for theory are questions about politics: Is there an experience of women that transcends the boundaries of class and race? How do differences of race or ethnicity affect the 'experience of women' and the definitions of female needs and interests around which we can organize or about which we write? How can we determine what that 'experience' is or was in the past? Without some way to think theoretically about experience, historians cannot answer these questions; without some way to think theoretically about the relationship of women's history to history, the potentially critical and destabilizing effects of feminism will be too easily lost and we will forsake the opportunity to radically transform the knowledge that constitutes the history and politics we practice.

Poststructuralism is not without its dilemmas for feminist historians. I think those who insist that poststructuralism can't deal with reality or that its focus on texts excludes social structures miss the point of the theory. But I do think that it does not give ready answers for historians to some of the problems it raises: how to invoke 'experience' without implicitly endorsing essentialized concepts; how to describe political mobilization without appealing to essentialized, ahistorical identities; how to depict human agency while acknowledging its linguistic and cultural determinations; how to incorporate fantasy and the unconscious into studies of social behavior; how to recognize differences and make processes of differentiation the focus of political analysis without either ending up with unconnected, multiple accounts or with over-arching categories like class or 'the oppressed'; how to acknowledge the partiality of one's story (indeed of all stories) and still tell it with authority and conviction. These are problems not solved by dismissing 'theory' or declaring it antithetical to 'politics'; rather they require sustained and simultaneous discussion (discussion that is at once theoretical and political) for in the end they are the problems of all those who write women's history, whatever their approach.

Notes

1 Judith Butler, *Gender Trouble: Feminism and the Subversion of Identity*, Routledge, 1989.
2 Denise Riley, *Am I That Name? Feminism and the Category of 'Women' in History*, Macmillan, 1988 (ED).
3 Judith Newton, '"History as usual?": feminism and the "New Historicism"', *Cultural Critique* 9 (1988), p. 93.

37.   Joyce Appleby, Lynn Hunt and Margaret Jacob

[from Telling the Truth About History, *Norton, 1994, pp. 223–37]*

Postmodernism and Historians

At first glance, it might seem unlikely that either Foucault or Derrida would have much influence on the practice of history. Both of them argued vehemently against any research into origins (perhaps the classic historical approach to any problem), and both advanced methods of discourse analysis that required none of the usual forms of grounding in economics, society, or politics. Both consequently have been accused of fostering nihilism. While Derrida seemed to offer no motive at all for the play of language, the only consistent 'cause' cited by Foucault for the formation of discourses was the Nietzschean will to power, usually expressed through institutions, rather than by individuals. Foucault's definition of his work as a history of the conditions for the 'production of truth' thus risked reducing all truth, and all his historical explanations of it, to an all-encompassing will to power – in many ways, the opposite of Derrida's motiveless play of language. In either rendering, women and men are stripped of the meaningful choices whose reality had once served to distinguish human beings from animals. Change comes about through unexpected and unpredictable slips in the fault lines of broad discursive configurations, through lucky breaks in the war of all against all, not through self-determined human action.

Despite much resistance to postmodernism, it has gained ground through the rising influence of literary theory in all forms of cultural studies in the last two decades. In the 1980s, Geertz pointed anthropologists in this direction by linking his 'interpretive theory' to what he called 'the Text analogy . . . the broadest of the recent refigurations of social theory'.[1] In the 'text analogy', culture is likened to a text or language. Like a text, it has to be studied as something in itself rather than as a transparent representation of some more basic set of codes such as economic or social trends. If culture is like a text or language, then it is presumably susceptible to all the criticisms leveled by Foucault and Derrida.

All historians of culture must grapple with how to relate the cultural artifact – text, painting, or steam engine – with the other beliefs, knowledge systems, interests, and structures affecting the human agents who gave rise to it. But postmodern theories of interpretation invariably go further than simply insisting on the integrity of the cultural artifact. They challenge all endeavors to relate culture (or discourse or text) to something outside or beneath it, either to nature or material circumstances, and in so doing they undermine the traditional foundations of knowledge claims in both the natural and the human sciences. If postmodern theories are taken seriously, there is no trans-historical or transcendent grounds for interpretation, and human beings have no unmediated access to the world of things or events. Taken at its word, postmodernism means that there can be no straightforward passageway to the world outside the text, nor, by implication perhaps, any access to the text by peoples or cultures foreign to it. 'Beauty', like 'truth', like 'reality', would lie in the 'eye', as it were, of language. Neither reality nor the individual knower stands outside of the cultural construction. The world, the knower, and knowledge are all profoundly relativized and cut off from the social processes that grind or swirl wordlessly around the bearer of culture. In this rendering, scientific knowledge becomes simply another linguistic convention, a form of discourse related to the excessively rationalist form of life in the West.

Reactions to postmodernist theories within history have varied widely. Traditionalists reject the new forms of theory just as they rejected all previous forms of theory as unnecessary, even unhealthy, intrusions into the domain of history. Social historians have resisted cultural theory as too removed from concrete social conditions, though in some instances social historians have themselves moved to embrace the new theories. As is so often the case with an academic discipline, the introduction of new theories has served to divide scholars into opposing camps. Our view is that the new cultural theories, including postmodernist ones, have helped, like their predecessors, to revitalize discussion about methods, goals, and even the foundations of knowledge. Provocative and unsettling, they raise questions that demand some new answers.

Some academic feminists have found postmodernist theories congenial because such theories underline the contingency, the human-madeness, and hence the changeability of cultural norms and practices. In the United States, in particular (and perhaps uniquely), women's history and gender studies have been at the forefront of the new cultural history. Feminist historians pioneered the use of anthropological insights, and now some of them are in the vanguard of those who utilize postmodern theories. The very notion of gender shows the influence of the cultural and linguistic term in the humanities. From its origins as a term of grammar, gender has come to refer in English increasingly to the cultural and social construction of sexual identity. In her influential collection of essays *Gender and the Politics of History*, Joan Wallach Scott insisted that 'a more radical feminist politics' required 'a more radical epistemology', which she found in postmodernist theory. Citing the approaches of Foucault and Derrida as models, she praised postmodernist theory for relativizing the status of all knowledge.[2]

The issues raised by the feminist use of postmodernist theory are characteristic of the debate about the text analogy and postmodernist theory more generally. Central to the debate has been the blurring of the distinction between text and context (or between language and the social world). Classic social theory rested on a heuristic separation of text and context. Something was taken as the thing to be explained (the text, the effect, or the dependent variable), such as the rise of capitalism, the workings of bureaucratic rationalization, or the increasing impersonality in modern society; something else was posited as the means of explanation (the context, the cause, or the independent variable), e.g., the Protestant work ethic, the spread of markets, or the increasing differentiation of functions in modern society. Denying the possibility of any separation of text and context (or cause and effect), postmodernist theory jeopardizes all social theorizing.

If postmodernist cultural anthropology is any guide, the concern with developing causal explanations and social theories would be replaced in a postmodernist history with a focus on self-reflexivity and on problems of literary construction: how does the historian as author construct his or her text, how is the illusion of authenticity produced, what creates a sense of truthfulness to the facts and a warranty of closeness to past reality (or the 'truth-effect' as it is sometimes called)? The implication is that the historian does not in fact capture the past in faithful fashion but rather, like the novelist, gives the appearance of doing so. Were this version of postmodernism applied to history, the search for truths about the past would be displaced by the self-reflexive analysis of historians' ways of fictively producing convincing 'truth-effects'. Similarly, people in the past who believed themselves to be engaged in the search for truth would have to be either indulged or disabused by the historian, their futile struggle seen to be analogous to the odyssey to which any superstition or self-delusion consigns its believers.[3] Relativism, possibly tinged with cynicism or arrogance, would characterize the historian's aesthetic stance toward such people, becoming the alternative to and replacement for respect. In the face of their myopia or futile discursive strategies, the ironic voice would overshadow the historian's wonder, presenting the passion to linger among human beings struggling to find truths as a quest for their 'truth-effects'.

Under the impact of postmodernist literary approaches, historians are now becoming more aware that their supposedly matter-of-fact choices of narrative techniques and analytical forms also have implications with social and political ramifications. Essays on the state of the discipline often have a canonical form all their own: first a narrative of the rise of new kinds of history, then a long moment for exploring the problems posed by new kinds of history, followed by either a jeremiad on the evils of new practices or a celebration of the potential overcoming of all obstacles. The literary form that the argument takes has a very strong influence on the way that evidence and arguments are presented.

Authors of essays about the 'new history' in the early twentieth century or about social history in the 1950s and 1960s often wrote in heroic and romantic terms of the advance of social and economic history, with the brave historian marching hand in hand with the forces of progress and democracy to do battle with backwardness and tradition. More recently, the ironic mode has become dominant among those historians, who, like other cultural critics, have wondered whether their work could ever be other than fragmentary and partial, with little relevance to the grander narratives of the past. Despairing of the validity of what they describe as macrohistories, they embrace irony and claim only to be writing microhistories.

Questions of form or technique justifiably extend to the chapters in this volume. In our emphasis on the need for narrative coherence, causal analysis, and social contextualization, as exemplified in our own narratives, we are attempting to go beyond the current negative or ironic judgments about history's role. We as historians are nonetheless making our own aesthetic choices, just as others have chosen comedy, romance, or irony for their writings. We are emphasizing the human need for self-understanding through a coherent narrative of the past and the need for admittedly partial, objective explanations of how the past has worked. In this sense, we have renounced an ironic stance. Rather than try to prove our superiority to past historians by focusing on their failures, we are trying to learn from their efforts to make sense of the social world. Rather than underlining the impossibility of total objectivity or completely satisfying causal explanation, we are highlighting the need for the most objective possible explanations as the only way to move forward, perhaps not on a straight line of progress into the future, but forward toward a more intellectually alive, democratic community, toward the kind of society in which we would like to live.

These are aesthetic or literary choices because they involve ways of organizing a narrative, but history is more than a branch of letters to be judged only in terms of its literary merit. Our choices are political, social, and epistemological. They are political and social because they reflect beliefs in a certain kind of community of historians and society of Americans. They are epistemological because they reflect positions on what can be known and how it can be known. With diligence and good faith they may also be at moments reasonably, if partially, true accounts of the distant and recent past.

The assumption of a clear hierarchy of explanation running from economy and society up to politics and culture was present in the Annales school, Marxism, and modernization theory, and it can still be seen in the table of contents of many social history monographs. We agree that the focus on culture and language undermines this hierarchical view by showing that all social reality is culturally constructed and discursively construed in the first instance. Culture can no longer be considered a phenomenon of 'the third level' in Annales terms, if the 'basics' of life (demography, economy) are themselves constructed in and through culture. In that sense, discursive or linguistic models throw into doubt the once absolutist forms of conventional historical explanation, and they thereby open up the way to new forms of historical investigation. Foucault's own work is perhaps the best-known example of such a new form with direct historical relevance.

We are not, therefore, rejecting out of hand everything put forward by the postmodernists. The text analogy and aspects of postmodernist theories have some real political and epistemological attractions. The interest in culture was a way of disengaging from Marxism, or at least from the most unsatisfactory versions of economic and social reductionism. Cultural and linguistic approaches also helped in the ongoing task of puncturing the shield of science behind which reductionism often hid. By focusing on culture, one could challenge the virtually commonsensical assumption that there is a clear hierarchy of explanation in history (that is, in all social reality), running from biology and topography through demography and economics up to social structure and finally to politics and its poor cousins, cultural and intellectual life.

Yet postmodernism has also raised its own set of concerns, just as every previous theoretical intervention did. Chief among them has been the problem of linguistic determinism or conflation, the reduction of the social and natural world to language and context to text. If historians give up the analogies of levels (the Annales school) or base-superstructure (Marxism), must they also give up social theory and causal language altogether? Paradoxically, as theory has developed from the days of Hegel and Marx, one trajectory that went from Nietzsche and Heidegger and on to the postmodernists has progressively shed any ambition to explain. As the exponents of that trajectory take aim at history, its original theoretical and empirical project, the explanation of long-term social and political development, then comes under attack. In other words, postmodernism throws into question the modern narrative form, proving once again that the philosophy of history does matter.

The Problem of Narrative

Philosophical questions about epistemological foundations inevitably touch upon the narrative form that gives cohesion to history as a discipline. Narrative continues to be fundamental, albeit in different ways, to history as a form of knowledge about human life, even though few professional historians now write what was classically known as narrative history – grand panoramic stories about the emergence of a new nation or major crises that threatened national identity. Despite the decline of grand narratives, history has retained a strong narrative cast, even in the most specialized monographs of social and cultural history. Like memory itself, every work of history has the structure of a plot with a beginning, middle, and end, whether the subject is social mobility in a nineteenth-century American city, the uses of art as propaganda in the Russian Revolution, or the analysis of the rise of postmodernist theory in historical writing. Thus, to argue for a return to narrative, as some traditionalists have done, is to miss the cardinal point that historians have never entirely departed from it.[4]

Not surprisingly, 'narrative' has become one of the charged code words of the current struggles over history. Those who resist the changes in the discipline, including the rise of social history, tend to defend narrative as the form of writing specific to history, while those who champion disciplinary innovation tend to demean narrative as an unsophisticated form of writing about the past or as simply another version of fiction camouflaged as history. More important than this essentially superficial debate about the place of narrative within the profession (superficial because it focuses on the most immediately evident form of writing rather than on its deeper significance) is the question of what have been called meta-narratives or master narratives.

A meta-narrative or master narrative is a grand schema for organizing the interpretation and writing of history. In earlier chapters we described three of the most important meta-narratives of modern history: the heroic model of progress through science, the epic of an unfolding American nation, and the idea of the 'modern'. Marxism, liberalism, even postmodernism itself are all examples of meta-narratives, for they all offer sweeping stories about the origins of American and Western problems and the direction that lives may take in the present, as well as remedies for the future. Of these philosophies of history, only postmodernism attacks meta-narrative along with the narrative form itself as inherently ideological and hence obfuscating. In the postmodernist view, present in the works of Foucault and Derrida, among others, history in general and narrative in particular are denounced as 'representational practices' by which Western societies produced individuals especially well suited to life in a postindustrial state.[5] (It isn't entirely clear why this is a bad thing.)

At best, in this line of postmodernist argument, narrative and metanarrative are useful fictions for modern industrial society, nothing more. At worst, they are insidious ways of hiding the partiality and propaganda aims of the author of the narrative and the normalizing tendencies of modern states and societies. For some postmodernists, all meta-narratives are inherently totalitarian. They cannot, by this overarching analysis, be in any sense true. One postmodernist proclaimed, 'History is the Western myth'.[6] In place of plot and character, history and individuality, perhaps even meaning itself, the most thoroughgoing postmodernists would offer an 'interminable pattern without meaning', a form of writing closer to modern music and certain modern novels.[7]

In the most extreme form of the postmodernist critique of narrative, special scorn is reserved for those who write for an 'ordinary educated public', since they turn the contradictions, political forces, and ideological tensions of history into 'disthought',[8] that is, a form of propaganda for the status quo. This is the ultimate *reductio ad absurdum* of postmodernist criticisms of history-writing. Such critics take to heart the postmodernist notion that history is irrelevant to identity (a position not shared, by the way, by Foucault, who attributed all identity to historical processes). They deny that story or narrative is one of the major ways in which human intelligence ascribes meaning to life. For them, the entire historiographical tradition simply fosters 'a consciousness that is never able to arrive at criticism'.[9] Narrative and critical thinking are incompatible.

Several different levels of argument are involved in these condemnations of meta-narratives: historiography as the tradition of history-writing over time; narrative as a form of historical writing; and storytelling as a form of ascribing meaning to social life. The most extreme postmodernist position denies the validity of all of them at once. Meta-narrative is denounced as myth, historiography dismissed as 'a mode of bureaucratic-ideological organization', narrative as a form of propaganda, and story or plot (beginning-middle-end as an essential way of viewing action in the world) as part of the 'myth that history is a condition of knowledge'. It is less clear, however, what such critics would have historians do instead, except, perhaps, that they ought not to write history at all or admit that in the end history is another form of fiction. As one contemporary philosopher puts the objection to this kind of nihilistic criticism, 'deconstruction without reconstruction is irresponsibility'.[10]

No one argues any longer, as Ranke seemed to do, that historical narrative in any way exactly mirrors past reality, 'as it actually was'. Historians cannot capture the fullness of past experience, any more than individual memories can; they only have the traces or residues of the past, and their accounts are necessarily partial. Even those who argue that narrative structure inheres in the events themselves and that narration actually constitutes action and experience grant that historical narratives do not simply mirror or reproduce the firsthand experience of reality.

Although most historians continue to believe that narrative is a universal mode of organizing human knowledge, others have questioned this position. One previous defender of narrative recently concluded that master narratives and narrative itself might be tainted with 'the guilt of culture and history'. He speculated that the death of history, politics, and narrative might all be aspects of another great transformation, similar in scope and effect to that which marked the initial emergence of Greek thought.[11] Similarly, it has been argued that postmodern narrative will no longer rely on the time of Newton, 'the time of history . . . the time of clocks and capital'. Instead, it will collapse the subject and object of knowledge and with it the distinction between 'invention and reality'.[12]

It is probably impossible to develop an airtight defense of narrative and meta-narrative (in Newtonian time). One commentator recently acknowledged, 'There is no global defense of the narrative form that will insulate it, once and for all, from skeptical doubts'.[13] Similarly, philosophical efforts to define precisely the workings of causal analysis in historical explanation have become hopelessly entangled in debates about general laws of explanation and history's relationship to the natural sciences. If the nature of the particles that make up physical reality is up for grabs in contemporary philosophical and scientific thought, then the concept of a once-lived reality in the past and its relation to historical representations is even more vexed. Yet the mere existence of questions and doubts does not prove the inherent falseness of the narrative form with its incorporation of causal language.

We see no reason to conclude that because there is a gap between reality and its narration (its representation), the narration in some fundamental sense is inherently invalid. Just because narratives are human creations does not make them all equally fictitious or mythical. In our last two chapters, we will examine the ways in which historians determine the truth or falseness of their narrative creations. Suffice it to say for now that in our view, narrative is essential both to individual and social identity. It is consequently a defining element in history-writing, and the historiographical tradition, as we have reviewed it briefly here, is an important element in identity, both for historians in a profession and for citizens in modern societies. We believe that historians must try to develop new and better social theories or new and better meta-narratives, even while making problematic their old ones. Just as the meta-narrative of progress replaced that of Christianity in the West, so too it is possible to believe that people will want to develop new meta-narratives in order to prepare for the future. New experiences will always require new interpretations and new explanations.

Postmodernism is in fact one such meta-narrative, and many commentators have pointed to its unstated reliance on a narrative of modernism to make its point. As one historian reminds us, to proclaim the end of historical meta-narratives is itself 'a (quite totalizing) piece of historical narrative'.[14] Rejecting all meta-narratives cannot make sense, because narratives and meta-narratives are the kinds of stories that make action in the world possible. They make action possible because they make it meaningful. Postmodernism offers another interpretation of meaning, including historical meaning, even as it claims to contest the foundations of all meanings. There is no action without a story about how the world works, and action is all the more deliberative if the stories are all the more theorized. The stories will always be changing (they are in fact stories about how change works), but historians will always have to tell them in order to make sense of the past, and it matters whether they tell them well – as truthfully and fully as possible – or not.

The move toward the most radically skeptical and relativist postmodern position inevitably leads into a cul-de-sac. Dismissals of history, politics, and narrative as hopelessly modern ideas, now outmoded in the postmodern world, might seem up-to-date, but history, politics, and narrative are still the best tools available for dealing with the world and preparing for the future. A similar kind of crisis that foreshadows a turning away from the postmodern view can be seen in almost every field of knowledge or learning today. Postmodern art often consists of critiques of the function of art and especially past art (the mounds of shopping carts piled around the statue of Mozart in downtown Salzburg, for instance, in the year of the Mozart bicentenary) rather than new art. Similarly, postmodern history too often seems to consist of denunciations of history as it has been known rather than of new histories for present and hence future time. Periodic exercises in theory have an undeniably useful function as criticism of unself-conscious assumptions about art or history or science, but postmodernism cannot provide models for the future when it claims to refuse the entire idea of offering models for the future. In the final analysis, then, there can be no postmodern history.

Notes

1 Clifford Geertz, 'Blurred genres: the refiguration of social thought', in his *Local Knowledge*, Basic Books, 1983, p. 30.
2 Joan Wallach Scott, *Gender and the Politics of History*, Columbia University Press, 1988, p. 4.
3 Phyllis Mack, *Visionary Women: Ecstatic Prophecy in Seventeenth-Century England*, University of California Press, 1992, pp. 6–7.
4 See Hayden White, *The Content of the Form*, Johns Hopkins University Press, 1987, pp. 26–7. For an account of the attempt to revive narrative, see Peter Novick, *That Noble Dream: The 'Objectivity Question' and the American Historical Profession*, Cambridge University Press, 1988, pp. 622–5.
5 White, *Content of the Form*, p. 5.
6 Descombes, as quoted in Pauline Rosenau, *Post-modernism and the Social Sciences*, Princeton University Press, 1992, p. 62.
7 Elizabeth Deeds Ermarth, *Sequel to History: Postmodernism and the Crisis of Representational Time*, Princeton University Press, 1992, p. 212.
8 Sande Cohen, *Historical Culture: On the Recoding of an Academic Discipline*, University of California Press, 1986, p. 326.
9 Ibid., p. 77.
10 Hilary Putnam, *Renewing Philosophy*, Harvard University Press, 1992, p. 113.
11 White, *Content of the Form*, pp. 1, 168.
12 Ermarth, *Sequel to History*, p. 22.
13 Andrew P. Norman, 'Telling it like it was: historical narratives on their own terms', *History and Theory* 30 (1991), p. 128.
14 William Reddy, 'Postmodernism and the public sphere: implications for an historical ethnography', *Cultural Anthropology* 7 (1992), p. 137.

The new Cultural History

The positive impact of Postmodernism on the practice of history is to be measured primarily in terms of the remarkable rise of cultural history, from a marginal specialism in the 1970s to an increasingly dominant role today. The questions of meaning and representation with which the new cultural history is mainly concerned are now addressed to a formidable range of subject-matter, from political campaigns to the history of the book, and from sexuality to militarism. Mark Poster attributes these changes primarily to Postmodernism's emphasis on the materiality of texts. He welcomes the resultant destabilising of both social history and intellectual history. He welcomes above all the new study of identities which, instead of working within a given framework of class and nation, seeks to uncover the construction not only of these identities, but of the self as an autonomous agent.

Robert Darnton makes a rather different case for the centrality of culture in historical work. His starting point is the impeccably historicist notion of the otherness of the past and the 'culture shock' engendered by close encounters. But in seeking intellectual resources for the demanding work of cultural translation, Darnton turns not to critical theory but to anthropology. Anthropologists like Clifford Geertz treat culture as central to the societies they study, and as the code for understanding how they function. Darnton's own writings on French cultural history under the *ancien régime* have been informed by this model. He insists that historians should abandon the practice of treating culture as an add-on, automatically subordinate to economy and society.

38. Mark Poster

[from Cultural History and Postmodernity: Disciplinary Readings and Challenges, *Columbia University Press, 1997, pp. 3–12]*

Since the 1960s the discipline of history has grudgingly made room for the new genre of "social history." In the 1980s another new genre has emerged among historians, this one called "cultural history."[1] The profession's acceptance of social history followed a ragged course characterized by stages of denial, resistance, debate, approval, and, finally, hegemony. In the course of two decades social history changed from a scorned, marginal discourse referred to by leading political historians as "pots and pans history" into the prevailing norm of the field. The generation of young historians in the 1960s and 1970s who took some risks with their careers by practicing social history now to a considerable extent dominates the discipline. And this generation is currently defending its way of doing history against the new challengers, the cultural historians. In some cases, the senior generation of historians, such as Gertrude Himmelfarb, who predated the wave of social history and generally opposed it during the 1970s, now adamantly defend the current regime, including Marxist versions, against the new trend.[2]

The introduction of social history into the discipline brought with it a series of methodological innovations. Historians attended to the procedures of the social sciences: explanatory strategies shifted from narrative to analysis; evidence changed from the direct quotation of individuals to quantitative documentation; topics and problems concerned not political and intellectual elites but large groups and massive institutions of daily life; above all, the subjects of history were expanded from the political and intellectual elite to the working classes, women, the poor, criminals, and minority ethnic and racial groups. Taken together, these novelties constituted an epistemological break or paradigm shift of serious proportions. Yet I contend that aspects of the fundamental relation of the historian to the past were untouched by the upheaval. In particular, the shift from political to social history maintained a central feature of historiography: truth as the unmediated relation of the historian to the past.

The turn to social history also meant in particular a preference for "history from below," as its premier practitioner, E.P. Thompson, termed it.[3] This apparent change in direction, a focus on the bottom of the social order rather than a view from above, nonetheless retained a humanist view of the historical agent. Paraphrasing Marx for the discipline of history, Thompson wrote lines that few historians—liberal, conservative, or Marxist—would contest: "Men make their own history. They are part agent, part victim: it is precisely the element of agency which distinguishes them from the beasts, which is the *human* part of man."[4] Thompson thus spoke for a broad consensus of the discipline, even though social historians conceived their work as a radical departure from the ways of the older generation. Humanist to the bone, social and political historians alike defined history as the free and determined acts of agents. Masters and victims of their fates, these historical agents were the main characters in the drama of modern society, in both its capitalist and its socialist versions. The secret collusion of social and political historians rested in their fundamental unity on the question of the subject or agent, one that, to quote Thompson once more, "was present at its own making."[5] This fullness of presence of the individual or group to itself in its experience is the hallmark of the culture of modernity in the West. Any discourse that pretends to be critical of the prevailing order, call it "modern" or call it "capitalist," must begin by putting this figure of the self into question. This is what social and political historians have not been able to do, and this is the exact purpose of cultural history in its poststructuralist versions.

In both the "old" political-intellectual history and the "new" social history, the historian sought to attain the truth about the "real."[6] The records examined by the historian—diplomatic correspondence or local archives—were taken as transparent mediations between the past and the present. Textuality, writing, discourse, terms that poststructuralists have made into indications of a problematic, did not intercede between the historian and the representation of the past. Written traces were merely the occasion in which the gaze of the historian perceived directly the real that once was. The events and structures of the past drew all the attention of the old political historian and the new social historian. To read closely the documents as internally articulated signifiers, to take them seriously on their own structural terms, to consider self-reflexively their rhetorical shaping powers over the reader, to allow the text a material role in constituting historical knowledge: these are negligible digressions not suitable for the political or social historian impatient to recapture the "real." Like historical documents, the historian's discourse was itself another more or less elegantly composed transparent mediation. When Hayden White suggested otherwise in *Metahistory*[7]—that the trope embedded in the historical text greatly shaped its meaning—he was virtually ejected from the guild.

The new cultural history upsets this configuration of truth. It often does so by resorting to poststructuralist interpretive strategies and raising the issue of feminist and anticolonial discourse. The topic of women, for example, may provide the occasion for reexamining the relation of the historian to the truth because women have been figured in Western history as other to the truth, as outside the couplet truth-real. Writing the history of women, subjects who by and large have not authored the documents or at least those taken seriously by earlier generations of historians, as Joan Scott points out, calls attention to the text as noise, as interference between the historian and the truth, in addition to opening a new domain of the history of women.[8] Similarly, poststructuralist theory directly problematizes the text as mediation. In Derrida's case, the text is as much an indication of the absence of the real as it is itself an inscription of reality. For Foucault, as I will subsequently show, the textual document is material in the sense that discourse is productive of practice. Cultural history, then, challenges historians to confront what hitherto has remained buried in realist or logocentric assumptions of the representational power of writing, that is, the productive materiality of the text, the sense in which history as past event is always mediated by written documents and history as a form of knowledge is always itself a discourse.

There is another way of addressing the issue of epistemological self-consciousness and its relation to poststructuralist theory within the discipline of history. Historians often do not see the relevance of poststructuralist theory to their work because as a rule they do not seriously question what they do as a form of knowledge.[9] As long as historians fail to write texts that call into question the issue of knowledge and of their role in its production, poststructuralism will appear to them to be opaque, esoteric, and irrelevant. For in the first instance poststructuralism is a means of bringing into the open and putting into doubt the way a text organizes itself as a form of knowledge, as truth. Some poststructuralists, notably Derrideans, raise this issue for properly epistemological reasons. Others, like Foucault, with whom I am most in sympathy, raise the issue for political reasons as well.

The question of the truth claims of texts is particularly relevant at this time, it could be shown, because certain forms of discourse in the social sciences have become, in the contemporary university and the welfare state, inextricably merged with structures of domination. Therefore the failure to question the truth claims of the historian's writing or text operates by default to legitimize those forms of domination, to give cultural force to the hegemonic configuration of representationality. In other words, impatience with the issue of the truth status of one's text, the urge to get on with the seemingly more important business of analyzing change and attributing causes to events, is a form of representation that inadvertently plays into the hands of the established power structure and functions in a conservative way to authorize increasingly questionable and ubiquitous forms of representational discourse. Historical "explanations," for example, inscribe reason into the past in a manner that both controls it and introduces into it an instrumentality that mirrors that of the prevailing state and economic system. This effect of a certain form of representational discourse, I argue, applies even to those types of historical writing, such as historical materialism, that wish to be understood as critical or revolutionary.

In fairness, it might be noted that historical writing in turn raises questions for poststructuralism, especially in its deconstructionist variant. Historians are often masters of contextualization, practitioners of the art of tracing connections between different registers. Many deconstructionists, once outside the written text, seem uncertain and confused, overcome by what appears to them an infinite array of possible contextual relations, each with equally legitimate claim to the standing of "the context." This sense of confusion, or recognition of multiplicity, safeguards deconstruction from simplistic reductions. But it also may incapacitate it in the areas of history and politics by weakening its ability to present forceful, compelling interpretations of practices. Moreover, deconstruction may be responsible for its relative inability to treat the question of context: its very strength as a strategy of reading texts may produce a theoretical weakness when the object of analysis is not properly textual. Its insight is also blindness.

Weakening Oppositions and Blurred Distinctions

The field of cultural history as distinct from both intellectual history and social history may be configured in numerous ways. Roger Chartier, for instance, offers a starting point for a definition of cultural history as the calling into question of three traditional distinctions in intellectual and social history: high versus popular culture, production versus consumption, and reality versus fiction.[10] And surely these oppositions form an excellent starting point for thinking about a new cultural history as distinct from intellectual and social history. In relation to the first distinction, intellectual history drew its borders around the great works of thought, literature, and to a lesser extent the arts; popular culture, to the contrary, has been studied commonly by social historians using quantitative analysis or searching for indications of resistance against oppression. At times these clear lines between the subdisciplines of intellectual and social history were transgressed, as Robert Darnton did in the direction of a social history of intellectual life in his study of the diffusion of the Encyclopedia.[11] But these exceptions have been rare.

Chartier discusses the second distinction, that between production and consumption, in relation to intellectual and artistic creation versus reception. Before the recent interest in cultural history, creation was understood as the domain of intellectual history, and reception or reading was seen as part of social history. The production/consumption distinction goes to the heart of modern culture since it speaks to the profound value modernity places on the active, Faustian moment associated with the former term and the general disregard even antipathy in which the latter term, associated with passivity, is held. The rise of postmodern culture, with its fascination with consumerism and digital communications, with hypertext programs inverting readers into authors, dissolves the older priorities along with the binary opposition underlying them. At the theoretical level, Michel de Certeau in France and Cultural Studies in England demonstrated the "active" component of daily life among the popular classes. Walking in a city, reading a magazine, watching television, even participating in a fan club were reinterpreted as creative practices that resist hegemonic flows of imposition and constraint.[12]

Chartier's distinction between reality and fiction speaks to the stability of representational practices in the modern period, the sense that texts firmly point outside themselves to referents that are understood as distinct. This opposition relies on the Cartesian dualism of bodies and minds in which individuals are subjects metaphysically distinct from objects. Intellectual history treats subjects and their spiritual creations, literary and philosophical representations of external worlds. Social history inevitably configures its field as one of objects, material things determined by laws, forces, and tendencies (even though the agent of the social historian is surely a Cartesian subject). Cultural history emerges as a possibility when this distinction begins to collapse, when the performative aspects of language are recognized. In Chartier's words, "What is real, in fact, is not (or not only) the reality that the text aims at, but the very manner in which it aims at it in the historic setting of its production and the strategy used in its writing."[13] Texts do more and less than represent: they configure what they point to, and they are configured by it. To the extent that discourse configures what it indicates, it is a fiction as much as a representation. When reality and fiction are seen as permeable to one another, material reality has a cultural component, and culture is material.

While these distinctions do not sharply delineate all that is at stake in the new field of cultural history, they are helpful in outlining a changed context for debate. They suggest directions for study; they hint at new perspectives and new topics; they validate imaginative proposals and open the gates to hetero-dox formulations, tearing down the defenses of disciplinary stability. One might now comb the archives for documents on advertising or cosmetics or comic books, topics earlier regarded as of grand vulgarity, of stupendous banality, and still discover through their investigation the key to working-class politics or women's identity or a youth culture imaginary. What is perhaps worse from the standpoint of the stable dichotomy of intellectual and social history, one might also mix the levels, the types of discourses, the realms of high and low. Thus cultural history may study the influence of the legal system on the development of psychoanalysis, or the relation of a play by Shakespeare to colonial life in Virginia, or the connection between modernist art and psychology and of both with advertising. A vertiginous array of possibilities confronts the would-be cultural historian.

Cultural History and Subject Constitution

Cultural history's fluid multiplication of research agendas is salubrious for the discipline of history. Productive affinities link cultural history to emerging perspectives such as discourse analysis, deconstruction, new historicism, and cultural studies. Connective tissues bind the subdiscipline to theoretico-political clusters such as postcolonialism, subaltern studies, queer theory, and feminist studies. Amid the proliferating proposals and initiatives, one prob-lematic stands out in my mind as a most promising line of study in cultural history: that is, the question of the construction of the subject. Cultural history might then be understood as the study of the construction of the subject, the extent to which and the mechanisms through which individuals are attached to identities, the shapes and characteristics of those identities, the role the process of self-constitution plays in the disruption or stabilization of political formations, and the relation of all these processes to distinctions of gender, ethnicity, and class.

The issues at stake in this cultural history are profound. For as long as historians presuppose that their task is to discover or investigate agents and victims, to resurrect for the present age fully formed agents in the past bearing and resisting burdens of oppression, there can never be a historiography that is critical of modernity simply because a world of agents and victims is its chief cultural figure, its great ideological myth. Historians may contribute to the delineation of the limits of the modern only by studying how such a cultural figure (the individual or group as agent/victim) was constituted. This task, I propose, is the preeminent one for cultural history: to trace the construction of the autonomous agent, with due attention to its differential predecessors, and to estimate the extent to which it may be at a point of decline, in other words, the extent to which a postmodern cultural figure, one yet to be clearly defined, may be emerging. Such a project of cultural history benefits from the critique of Western culture at the heart of poststructuralist theory, especially in the Foucaultian and Derridean forms. It also finds natural allies in those discursive orientations that derive from a position of exteriority with respect to the cultural dominant of the modern West, that is, postcolonialism, subaltern theory, feminist theory, and queer theory. And this cultural history would benefit from certain advances already at play in disciplines from literature to sociology such as new historicism and cultural studies. Finally, one must understand my proposal for a cultural history not as supplanting or displacing social and political history but as challenging them, as animating the discipline by the introduction of a different way of doing history, a different set of epistemological protocols.

The question I raise under the banner of cultural history for my colleagues who have critical ambitions is then the following: if modern society claims to promote the freedom of the individual, how can one define its limits except by showing that "free individuals" are historical constructions? Otherwise the historian projects a figure of the free individual into the past, duly noting and regretting the unjust impositions upon it yet confirming the great myth of modernity. The truly historical task is not to find in the past suffering workers and victimized women so that all may recognize the evils of the system. Instead the problem is to describe the mechanisms through which such people were constituted as subjects in relation to the measure of stable, centered autonomy; to show how the discursive figure of the universal, free individual was paradoxically able to designate these groups and others as outside the universal and as unfree, to show that modern freedom has always only been possible through its exclusions. This task will reveal that the modern nation has always been a forced and false unity, a seductive goal whose only realization must be its systematic undoing. Cultural historians contribute to a critical history when they show not that certain groups were wrongly excluded from the nation but that the proper goal of emancipation is for all to strive for such exclusion.

Notes

1 See Lynn Hunt (ed.), *The New Cultural History*, Berkeley, 1989; Roger Chartier, *Cultural History: Between Practices and Representations*, trans. Lydia Cochrane, Polity, 1988.
2 Gertrude Himmelfarb, *On Looking into the Abyss*, Knopf, 1994 (ED).
3 E.P. Thompson, 'History from below', *Times Literary Supplement*, 7 April 1966, pp. 279–80.
4 E.P. Thompson, 'Socialist humanism: an epistle to the Philistines', *The New Reasoner* 1 (1957), p. 122.
5 E.P. Thompson, *The Making of the English Working Class*, Penguin, 1968, p. 9.
6 Peter Novick, *That Noble Dream: The 'Objectivity Question' and the American Historical Profession*, New York, 1988.
7 Hayden White, *Metahistory: The Historical Imagination in Nineteenth-Century Europe*, Baltimore, 1973.
8 Joan Wallach Scott, *Gender and the Politics of History*, New York, 1989.
9 Robert Berkhofer, *Beyond the Great Story: History as Text and Discourse*, Cambridge, 1995. See also Dominick LaCapra, *Soundings in Critical Theory* (Ithaca, 1989), and *History, Politics and the Novel* (Ithaca, 1987).
10 Chartier, *Cultural History*, p. 37. I have altered slightly the terms of Chartier's binary oppositions.
11 Robert Darnton, *The Business of Enlightenment*, Cambridge, 1979.
12 Michel de Certeau, *The Practice of Everyday Life*, trans. Steven Rendall, Berkeley, 1984.
13 Chartier, *Cultural History*, p. 44.

39. Robert Darnton

[from The Great Cat Massacre and Other Episodes in French
Cultural History, *Allen Lane, 1984, pp. 11–15, 250–3]*

This book investigates ways of thinking in eighteenth-century France. It
attempts to show not merely what people thought but how they thought
—how they construed the world, invested it with meaning, and infused it with
emotion. Instead of following the high road of intellectual history, the inquiry
leads into the unmapped territory known in France as *l'histoire des mentalités*.
This genre has not yet received a name in English, but it might simply be called
cultural history; for it treats our own civilization in the same way that anthropologists study alien cultures. It is history in the ethnographic grain.

Most people tend to think that cultural history concerns high culture, culture with a capital *c*. The history of culture in the lower case goes back as far as
Burckhardt, if not Herodotus; but it is still unfamiliar and full of surprises.
So the reader may want a word of explanation. Where the historian of ideas
traces the filiation of formal thought from philosopher to philosopher, the
ethnographic historian studies the way ordinary people made sense of the
world. He attempts to uncover their cosmology, to show how they organized
reality in their minds and expressed it in their behavior. He does not try to
make a philosopher out of the man in the street but to see how street life
called for a strategy. Operating at ground level, ordinary people learn to be
"street smart"—and they can be as intelligent in their fashion as philosophers.
But instead of deriving logical propositions, they think with things, or with
anything else that their culture makes available to them, such as stories or
ceremonies.

What things are good to think with? Claude Lévi-Strauss applied that
question to the totems and tatoos of Amazonia twenty-five years ago. Why
not try it out on eighteenth-century France? Because eighteenth-century
Frenchmen cannot be interviewed, the skeptic will reply; and to drive the

point home, he will add that archives can never serve as a substitute for field work. True, but the archives from the Old Regime are exceptionally rich, and one can always put new questions to old material. Furthermore, one should not imagine that the anthropologist has an easy time with his native informant. He, too, runs into areas of opacity and silence, and he must interpret the native's interpretation of what the other natives think. Mental undergrowth can be as impenetrable in the bush as in the library.

But one thing seems clear to everyone who returns from field work: other people are other. They do not think the way we do. And if we want to understand their way of thinking, we should set out with the idea of capturing otherness. Translated into the terms of the historian's craft, that may merely sound like the familiar injunction against anachronism. It is worth repeating, nonetheless; for nothing is easier than to slip into the comfortable assumption that Europeans thought and felt two centuries ago just as we do today—allowing for the wigs and wooden shoes. We constantly need to be shaken out of a false sense of familiarity with the past, to be administered doses of culture shock.

There is no better way, I believe, than to wander through the archives. One can hardly read a letter from the Old Regime without coming up against surprises—anything from the constant dread of toothaches, which existed everywhere, to the obsession with braiding dung for display on manure heaps, which remained confined to certain villages. What was proverbial wisdom to our ancestors is completely opaque to us. Open any eighteenth-century book of proverbs, and you will find entries such as: "He who is snotty, let him blow his nose." When we cannot get a proverb, or a joke, or a ritual, or a poem, we know we are on to something. By picking at the document where it is most opaque, we may be able to unravel an alien system of meaning. The thread might even lead into a strange and wonderful world view.

This book attempts to explore such unfamiliar views of the world. It proceeds by following up the surprises provided by an unlikely assortment of texts: a primitive version of "Little Red Riding Hood," an account of a massacre of cats, a bizarre description of a city, a curious file kept by a police inspector—documents that cannot be taken to typify eighteenth-century thought but that provide ways of entering into it.

....

The notion of reading runs through all the chapters, for one can read a ritual or a city just as one can read a folktale or a philosophic text. The mode of exegesis may vary, but in each case one reads for meaning—the meaning inscribed by contemporaries in whatever survives

of their vision of the world. I have therefore tried to read my way through the
eighteenth century, and I have appended texts to my interpretations so that my
own reader can interpret these texts and disagree with me. I do not expect to
have the last word and do not pretend to completeness. This book does not
provide an inventory of ideas and attitudes in all the social groups and geographical regions of the Old Regime. Nor does it offer typical case studies, for
I do not believe there is such a thing as a typical peasant or a representative
bourgeois. Instead of chasing after them, I have pursued what seemed to be
the richest run of documents, following leads wherever they went and quicken-
ing my pace as soon as I stumbled on a surprise. Straying from the beaten path
may not be much of a methodology, but it creates the possibility of enjoying
some unusual views, and they can be the most revealing. I do not see why
cultural history should avoid the eccentric or embrace the average, for one
cannot calculate the mean of meanings or reduce symbols to their lowest
common denominator.

This confession of nonsystematism does not imply that anything goes in
cultural history because anything can pass as anthropology. The anthropological mode of history has a rigor of its own, even if it may look suspiciously
like literature to a hard-boiled social scientist. It begins from the premise
that individual expression takes place within a general idiom, that we learn to
classify sensations and make sense of things by thinking within a framework
provided by our culture. It therefore should be possible for the historian
to discover the social dimension of thought and to tease meaning from documents by relating them to the surrounding world of significance, passing
from text to context and back again until he has cleared a way through a foreign
mental world.

This kind of cultural history belongs to the interpretive sciences. It may
seem too literary to be classified under the *appellation contrôlée* of "science"
in the English-speaking world, but it fits in nicely with the *sciences humaines*
in France. It is not an easy genre, and it is bound to be imperfect, but it should
not be impossible, even in English. All of us, French and "Anglo-Saxons,"
pedants as well as peasants, operate within cultural constraints, just as we
all share conventions of speech. So historians should be able to see how
cultures shape ways of thinking, even for the greatest thinkers. A poet or
philosopher may push a language to its limits, but at some point he will
hit against the outer frame of meaning. Beyond it, madness lies—the fate of
Hölderlin and Nietzsche. But within it, great men can test and shift the boundaries of meaning. Thus there should be room for Diderot and Rousseau in
a book about *mentalités* in eighteenth-century France. By including them
along with the peasant tellers of tales and the plebeian killers of cats, I have

abandoned the usual distinction between elite and popular culture, and have tried to show how intellectuals and common people coped with the same sort of problems.

....

Having made this quick trial run through eighteenth-century culture, can we draw any conclusions about the history of *mentalités*? The genre remains obscure, although the French have tried to surround it with prolegomena and discourses on method. The most revealing of their programmatic statements is an essay by Pierre Chaunu: "Un Nouveau Champ pour l'histoire sérielle: Le Quantitatif au troisième niveau" ("A New Field for Statistical History: Quantification at the Third Level.") Chaunu makes explicit a set of assumptions that can be found almost everywhere in recent French historiography, that unites Marxists and revisionists, that determines the structure of the best doctoral theses, and that is inscribed in the title of France's most influential historical journal, *Annales: Économies, sociétés, civilisations*—namely, that one can distinguish levels in the past; that the third level (culture) somehow derives from the first two (economics and demography, and social structure); and that third-level phenomena can be understood in the same way as those on the deeper levels (by means of statistical analysis, the play of structure and conjuncture, and considerations of long-term change rather than of events). This historiographical tradition, usually identified loosely as the "*Annales* school," has contributed enormously to our understanding of the past—more, I should think, than any other trend in history writing since the beginning of this century. But all three of its assumptions strike me as dubious, and I would especially question the third.[1]

The French attempt to measure attitudes by counting—counting masses for the dead, pictures of Purgatory, titles of books, speeches in academies, furniture in inventories, crimes in police records, invocations to the Virgin Mary in wills, and pounds of candle wax burned to patron saints in churches. The numbers can be fascinating, especially when they are compiled with the masterly hand of a Michel Vovelle or a Daniel Roche. But they are nothing more than symptoms produced by the historian himself, and they can be interpreted in wildly different ways. Vovelle sees dechristianization in the drop in the graphs of masses said for souls in Purgatory; Philippe Ariès sees a tendency toward a more inward and intense form of spirituality. To the secular left (Vovelle, Roche, Roger Chartier), the statistical curves generally indicate *embourgeoisement* of world view; to the religious right (Ariès, Chaunu, Bernard Plongeron), they reveal new patterns of family affection and charity. The only point of agreement seems to be the dictum of Ernest Labrousse:

"Everything derives from the curve." Labrousse's work represents the supreme "discourse on method" of modern French historiography, according to Chaunu; but it misrepresents cultural phenomena. Unlike the price series of economics, the vital statistics of demography, and the (more problematic) professional categories in social history, cultural objects are not manufactured by the historian but by the people he studies. They give off meaning. They need to be read, not counted. Despite its strong start fifteen years ago, the history of *mentalités* seems to be running out of momentum in France. If so, the explanation may lie in an overcommitment to the quantification of culture and an undervaluation of the symbolic element in social intercourse.[2]

The French formula, with its implicit references to Marxism and structuralism, never had much appeal to the tribes identified as "Anglo-Saxon" in France. But cultural history has its problems within our own tradition. How many of our books begin by sketching the social background of the subject and end by filling in the culture? This tendency runs through the entire series on *The Rise of Modern Europe* edited by William Langer, the most eminent American historian of his generation, and especially through the volume written for the series by Langer himself.[3] It makes sense to us as a mode of exposition, but it does so because of an unspoken assumption that if we can get the social setting right the cultural content will somehow follow. We structure our work in a way that implies that cultural systems derive from social orders. Perhaps they do, but how? The question must be confronted, yet it is rarely recognized. And if we fail to face up to it, we may fall into a naïve kind of functionalism. Keith Thomas begins his magisterial *Religion and the Decline of Magic* with a chapter on the harsh and uncertain conditions of life in the sixteenth and seventeenth centuries, when witchcraft flourished, and ends it with a chapter on the improved conditions in the eighteenth century, when it died out.[4] He seems to imply that social conditions determined popular beliefs. But when confronted with so bold and bald a proposition, he backed down—and wisely so, for it would have committed him to a simple, stimulus-and-response view of attitude formation and it would not even have made sense of the chronology. Life in English villages did not improve dramatically between 1650 and 1750. Indeed, attitudes often changed during periods of relative stability and remained relatively stable during times of upheaval, as Lawrence Stone discovered in his study of English family life.[5] Philippe Ariès found the same tendency in France, and even Michel Vovelle confessed to an inability to correlate religious attitudes with social change at the end of his massive *Piété baroque et déchristianisation*.[6]

I mention these historians, not in order to snipe at them but because they are the best in the profession; yet whenever they try to join social and cultural history, they run into the same kind of problem. Perhaps a more successful juncture could be made by orienting cultural history in a new direction: toward anthropology. Of course, that suggestion is not really new. Keith Thomas made it long ago, and before him E.E. Evans-Pritchard urged anthropologists to turn toward history. Several anthropological books by historians and historical books by anthropologists have shown that the two disciplines are destined to converge.[7]

But how? The way to a thoroughly anthropological history remains unclear, and I doubt that historians can find one by taking bits and pieces from the neighboring discipline, or even by borrowing a full-fledged methodology. Anthropologists have no common method, no all-embracing theory. If merely asked for a definition of culture, they are liable to explode in clan warfare. But despite their disagreements, they share a general orientation. In their different ways among their different tribes, they usually try to see things from the native's point of view, to understand what he means, and to seek out the social dimensions of meaning. They work from the assumption that symbols are shared, like the air we breathe or, to adopt their favorite metaphor, the language we speak.

At the risk of putting words in the mouths of my own native informants, I think it fair to say that the preoccupation with language among anthropologists includes a concern for expressivity and style as well as lexicology and syntax, and that this concern applies to societies as well as individuals. Each of us speaks in his own manner, but we share the same grammar—all the more so as we are usually unconscious of it. Grammatical slips, or deviations from the idiom, can be detected by everyone, even the illiterate—unless the 'errors' belong to a popular dialect, in which case they are not erroneous—because some things are generally considered to be wrong and some things cannot be said. We can move from one language to another, but in doing so we accept new constraints and make new mistakes. We also adopt a different tone, enjoying the *je ne sais quoi* of *Sprachgefühl*. The untranslatability of such terms suggests that it is not extravagant to entertain the notion of tone and style in cultures—the sort of thing one senses in comparing expressions like "bloody-minded" and *grogneur* or cross-linguistic borrowings like *le fair-play anglais* and "French finesse" or cross-cultural insults like "French leave" and *capote anglaise*. Anthropologists may have overworked the concept of culture-as-language, but it provides a tonic to historians. For if culture is idiomatic, it is retrievable. And if enough of its texts have survived, it can be excavated from the archives. We can stop straining to see how the documents "reflect" their social surroundings, because they were imbedded in a symbolic world that was social and cultural at the same time.

Notes

1 Pierre Chaunu, 'Un nouveau champ pour l'histoire sérielle: le quantitative au troisième niveau', in Pierre Chaunu, *Histoire quantitative, histoire sérielle*, Paris, 1978, pp. 216–30.

2 Ernest Labrousse, *La crise de l'économie française à la fin de l'Ancien Régime et au début de la Révolution*, Paris, 1944, vol. 1, p. xxix.

3 William Langer, *Political and Social Upheaval, 1832–1852*, New York, 1969.

4 Keith Thomas, *Religion and the Decline of Magic*, Weidenfeld & Nicolson, 1971.

5 Lawrence Stone, *The Family, Sex and Marriage in England, 1500–1800*, Weidenfeld & Nicolson, 1977.

6 Philippe Ariès, *The Hour of Our Death*, trans. Helen Weaver, Allen Lane, 1981; Michel Vovelle, *Piété baroque et déchristianisation en Provence au XVIIIe siècle*, Paris, 1973.

7 Keith Thomas, 'History and anthropology', *Past and Present* 24 (1963), pp. 3–24; E.E. Evans-Pritchard, *Essays in Social Anthropology*, Faber, 1962.

Memory and culture

The reach of the cultural turn extends to one of our most fundamental faculties. Long the province of psychology, memory is now understood by many historians as cultural, in the sense of being as much collective as personal, and in its sensitivity to the broader culture in which it is embedded. Pierre Nora provides important historical perspective to the understanding of collective memory. In pre-industrial societies, he maintains, memory was grounded in stable small-scale communities and relatively spontaneous. The importance attached to history today is symptomatic of the decline of that kind of recall. Instead, collective memory has to be defined and promoted, not only by the writing of history, but by *lieux de mémoire* – specially designated sites through which society tries to bring to life a capacity for social memory which has been lost; Nora has documented the vast extent of this memorialisation in France in his multi-volume edited work, *Lieux de mémoire* (1984–92).

Today memory is no less central to political culture and social consciousness than it was in the peasant cultures of old. But because so much of it depends on cultural initiative and public policy, it is particularly contentious. As Katherine Hodgkin and Susannah Radstone observe, the question 'Who is entitled to speak for the past?' is an insistent element of cultural politics. It is articulated at many different levels, from the struggle to find ways of representing the Holocaust to the relatively mundane context of the local museum or public memorial. Contests about the meaning of the past are always contests about the meaning of present, which is what undermines the validity of memory as a 'tool of truth'.

40. Pierre Nora

[from 'Between Memory and History: Les Lieux de Mémoire',
Representations *26 (1989), pp. 7–12]*

The acceleration of history: let us try to gauge the significance, beyond metaphor, of this phrase. An increasingly rapid slippage of the present into a historical past that is gone for good, a general perception that anything and everything may disappear—these indicate a rupture of equilibrium. The remnants of experience still lived in the warmth of tradition, in the silence of custom, in the repetition of the ancestral, have been displaced under the pressure of a fundamentally historical sensibility. Self-consciousness emerges under the sign of that which has already happened, as the fulfillment of something always already begun. We speak so much of memory because there is so little of it left.

Our interest in *lieux de mémoire* where memory crystallizes and secretes itself has occurred at a particular historical moment, a turning point where consciousness of a break with the past is bound up with the sense that memory has been torn—but torn in such a way as to pose the problem of the embodiment of memory in certain sites where a sense of historical continuity persists. There are *lieux de mémoire*, sites of memory, because there are no longer *milieux de mémoire*, real environments of memory.

Consider, for example, the irrevocable break marked by the disappearance of peasant culture, that quintessential repository of collective memory whose recent vogue as an object of historical study coincided with the apogee of industrial growth. Such a fundamental collapse of memory is but one familiar example of a movement toward democratization and mass culture on a global scale. Among the new nations, independence has swept into history societies newly awakened from their ethnological slumbers by colonial violation. Similarly, a process of interior decolonization has affected ethnic minorities, families, and groups that until now have possessed reserves of memory but little or no historical capital. We have seen the end of societies that had long assured the transmission and conservation of collectively remembered values, whether through churches or schools, the family or the state; the end too of ideologies that prepared a smooth passage from the past to the future or that had indicated what the future should keep from the past—whether for reaction, progress, or even revolution. Indeed, we have seen the tremendous dilation of our very mode of historical perception, which, with the help of the media, has substituted for a memory entwined in the intimacy of a collective heritage the ephemeral film of current events.

The "acceleration of history," then, confronts us with the brutal realization of the difference between real memory—social and unviolated, exemplified in but also retained as the secret of so-called primitive or archaic societies—and history, which is how our hopelessly forgetful modern societies, propelled by change, organize the past. On the one hand, we find an integrated, dictatorial memory—unself-conscious, commanding, all-powerful, spontaneously actual-izing, a memory without a past that ceaselessly reinvents tradition, linking the history of its ancestors to the undifferentiated time of heroes, origins, and myth—and on the other hand, our memory, nothing more in fact than sifted and sorted historical traces. The gulf between the two has deepened in modern times with the growing belief in a right, a capacity, and even a duty to change. Today, this distance has been stretched to its convulsive limit.

This conquest and eradication of memory by history has had the effect of a revelation, as if an ancient bond of identity had been broken and something had ended that we had experienced as self-evident—the equation of memory and history. The fact that only one word exists in French to designate both lived history and the intellectual operation that renders it intelligible (distin-guished in German by *Geschichte* and *Historie*) is a weakness of the language that has often been remarked; still, it delivers a profound truth: the process that is carrying us forward and our representation of that process are of the same kind. If we were able to live within memory, we would not have needed to consecrate *lieux de mémoire* in its name. Each gesture, down to the most every-day, would be experienced as the ritual repetition of a timeless practice in a pri-mordial identification of act and meaning. With the appearance of the trace, of mediation, of distance, we are not in the realm of true memory but of history. We can think, for an example, of the Jews of the diaspora, bound in daily devo-tion to the rituals of tradition, who as "peoples of memory" found little use for historians until their forced exposure to the modern world.

Memory and history, far from being synonymous, appear now to be in funda-mental opposition. Memory is life, borne by living societies founded in its name. It remains in permanent evolution, open to the dialectic of remembering and forgetting, unconscious of its successive deformations, vulnerable to manipulation and appropriation, susceptible to being long dormant and periodically revived. History, on the other hand, is the reconstruction, always problematic and incomplete, of what is no longer. Memory is a perpetually actual phenomenon, a bond tying us to the eternal present; history is a representation of the past. Memory, insofar as it is affective and magical, only accommodates those facts that suit it; it nourishes recollections that may be out of focus or telescopic, global or detached, particular or symbolic—responsive to each avenue of conveyance or phenomenal screen, to every censorship or projection. History, because it is an intellectual and secular production, calls for analysis and criticism. Memory installs remembrance within the sacred; history, always prosaic, releases it again. Memory is blind to all but the group it binds—which is to say, as Maurice Halbwachs has said, that there are as many memories as there are groups, that memory is by nature multiple and yet specific; collective, plural, and yet individual. History, on the other hand, belongs to everyone and to no one, whence its claim to universal authority. Memory takes root in the concrete, in spaces, gestures, images, and objects; history binds itself strictly to temporal continuities, to progressions and to relations between things. Memory is absolute, while history can only conceive the relative.

At the heart of history is a critical discourse that is antithetical to spontaneous memory. History is perpetually suspicious of memory, and its true mission is to suppress and destroy it. At the horizon of historical societies, at the limits of the completely historicized world, there would occur a permanent secularization. History's goal and ambition is not to exalt but to annihilate what has in reality taken place. A generalized critical history would no doubt preserve some museums, some medallions and monuments—that is to say, the materials necessary for its work—but it would empty them of what, to us, would make them *lieux de mémoire*. In the end, a society living wholly under the sign of history could not, any more than could a traditional society, conceive such sites for anchoring its memory.

Perhaps the most tangible sign of the split between history and memory has been the emergence of a history of history, the awakening, quite recent in France, of a historiographical consciousness. History, especially the history of national development, has constituted the oldest of our collective traditions: our quintessential *milieu de mémoire*. From the chroniclers of the Middle Ages to today's practitioners of "total" history, the entire tradition has developed as the controlled exercise and automatic deepening of memory, the reconstitution of a past without lacunae or faults. No doubt, none of the great historians, since Froissart, had the sense that he was representing only a particular memory. Commynes did not think he was fashioning a merely dynastic memory, La Popelinière merely a French memory, Bossuet a Christian and monarchical memory, Voltaire the memory of the progress of humankind, Michelet exclusively the "people's" memory, and Lavisse solely the memory of the nation. On the contrary, each historian was convinced that his task consisted in establishing a more positive, all-encompassing, and explicative memory. History's procurement, in the last century, of scientific methodology has only intensified the effort to establish critically a "true" memory. Every great historical revision has sought to enlarge the basis for collective memory.

In a country such as France the history of history cannot be an innocent operation; it amounts to the internal subversion of memory-history by critical history. Every history is by nature critical, and all historians have sought to denounce the hypocritical mythologies of their predecessors. But something fundamentally unsettling happens when history begins to write its own history. A historiographical anxiety arises when history assigns itself the task of tracing alien impulses within itself and discovers that it is the victim of memories which it has sought to master. Where history has not taken on the strong formative and didactic role that it has assumed in France, the history of history is less laden with polemical content. In the United States, for example, a country of plural memories and diverse traditions, historiography is more pragmatic. Different interpretations of the Revolution or of the Civil War do not threaten the American tradition because, in some sense, no such thing exists—or if it does, it is not primarily a historical construction. In France, on the other hand, historiography is iconoclastic and irreverent. It seizes upon the most clearly defined objects of tradition—a key battle, like Bouvines; a canonical manual, like the *Petit Lavisse*—in order to dismantle their mechanisms and analyze the conditions of their development. It operates primarily by introducing doubt, by running a knife between the tree of memory and the bark of history. That we study the historiography of the French Revolution, that we reconstitute its myths and interpretations, implies that we no longer unquestioningly identify with its heritage. To interrogate a tradition, venerable though it may be, is no longer to pass it on intact. Moreover, the history of history does not restrict itself to addressing the most sacred objects of our national tradition. By questioning its own traditional structure, its own conceptual and material resources, its operating procedures and social means of distribution, the entire discipline of history has entered its historiographical age, consummating its dissociation from memory—which in turn has become a possible object of history.

It once seemed as though a tradition of memory, through the concepts of history and the nation, had crystallized in the synthesis of the Third Republic. Adopting a broad chronology, between Augustin Thierry's *Lettres sur l'histoire de France* (1827) and Charles Seignobos's *Histoire sincère de la nation française* (1933), the relationships between history, memory, and the nation were characterized as more than natural currency: they were shown to involve a reciprocal circularity, a symbiosis at every level—scientific and pedagogical, theoretical and practical. This national definition of the present imperiously demanded justification through the illumination of the past. It was, however, a present that had been weakened by revolutionary trauma and the call for a general reevaluation of the monarchical past, and it was weakened further by the defeat of 1870, which rendered only more urgent, in the belated competition with German science and pedagogy—the real victors at Sadowa—the development of a severe documentary erudition for the scholarly transmission of memory. The tone of national responsibility assigned to the historian—half preacher, half soldier—is unequalled, for example, in the first editorial of the *Revue historique* (1876) in which Gabriel Monod foresaw a "slow scientific, methodical, and collective investigation" conducted in a "secret and secure manner for the greatness of the fatherland as well as for mankind." Reading this text, and a hundred others like it, one wonders how the notion that positivist history was not cumulative could ever have gained credibility. On the contrary, in the teleological perspective of the nation the political, the military, the biographical, and the diplomatic all were to be considered pillars of continuity. The defeat of Agincourt, the dagger of Ravaillac, the day of the Dupes, the additional clauses of the treaty of Westphalia—each required scrupulous accounting. The most incisive erudition thus served to add or take away some detail from the monumental edifice that was the nation. The nation's memory was held to be powerfully unified; no more discontinuity existed between our Greco-Roman cradle and the colonies of the Third Republic than between the high erudition that annexed new territories to the nation's heritage and the schoolbooks that professed its dogma. The holy nation thus acquired a holy history; through the nation our memory continued to rest upon a sacred foundation.

To see how this particular synthesis came apart under the pressure of a new secularizing force would be to show how, during the crisis of the 1930s in France, the coupling of state and nation was gradually replaced by the coupling of state and society—and how, at the same time and for the same reasons, history was transformed, spectacularly, from the tradition of memory it had become into the self-knowledge of society. As such, history was able to highlight many kinds of memory, even turn itself into a laboratory of past mentalities; but in disclaiming its national identity, it also abandoned its claim to bearing coherent meaning and consequently lost its pedagogical authority to transmit values. The definition of the nation was no longer the issue, and peace, prosperity, and the reduction of its power have since accomplished the rest. With the advent of society in place of the nation, legitimation by the past and therefore by history yields to legitimation by the future. One can only acknowledge and venerate the past and serve the nation; the future, however, can be prepared for: thus the three terms regain their autonomy. No longer a cause, the nation has become a given; history is now a social science, memory a purely private phenomenon. The memory-nation was thus the last incarnation of the unification of memory and history.

The study of *lieux de mémoires*, then, lies at the intersection of two developments that in France today give it meaning: one a purely historiographical movement, the reflexive turning of history upon itself, the other a movement that is, properly speaking, historical: the end of a tradition of memory. The moment of *lieux de mémoire* occurs at the same time that an immense and intimate fund of memory disappears, surviving only as a reconstituted object beneath the gaze of critical history. This period sees, on the one hand, the decisive deepening of historical study and, on the other hand, a heritage consolidated. The critical principle follows an internal dynamic: our intellectual, political, historical frameworks are exhausted but remain powerful enough not to leave us indifferent; whatever vitality they retain impresses us only in their most spectacular symbols. Combined, these two movements send us at once to history's most elementary tools and to the most symbolic objects of our memory: to the archives as well as to the tricolor; to the libraries, dictionaries, and museums as well as to commemorations, celebrations, the Panthéon, and the Arc de Triomphe; to the *Dictionnaire Larousse* as well as to the Wall of the Fédérés, where the last defenders of the Paris commune were massacred in 1870.

These *lieux de mémoire* are fundamentally remains, the ultimate embodiments of a memorial consciousness that has barely survived in a historical age that calls out for memory because it has abandoned it. They make their appearance by virtue of the deritualization of our world—producing, manifesting, establishing, constructing, decreeing, and maintaining by artifice and by will a society deeply absorbed in its own transformation and renewal, one that inherently values the new over the ancient, the young over the old, the future over the past. Museums, archives, cemeteries, festivals, anniversaries, treaties, depositions, monuments, sanctuaries, fraternal orders—these are the boundary stones of another age, illusions of eternity. It is the nostalgic dimension of these devotional institutions that makes them seem beleaguered and cold—they mark the rituals of a society without ritual; integral particularities in a society that levels particularity; signs of distinction and of group membership in a society that tends to recognize individuals only as identical and equal.

Lieux de mémoire originate with the sense that there is no spontaneous memory, that we must deliberately create archives, maintain anniversaries, organize celebrations, pronounce eulogies, and notarize bills because such activities no longer occur naturally. The defense, by certain minorities, of a privileged memory that has retreated to jealously protected enclaves in this sense intensely illuminates the truth of *lieux de mémoire*—that without commemorative vigilance, history would soon sweep them away. We buttress our identities upon such bastions, but if what they defended were not threatened, there would be no need to build them. Conversely, if the memories that they enclosed were to be set free they would be useless; if history did not besiege memory, deforming and transforming it, penetrating and petrifying it, there would be no *lieux de mémoire*. Indeed, it is this very push and pull that produces *lieux de mémoire*—moments of history torn away from the movement of history, then returned; no longer quite life, not yet death, like shells on the shore when the sea of living memory has receded.

41. Katherine Hodgkin and Susannah Radstone

[from 'Introduction' to Katherine Hodgkin and Susannah Radstone (eds), Contested Pasts, *Routledge, 2003, pp. 1–6]*

The question of what it means to contest the past is one that has become increasingly charged in the last few decades. It reveals certain presuppositions about the relationship between the present and the past, which have both historical and political purchase; and the discourse of memory has come to have a central part in thinking about that relationship. The idea of contest in the literal sense is apparently a straightforward one: it evokes a struggle in the terrain of truth. If what is disputed is the course of events – what really happened – new answers, particularly by groups whose knowledge has previously been discounted, may challenge dominant or privileged narratives. But to contest the past is also, of course, to pose questions about the present, and what the past means in the present. Our understanding of the past has strategic, political, and ethical consequences. Contests over the meaning of the past are also contests over the meaning of the present and over ways of taking the past forward. Ideas of restitution and reparation, evoking both financial or political justice and more abstruse compensations such as recognition of wrongs done, or readiness to hear and acknowledge hidden stories, all draw on a sense that the present is obliged to accommodate the past in order to move on from it (itself, of course, a historically specific way of thinking about history).

The focus of contestation, then, is very often not conflicting accounts of what actually happened in the past so much as the question of who or what is entitled to speak for that past in the present. The attempt to resolve meaning in the present is thus often a matter of conflicts over representation: where a memorial should be sited, what artefacts a museum should include, whose views should be sought in television interviews. In these debates the contest is often over how truth can best be conveyed, rather than what actually happened. There may be agreement as to the course of events, but not over how the truth of those events may be most fully represented, or what should be the explanatory and narrative context that would make sense of a given episode. And if these arguments are partly historical, memory, in such debates, occupies a particular place. In all the debates over the relationship between memory and history, one constantly recurring theme is that although history is about the present, so too is memory, and much more directly. Memory is still live and active, still charged with the weight of these contests, and it is to memory that one should turn in order to reveal 'what really happened'.

The appeal to memory in determining the truth of the past, then, is widespread. But it is also problematic: both 'memory' and 'truth' here are unstable and destabilising terms. To privilege memory as a tool of truth, through which the statements of authority may be subverted or contradicted, we must assume a direct correspondence between the experience and how it is remembered. The person who remembers, in this model, is able to know and tell the truth of the event, because s/he was there at the time. Experience is the guarantee of certainty; distortion an ideological weapon, opposed to the real facts, and imposed by ideological means (media, academy . . .). But for history as for other disciplines, after the critical revolutions of the last decades, the answer cannot be so straightforward. Not only the reliability of memory and experience as exact records of the past, but also the very notion of historical truth, have come into question; the past is constituted in narrative, always representation, always construction. In so far as historians have engaged in memory studies, indeed, they have done so primarily because the concept of memory seems to offer a more cautious and qualified relation to the past than the absolute assertion that for some is associated with history. Working with the concept of memory – provisional, subjective, concerned with representation and the present rather than fact and the past – suggests a way out of the impasse into which historiography might have been driven by the poststructuralist assault on truth.

But if the vocabulary of memory is found with increasing frequency in historical work, this still could not be said to make it more than a minority interest for historians. The relation between memory and history is complex, and has been constituted in many different ways by historians and others in the last few decades.[1] And yet it remains a curiously unrealised relation, as if conversations or conceptualisations are taking place independently of one another, and with little mutual awareness. Within the field of memory studies, 'history' is a key reference point, invoked both in titles and in discussion.

A glance at a few titles gives an indication of the characteristic juxtapositions: Felman and Laub's *Testimony: crises of witnessing in literature, psychoanalysis and history* (1992), for instance, or Vivian Sobchack's 1996 collection *The Persistence of History: cinema, television and the modern event*. But 'memory studies' itself, despite its interdisciplinary potential and despite the way in which the idea of memory has become dispersed across many different fields (anthropology, psychology, sociology) is located most firmly in disciplines most accustomed to a concern with representation: literature, film studies, cultural studies.

Arguments about the relation between history and memory have thus to a surprisingly large extent (and of course with exceptions) taken place outside the historical profession. 'History', prominent though it is in these debates, stands for a certain notion of truth and a certain notion of referentiality, to be summoned up as a tool in arguments going on elsewhere, rather than identifying the place where the argument is happening. The academic discipline of history has engaged with issues of memory much less than a brief survey of 'memory studies' might lead one to expect. There have been journal articles and special features, and the word appears in conference titles more than it used to. But a brief survey of recent works on historiography suggests that memory has had surprisingly little impact on historical writing or on theorisations of history.[2] Curiously, although it is often assumed that the rise of 'memory' goes alongside that of 'poststructuralism' (presumably leaving 'history' tied to 'empiricism'), poststructuralist historiographies seem particularly uninterested in memory. With few exceptions, theoretically informed historiographical studies tend to locate memory as a sub-category of oral history, or to ignore it altogether. Of two recent critical readers on history and theory, for example – Geoffrey Roberts's *History and Narrative Reader*, on 'the history and narrative debate' since 1960, and Anne Green and Kathleen Troup's collection *The Houses of History: a critical reader in twentieth-century history and theory* – the first has no index entry for memory, and the second directs the searcher to 'see oral history'. The idea of history, it seems, has been more important to memory studies than vice versa.

In this sense one might argue that the challenge represented by Raphael Samuel's *Theatres of Memory* (1994), widely cited though the book is, has never really been taken up. The book's concern with how the past is represented and engaged with in the present through an extraordinary variety of forms – television, fashions in interior decoration, historical walks, family histories, local museums, school textbooks – has certainly been followed through; but the field is identified primarily as 'public history' – history in the public sphere – not as 'memory', in the sense that Samuel used it. Public history may cover very similar ground to that of *Theatres of Memory*, and may indeed draw on memory discourses; its field might be identified as social or cultural memory, it might look at memorial discourses in museums, and so on. But the very fact that this field has come to be known as 'public history' must say something about the discomfort historians continue to feel in working with the concept of memory. And Samuel's central suggestion, that history might use memory actually to rethink its own conceptual and disciplinary boundaries and practices, and to acknowledge common characteristics rather than setting up the two as opposites, does not appear to have found much of a following. Bill Schwarz's discussion of memory and historical time, in our companion volume *Regimes of Memory*, is a rare example of a historian suggesting that memory might be integrated into historiography.[3] Often, it seems, history is willing to question the epistemological status of its object of study – the past – but less ready to engage with how 'the past' itself is variously conceptualised and constituted as history, memory, or archive.

The remainder of this introduction, then, returns to the question of the relation between history and memory, in the larger framework of the relation between the past and the present: in what fields has the encounter between history and memory been staged? What problems emerge in that encounter? And what is at stake in contests over the past? Implicit in these debates are questions about the social and individual dimensions of memory, and the media through which memory is experienced, produced or conveyed.

Witnessing history (1): the spoken word

One major exception to the relative reserve of history confronted with memory, of course, is the field of oral history, in which the concept of memory – the idea of memory *as* concept, rather than as given phenomenon – has been increasingly significant over the last couple of decades. This is hardly surprising. Oral historians, whose work involves soliciting the memories of the living, are ideally placed to reflect on and theorise the issues that the processes of remembering and retelling bring forward; and over the last few decades, there has been a shift in the preoccupations of oral history, involving an increasing attentiveness to issues of memory.[4] In its origins, however, oral history's view of memory was less complex. It laid claim precisely to an authentic truth excluded from the historical record.[5] It solicited the voices of those who have been silent and ignored throughout the centuries: the poor and powerless, workers and women, who seldom have speaking parts in the historical drama. It attended to the private, the domestic, the details of daily life, rather than to great events. And it found in the memories evoked a counter-narrative, a corrective to the simplifying and patronising assumptions of the traditional makers of history.

Thus, in the first instance, oral history offers a validation of memory as *more* true and more reliable than other records: these people know what it was like, because they were there. Early distrust of oral history, indeed, expressed itself at times precisely as contempt for the rememberers: old men drooling about their youth, in A.J.P. Taylor's notorious phrase.[6] And it is as a popularising and democratic form of history that it has become most widespread. Along with family history – and often closely allied to it, as family historians tape-record ancient relatives to fill out the picture and get crucial genealogical details before death snatches them out of reach – it has become a grass-roots practice. Schoolchildren are encouraged to interview their grandparents (as Graham Carr notes in this volume); local enthusiasts publish booklets in small presses recording *Memories of Old Poplar*, or *Memories of Highgate from a Keeper's Lodge*, to be sold in local shops and libraries, used by schoolchildren (again) for projects, and so on.

All this activity is founded on, and confirms, a belief that one's own memory is more to be relied on than other forms of knowledge: if I remember something, it must be true; this vivid picture in my mind could not have sprung up at random. But it is precisely in revealing the ways in which memory, even when it seems most real and definite, is not a certain guarantee of truth, that oral history has developed into such a fruitful area for thinking about memory. This is not to return to a dismissive approach to those whose accounts of the past have previously been ignored. If at times people claim memories of what evidently never happened, or happened other than how they remember it, this does not mean their memories are invalid or irrelevant, but that different questions need to be asked. The focus of historical analysis shifts from the notion of memory as either 'true' or 'mistaken', to an emphasis on memory as process, and how to understand its motivation and meaning. How do people recollect events they were involved in or witnesses to, and what can be learned from their narratives? These are the questions now posed by oral history, as several contributors to this volume point out. The very fact that there are divergences, inconsistencies, different versions at different times, is in itself revealing both about the culture in which these memories have been built and emerge, and about the workings of memory itself.[7] The idea of memory as a tool with which to contest 'official' versions of the past, too, shifts from an opposition between the subordinate truth versus the dominant lie, to a concern with the ways in which particular versions of an event may be at various times and for various reasons promoted, reformulated, or silenced. This is not to deny that the dominant versions of the past are inextricably entangled with relations of power in society, but rather to refocus the question around the many ways in which conflict and contest can emerge.

Such work also reminds us that memory is not only individual but cultural: memory, though we may experience it as private and internal, draws on countless scraps and bits of knowledge and information from the surrounding culture, and is inserted into larger cultural narratives. This is a relationship that goes both ways, of course. If individual memories are constructed within culture, and are part of cultural systems of representation, so cultural memories are constituted by the cumulative weight of dispersed and fragmented individual memories, among other things. We may 'remember' the 1960s, or the Second World War, in our own lifetimes; but it would be impossible to remember them without seeing them in the framework established subsequently of what a given decade or event *means*. And what it means is itself an occasion for cultural struggle. If history and oral history are now both inclined to be more cautious about the notion of an absolute historical truth, there remains nonetheless a sharp sense that it is possible to tell lies about the past; and that the meanings and narratives of the past that we live with are of critical importance in establishing our sense of ourselves and our cultures.

Moreover, while the model of authorities imposing false histories (to be countered by memory) may be too simple, it is clear that questions of power and authority do not disappear in thinking about what versions of history come to be identified as true. For history and memory are not abstract forces: they are located in specific contexts, instances, and narratives, and decisions have always to be taken about what story is to be told. Memory as it is invoked in schools, museums, and mass media may be forwarding political agendas which serve particular ideas about the virtues of the nation, the family, or the current government, as several of the pieces in this volume demonstrate. The appeal to memory itself (as opposed to its content) may carry particular ideological assumptions about history and subjectivity, as we shall see below. Thus moving away from a model of 'truth' vs. 'distortion' does not imply moving away from a sense that memory is political; it remains a site of struggle over meaning.

....

Witnessing history (2): trauma and history

If oral history is one field in which the notion of memory has been a focus for special interest, another area particularly associated with the vocabulary of remembrance is that of holocaust studies. The two, indeed, at times are hard to separate out. A cluster of politically and emotionally charged concepts – witnessing, testimony, trauma, silence, memory, history, denial – keep recurring in discussions of the holocaust, not so much in relation to the historical event as to its memorial afterlife.[8] Trauma theory, the 'home' of this cluster, in its origins a discourse relating to the psychology of individuals, has become an explanatory apparatus through which to apprehend and analyse the past; partly through the frame of the individual memory, but also through a more general set of arguments about representation, what could be said, what could be remembered and how.[9] Founded on the notion of an originary traumatic event, however, trauma theory returns us to precisely the problems about the nature of the event that memory as it stands in relation to history helps us to rethink. Memory cannot be seen as a simple evasion of the problem of referentiality, since it is itself a referential system. But its relation to historical 'events' is complex and mediated, involving fantasy and wish rather than simply recording what happens. If memory slides uncertainly along a line with history and fantasy at either end, trauma theory has difficulty in acknowledging the place of fantasy.

At the heart of the idea of traumatic memory, as it developed particularly in relation to the sexual abuse of children, is the idea of unrepresentability. Following a terrible event, it suggests, memory goes into crisis, and refuses the knowledge of what has happened. The theoretical crux is the idea of something that cannot be thought, that is inaccessibly closed to memory, because the psychic wound inflicted by the event was intolerable. Thus the notion of trauma complicates referentiality by interposing the disruptions of memory between the event and its representations. But whereas for oral history, as we have seen, those disruptions are intrinsic to memory itself (which distorts, conflates, masks, omits), for trauma theory it is a specific event that disrupts a memory that would otherwise – in its healthy state – be unperturbed. Underpinning the theory of traumatic memory is a particular narrative of the psychic consequences of a real event; and the debates around what can and cannot be spoken, remembered, represented, take place in relation to arguments about whether that event happened or not – so, once again, in the context of a contested past, in which neither events nor their meanings can straightforwardly be known.[10]

Notes

1   See for example Jacques Le Goff, *History and Memory*, trans. Steven Randall and Elizabeth Claman, New York, 1992; Pierre Nora, 'Between memory and history' (see extract 40, ED); and Raphael Samuel, *Theatres of Memory*, Verso, 1994.

2 For a different perspective, see Kerwin Lee Klein, 'On the emergence of *Memory* in historical discourse', *Representations* 69 (2000).

3 Bill Schwarz, '"Already the past": memory and historical time', in Susannah Radstone and Katherine Hodgkin, *Regimes of Memory*, Routledge, 2003.

4 See Robert Perks and Alistair Thomson (eds), *The Oral History Reader*, Routledge, 1998, which includes important essays by Luisa Passerini and Alessandro Portelli.

5 For an overview, see Paul Thompson, *The Voice of the Past: Oral History*, Oxford University Press, 2nd edn, 1988.

6 'In this matter I am an almost total sceptic . . . Old men drooling about their youth – No.' A.J.P. Taylor, quoted in Thompson, *Voice of the Past*, p. 70.

7 See Alessandro Portelli, *The Death of Luigi Trastulli and Other Stories: Form and Meaning in Oral History*, New York, 1991; Luisa Passerini (ed.), *Memory and Totalitarianism*, Oxford University Press, 1992.

8 E.g. Dominick LaCapra, *Representing the Holocaust: History, Theory, Trauma*, New York, 1994; Cathy Caruth, *Unclaimed Experience: Trauma, Narrative and History*, Baltimore, 1996.

9 On trauma theory, see Susannah Radstone, 'Screening trauma: *Forrest Gump*, film and memory', in Susannah Radstone (ed.), *Memory and Methodology*, Berg, 2000; Thomas Elsaesser, 'Postmodernism as mourning work', *Screen* 42 (2001); Paul Antze and Michael Lambek (eds), *Tense Past: Cultural Essays in Trauma and Memory*, Routledge, 1996.

10 See Ann Scott, *Real Events Revisited: Fantasy, Memory and Psychoanalysis*, Virago, 1996; Radstone, 'Screening trauma'.

Part Seven

Beyond Academia

This anthology concludes with two eloquent reminders that the debates of historians concern not only the profession but the wider society of which they are members. If history offers learning and instruction (as argued in Part Four), then its practitioners must give attention to how they communicate their findings to a wider audience. In his inaugural lecture of 1957, H.R. Trevor-Roper argued that most undergraduate history teaching should be geared not to research, but to the requirements of an educated laity. By this he did not mean that historians should pander to fashionable ideologies, but rather that they should assert their professional authority. Trevor-Roper's taste for controversy ensured that his own work received considerable public attention.

Gerda Lerner approaches the issue from a much more radical perspective. She was a refugee from Nazism and later became a formative influence on American women's history. Lerner calls for a much more interactive relationship between historians and the world outside academe. Historians should gain experience of other areas of professional life; they need to acknowledge the contribution made by popular forms of historical enquiry; above all they should take more seriously their role as teachers. Women's history has been more successful than most branches of history in straddling the divide between academic and popular audiences (see Lerner's own *The Majority Finds Its Past*, 1979).

Ultimately the debates which this book has reviewed will be futile unless they influence the history available to the general public. In each generation the call for greater accessibility and greater accountability on the part of historians has to be repeated.

42. H.R. Trevor-Roper

[from 'History: professional and lay' (1957), reprinted in Hugh Lloyd-Jones, Valerie Pearl and Blair Worden (eds), History and Imagination, *Duckworth, 1982, pp. 7–12]*

The view which I wish to express springs from the conviction that history is a humane study and that the study of the humanities requires a different method from the study of the sciences. It may be that human history will one day be reduced to an exact science; but at present, although scientific laws are relevant to it and condition its course, these laws are the laws of other sciences – of economics or geography or statistics – they are not the laws of history. Indeed, if history ever should become an exact science, with established laws of its own, we should then cease to study it as we do: we should apply it, as a form of engineering, and its study as a 'humanity' would be left to those heretics who, still believing in the freedom of the human will, might hope to disprove that grim conclusion. This being so, I am obliged to ask what is the difference in method between the study of humane subjects like history and exact sciences like engineering, and I conclude that this difference can be expressed, and I shall therefore try to express it, very simply.

The difference, as it seems to me, essentially concerns the position of the laity. Exact sciences require specialisation and all the apparatus of specialisation, even if such specialisation carries them beyond the bounds of human interest or lay understanding. The fact that a branch of physics or mathematics may be quite beyond the interest or comprehension of an educated layman in no way invalidates it, because the validity of such subjects does not depend on lay interest or lay comprehension. Even if no layman can understand them, they will still be taught by professionals to professionals from generation to generation. The exact scientists are a kind of pre-Reformation clergy, and their function is to perform their miracles, to continue their Church, not to make themselves intelligible to laymen: for their control of the means of salvation and damnation makes the lay world so dependent on them that it will tolerate and subsidise them even without understanding.

But the humane subjects are quite different from this. They have no direct scientific use; they owe their title to existence to the interest and comprehension of the laity; they exist primarily not for the training of professionals but for the education of laymen; and therefore if they once lose touch with the lay mind, they are rightly condemned to perish. I know it will be answered that all knowledge, including humane knowledge, advances by means of technical specialisation. I do not dispute this answer; for I do not dispute that exact sciences contribute to humane subjects. But since they merely contribute to humane subjects and have not yet absorbed them, it follows that such technical specialisation in respect of them has no value in itself; it owes whatever value it has entirely to that degree to which it makes those subjects clearer, more comprehensible, and more interesting to the intelligent laity. I do not dispute that by a completer professionalism we may arrive at a more perfect knowledge of history or literature: I merely state that that perfect knowledge may be so fine and so uninteresting that nobody, except its discoverers, will wish to possess it. If we believe, as I do, that a knowledge of history and literature is essential to a civilised society, this would be a great loss.

Consider the case of classical studies. A century ago our ancestors knew far less than we can know (if we want to know) about the civilisation of Greece and Rome; and yet somehow, in spite of the more copious fountains which now break out before our feet, we seem strangely exempt from thirst. The study of the classics is now described as 'too narrow'. I do not believe that a study which was wide enough to educate Gladstone and Derby and Asquith and Curzon is too narrow for us. What has happened is not that the subject has lost its value but that a humane subject has been treated as an exact science: professional classical scholars have assumed that they are teaching only other professional classical scholars; consequently they have killed the classics. When I see a Greek tragedy, one of the greatest works of human literature, a tragedy no longer than a single book of *Paradise Lost*, put out into the world with a commentary of three large octavo volumes round its neck, weighing in all nearly half a stone, I fear the poor thing will not get far: it will languish and die, die of strangulation and neglect in some corner of a forgotten bookshelf. If an interest in the classics survives today, apart from the subsidies which they enjoy from the past, that may well be due rather to the enterprise of Sir Allen Lane and his Pelican Books, where they appear, purged of otiose learning, reanimated by lay interest, than to the heavy cossetting of professional scholars.

Similarly, unless we take heed, there is a danger that philosophers may kill philosophy, philologists literature, and historians history. Armies of research students, organised by a general staff of professors, may in time have mapped out the entire history of the world. We may know, or be able to know, what every unimportant minor official in a government office did every hour of his day, what every peasant paid for his plot in a long extinct village, how every backbencher voted on a private bill in an eighteenth-century parliament. Our libraries may groan beneath volumes on medieval chamber administration and bed-chamber administration. But to what end? Just as the layman now turns aside from the great civilised nations of antiquity whose living literature has been stifled with dead learning, and goes a-whoring after the barbarous despotisms of ancient Assyria or the savage empires of pre-Columbian America – peoples of bloody history and no literature at all – so he will turn aside from us and seek interest and enlightenment elsewhere. He may not seek it in such edifying sources; but it will not be for us to complain, who will have driven him away.

This, after all, is what happened in the sixteenth century to the Church which presumed too much on its monopoly of what is supposed an exact magical science. Its endowments were fat as never before; the material for study was growing with the passage of time and the elongation of tradition; and armies of disciplined theologians, fondling their subject with minute expertise, had encrusted it with a rich commentary of scholasticism. And yet somehow the laity would not take it. They declared that religion too was a humane subject, that the laity, not the clergy, are the measure of the Church, and that experts exist to serve others, not themselves. So all that great weight of tradition and scholasticism which clogged and cluttered the free spaces of the intellectual world was suddenly found to be otiose, and the lay spirit of man, the spirit that sought not a self-perpetuating apostolic succession of warranted experts but guidance and education for the lay mind, freedom to move in a present which had become overcharged with the cumber of the past, a clear path back to the pure sources of truth which had since been choked with learned rubbish, turned aside from that tradition, rejected that scholasticism, and, by emancipation from it, enabled the world's great age to begin anew.

For every enlightenment entails a certain disposal of waste learning, and the study of history can sometimes progress as well by forgetting as by remembering the past. Just as, in economic life, societies advance by gradual inflation which frees the present from some part of the burden it has inherited, even if it also mortifies those who have invested their savings in such dwindling securities, so, in historical study, we march similarly forward, constantly devaluing some of our own pious savings, even if that process is also mortifying to those who have invested too heavily in them. At every onward stage there is a cry from the backwoods: from the annuitants who are landed with Dalton's $2\frac{1}{2}$%s and from the antiquaries who have locked up their intellectual capital in depreciated scholiasts. But somehow these plaintive voices are soon forgotten. Duns, in the sixteenth century, is put unlamented in Bocardo; in the seventeenth century we find ourselves agreeing with Milton's summary dismissal of the early Fathers as 'marginal stuffings'; and in the eighteenth with Goldsmith, who watched the advance of polite learning at the expense of those who had vainly absorbed 'Metrodorus, Valerius Probus, Aulus Gellius, Pedianus, Boethius and a hundred others, to be acquainted with whom might show much reading but little judgment'.

This is the lesson which we must always remember when we demand, as we so often do, more and more research, more and more funds for research, more and more professionalism and specialisation in humane subjects. For humane subjects, called into being ultimately to serve the laity, not to discover some recondite but unimportant truth, can only bear a limited amount of specialisation. They need professional methods, but always for the pursuit of lay ends.

Of course, in the great battles between tutors and professors which ended fifty years ago, I do not believe that Dr Pusey and his allies were fighting to keep humane subjects from professionalisation. Far from it. They were fighting, or some of them were fighting, and he certainly was fighting, to defend clerical monopoly, clerical privilege, clerical bigotry, against the humane, liberal, 'infidel' state. They were resisting the reforms of a progressive government in the same spirit of stagnant reaction in which their predecessors had resisted the gifts of the Whig monarchy. They were the heirs of Gibbon's tutors, those immortal 'monks of Magdalen', 'sunk in prejudice and port', whose 'dull and deep potations excused the brisk intemperance of youth' and whose 'constitutional toasts were not expressive of the most lively loyalty for the house of Hanover'. And on the other hand the intruded professors often represented, even from the beginning, even in the eighteenth century, some trace at least of the enlightenment, the urbanity, the cosmopolitanism of the Whig world against the clerical incivility of Tory common-rooms. Who would not prefer the friends and patrons of Pope, Handel, and Rysbrack to snarling old antiquaries like Antony Wood and Thomas Hearne, the hermit-crabs of Merton College and St. Edmund Hall? Nevertheless, the wars which are ultimately decided are seldom the same wars which were first declared, and the long struggle which the heads and tutors fought in the last century to preserve their sacred college arks against an infidel, upstart professoriate has led to a result very different from their aims. By keeping the direction of historical and all other humane studies in the hands of those responsible for teaching, not research, it has provided at least the machinery whereby the creeping paralysis of professionalism can be kept at bay. Time has shown that the real danger of a German professoriate is not 'infidelity': it is the removal of humane studies into a specialisation so remote that they cease to have that lay interest which is their sole ultimate justification.

But if we have the machinery, have we, what is equally necessary, the spirit to drive that machinery in that direction? That spirit, I venture to suggest, must still be a spirit of research. Since I have spoken against professionalism – or rather, against independent professionalism, professionalism for its own sake – allow me to say a word in favour of research – genuine, productive research. For although I believe that history, unless it is taught by men ever conscious of the lay interest, loses its title to be taught at all, equally I believe that it cannot capture that lay interest unless it is perpetually refreshed from outside, by research. Research is not the same as professionalism. Professionalism is that private expertise which carries the details of a subject progressively farther away from lay comprehension; research (as I am using the term) is the digging of new channels whereby fresh and refreshing matter flows into old courses. For even the purest water, if it remains stagnant for long, loses its taste, nor can it be revived merely by being stirred or analysed or distilled. What is needed is a new body of water flowing into it. It is not enough merely to be rejoined, at intervals, by its own temporarily separated back-waters: the water must be fresh, cold, stimulating. It must flow in from outside sources, and its impact must be perceptible, causing sudden shock, gradual adjustment, and the pleasant gurgle of controversy.

Whence shall such tributary streams come? At different times they have come from different sources, and sometimes, of course, from very slender sources. Refreshment has drained silently in through the spongy earth as well as rattled noisily in through wide, pebbled streams. But I wish to make one general point, and that is, that the greatest refreshment has always been brought in by the laity. I do not mean the laity absolutely, but the laity in respect of purely historical studies: for a man is a layman in respect of those studies even if he is a professional in some other branch of learning. The clergy, in any subject, by a kind of natural law, tend to bury themselves deeper and deeper in the *minutiae* of their own dogma; thus buried, they tend to forget the outer world which may be radically changing around them; and often it takes the less concentrated mind of the layman, who is more aware of these changes, sometimes even his impatient boot, to bring them up to date. The lay spirit not only forces the unwilling professional to jettison, at intervals, his past accumulations; it also poses new problems and suggests new methods and new purposes derived from other disciplines, other sciences.

Consider biblical studies. What advance was made by any of those numer-ous professional theologians of the early sixteenth century, those monks and canons and apologists and 'Obscure Men' with their portentous learning, comparable with that of Erasmus? They accused him of levity, flippancy, irreverence (today they would accuse him of 'journalism'); they denounced as cowardly and indecent the nimble strategy with which he circumvented and destroyed their floundering monkish cataphracts. In fact he used professional methods – more professional than theirs – but directed by a lay spirit. A century later that great lay scholar John Selden was able to say that 'laymen have best interpreted the hard places in the Bible', and he listed their names: Pico della Mirandola, Scaliger, Grotius, Salmasius, Heinsius. Later centuries only illustrate the same point. The study of the Bible and of Christian antiquities owed more, in the eighteenth century, to Porson and Gibbon than to Chelsum and Travis, and, in the nineteenth, to Darwin and Lyell than to Pusey and that Theban Legion of eleven thousand clergymen who, with him, sought government sanction for the threatened doctrine of everlasting damnation. If we turn to our own subject, it is the same. Conceive, if you can, modern history without the contributions of economists like Adam Smith, Simiand, and Keynes, sociologists like Marx, Weber, and Sombart, philosophers like Hume and Hegel, scholars of culture and art-history like Burckhardt and Mâle, even anthropologists and psychologists like Frazer and Freud. None of these were professional historians. And yet but for their work the study of history would have dried up and perished long ago.

For it is the essence of humane studies, since their central object is the study of man, that they all flow down towards that centre, even though the professionals in each of them have a natural tendency to move upstream in search of distant sources and sometimes to get lost on the way. And many exact sciences too flow in to refresh that same stream. The sciences of population, of epidemics, of climate, and of price-history are now recognised to be essential to the understanding of history, and of course the enthusiastic experts in these subjects often seek to lead us up these tempting tributaries which they have explored. But we must be firm. We may send surveying parties up them, we may make brief journeys up them ourselves, but we must remember that our ultimate purpose is to contine downstream, taking note of these new waters which are constantly supplying us, but never forgetting the main direction in which we are going, or ought to be going: the study not of circumstances, but of man in circumstances.

43. Gerda Lerner

[from 'The necessity of history' (1982), in her Why History Matters, *Oxford University Press, 1997, pp. 122–8]*

Today, what does it mean to be a professional historian?
The world in which we now practice our profession is a vastly different world from that in which our profession was first institutionalized. It might be well to remember that written and interpreted history is, of itself, a historical creation, which arose with the emergence of ruling elites. From the time of the king lists of Babylonia and Assyria on, historians, whether priests, royal servants, clerks and clerics or a professional class of university-trained intellectuals, have usually ordered the past within a frame of reference that supported the values of the ruling elite, of which they themselves were a part. The grand unity of design so evident in the history writing of the past has always been based on the commonly held values of those in power. In Western civilization, for many centuries, Christianity provided the common context for the cultural tradition. Later as nationalism developed, national history provided the needed coherence and legitimizing ideology. A teleological framework, in which history was the working out of God's consciousness, gave way to an evolutionary framework, in which history became a story of progress. For American history, manifest destiny and mission long provided an ordering framework, as did confidence in laissez-faire economics and liberal politics. Other commonly held assumptions, such as white superiority and male supremacy, were implicit in the culture, but unacknowledged.

Recent American historiography has reflected the breakdown of commonly held values in the assertion by previously submerged and invisible groups of their right to be heard and to have their own past recorded and interpreted. New technology, which has produced the tape recorder and the computer, has opened new fields, such as oral history and cliometrics. New conceptual frameworks, such as those provided by the social sciences and by psychology, have added to differentiation and specialization.

Historical scholarship has never been more sophisticated, more innovative and more interesting. Specialization and a multiplicity of conceptual frameworks have not weakened historical studies. On the contrary, new groups that have hitherto been 'out of history' but are now entering historical inquiry as objects and subjects, have invigorated academic life and form a link to new constituencies outside of the academy. Yet many thoughtful observers have noticed the gap between academic historical scholarship and the public's seemingly insatiable appetite for popular history in its various forms. This phenomenon began early in this century with the media revolution – the dramatic change in the way the society related to past and current events due to the technological innovations embodied in the mass media.

Photography as a mass art form, popular journalism, radio, film and television have profoundly affected the relationship of people to the past. This has never been more sharply evident than in recent decades, when the first generation of youths entirely raised in the age of television have begun to enter adulthood and public life. Members of the 'TV generation', and probably all generations succeeding it, connect more readily with the visual symbol than with the written or spoken word. They are discouraged from giving sustained and thoughtful attention to the past by being daily exposed to the mass-media way of perceiving the world. The rapid succession of superficial problems instantly solved, which is the mainstay of both television fare and the advertising that sustains it, induces the viewer to assume that there are simple and readily available solutions to every problem. The constant reiteration of 'news', presented in flashes and headlines, induces in the public a present-mindedness, which finds reinforcement in the other mass media and in advertisement. The short-range interpretation of events by television pundits and journalists discourages perspective and in-depth analysis. Present-mindedness, a shallow attention to meaning, and contempt for the value of precise definition and critical reasoning are characteristic attitudes produced by mass-media culture. All of them run counter to the mind-set of the historian and to the values and perspective historical studies provide.

Yet the beneficial aspects of education by television – the enormous increase in accessible information, the stimulation and immediacy of entering other lives, the exposure to the variety and richness of human societies and cultures – all feed the public's hunger for a meaningful understanding of the past and for coherent explanations of present-day phenomena. A variety of beneficial historical activities are manifestations of this public interest: genealogy, the vogue for historic spectacles, the popularity of historic-site reconstructions, the search for 'roots' through family or ethnic group history. On a shallower level, there is the mass appeal of historical fiction and of new forms that deliberately challenge the boundaries of fact and fiction, such as the docudrama and the docu-film. The public's interest in the past is also reflected in shoddy and surrogate cultural manifestations, such as the nostalgia craze for old records, films and magazines, or in the fashion industry's endless recycling of a past, which it neatly divides into decade-long units. We may deplore the quality of the end product, or we may seek to influence and improve it, but we dare not ignore the concern, interest, enthusiasm of broad new audiences for history.

Without relaxing our standards of accuracy and our commitment to scholarship, we must accept that there are many roads to historical understanding. We must be open to the ways in which people now relate to the past, and we must reach out to communicate with them at their level. We should rejoice at the surfacing of the lost past of women, nonwhite people, and minorities and use every opportunity open to us to encourage members of these groups to participate in the definition of their past with the best skills academic training can provide. In turn, we should allow our own thinking and interpretations to be enriched by the viewpoint and perspective they bring to historical scholarship. We should continue to broaden our definitions of training and accreditation to include applied fields, such as museum and preservation work, train specialists equipped to work as historians in government and business and strive to train biographers and historian/writers, expanding that concept to include writers in the mass media.

A broader understanding of our professional roles is already under way. It is reflected in the increasing participation at all levels of our own organization by historians employed outside of the academy. We may, in time, welcome a new model of professional life in which one can, at various stages of one's career, move freely in between the academic world and the public sector, literary freelance work or business consultancies. Restructuring careers so as to allow historians to move in and out of academe *by choice* might strengthen and energize us.

As we adapt to changing public needs and explore various modes of communication, we must hold fast to our commitment to scholarly and theoretical work. Most of us have and will continue to spend part or most of our lives as scholars. If society increasingly devalues such work and inadequately understands it, we must reaffirm our dedication to scholarship with increasing confidence and assertiveness. Each of us individually, and through our organizations, must be effective publicly in defense of scholarship and of the priceless archival resources on which it rests. Our nation's heritage and its very future are threatened, when shortsighted political decisions undercut the funding for historic documentary projects, for record preservation, and for the National Archives. Freedom of information for scholars and open access to records of government and bureaucracies are causes we must defend with as much vigor as we defend our right to free speech.

As we examine our relationship to the society at large, we see that insofar as we function as fact finders about the past and as re-creators of past worlds (or model builders), the need of society for our skills is as great as ever. It is our function as interpreters of the past, as meaning givers, that has become most problematical. History as cultural tradition and legitimizing ideology and history as explanation have increasingly come under questioning. Again, the causes are societal and historic. The scientific revolution of the 20th century has undermined the claim of history to being, together with philosophy, the universal field of knowledge for ordering the human experience. The facile slogan of the 1960s, which declared history 'irrelevant', reflected a perceived discontinuity between industrial and postindustrial society. The explosion of scientific knowledge and of technical control over the environment has made it possible to envision a future dominated by scientific knowledge and technical expertise. For such a future, it appears, the past cannot serve as a model. In its most pragmatic manifestation, this kind of thinking has led to the substitution of 'Social Studies' for history in many American school systems. At a more advanced and theoretical level, this kind of thinking is evident in a debate among sociologists, philosophers and historians, some of whom argue that history has been superseded by science as a means of ordering human experience and orienting the individual within society. Most historians would answer that, despite great strides in science and technology, human nature has not essentially changed. Historically formed institutions continue to provide the structures within which the new knowledge and technologies are organized. Historically determined political institutions continue to allocate labor and resources to science and technology, so that those holding and organizing 'the new knowledge' operate within the constraints of tradition.

Those arguing the irrelevance of history define history too narrowly, by focusing on history as the transmitter of tradition, as the means for legitimizing the status quo, as the ideology of a ruling elite. But history, as we have discussed earlier, has many other than merely legitimizing functions. It is possible that what we now perceive as 'the crisis of history' is merely the coming to an end of the function of history as elite ideology.

Another important strand of 20th-century thought can help us in reorienting history in the modern world. The major upheavals of our time – wars, the Holocaust, the nuclear and cybernetic revolutions, and the threats to the ecological balance – have made us aware of the limited use of rational thought in politics and social planning. Irrationality in political and social behavior may make it more urgent than ever to understand the process of Becoming and the limits placed upon the present by past decisions and choices. Psychoanalysis has directed our attention to the power of the irrational and unconscious in motivating human behavior. Sigmund Freud showed us how the past of the individual, suppressed and made unconscious through faulty interpretation, can exert a coercive force over present behavior. 'Healing' of such compulsive behavior occurs through the mental process of bringing past events to awareness and reinterpreting them in light of a new – and better – understanding derived from present circumstances. This process is akin to the work of the historian in reinterpreting past events in light of present questions. The denied past of the group, as well as of the individual, continues to affect the present and to limit the future. We, as historians, might take up the challenge offered by analytic theory and seek to work toward a 'healing' of contemporary social pathology, using the tools of our craft imaginatively and with a new sense of direction. We are, after all, not a small group of clerks and mandarins guarding secret knowledge in the service of a ruling ideology, but people with special skills, who translate to others the meaning of the lives and struggles of their ancestors, so that they may see meaning in their own lives.

We do this best in our function as teachers. Most of us, for much of our professional lives, are teachers; yet this activity is the one we seem least to appreciate in ourselves and in others. Our habitual performance at the lectern has, in some aspects, been superseded by the intervention of printing, and many of us, sensing the basic incongruity of the manner in which we conduct our work, have fallen back on being performers, seeking to catch the reluctant attention of an audience more accustomed to the frenetic entertainment style of the mass media.

In fact, the teacher as performer acts within an ancient and valid tradition. Above all, we seek to tell a story and tell it well – to hold the audience's attention and to seduce it, by one means or another, into suspending disbelief and inattention. We seek to focus concentrated attention upon ourselves and to hold it long enough to allow the students' minds to be directed into unexpected pathways and to perceive new patterns. There is nothing shabby about this performance aspect of the teacher's skill, this trick of the magician and the artist. When we succeed in our performance role as teachers, we extend the learner's thoughts and feelings, so that he or she can move into past worlds and share the thoughts and values of another time and place. We offer the student the excitement of puzzle solving in our search for evidence and the sense of discovery in seeing general design out of the mass of particulars.

Lastly, we also teach, as master craftsmen and craftswomen, imparting particular skills to the uninitiated. The ability to think and write with clarity, the habit of critical analysis, the methodology of history, the painstaking patience of the researcher – all these skills are transmitted by the ancient method of transference from master to apprentice. As we allow students to see the historian at work, we become role models, and if we are so inclined, we lighten the students' task by demystifying our knowledge, sharing its 'tricks' and openly acknowledging its shortcomings. The craftsmanship aspect of teaching connects us with the craftsmanship of other workers, those who labor with their hands and those who work with their minds. As teaching and researching historians, we work as did the master stonemasons and wood-carvers on the great medieval cathedrals and the ancient Mayan or Buddhist temples or the women who wove the great Bayeux tapestry: we do our own particular work, contributing to a vast, ongoing enterprise. In our own perform-ance and in the standards we set for students we can represent dedication to understanding the past for its own sake and in its own light. In an age of alienation we can impart a sense of continuity to the men and women we teach. And we can help them to see the discontinuities in a larger perspective.

The problem of discontinuities has never loomed larger than in this gener-ation, which is the first generation in history forced to consider the possibility of the extinction of humankind in a nuclear war. The possibility of disconti-nuity on such a vast scale staggers the imagination and reinforces the need of each individual to know his or her place in history. Now, as never before, we need to have a sense of meaning in our lives and assurance of a collective con-tinuity. It is history, the known and ordered past, that enables us to delineate goals and visions for a communal future. Shared values, be they based on con-sensus or on the recognition and acceptance of many ways of form-giving, link the individual to the collective immortality of the human enterprise.

The historian professes and practices such knowledge and imparts it to others with passion and an abiding confidence in the necessity of history. In these times, more than ever, it is good to be a historian.

Further Reading

General

John Tosh (with Sean Lang), *The Pursuit of History: Aims, Methods and New Directions in the Study of Modern History*, 4th edn, Longman, 2006

Ludmilla Jordanova, *History in Practice*, 2nd edn, Hodder Arnold, 2006

Anna Green & Kathleen Troup (eds), *The Houses of History*, Manchester University Press, 1999

Stefan Berger et al. (eds), *Writing History: Theory and Practice*, Hodder Arnold, 2002

Beverley Southgate, *History: What and Why?*, Routledge, 1996

History for its own Sake

Michael Bentley, *Modern Historiography*, Routledge, 1999

Peter Novick, *That Noble Dream: The 'Objectivity Question' and the American Historical Profession*, Cambridge University Press, 1988

G.R. Elton, *Return to Essentials*, Cambridge University Press, 1991

J.H. Hexter, *On Historians*, Harvard University Press, 1979

Political Histories

Sydney Pollard, *The Idea of Progress: History and Society*, C.A. Watts, 1968

Peter Mandler, *History and National Life*, Profile, 2002

Raphael Samuel, *Island Stories: Unravelling Britain*, Verso, 1998

Marc Ferro, *The Use and Abuse of History, Or How the Past is Taught*, Routledge & Kegan Paul, 1984

Harvey J. Kaye, *The British Marxist Historians*, Polity, 1984

E.P. Thompson, *The Poverty of Theory*, Merlin Press, 1978

The New Radicalism

Raphael Samuel (ed.), *People's History and Socialist Theory*, Routledge, 1981
Laura Lee Downs, *Writing Gender History*, Hodder Arnold, 2004
Sue Morgan (ed.), *The Feminist History Reader*, Routledge, 2006
Bonnie G. Smith, *The Gender of History: Men, Women, and Historical Practice*, Harvard University Press, 1998
Paul A. Cimbala & Robert F. Himmelberg (eds), *Historians and Race*, Indiana University Press, 1996
Catherine Hall & Sonya O. Rose (eds), *At Home with the Empire*, Cambridge University Press, 2006

Learning from Historical Perspective

Gordon Connell-Smith & Howell A. Lloyd, *The Relevance of History*, Heinemann, 1972
John Tosh, *Why History Matters*, Palgrave Macmillan, 2008
Jeremy Black, *Using History*, Hodder Arnold, 2005

History as Social Science

Peter Burke, *History and Social Theory*, Polity, 1995
Eric Hobsbawm, *On History*, Weidenfeld & Nicolson, 1997
Adrian Wilson (ed.), *Rethinking Social History: English Society 1570–1990*, Manchester University Press, 1993
Pat Hudson, *History by Numbers*, Arnold, 2000

The Cultural Turn

Keith Jenkins, *On 'What Is History?': From Carr and Elton to Rorty and White*, Routledge, 1995
Alun Munslow, *Deconstructing History*, Routledge, 1997
Hayden White, *Metahistory: The Historical Imagination in Nineteenth-Century Europe*, Johns Hopkins University Press, 1973
Richard J. Evans, *In Defence of History*, Granta, 1997
Lynn Hunt (ed.), *The New Cultural History*, California University Press, 1989
Simon Gunn, *History and Cultural Theory*, Longman, 2006
James Fentress & Chris Wickham, *Social Memory*, Blackwell, 1992
Raphael Samuel, *Theatres of Memory*, vol. I, Verso, 1994

Beyond Academia

Ian Tyrrell, *Historians in Public: The Practice of American History, 1890–1970*, University of Chicago Press, 2005

Index